THE RACE TO THE WHITE CONTINENT

Also by Alan Gurney

Below the Convergence:
Voyages toward Antarctica 1699–1839

DONATED IN MEMORY

OF

ALLEN MENDEZ

BY

HIS FAMILY

THE RACE TO THE
WHITE CONTINENT

ALAN GURNEY

W • W • NORTON & COMPANY • NEW YORK • LONDON

The text of this book is composed in Galliard with the
display set in Caslon Openface and Shaded,
Shell Roundhand, and Helvetica Black
Composition by Allentown Digital Services Division of
R. R. Donnelley & Sons Company and
Manufacturing by Haddon Craftsmen, Inc.

Library of Congress Cataloging-in-Publication Data
Gurney, Alan.
The race to the white continent:
voyages to the Antarctic / Alan Gurney.
p. cm.
Includes bibliographical references (p.) and index.
ISBN 0-393-05004-1
1. Antarctica—Discovery and exploration. I. Title.

G860.G84 2000
919.8'904—dc21   00-038673

ISBN 0-393-32321-8 pbk.

W. W. Norton & Company, Inc.
500 Fifth Avenue, New York, N.Y. 10110
www.wwnorton.com

W. W. Norton & Company Ltd.
Castle House, 75/76 Wells Street, London W1T 3QT

1 2 3 4 5 6 7 8 9 0

To the memory of Richard Hakluyt (1552–1616),
geographer, clergyman, scholar, and spy

Contents

THE RACE TO THE
WHITE CONTINENT

Introduction

HE SHADOWS of an air-raid shelter lit by a swaying oil lamp, the earth quaking under the sticks of bombs from enemy planes remain an enduring childhood memory of World War II. Such entertainment, my experience of life being limited, enthralled me. My mother and older sister must have been terrified.

Childhood pleasures during the war years were basic. With petrol rationed the roads were empty and the trains crowded. But the countryside felt more spacious than today, and I busied myself with the time-hallowed pursuits of small boys: the making of primitive bows and arrows, catapults, toilet paper boats for the bath (British toilet paper in those days had the waterproof quality and texture of waxed paper), and more substantial balsa wood models to float in ponds and down streams. With a father in the RAF, I became adept at identifying warplanes by their engine noise.

If ration books dominated my mother's life, books of every description dominated mine. And the reading was omnivorous. The printed word, carrying me into strange and different worlds, fascinated me: *Three Men in a Boat* by Jerome K. Jerome; *Wind in the Willows* by Kenneth Grahame; the works of Rudyard Kipling, Arthur Ransome, Robert Ballantyne, Robert Louis Stevenson, P. G. Wodehouse (still a favorite), Richmal Crompton. A. A. Milne and Christopher Robin were spit out with distaste. W. C. Sellar and R. J. Yeatman with their *1066 and All That* put English history into perspective.

Into this rather predictable juvenile soup went meatier items: George Orwell's *Animal Farm;* Erich Maria Remarque's *All Quiet on the Western Front* (read by the light from a surreptitious and guttering candle in my bedroom, which added much to the First World War atmosphere).

Then came the books on sailing: *The Riddle of the Sands* by Erskine Childers, an adventure novel based on Childers's own sailing experience and still one of the classic books on small boat cruising; Alain Gerbault's *The Fight of the "Firecrest,"* a narrative of Gerbault's single-handed 101-day passage from the Mediterranean to New York in a thirty-nine-foot cutter. Gerbault, a Frenchman, had flown in the Flying Corps during the Great

War, and during those years, he wrote, a "young American, an aviator in my squadron, the 31st French, lent me some of Jack London's books. It was in reading *The Cruise of the 'Shark'* that I first learned it was possible to cross the ocean in a small boat." The result had been Gerbault's 1924 Atlantic crossing.

More sailing books followed. Two of them were by E. F. Knight: *The Cruise of the "Falcon"* and the *Cruise of the "Alerte."* Knight, an English barrister, had developed a passion for small boat sailing after reading John Macgregor's *A Thousand Miles in a Rob Roy Canoe.* Grown tired of pettifogging legal quibbles, Knight with three other barristers and a fifteen-year-old cabin boy had sailed the *Falcon,* a forty-two-foot yawl, into the South Atlantic and up the Paraná and Paraguay rivers to Asunción. This being 1880, with brigands still roaming South America, Knight had "procured all necessary charts, directories, nautical instruments, stored away some nine months' provisions, decorated the main cabin walls with arms for defence and sport—Martini-Henry rifles, cutlasses, and revolvers, and purchased a small brass swivel gun with grape and canister."

A few years later Knight was back in the South Atlantic, this time aboard the *Alerte,* searching for buried treasure (shades of *Treasure Island*) on Trinidad Island, some seven hundred miles off the Brazilian coast.

Such reading determined me that I too one day would sail across the world's oceans in a small yacht. But I would be better prepared than one of the *Falcon*'s barristers, a sailing neophyte who had stepped aboard sporting kid gloves and a top hat, gazed around, and then said: "What a lot of strings there are about this boat! I shall never know the use of them all." He never did.

One day, rather self-conscious in my new long trousers (for my generation the change from short to long trousers marked a rite of passage, the metamorphosis from childhood into boyhood), I came across the volumes of Richard Hakluyt's *Principal Navigations, Voyages, Traffiques and Discoveries of the English Nation.*

Hakluyt died in 1616, the same year as Shakespeare. The *Principal Navigations* is not a seamless narrative but, like a treasure chest, can be dipped into at whim and the individual tales savored with delight. Here, in Hakluyt's pages, those tough, pugnacious, spade-bearded Elizabethan ruffians stepped from their portraits and came alive: Sir Francis Drake, Sir Walter Raleigh, Thomas Cavendish, John Davis, Martin Frobisher. Among these major stars swam lesser luminaries. Such a one was John Fox (born in Woodbridge at the Crown Inn, a hostelry that still serves the hungry and thirsty traveler), who sailed as gunner aboard the merchant ship *Three Half Moons.* Taken by a Turkish fleet, Fox and his companions spent fourteen years heaving on oars in the galleys. One year, with the vessels laid up for winter at Alexandria, Fox and two other Englishmen organized a mass escape of more than 260 Christian galley slaves. Seizing a vessel, but with few provisions, they sailed into the Mediterranean. After a month at sea—eight of the men died—they finally reached Crete: "Where they were made much of by the Abbot and monks there, who caused them to stay there, while they were well refreshed and eased." The admiring monks kept Fox's sword "and hung it up for a monument." Fox went on to fight against the Spanish Armada. He died in 1594 leaving ten pounds to the poor of Woodbridge.

But Hakluyt's work was more than a collection of adventure stories. Here lay advice about safe harbors, anchorages, courses to be sailed, dangers to be avoided, advice about fitting out a whaler; advice on the natural history, products and customs of countries; essential words in native tongues. This was a reference book used by seamen, merchants, traders, and diplomats, an early trade manual that found its way into sea chests and nestled next to logbooks, ledgers, the Bible, and the Book of Common Prayer.

It was also read by playwrights.

One warm spring day, the rooks cawing in the trees, the classroom redolent of chalk dust and grubby schoolboys, all of us yearning to be outside but forced to concentrate our wandering minds on Shakespeare's *Macbeth*, I came across one of the witches cackling that the husband of a "rump-fed ronyon" is "to Aleppo gone, master o' the Tiger." Only the previous day I had read, in Hakluyt, of the journey taken by Mr. Ralph Fitch, merchant of London, to Goa and Siam. Fitch had sailed from London to Tripoli in the *Tiger* "and thence took the way for Aleppo." In a blinding flash it came to me that Shakespeare had also read Hakluyt. England's literary ornament was made human. He was flesh and blood like me. We had shared the same book.

It was the dedication to Sir Francis Walsingham (chief of Queen Elizabeth's espionage service) where Hakluyt had me hooked, netted, and landed:

Right Honourable, I do remember that being a youth . . . it was my hap to visit the chamber of Mr. Richard Hakluyt my cousin, a gentleman of the Middle Temple, well known unto you, at a time when I found lying open upon his board certain books of Cosmography, with a universal Map: he seeing me somewhat curious in the view thereof, began to instruct my ignorance, by showing me the division of the earth into three parts after the old account: he pointed with his wand to all the known seas, gulfs, bays, straits, capes, rivers, empires, kingdoms, dukedoms and territories of each part, with declaration also of their special commodities, and particular wants, which by the benefit of traffic, and intercourse of merchants, are plentifully supplied. From the map he brought me to the Bible, and turning to the 107 Psalm, directed me to the 23 and 24 verses, where I read, that they which go down to the sea in ships, and occupy by the great waters, they see the works of the Lord and his wonders in the deep, &c. Which words of the prophet together with my cousin's discourse (things of high and rare delight to my young nature) took in me so deep an impression, that I constantly resolved, if ever I were preferred to the University, where better time, and more convenient place might be ministered for these studies, I would by God's assistance prosecute that knowledge and kind of literature, the doors whereof (after a sort) were so happily opened before me.

Hakluyt's course was set. As a scholar at Oxford he learned Greek, Latin, Spanish, Portuguese, and French. He later became the first ordained lecturer on geography at Oxford and introduced the use of the globe into English schools. In his thirties he accompanied Sir Edward Stafford to France, where "during my five years abroad with him in his dangerous and chargeable residency in Her Highness's service, I both heard in speech and read in books other nations miraculously extolled for their discoveries and notable enterprises by sea, but the English of all others for their sluggish security. . . ."

Hakluyt determined to set the record straight: "For it cannot be denied but as in all former ages, they have been men full of activity, stirrers abroad, and searchers of the most remote parts of the world."

The phrase "stirrers abroad, and searchers of the most remote parts of the world" was unforgettable. And so, from a happy reading of years ago, and as a doff of the hat to Richard Hakluyt, I decided to name this book *Stirrers Abroad*. Authors, it should be remembered, look upon their book titles as a young mother looks upon her firstborn child. Jim Mairs, my editor at W. W. Norton and book midwife, took one look at this title and growled some uncomplimentary comments about expatriates languidly stirring their gin and tonics under tropical skies. *Stirrers Abroad,* having barely drawn a breath, was then exposed on the hillside to the withering blasts of Marketing and Publicity. It died.

Nevertheless, these stirrers abroad—all gulpers of brandy, whiskey, or rum—are not bound by the narrow confines of nationality. Here, on the following pages, are men from many nations who searched into the most remote parts of the world in the last days of sail, all of them worthy of entry into Hakluyt's *Principal Navigations, Voyages, Traffiques and Discoveries. . . .*

Prologue

I N THE SUMMER of 1784 the official account of Captain James Cook's voyage in search of a Northwest or Northeast Passage from the Pacific to the Atlantic was bought by an expectant public. Priced at four and half guineas (four months' wages for an able seaman in the Royal Navy), it sold out in three days. The first two of the three quarto-size leather-bound volumes, based on Cook's journals, had been edited by John Douglas, canon of Windsor, and the final volume had been written by Captain James King of HMS *Discovery*. Cook, a famous man after his two previous circumnavigations, had been killed and dismembered in 1779 by the natives of Hawaii. This perhaps went some way to explain why the story of his final voyage had been awaited so eagerly.

To aid the armchair sailor, the three volumes were accompanied by a world map, three feet by two feet, drawn on the Mercator projection. This elegant piece of draftsmanship had been drawn by Lieutenant Henry Roberts—he had sailed on two of Cook's expeditions—and showed the tracks of Cook's three voyages.

Fifty years after its publication anyone with a geographical bent, gazing at Roberts's map, would have found little to add or change. New Holland had taken on the name Australia, and Van Diemen's Land, shown as part of the mainland, had proved to be an island. With a nice sense of symmetry, Banks Island, off New Zealand's east coast, had proved to be a peninsula. And the northwest coast of North America would have required many changes after Captain George Vancouver's 1792–94 survey.

At the bottom of Roberts's map—which stopped at 72°S latitude—stretched a huge blank. No coastline was shown: just "THE ANTARCTIC OCEAN" writ large across the blank. Notations in small print, following Cook's track, showed the reasons why no coast had been discovered: "Many Isles & firm fields of Ice; Islands of Ice innumerable; Firm Field and Vast Mountains of Ice." Where these were printed, Cook's south-going track turned north.

Since Cook's time, however, stretches of coastline and desolate islands had been discovered in that huge blank. Most of the discoveries had been made by sealers looking for elephant seals and fur seals. By the 1830s the seals had been virtually exterminated from the grim lands and islands washed by the Antarctic Ocean.

But the preponderance of discoveries by sealers was about to change. During the 1830s three national expeditions—American, British, and French—were organizing themselves to tackle Cook's "Firm Field and Vast Mountains of Ice."

That three government expeditions had the world's most remote and inhospitable ocean in their sights at the same time is a matter of some wonder. But the old antagonists had now changed into commercial, political, and scientific rivals. France, still smarting after its defeat in the Napoleonic Wars, had become the second most powerful naval prescence in the Pacific after Great Britain, while no part of the Indian or Pacific oceans lay untouched by American whaling ships and merchant traders. For both the French and Americans the advancement of the tricolor and Old Glory beyond the farthest south reached by James Cook and the sealer James Weddell—even perhaps to the South Pole itself—was a matter of patriotic and national prestige. For the British, having reached the north magnetic pole, bagging both the south magnetic pole and the geographic pole represented a scientific and exploring crusade.

The stage was set, the players were in the wings, for the last great sailing exploration expeditions under sail.

Chapter 1

The Background

ABLE-WHACKETS. A popular sea-game with cards, wherein the loser is beaten over the palms of the hands with a handkerchief tightly twisted like a rope. Very popular with horny-fisted salts.

ADVANCE MONEY. In men-of-war and most merchant ships the advance of two months' wages is given to the crew, previous to going to sea; the clearing off of which is called *working up the dead horse.*

Admiral W. H. Smyth, *The Sailor's Word-Book,* 1867

HE WORLD of the 1830s still held great mysteries. South America, Africa, and Australia, all with their forbidding and hostile interiors. Tibet, sprawling across the roof of the world, guarded by deserts and mountains and ruled by a god-king. The closely shuttered islands of a feudal Japan, its only window open to Europeans with the Dutch trading post at Nagasaki. Ancient China with its contempt for the inquisitive, acquisitive, hairy foreign devils clinging like leeches—and closely watched—in their enclaves at Macao and Canton. All these were a palimpset that explorers, travelers, merchants, adventurers, and rogues could mark for fame or fortune.

For the seaman lay the vast stretches of the Pacific and Indian oceans with their pinpricks of reefs, islands, and atolls. The reefs were dangerous, but the islands and atolls provided opportunities for the adventurous trader and souls for the adventurous missionary. The seas themselves in certain areas were rich in whales for the taking. Then lay the polar regions, perhaps the greatest mystery of all. From all else came whispers of human activity: strange customs, different gods. From the polar regions came nothing but ice.

Beyond the cordons of ice guarding both Arctic and Antarctic lay an unexplored area the size of Africa and Australia combined. In the third century B.C. Pytheas, a trader from Marseilles, had sailed north and brought back strange stories of a *mare concretum*—a frozen sea—to a skeptical Mediterranean world. Since then the lands and seas rimming this improbable region had produced ivory, furs, cod, whalebone, and whale oil. The tantalizing lure of a northern sea route to the riches of the East had drawn European seamen and merchants—mainly English, Dutch, and French—to search for a Northwest and Northeast Passage. The Arctic ice always defeated them. But memorializing their efforts, their names lay engraved on Henry Roberts's map: Baffin's Bay, Hudson's Bay, Davis's Strait.

The south had waited longer for its Pytheas. In 1700 Edmond Halley had made the first drawing of an Antarctic tabular iceberg—the large flat-topped icebergs calved from the floating ice shelves rimming Antarctica—when commanding the *Paramore* on a voyage to collect information on magnetic variation. But it was not until 1775, with James Cook's circumnavigation of Antarctica in the *Resolution*, that the full enormousness of the southern pack ice was first realized.

What lay beyond these northern and southern barriers of ice was a matter of educated and uneducated speculation. More ice? Land? An open polar sea?

James Cook, the first seaman to probe both Arctic and Antarctic ice, had his own ideas. In February 1775, nearing the completion of his Antarctic circumnavigation—a voyage that finally laid to rest the centuries-old speculation of a *terra australis incognita*, an unknown southern continent—he wrote in his journal: "That there may be a Continent or large tract of land near the Pole, I will not deny, on the contrary I am of the opinion there is, and it is probable that we have seen part of it. The excessive cold, the many islands and vast floats of ice all tend to prove that there must be land to the South. . . ."

Three years later, on his last voyage in the *Resolution*, this time in the Arctic Ocean between Asia and North America, he was again halted by ice. Roberts's map bears a terse notation: "The further progress of the Ships Northward was render'd impossible by the Ice extending from Continent to Continent." From Icy Cape in Alaska to Cape North in Siberia, the *Resolution* and the *Discovery* had ranged and probed the implacable ice front, pack ice that threatened to sweep them against the low-lying shores of either continent. This ice was very different from the ice floes that Cook had seen in the Antarctic. This was old ice with floes rafted one upon another, sometimes to a thickness of thirty feet.

On 27 August 1778 an entry that summed up Cook's thoughts on this northern ice went into his journal: "It appeared to me very improbable that this ice could be the produce of the preceding Winter alone, but rather that of a great many." A few sentences later he ended his speculations: "Thus it may happen that more ice is distroyed in one Stormy Season, than is formed in several Winters and an endless accummulation prevented, but that there is always a remaining store, none who has been upon the spot will deny and none but Closet studdying Philosiphers will dispute." Cook's acerbic "Closet studdying Philosiphers" is a barbed reference to the Honorable Daines Barrington, a man whom Cook must have regarded as a particularly mischievous troll sent to try him. A dispassionate observer can only agree.

Although of the same age, Barrington, the son of a viscount, and Cook, the son of a farm laboror, stand in stark contrast with each other. Cook demonstrates to a perfect degree what J. R. L. Anderson has termed the Ulysses factor—the characteristics, the weft and the warp, that make a great explorer: courage, practical competence, imagination, leadership, endurance, self-sufficiency, the compulsion to cross the next range of mountains, to ford the next river, to double the next headland, and the self-confidence when to admit defeat. Cook, in a rare moment, revealed himself in a telling journal entry on 30 January 1774. Halted by the Antarctic ice at 70°15′S latitude—the farthest south that any ship had sailed—he wrote: "I whose ambition leads me not only farther than any other man has been before me, but as far as I think it possible for man to go, was not sorry at meeting with this interruption, as it in some measure relieved us from the dangers and hardships, inseparable with the Navigation of the Southern Polar regions."

Barrington demonstrates to a perfect degree what might be called the Magpie factor: the compulsion to collect random facts, ideas, information, and statistics on a subject and then bind the whole together to form a rickety, speculative theory.

The books, tracts, and articles flowed from this lawyer, antiquary, and naturalist's pen. Jeremy Bentham considered him as a lawyer to be "a very indifferent judge." As an antiquary he wrote on the Flood (an article attacked by the *Gentleman's Magazine*); on Dolly Pentreath, the last person to speak the Cornish language (an article ridiculed by Horace Walpole); on Julius Caesar's landing in Britain and the passage of the Thames; on the antiquity of cardplaying ("Barrington is singularly unfortunate in his speculations about cards," wrote William Chatto in his *History of Playing Cards*). As a naturalist he designed a form for keeping records and sent a copy to the Reverend Gilbert White at Selborne. (Of the 110 letters that make up White's classic *Natural History and Antiquities of Selborne*, 61 are addressed to Barrington.) "I have," Barrington ruefully admitted, "perhaps published too many things."

A man from an influential family—one brother a respected post captain in the Royal Navy, another a bishop, yet another a secretary at war—and with a wide circle of influential friends, Barrington had been instrumental in obtaining for Johann Forster and his son Georg the positions of naturalists aboard Cook's *Resolution* after Joseph Banks, the intended naturalist, had stormed off in a fit of pique. Forster, pedantic, humorless, quarrelsome, harboring grudges, had proved a constant irritant on the three-year voyage that circumnavigated Antarctica.

Barrington's influence also made itself felt in the Arctic. The same year, 1773, that Forster was sourly eyeing the Antarctic pack ice, two more Royal Navy vessels, the *Racehorse* and the *Carcass,* sailed north from Spitsbergen before being stopped by pack ice. This expedition—much against the advice of Greenland whalers—was attempting to sail through the pack to a theoretical open polar sea. The expedition can be considered the brainchild of Daines Barrington. The viscount's son, never having seen it, had pitched upon the Arctic Ocean as one of his many hobby-horses. The polar sea was an open sea, according to Barrington.

Intrigued by a theory of the Swiss Samuel Engel that seawater never froze and that all polar ice came from the breakup of frozen rivers, Barrington had entered into a long correspondence with the land-locked Engel. This type of speculation was pure catnip to Barrington. Powerful friends in the Admiralty and the Royal Society set the *Racehorse* and the *Carcass* on their course for the North Pole. The singular failure of the expedition—the two vessels barely escaped from the pack ice, and a young Horatio Nelson barely escaped from a polar bear—also failed to dampen Barrington's infatuation with the open polar sea. Quite the reverse. He resumed his lobbying, this time for an expedition to search for a Northwest or Northeast Passage from the Pacific. The astronomer royal Nevil Maskelyne, Lord Sandwich at the Admiralty, Joseph Banks, and Dr. Daniel Solander—the latter two still basking in the glow of their 1768–71 *Endeavour* voyage with Cook—all were dragooned into helping Barrington. By March 1774 Barrington was happily informing the secretary of the Royal Society that the voyage "will be undertaken after the return of Capt. Cook in 1775; when a similar expedition will be fitted out, which will in general follow the outline proposed by the Council of the Royal Society to the Board of Admiralty." Here, in embryo, lay the flesh and bones of Cook's last fatal voyage.

The *Resolution* sailed from Plymouth on 12 July 1776. Barrington continued to publish articles and tracts about the open polar sea. Republished in 1781 and 1818, they had a profound effect on British and American theories on the nature of the polar regions, theories advanced by men whom Cook would have instantly pigeonholed as more closet studying philosophers.

Cook's pioneering voyage into the high southern latitudes was followed by others. The seamen who speculated upon the source of this ice, the vast fields of compacted floes, the huge flat-topped icebergs that could be counted by the hundred from deck level, all these men, men with questioning and inquiring minds, had their own ideas on the source of the ice and what lay close to the South Pole.

Thaddeus Bellingshausen, commander of the 1819–21 Russian naval expedition that circumnavigated Antarctica, thought it an ice-covered sea with the ice attached to shallows and islands. The sealer James Weddell's farthest south—achieved in his eponymous sea, a sea clear of ice—led him to believe that the remaining miles to the pole would be ice-free. However, the season's being late, the wind contrary, rations short, Weddell had reluctantly made the prudent decision to turn north for the island of South Georgia. A decade later, in 1832, during the third circumnavigation of Antarctica, John Biscoe, on a sealing voyage, having sighted land in both the Indian Ocean and Pacific Ocean sectors—land some three thousand miles apart—wrote to Captain Francis Beaufort at the British Hydrographic Office that it was his considered opinion that these widely separated coastlines formed "the headlands of a Southern Continent."

An ice-covered sea, an open sea, a polar landmass: Even the pragmatic seamen held divided opinions on what lay close to the South Pole. But all these men would have agreed with Cook's candid opinion of Antarctic sailing:

The risk one runs in exploring a coast in these unknown and Icy Seas, is so very great, that I can be bold to say, that no man will ever venture farther than I have done and that the lands which may lie to the South will never be explored. Thick fogs, Snow storms, Intense Cold and every other thing that can render Navigation dangerous one has to encounter and these difficulties are greatly heightened by the enexpressable horrid aspect of the Country, a Country doomed by Nature never once to feel the warmth of the Suns rays, but to lie for ever buried under everlasting snow and ice. The Ports which may be on the Coast are in a manner wholy filled up with frozen Snow of a vast thickness, but if any should so far be open as to admit a ship in, it is even dangerous to go in, for she runs a risk of being fixed there for ever, or coming out in an ice island.

Reading that grim paragraph would be enough to convince any mariner to steer clear of the high southern latitudes. But Cook's widely read journals had also written of the Pacific and its whales, of the American northwest coast and its sea otters and fur seals, of New Zealand with its flax and timber, of Tahiti with its breadfruit and hogs. Here, for sharp-nosed merchants, were trading possibilities. As the years went by, the whaleships and traders moved into the Pacific and Indian oceans.

Chapter 2

Blubber Hunters and Traders

BACK OFF ALL. The order when the harpooner has thrown his harpoon into the whale. Also, to back off a sudden danger.

BOTH SHEETS AFT. The situation of a square-rigged ship that sails before the wind, or with the wind right astern. It is said also of a half-drunken sailor rolling along with his hands in his pockets and elbows square.

Admiral W. H. Smyth, *The Sailor's Word-Book,* 1867

RIOR TO THE AMERICAN CIVIL WAR a handful of small New England ports and islands burst out from the grim provincialism of their puritanical shores and became the world's paramount whale oil and whalebone marketplace. More than three-quarters of the world's whaling fleet sailed under the Stars and Stripes. Their more fastidious merchant marine colleagues disparagingly called these whalemen and their vessels blubber hunters.

A theatrical air surrounds nineteenth-century prints of the blubber hunters at work. Convention dictates the whaleship be set as the backdrop, hove to, a dead whale alongside, black smoke billowing from the tryworks as the blubber is reduced to oil. Front stage is full of action. Here are whales—invariably sperm whales with bulbous heads and dangerous toothed jaws—harpooned and lanced, roiling and thrashing the waters in their death throes, blood spouting from their blowholes. Some fight back. The fearsome jaws bite into fragile open whaleboats. Men tumble out. Spars, oars, whale line tubs, and men bob in the water. Flukes thrash the air and sea. Men, whale gear, splinters of boat, all explode skyward.

The print's central message is uncannily close to that of a prehistoric rock painting showing men hunting mammoths with spears or, nearer our time, the bas-relief of Fifth Dynasty Egyptians hunting hippopotamus

South Sea whale fishery, 1825

"Yes, there is death in this business of whaling—a speechlessly quick chaotic bundling of a man into Eternity." —Herman Melville

(Aquatint by Thomas Sutherland after William Huggins)

from papyrus reed boats with harpoon and line. Samuel Colt might have patented his six-shot breech-loading revolver, but his countrymen's techniques, in hunting the world's largest animal, were little removed from those of the Stone Age.

The nineteenth-century descendant of the ancient Stone Age hunter, braced in the bow of his whaleboat, arms drawn back, hands grasping the harpoon, poised to plunge the weapon into the whale's body, was in a very literal sense the point man for an industry that provided a livelihood for tens of thousands of American men and women.

The New England whaling ports provided the infrastructure that kept the blubber hunters, men and ships, at sea. Here were shipyards for building and repair, loud with the noise of mallet and hammer, saw and adz, sweet with the smell of wood shavings, tar, and paint. Ship chandlers' shelves and floors were crammed to overflowing with a cornucopia of stores and equipment, the buildings pungent with the aroma of tarred hemp rope. Men worked in cool and airy sailmakers' lofts and lengthy rope walks. Blacksmiths worked furnaces and forges to fashion harpoons, lances, flensing knives, blubber hooks, and blubber spades. Coopers shaved staves for the barrels and the kegs that lay piled on wharves. Boardinghouses, inns, and brothels catered to the physical desires and comforts of whalemen returned from a four-year voyage and those about to sail. The more material needs of the whalemen—especially the raw, green hands from the Vermont and the New Hampshire backwoods—were catered to by the avaricious and predatory outfitters. The whalemen called them land sharks. (So general was the term that the New Bedford Outfitters' Association resorted to fines in an attempt to stop its members from calling themselves land sharks during their meetings.) The outfitters also ran sweatshop clothing operations. Local women were supplied with cheap fabrics for the sewing, at piece rates, of shirts, jackets, and trousers. These in turn were sold to the whalemen, with the outfitter pocketing a very handsome profit.

These exploited whalemen roamed the world's oceans, seeking out sperm whales, right whales, bowhead whales, and elephant seals. In their wandering among the islands of the Pacific and Indian oceans the whalemen, with evenhanded abandon, spread rum, whiskey, firearms, and venereal disease. Some of the islanders, looking upon their visitors as undesirable aliens who molested their women, massacred them—and sometimes ate them.

The massacre of the whales, however, provided the oil that lit the lamps of the Conestoga wagons and the advancing western frontier settlements, lit the offices, streets, factories, and light beacons of the eastern seaboard. Bright, clean burning spermaceti candles replaced smoky, guttering tallow candles in the home. The lower-grade oil from the right whale and bowhead whale lubricated the clattering machinery of the mills.

Baleen (the fibrous plates acting as food filters in the mouths of the right whale and the bowhead whale) provided the strips of strong, springy whalebone sewn into corsets and stays that cinched and shaped the female figure. Baleen provided hoops for crinolines and struts for the parasols that protected delicate female skin from bright sunlight, skin that had been cleansed and soothed with spermaceti-based soaps and ointments, skin then dabbed with perfume fixed with ambergris.[1]

The menfolk of these cleansed, perfumed, constricted ladies rode on whalebone sprung carriages, and swung whalebone buggy whips. They wore gloves, leather boots, and wool clothing all cured and carded with whale oil. This industry, in short, was one guaranteed to send today's conservationists, environmentalists, and anthropologists into hysterical fits of the vapors.

The wealth produced by this reprehensible—to modern-day perceptions—industry (a description that would have raised the blood pressure of a nineteenth-century mercantile Yankee; only the shoemaking and the cotton industry outranked whaling in Massachusetts) may be seen in the graceful architecture of the New England towns closely identified with whale oil and whalebone. But the towns, with their elegant Greek Revival buildings lining tree-shaded and tourist-haunted streets, stand in stark contrast with the whaleships that once sailed from them. Dumpy-looking vessels, heavily constructed, flat-sheered, bluff-bowed, wide of beam, three-masted with lookouts at the mastheads spying for whales, whaleboats slung in heavy wooden davits and resting on cranes, spars and sails grimy with soot from blubber smoke: All these made whaleships instantly recognizable. Even more so when they were cutting in the whale: the dead whale alongside, men balancing on a plank platform rigged out from the hull and slicing the blubber into strips with razor-sharp blubber spades, the whale slowly revolving as the blubber was ripped off in a long strip, hauled aboard by a heavy tackle rigged to the main yard. On deck the blubber was chopped into blocks and then thinly sliced (but held at the skin like the spine of a book, blocks known as bible leaves to whalemen) before being heaved into the smoking try-pots—iron cauldrons held in a rectangular brick structure with a fire underneath fed on scraps of shriveled blubber—the thick black smoke curling through the masts, sails, and rigging. At night with their try-pots at full cook, fires flaming under the cauldrons, the whaleships resembled miniature floating infernos. Such uncouth craft, the merchant seamen claimed, were built by the mile and cut to the length required.

The only sweet curved lines of these slow-moving plebeian seagoing hunters lay in their whaleboats. Graceful, double-ended craft with raking stem and stern, swooping buoyant sheer, twenty-eight to thirty feet overall, they hung in their davits ready for instant lowering: two or three boats to port and one at the starboard quarter, that side being left clear for the cutting in of the whale carcass.

So many of these lightly built and graceful craft were required by the whaling fleet that they can claim to be one of the world's earliest mass production line of boats. Builders would steam bend frames and stems, cut planks, thwarts, and knees, all to be stockpiled for a production run. One New Bedford builder, James Beetle, told of getting a verbal order for forty boats from one whaleship owner. Beetle's whaleboats bore his burned-in brand name and a carved-in serial number.

Stowed in the open hull of these craft, perfect for their purpose, lay the simple but effective hunting gear: There were harpoons—irons—for the initial spearing and lances for the final killing. Two whale line tubs holding three hundred fathoms of carefully coiled, lightly tarred three-strand hemp rope the thickness of a thumb. A wooden drogue for hitching to the whale line to slow and tire a harpooned whale. Several ten-foot pointed staffs with flags—waifs—for marking the ownership of the dead whale. A boat blubber spade for cutting a hole in the whale's lips or flukes (through the hole went a toggle and line for towing the animal back to the whaleship). Six ash oars, five for rowing and the sixth, considerably longer, for steering. Six paddles; a wooden piggin for bailing; a freshwater keg; a

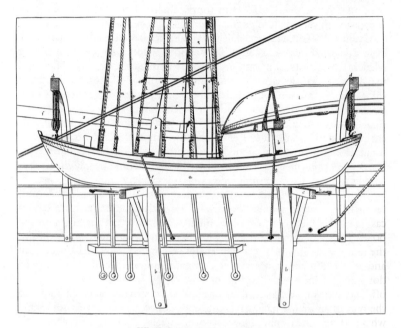

Whaleboat on the cranes

"The three boats dropped into the sea; while, with a dexterous, off-handed daring, unknown in any other vocation, the sailors, goat-like, leaped down the rolling ship's side
into the tossed boats below."   —Herman Melville
(Illustration from *The Fisheries & Fishing Industries of the United States,* 1887)

lantern keg containing lantern, tinderbox, matches, candles, pipes, tobacco, biscuits. Several thick-padded canvas rectangles—nippers—for hand
protection when gripping the whale line once the whale had been struck.
A bucket for wetting the whale line as it surged around the loggerhead,[2]
for a struck and sounding whale could take out whale line so fast that the
friction often ignited the timber post. Spars, sails, rigging, compass,
boathook, grapnel, hatchets, and knives completed the outfit.

Six men formed the whaleboat's crew. All played a specific part in the
highly choreographed performance that lay in whale killing. Warships had
their gun drill; whaleships had their boat drill.

The two leading players in this marine ballet were the boatheader and
the boatsteerer. The boatheader (one of the mates and sometimes the
captain) commanded and steered the whaleboat on its approach to the
whale. The boatsteerer rowed in the forward position and harpooned the

whale. When the boat was fast to the whale, the two men changed positions, the boatsteerer moving aft to the long steering oar and the boatheader forward to lance and kill the whale. It was an acrobatic exchange calling for sure footwork and balance in a wildly pitching and rolling whaleboat encumbered with an obstacle course of men, oars, thwarts, masts, sails, and whale line.

Aft of the boatsteerer rowed the bowman; the most experienced foremast hand, he helped the boatsteerer in stepping and lowering the mast. Aft of the bowman came the midship oarsman, usually the most inexperienced hand on board. Aft of him came the tub oarsman, who wetted the whale line as it smoked around the loggerhead. The stroke or after oarsman coiled the whale line as it was hauled inboard, and he caught and secured the mast when it was lowered. He also bailed.

"Lower away there, d'ye here?" was the invariable call to action that set the men in motion. Line tubs were loaded aboard, gripes and tackles cast off; the whaleboat was raised slightly, and the cranes were swung inboard. The mate and boatsteerer went down in the boat as it was lowered, the mate aft by his steering oar and the boatsteerer forward. Once afloat and rocking in the swell, the four remaining crew members scrambled down the chains and took their appointed places. Davit tackles were cast off, oars shipped, and the whaleboat pulled away from the mother ship. If the whales lay downwind, the mast was stepped and sails were set. If the whales lay upwind, the long row started. The whale line was now led from the tub, around the loggerhead, and then forward between the rowing men to the bow chock and then hitched to the harpoon. The slim, narrow craft, fully armed, ash oars bending under the strain, creaming toward her target, was now a deadly missile set on its course.

The result of this conflict—a half ton of human muscle against sixty tons of whale—invariably ended in death. For the whaleman the means were various: a simple drowning; a bone-crunching death from flukes or jaws; or—"a speechlessly quick chaotic bundling of man into Eternity," according to Herman Melville—being snatched by a foul turn of the racing whale line and plucked overboard.

Some whales died quickly and quietly. Some sounded and set off at speed underwater, towing the whaleboat in a mad careering white-water run, the famous "Nantucket sleigh-ride." Others fought back with the ferocity shown in the whaling prints. But the whale's end usually came with the flurry, the final furious swimming in a narrowing circle, spouting blood, before rolling "fin out," dead. Old whalemen claimed that the final moment always came as the whale faced the sun.

The first Pacific sperm whale was taken in 1789. The whaleship was the *Amelia*, owned by the English whaling firm of Samuel Enderby but officered by Nantucket men. The first mate, Archaelus Hammond, lanced and

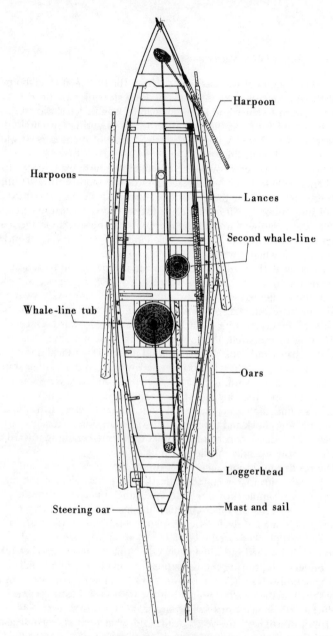

Harpoon

Harpoons

Lances

Second whale-line

Whale-line tub

Oars

Loggerhead

Steering oar

Mast and sail

Whaleboat equipment

"For lightness and form, for carrying capacity compared to its weight and sea-going qualities, for speed and facility of movement at the word of command . . . the whaleboat is simply perfect."

—William Davis

(Illustration by author. Simplified from drawing in
The Fisheries & Fishing Industries of the United States, 1887)

killed the whale off the Chilean coast. It was the first of many. The *Amelia* returned to England with her hold packed with barrels of sperm oil. Two years later, the floodgates creaking open, nine whaleships were working the Pacific. A half century later hundreds of New England whaleships and thousands of men were crisscrossing the Pacific and creating havoc among the islands and islanders. Men from Nantucket, New Bedford, New London, and Fairhaven were more at home in the South Sea Islands than on Boston Common. Honolulu, Lahaina, and Papeete, with their grogshops, gaming houses, and brothels, became the Pacific's red-light districts. A flavor of the problems that beset these ports may be seen in the code of offenses and penalties drawn up by Honolulu's harried forces of law and order.

Hanging, as a murderer, for knowingly and maliciously violating these laws whereby a contagious disease is communicated on shore.

$60.00 fine on any captain who leaves on shore any men without written leave from the Government.

$10.00 for coming ashore with a knife, sword-cane, or any other dangerous weapon.

$2.00 for every seaman seized ashore after 9:30 P.M., at firing of second gun from fort.

$1.00 to $5.00 for hallooing or making a noise in the streets at night.

$6.00 for striking another in a quarrel.

$5.00 for racing or swift riding in the streets or frequented roads.

$6.00 for desecrating the Sabbath for the first time; $2.00 for second time; and fine doubled for every repetition.

$6.00 for catching deserter near harbor; $12.00 if 10 miles off.

$6.00 for drunkenness.

$10.00 for lewd, seductive, and lascivious conduct.

$5.00 for fornication.

$30.00 for adultery.

$50.00 for rape.

The initial whaling ground discovered by the *Amelia*—the On-Shore Ground off the coasts of Chile and Peru—had, fifty years later, expanded to fifteen whaling areas. The most important included the Off-Shore Ground, bounded by the 5°S and 10°S latitudes and 9°W and 120°W longitudes; the Middle Ground, between New Zealand and Australia; the Japan Ground, between the Japanese coast and the Bonin Islands; the On-the-Line Grounds, running along the equator between South America and the Gilbert Islands—more than a quarter of the Earth's girth. In addition were areas off the northwest coast of North America; the North Pacific between 27°N and 35°N latitudes; the South Pacific between 21°S and 27°S latitudes; grounds close to the Hawaiian, Society, Samoan, Fiji, and Kingsmill islands; and off the coasts of southern Australia and New Zealand.

A typical whaleship voyage would sail from New England in early summer, double Cape Horn, and cruise the On-Shore Ground. The whaleship would then recruit—barter or buy fresh provisions and supplies—at a convenient Chilean or Peruvian port before sailing in November to the Off-Shore Ground. Two or three months would be spent cruising there before sailing for the Marquesas followed by a great clockwise sweep through the Pacific: along the Equator, the Japan Ground, the northwest coast of North America, before ending at Hawaii to recruit for the next season on the Off-Shore Ground.

A vessel leaving New England in the fall would sail via the Cape of Good Hope to arrive at the New Zealand grounds not later than March and would cruise there for six to eight weeks until the southern winter set in. Then it was north and a cruise eastward between 22°S and 28°S until the South American coast was reached. After recruiting, the whaleship would sail in November for the Off-Shore Ground.

A mixture of honor, pride, and greed kept the whaleship masters—often part owners—at this ocean wandering until all the barrels were full. Voyages could last four years. Whalemen's wives saw little of their husbands. One woman, married for eleven years, had her husband home for only one year's worth of scattered days. Captain George Gardener of Nantucket spent thirty-seven years at sea, sailed a million miles, and was under his own roof only four years and eight months.

The Pacific whalemen—in the perverse way of cliques within a group—spoke with contempt of their Atlantic whaling brethren (from Provincetown for the most part and called plum-puddings) who took voyages numbered only in months rather than years.

One tale has a veteran master, used to long Pacific voyages, forced to take a cruise aboard a plum-pudding. Regarding this voyage as no more than a short interlude, he sailed without bidding farewell to his wife. "Because," as he remarked, "I'll only be gone for a year." His imperturbable wife, needless to say, had the last word. On his return, spotting his arrival from a window, she met him at the door with a bucket. "Now fill this at the pump" was her sole greeting. "Supper will be ready in a few minutes."

Letters between whalemen and their family and friends at home were as haphazard as the whaleship's wanderings. Outward-bound vessels would carry letters addressed with laconic simplicity: "Obed Starbuck, Ship *Diana*, Pacific Ocean." One wife wrote more than a hundred letters to her husband during his three-year voyage. Only six were received. The Galápagos Islands, being much frequented by whaleships for stocking up with turtles, had a crude mailbox on Charles Island. Here outward-bound and homeward-bound vessels would leave and pick up messages.

Such an idiosyncratic mailing system led to many fo'c'sle stories. One such correspondence, brief in content but lengthy in time, between a laconic Nantucket wife and her equally laconic husband in the Pacific was reputed to have run as follows: "Dear Abner, Where did you put the axe? Love, Judith." Sixteen months later the reply arrived in Nantucket: "Dear Judith, What do you want the axe for? Love, Abner." In the Pacific, more than a year later, Abner heard again from his wife: "Dear Abner, Found the axe. What did you do with the hammer? Love, Judith."

An Old Testament aura surrounds New England whaling. Here is a wandering tribe of Israelites complete with Abners, Obeds, Ezras, Isaiahs, Ishmaels, Jeremiahs, Ezekiels, Michas, Obidiahs, Daniels, Malachis. *Hierarchic* is the adjective that comes to mind when one thinks of a sailor's structured shipboard life, *hierarchic* and *patriarchic* when one thinks of the New England whaleman's.

It was primarily tidewater New England—up until the middle of the 1820s—that supplied the menfolk who manned the whaleships. For a village youth from the Massachusetts coastline, Long Island, Martha's Vineyard, and Nantucket, it was the road to local fame, fortune, and prestige. The route was clearly marked: cabin boy, foremast hand, boatsteerer, mate, captain, owner, whaling merchant.

Nantucket stands as the paradigm of a society where whaling was central to community life, where the way to a girl's heart was to have darted harpoon or lance and killed a whale, where every boy coveted the chockpin[3] worn on a boatsteerer's coat lapel as a mark of his rank. Here was an island where Herman Melville's Quakers, those "most sanguinary of all sailors and whalehunters . . . fighting Quakers . . . Quakers with a vengeance," played a leading role and where the community shared in the ownership of the vessel: "widows, fatherless children, and chancery wards; each owning about the value of a timber head, or a foot of plank, or a nail or two in the ship." When the ship sailed, it was certain that many of the crew were related to the captain, a floating patriarchical tribe.

The whaleship's hierarchy was repeated aboard the smaller whaleboat. The dangerous, and seemingly needless, changing of positions by the boatsteerer and the boatheader after the harpooning of the whale was strictly hierarchical. W. J. Dakin, in his *Whalemen Adventurers,* thinking this a curious maneuver, asked an old whaleman to explain it. The harpooning and killing of the whale, said the old fellow, were two different skills. The killing belonged to the more experienced boatheader and was therefore his by right. The sacrifice, in short, had to be performed by one of the high priests.

The trinity of the whaleboat—boatheader, boatsteerer, foremast hands—was repeated aboard the whaleship. The officers—captain and mates—slept and ate aft. Forward of the officers' cabins came the steerage; here slept the boatsteerers, cooper, and carpenter. The most numerous body of men, the foremast hands, lived forward in the fo'c'sle. Here some dozen to a score of men slept and ate in a nautical Dickensian cellar slum. Crude, rough lumber bunks in tiers lined the hull of the triangular compartment. Access was by a hatch in the deck, the only source of light and ventilation, that had to be closed in foul weather. Well might Frank Bullen, a young seaman desperate for a berth, find himself "booked for a sailor's horror—a cruise in a whaler." Another green hand, J. R. Browne, wrote that his whaler's fo'c'sle was "black and slimy with filth, very small . . . filled with a compound of foul air, smoke, sea-chests, greasy pans, tainted meat, Portuguese ruffians and sea-sick Americans." Browne thought Kentucky pigsties far cleaner.

The messing arrangements for the fo'c'sle were as crude as the accommodation. Salt pork or salt beef—known with good cause as salt horse to the whalemen—formed the basis for the perennial stew known as lobscouse. The cook dumped the boiled meat into a wooden kid, coffee into a bucket, and then yelled for it to be taken forward by a couple of foremast hands. The men hunkered down on the deck or in the fo'c'sle and grabbed what they could. In more civilized fo'c'sles one man would spear a chunk of meat, and another, with his back turned, would call out whose portion it should be. Every man had a tin plate, a tin mug, a fork, and his sheath knife. Utensil cleaning was simple. The plates were hung in nets and cleaned by the omnipresent cockroaches.

Messing for the officers and steerage was conducted with a touch more polish but with an etiquette worthy of a hidebound guards regiment or primitive South Sea island tribe. The officers ate aft in the great cabin and were served at a covered table by a steward and ate off heavy chinaware. But a strict pecking order prevailed. The captain was the first to enter, be seated, and then be served. The mates followed in strict order of rank. Finishing and rising from the table were in inverse order. First to finish and leave (having gobbled his meal) was the lowliest mate. After the captain had left, the steward would remove the canvas tablecloth, butter dish, and sugar pot. The sugar pot would be replaced with a molasses jug. Only officers sweetened their coffee with sugar and spread butter on their hard and soft tack. The steward would then wait for the entry of the boatsteerers.

Whaleships were notorious for their dreary, monotonous diet. And tightfisted Yankee owners, with a calculating eye cocked on the ledger books, saw no reason to improve it. Any changes to the salt horse could be effected at sea with fish, porpoise, and turtles from the Galápagos Islands. Old hands would tell the green hands that the turtles were reincarnated ships' captains.

Green hands were also considered credulous fair game by shipping agents, outfitters, and owners. William Davis, in his *Nimrod of the Sea*, described how he was inveigled by an owner into signing aboard the whaleship *Chelsea* in the 1830s:

You think you'll like the sea? Of course you will. Nice life—very, if you take it right. Been aboard the *Chelsea* yet? Yes; a good ship the *Chelsea*, and such a sailer! A regular Baltimore clipper; easy times aboard that ship. You've trade-winds most of the way to Cape Horn; trade winds you know, are steady; as fixed, sir, as the needle to the pole, as the poet has it. And then there's the Pacific! Grand sea that; all about Juan Fernandez, Magellan, and the Southern Cross it's as calm and smiling as a mill-dam—so smooth that the illimitable sea seems a boundless oil-tank; where you see reflected in it the belt of Orion and the Pleiades. The thought almost tempts me to run out on a voyage, just to see that whaleman's heaven.

Do you know that you get fresh beef at sea? Yes, sir, you do. Porpoises are to be had for the catching. Porpoises has muscle in it; you'd stiffen up on porpoise. And albatross too, big as geese; a little oily, but you'll get used to that. It makes a man waterproof to eat albatross.

Ah! you've signed. That's a good Bill; there's a captain's berth ahead, if you earn it. Now run down to Mr. Strong in the basement; he'll finish your outfit in a jiffy. . . .

This silver-tongued orator was Thomas W. Williams, who founded a successful whaling firm in New London and was also elected to Congress. A portrait shows him to be clean-shaven, innocent of eye, and with a mane of silver hair. He looks like a guileless and distinguished bishop. J. R. Browne had signed aboard a whaler after seeing a notice on a New York shipping office door:

WANTED IMMEDIATELY!!!
Six able-bodied landsmen, to go on a whaling voyage from New Bedford. Apply at stairs before 5 o'clock P.M.

The agent proved to be "an excessively polite old gentleman of prepossessing appearance"—and one with an obviously well-polished sales patter:

"Whaling gentlemen, is tolerably hard at first, but it's the finest business in the world for enterprising young men. If you are *determined* to make a voyage, I'll put you in the way of shipping in a most elegant vessel, well fitted: that's the great thing, well fitted. Vigilance and activity will insure you rapid promotion. I haven't the least doubt but you'll come home boatsteerers. I sent off six college students a few days ago, and a poor fellow who had been flogged away from home by a vicious wife. A whaler, gentlemen," continued the agent, rising in eloquence, "a whaler is a place of refuge for the distressed and persecuted, a school for the dissipated, an asylum for the needy! There's nothing like it. You can see the world; you can see something of life!"

Here, from owner and shipping agent, is a suave deceitfulness on a heroic scale worthy of W. C. Fields at his screen best.

If Yankee shipowners were parsimonious in their provisioning, they also balked at paying for a ship's surgeon. The ailments and injuries of the whalemen serving aboard American whalers (British whaleships carried surgeons) were taken care of by the captain.

The doctoring was done by numbers. Every vessel carried a small medicine chest filled with numbered bottles containing common drugs and potions. It also contained a small booklet. A seaman reporting sick would describe his symptoms, and the captain would thumb through the booklet until he came across something that corresponded. The booklet gave him a number. The dosage came from the numbered bottle. (Little different, in fact, from modern family doctoring.) Some captains thought this time-wasting pandering to a seaman's whim. All men reporting sick were merely given a dose of Glauber's salt, calomel, or castor oil. Some concocted their own specific with a plug of tobacco soaked in whale oil. The seaman was required to down the mixture every few hours until cured. Surgery was equally crude. No surgical instruments were provided, and the captain made do with carving knives, carpenter's saws, and chisels. Some patients, amazingly enough, survived the butchery.

A whaleman's life at sea, his living in cramped and filthy quarters, with its monotonous diet, harsh discipline, long hours of grueling and dangerous work interspersed with days of boredom, had few solaces. One of them was storytelling; another was the painstaking working of sperm whale teeth into decorated articles, scrimshaw. The main solace, however, was tobacco. One whaleship's slop chest held thirty-eight boxes of tobacco totaling 4,329 pounds. It cost the owners sixteen cents a pound and was sold to the whalemen at forty cents a pound.

This gargantuan consumption of tobacco makes sense when seen against the peculiarly American habit, noted by all foreign visitors, of tobacco chewing and spitting. Fanny Trollope found the spitting incessant and that "this most vile and universal habit of chewing tobacco is the cause of a remarkable peculiarity in the male physiognomy of Americans; their lips are almost uniformly thin and compressed . . . the habit above mentioned, which pervades all classes (excepting the literary) well accounts for it, as the act of expressing the juices of this loathsome herb, enforces exactly that position of the lips, which gives this remarkable peculiarity to the American countenance." Charles Dickens called Washington "the head-quarters of tobaccoo-tinctured saliva," a city where notices in the public buildings implored visitors "to squirt the essence of their quids, or 'plugs,' as I have heard them called by gentlemen learned in this kind of sweetmeat, into the national spittoons, and not about the bases of the marble columns."

Ashore the whaleman's solace was found in the grogshop, gaming house, and brothel. Their locations throughout the Pacific and Indian oceans loomed large in the fo'c'sle's lurid anecdotes. Care had to be taken in exotic Zanzibar. Here was a harbor filled with Arab dhows, refuse, and bloated bodies. This was a slave market town, and its filthy narrow streets were crowded with a jostling crowd of burnoused Arabs, coffee-colored Swahilis, file-toothed Africans, Indians, and Persians with calculating eyes. Three-quarters of the population were rotted with venereal disease, and the vile smell of putrid fish and copra and the open sewers all hinted at endemic diseases and fevers; a whaleman could die of dysentery or yellow fever in a few days if imprisoned in the notorious coral-walled fort. The disreputable Rocks area of Sydney also called for caution. This was a thieves' kitchen filled with muggers, deserters, hoydenish prostitutes, pigs, rats, raw sewage, grogshops, and brothels in equal proportion. The prostitutes had a habit of slipping their marks knockout drops—usually laudanum—and then emptying their pockets. It made the Five Points area of New York and Boston's Ann Street look like a Sunday in Philadelphia.

East, across the stormy Tasman Sea, lay New Zealand's Bay of Islands, a favorite haunt of whaleships, sealers, and traders. This was the South Pacific's catchment area for a polyglot collection of rogues, adventurers, runaway seamen, and escaped convicts. One observer called this lowlife white population "the veriest refuse of civilized society," an opinion shared by Charles Darwin. The *Beagle* spent a week in the bay, and on sailing, Darwin wrote: "I believe we were all glad to leave New Zealand. It is not a pleasant place. Amongst the natives there is absent that charming simplicity which is found at Tahiti; and the greater part of the English are the very refuse of society." But ashore, for seamen, were billiard halls, skittle alleys, grogshops, and brothels. Thousands of miles northward lay Papeete, Honolulu, and Lahaina, all with similar delights for the whalemen.

Gambling, drinking, and fornication required money. No wages were paid to the whalemen, but each man signed on for a proportion of the profits—the lay. A captain might receive 1/15; the first mate 1/25; the second mate 1/40; the third mate 1/50; boatsteerers 1/100; experienced foremast hands 1/175; green hands 1/200.

The lay, however, had a disconcerting way of shrinking under the deductions levied by the owners and the whaleship's captain. Automatic deductions included a 10 percent charge of the lay for "leakage and shrinkage" of the whale oil; a 3 percent insurance charge; a loading and unloading charge; a "Medicine Chest" charge of $10; the outfitter's charge plus interest; cash advanced during the voyage plus interest; items bought from the slop chest (sold to the seaman at double the owner's cost) plus interest. Interest was charged at 1 per cent per month. With this creative accounting a $250 lay for a four-year voyage could be reduced to $50. Some foremast hands returned from a voyage and found themselves *owing* money to the owners.

By the middle of the 1830s a whaleship's crew had changed for the worse. From being close-knit New England provincial it had become—particularly in the fo'c'sle—a cosmopolitan lowlife cast from John Gay's *Beggar's Opera*. Here were drunkards, escaped criminals, vagrants, ne'er-do-wells, and men escaping from creditors or family. Charles Tucker, a New Bedford whaling merchant, wrote that "it has of late become very fashionable for sailors to assume some fictitious name by which they ship and are known by before they sail." (Crew lists show that a remarkable number of old-fashioned American aristocracy went whaling: John Quincy Adams, Samuel Adams, George Washington, Thomas Jefferson, etc.)

One fo'c'sle contained two boys who had run from a house of correction; two reprobate youths from wealthy families who had been packed off to sea in the pious hope of bringing about reform; an orphan with no known relatives; two down easters from the Maine coast; an Irishman just landed in the United States; an English printer who had been shanghaied in New York; a Dutchman; and eight Portuguese. All the boatsteerers were Portuguese except for one New Zealand Maori.

Youth and inexperience characterized the fo'c'sle. One vessel left New Bedford in 1832 with fourteen foremasthands of whom only four had ever been to sea. The afterguard, mates and captain, still tended to be Yankee stock, but the gulf had widened between them and the fo'c'sle. Discipline became tougher and more brutal, with bucko mates delivering it with fist, boot, and belaying pin. Floggings were common. The seaman was strung up by his wrists (more sadistic captains preferred the thumbs) to the weather rigging, toes just touching the deck (when the ship rolled, the man would be suspended by wrists or thumbs), back bared, and flogged with a knotted rope end. Confinement in the run was another punishment. This was a small hellish place, a crouching-room-only cell under the deck without light or ventilation. Diet was hardtack and water.

This was a Foreign Legion of the seas—but one without its esprit de corps. Brutal officers, bad beef, bad pork, and worse biscuit led to desertions on a grand scale. The *James Maury,* during one voyage, had two mates, three boatsteerers, and a large proportion of the foremasthands desert. A whaleship's single cruise often required hiring the equivalent of three, four, or even five complete crews. The literary world's most famous deserter, the twenty-two-year-old Herman Melville, jumped ship with a companion when the *Acushnet* was anchored off Nuku Hiva in the Marquesas Islands.[4]

The replacements for these deserting seamen (three men in ten deserted) came from the natives of the Pacific islands; the rogues and riffraff of the South American coast; and the beachcombers, those dissolute and improvident whites who, for a large part, were made up of convicts from New South Wales and runaway seamen. The nicknames of these foremasthands reel off the tongue like a host of characters in a picaresque novel: Bembo, Jingling Joe, Long Jim, Flash Jack, Black Dan, Navy Bob, Red Sandy, Long-legged Bill, Big-foot Jack, Chaw-o'-tobacco Jim, Handsome Tom, Bully Clincher.

Mutiny, for a desperate crew, was the one irrevocable step beyond desertion, one, if blood had been shed, toward the hangman's noose. And every whaleship officer, after the violently bloody 1824 mutiny aboard the *Globe* of Nantucket, must have kept a wary eye cocked for potential troublemakers.

This was a dreadful affair that makes the *Bounty*'s mutiny look like a squabble at a primary school picnic. The mutiny had been led by Samuel Comstock, a Nantucket boatsteerer, and included beachcombers hired at Honolulu to replace six deserters. The captain and the three mates were slaughtered in their cabins, and their bodies, one man still barely alive, thrown overboard. The killing continued with the steward, convicted by a kangaroo court of treachery, hanged at the foreyard. At Mili Atoll in the Marshall Islands, Comstock was shot and killed by some of the mutineers. The Mili Atoll natives, angered by the mutineers' treatment of their women, then massacred loyalists and mutineers—except for two youths, Cyrus Hussey of Nantucket and William Lay of Saybrook. Six loyalists aboard the *Globe* cut the anchor cable and sailed across the Pacific to Chile, where they told their story to the U.S. consul. (So far the story is a body-strewn Shakespearean tragedy. Hollywood now takes over.)

The U.S. schooner *Dolphin* was ordered to Mili Atoll, where on the beach of one of the islands a search party made a find. The beach, wrote Lieutenant Hiram Paulding, "was strewed with several hundreds of staves of beef and pork barrels, and old pieces of canvas and cloth. In advancing further, they found a skeleton, lightly covered with sand, and a box containing a few Spanish dollars." Hussey and Lay, who were being spirited from island to island by the natives, were eventually tracked down and rescued by Paulding in two daring beachfront confrontations with the natives. The youths had spent almost two years on the islands, were burned almost black, had been tattooed from neck to feet, spoke the native language but, having been kept apart from each other, had almost lost their English. Within five years their account of the mutiny and Paulding's narrative of the search had been published. For whalemen it was a warning that mutineers would be searched out by the government. For writers of tales set in the South Seas the two books provided a treasure trove of gems for picaresque adventure stories.

The late Saul Steinberg's cover illustration for the 20 March 1976 issue of the *New Yorker* magazine brilliantly encapsulated the New Yorker's perspective of North America and the rest of the world. In the foreground, looking west, lies a section of midtown Manhattan—Ninth and Tenth avenues clearly marked—with the sidewalks full of bustling people and the streets full of cars. Beyond the Hudson River stretches North America. The United States is shown as a neat green rectangle with Canada on the right and Mexico on the left. A few names are sprinkled across the green rectangle: Jersey, Texas, Utah, Nebraska, Kansas City, Chicago, Washington, D.C., Los Angeles, Las Vegas. Beyond lies the Pacific Ocean with three lumps on the horizon marked China, Japan, Russia.

New Yorkers took this illustration to their calloused hearts. Within months it was on sale as a poster. (The drawing is full of sly digs at the rest of America—apparent only to a New Yorker. The despised state of New

Jersey is merely Jersey; San Francisco does not appear; Chicago's initial *C* is in lowercase.)

A Steinberg perspective of the 1830s, for a New England merchant trader, would have required more prominence to be given to the Pacific Ocean and China. The very profitable China trade brought to America tea, porcelains, lacquer ware, silks, and nankeens, all luxury goods fetching a high price. But other than silver specie what did the Chinese require in exchange for their products? The manufactured goods of the "flowery-flag devils"—Americans—were thought primitive and crude. Other items had to be found to tempt the Chinese. In exchange went smuggled opium, which floated up the Canton River and into the Celestial Empire on a silent tide of squeeze—bribes. Most of the opium came from India and was brought in by British (mainly Scots) and American traders, with Boston merchants shipping in nearly all the Turkish opium production. Ginseng root (from New England), bêche-de-mer, the skins of fur seal and sea otter, sandalwood, pearls, mother-of-pearl, and tortoiseshell also found a ready market.

All these items, except for the opium and ginseng, came from the seas and islands of the Pacific. Seal and otter skins made luxurious and warm winter clothing for the wealthy Chinese. Pearls decorated the concubine's neck, and tortoiseshell combs held her hair. Mother-of-pearl was inlaid into cabinets and caskets. A potency tonic was made from ginseng root. Bêche-de-mer, a sea slug found in shallow waters, was smoke-dried and looked like a small brown sausage. The Chinese thought it a powerful aphrodisiac and added it to soups. Salem vessels and traders dominated the trade on the Fiji Islands. It was a labor-intensive business with hundreds of canoe-borne natives scouring the reefs and shallows for the slugs, which were then gutted and boiled in large iron pots by a second group of natives. The smoking and drying house was a large structure about a hundred-feet long and twenty feet wide. A ditch filled with burning timber ran the full length of the building. The cleaned slugs were then spread on racks and smoke-dried. A third group of natives was employed in the endless task of cutting timber and tending the fire.

This concentration of people—natives and ship's crew—required considerable quantities of food. The chiefs' baking ovens were kept hot and supplied with yams and pigs from the surrounding islands. Bêche-de-mer trading in the Fiji Islands was considered dangerous. These were the archetype cannibal islands. Sailors and traders walked warily, protected their backs, made sure their holstered pistols were loose and primed. White "long-pig" had been known to go into those hot baking ovens even though the natives cheerfully admitted that they favored darker flesh. White man's flesh, they claimed, was too salty.

Bêche-de-mer might raise a mandarin's libido, but a large stand of sandalwood could bring a different type of lust into a Yankee trader's eyes.

A small paragraph in the 9 October 1812 edition of the *Newburyport Herald and Country Gazette* holds the clue: "The ship Hunter, Rogers, of Boston has arrived at Whampoe from an Island Capt. R. discovered, near Fegee Islands with a cargo of sandal wood the first cost of which was 800 dls which he sold for 80,000 dls. this is making money with a witness!" Sandalwood was much prized by the Chinese. This sweet-smelling wood was used for joss sticks, fans, fine cabinet work, and chairs. Sandalwood oil was distilled from the shavings and went into perfumes. Buddhists burned it for incense, and Indian Brahmins used it in a paste for caste marks. But the trade in this sweet-smelling wood could also carry with it the stench of death.

In 1839 two missionaries were killed on the beach at Eromanga when the natives thought their vessel a sandalwood trader. The sandalwooders, said the natives, had recently killed a number of their people and plundered their plantations. A few years after the missionaries' deaths three sandalwood vessels arrived at the island. Aboard the vessels were sixty Tongans, recruited, according to the schooner *Sophia*'s mate, "to cut sandalwood and to protect our vessels while in the New Hebrides." The whites stayed aboard their vessels, and the armed Tongans went ashore to cut sandalwood. A fight developed, and about sixty islanders were killed by the Tongans. The survivors, men, women, and children, were then herded into two caves. Wood and roof thatch were then piled at the entrances and set alight. (A missionary account called it a "savoury roast.") The Tongans returned to their woodcutting.

Hawaii's vast stands of sandalwood had been discovered in the 1790s. The wood held no special value for the Hawaiians—but an enormous value for the Boston merchants who came to dominate the trade. Within forty years the forests had vanished. The natives, however, had been introduced to the financial black magic of promissory notes (American warships visited the islands to enforce payment and protect American commerce), and the bewildered King Kamehameha to the alien facts of national debt. Clapboard New England houses lined dusty streets, and righteous Boston mission zealots, scandalized at the sight of half-naked girls lounging aboard ships, set up laws forbidding the girls from swimming out to vessels riding at anchor. An armed whaleship crew, outraged at what they thought missionary meddling, laid siege to a Lahaina mission house.

Another man of the same mind, the rough and ready Lieutenant John Percival—"Mad Jack" to his crew—commander of the schooner *Dolphin* in the search for the *Globe*'s mutineers, sailed into Honolulu in 1826. It was the first American naval vessel to visit the islands. Mad Jack thought the missionary edict idiotic and threatened to shoot the Reverend Hiram Bingham, whom he held responsible. Mad Jack had the mission schools emptied, much to the delight of both girls and sailors. Word of this soon came to respectable ears in Washington, and Percival's career was wrecked.

Thirty-five years later the missionaries were still savoring their triumph in *The Friend:* "The *Dolphin* was upon her return passage from the Mul-graves, when she touched at Honolulu, and those disgraceful scenes oc-curred, which gave Lieut. Percival an unenviable notoriety, and prevented him from obtaining the command of another vessel for nearly twenty years. He still lives, and in his old age doubtless regrets the mad freaks of his youth." For good or ill, Hawaii had entered the free trade evangelical nineteenth century.

If the "Nantucketois," as Thomas Jefferson called them, dominated the world's whaling grounds, Salemites could be found, thumbs tucked into waistcoats, smoke wreathing from seegars, haggling over cargoes on waterfronts spread around the globe from the Atlantic to the South China Sea. Salem ships packed their holds with peppers from Sumatra, coffee from Arabia, cloves and spices from Zanzibar, tea from China, and pipes of wine from Madeira. The trade goods sliding along this web of com-merce included coarse American cotton cloth—cheap cotton garments and blankets were known as merikani throughout East Africa—tobacco, beads, trinkets, mirrors, knives, axes, rum, ammunition, bullet molds, and muskets.

New Zealand's Maoris soon came to realize that the powerful god and religion of the white man was the *pu*—the musket. An even more powerful god was the *tupara*—the double-barreled musket. The Maoris, a belligerent race with a fearsome reputation for cannibalism, were con-verted. Sydney had an economy based on rum; the Bay of Islands soon had its economy based on the musket. Trading, sealing, and whaling vessels needing fresh provisions from the Maoris found the exchange rate to be one musket for 120 baskets of potatoes and 10 large hogs. The mission-aries also needed provisions. But they soon found their axes, hoes, and blankets a much-devalued currency. They too joined the musket economy. The Maoris set out to settle old scores.

A formidable Maori chief, Hongi Hike, had returned to New Zealand in 1819 after a visit to England. At Sydney he had exchanged all his Lon-don presents for three hundred muskets. The canny Hongi had noted that Britain was ruled by one chief, King George IV, and decided that New Zealand should be ruled by one chief, Hongi. Augustus Earle met the tat-tooed Maori in 1827. "So mild was the expression of his features," wrote Earle, "that he would have been the last man I should have imagined ac-customed to scenes of bloodshed and cruelty." Nevertheless, during the 1820s and early 1830s this mild-featured chief set in motion fierce inter-tribal wars that led to the slaughter of some forty thousand Maoris.

A by-product of this killing was an increase in one item of the Pacific's "curio" trade. (Ishmael, of Herman Melville's *Moby Dick,* first hears of this trade at the Spouter Inn when the landlord explains the reason for the ab-sence of Queequeg, Ishmael's unknown bedmate: "But be easy, be easy, this here harpooner I have been tellin' you of has just arrived from the south seas, where he bought up a lot of 'balmed New Zealand heads [great curios, you know], and he's sold all on 'em but one, and that one he's trying to sell tonight, 'cause to-morrow's Sunday, and it would not do to be sellin' human heads about the streets when folks is goin' to churches. He wanted to, last Sunday, but I stopped him just as he was goin' out of the door with four heads strung on a string, for all the airth like a string of inions.")

Cannibalism, tattooing, and the preserving of human heads all were part of Maori culture. The New Zealanders were also well aware of the perplexing European desire for Maori canoe paddles, war clubs, and primitive tools. Preserved human heads, particularly finely tattooed ones, came high on the European collector's list. (Abel Dupetit-Thouars, a French naval officer, wrote that he had seen, in 1825, two New Zealand heads for sale in Rio de Janeiro at six thousand francs.) The Maoris, catering for the market, soon turned it into an industry. Chiefs had the most elaborately tattooed and therefore the most valuable heads. This tended to limit the supply, and some heads were tattooed after death (this near counterfeiting could be detected by an expert). Some fine heads, still on their owners' shoulders, would be pointed out by a chief to a valued curio-collecting trader. On the trader's return trip the preserved head would be ready and waiting. This parading of wares sometimes failed. One keen observer of the New Zealand market, F. E. Maning, wrote that "a scoundrel slave had the conscience to run away with his own head after the trouble and expense had been gone to to make it more valuable."

The Reverend Samuel Marsden (the convicts' "flogging parson" of New South Wales and the protégé of the evangelical William Wilberforce) recorded the visit of a Maori chief to the *Prince of Denmark* at Sydney. Laid out for sale on the cabin table were fourteen tattooed heads.[5] The chief recognized them all. His late friends had become curios. It was this incident that lead the New South Wales governor to issue, in 1831, a general order forbidding, at least officially, this macabre trade.

The same year, 1831, half the world away from Sydney and in New York's Mariner's Church, an audience of seamen—an audience, according to the *New York Observer,* "over which solemnity reigned"—sat shoulder to shoulder and listened to a sermon based on the text "But truly, as the Lord liveth, and as thy soul liveth, there is but a step between me and death." After the sermon the seamen listened to the minister tell the story of the schooner *Antarctic,* just returned to New York, and the fate of her crew, who had sailed from the city in 1829. Bound on a voyage into the Pacific in search of fur seals, the schooner had sailed with twenty-three men and one woman. Even though virtue hovered over the *Antarctic,* for the schooner had carried "bibles and tracts . . . that the means of religious instruction might not be wanting when they should be far from the doors of a Christian sanctuary and the voice of the living preacher be lost in un-measured distance" and "no ardent spirits whatever had been admitted on board as an article of drink," six of the crew had died of fever and thirteen had been killed by Solomon Islanders. (The *Antarctic* had found no fur seals, and the seamen were ashore on the island to gather bêche-de-mer.)

Abby Jane Morrell, the captain's wife, had sailed and survived the *Antarctic*'s hair-raising voyage. Such a voyage had enough exciting in-gredients to make an armchair sailor's eyes bulge like gooseberries. This was book material. Abby Jane Morrell wrote one. In it, along with the page-turning events, she confessed to being "mortified" on finding her husband navigating—even out from New York's harbor—with English charts. Mrs. Morrell could not understand why the U.S. government did not print charts and sailing directions. "It were well," she wrote, "that we should do something for the world whose commerce we enjoy. . . . We have now a name to support, and what have we done to raise its glory?"

Mrs. Morrell's opinion was an echo of one held by John Quincy Adams. As President Adams he had urged Congress to launch, among other admirable and worthy causes, an exploring expedition. British, French, and Russian naval voyages had made enormous contributions to the "improvement of human knowledge" and the people of the United States had been "partakers of the improvement." Americans, according to Adams, as feeders at this banquet of knowledge, "owe for it a sacred debt." Adams's pleading fell on deaf ears. Congress's attitude was summed up in an editorial in a December 1825 edition of the *Richmond Enquirer*. "If we are in *debt* to Europe for her scientific discoveries," huffed the patriotic ed-itor, "how much does she *owe* us for the *splendid* example we have fur-nished of a *free government?*"

But, the blustering chauvinism notwithstanding, the truth lay in the unpalatable fact that the free government's naval and merchant ships sailed with foreign charts—and, even more unpalatable, mainly British charts.

When the Richmond editor was composing his editorial, HMS *Bar-racouta* and HMS *Leven* were coming to the end of a five-year survey of the African coastline. It was a survey achieved at an appalling cost in lives. Fever and disease had been the seamen's lot, and the lines

> Beware and take care of the Bight of Benin:
> There's one comes out for forty goes in!

held a dreadful truth. A dead seaman's possessions, according to a Royal Navy tradition, were sold at a shipboard auction to his messmates. At times during the five-year survey the possessions changed hands twice a week. The three hundred fair charts of the thirty thousand miles of sur-veyed coastline, according to one writer in the Royal Geographical Soci-ety's *Journal*, had been "drawn and coloured with drops of blood."

The *Barracouta* and the *Leven* were but two of the many Royal Navy vessels spread around the world with their launches, gigs, and cutters poking up rivers and into bays, the seamen hauling on oars and wearily heaving the lead line for soundings, the officers scribbling into notebooks, busy with chronometers, plane tables, sextants, and theodolites—and sometimes assisted by a gunner, happily playing with some fearsome fireworks in the shape of Congreve rockets.[6]

During the 1820s the Admiralty sent out twenty-six vessels on surveying and exploratory voyages and published its first chart catalog. The hydrographer, Captain Thomas Hurd, answered his bureaucratic masters on a question of candles. An excessive amount of money, they claimed, was being spent on candles by Hurd's survey vessels. Hurd wearily pointed out that the daylight hours were spent surveying. The day's work was then put down on paper during the evening and night hours, and for this, a fact not apparently clear to the chairbound, "a strong light is necessary."

A return of "light for light" had been President Adams's elegant phrase when urging Congress to loosen the purse strings and repay the sacred debt. A refusal, he said, would sentence America to perpetual inferiority.

The light eventually was returned. But its source was unlikely, its initial glow feeble, and Washington's political winds came close to blowing it out.

NOTES

1. Ambergris is a waxy aromatic substance sometimes found in a sperm whale's intestine. Expelled from the gut, it can also be found floating at sea. Soluble in alcohol, it was used as a fixative in perfumes. Some Muslim countries considered it an infallible aphrodisiac.

2. The loggerhead was a vertical wood post, offset to starboard, and set about three feet forward of the stern. The whale line was led from its tub, taken on a few turns around the loggerhead, and then led forward to the bow chock.

3. The chock-pin was a small wooden or bone peg that prevented the whale line from jumping out of the bow chock.

4. After a few weeks on the island Melville joined the Sydney whaleship *Lucy Ann*. At Tahiti he signed a round robin with other crew members declaring the ship to be scurvy-ridden and unseaworthy, and they all refused to take the vessel to sea. For this mutinous behavior the crew was jailed. Melville escaped with a companion, and together they explored Tahiti and Eimeo. Melville then signed aboard the Nantucket whaleship *Charles and Henry* and was discharged at Lahaina in the Hawaiian Islands.

5. A New Zealand missionary, the Reverend William Yate, in his *An Account of New Zealand*, has a detailed description of the Maori preserving method:

> When the head has been cut from the shoulders, the brains are immediately taken out, through a perforation behind, and the skull carefully cleansed inside from all mucilaginous and fleshy matter. The eyes are then scooped out; and the head thrown into

boiling water, into which red hot stones are continually cast, to keep the heat. It remains till the skin will slip off, and it is then suddenly plunged into cold water, whence it is immediately taken, and placed in a native oven, so as to allow the steam to penetrate into all the cavities of the interior of the skull. When sufficiently steamed it is placed on a stick to dry; and again put into an oven, made for the purpose, about the dimensions of the head. The flesh, which easily slips off the bones, is then taken away; and small sticks are employed, to thrust flax, or the bark of trees, within the skin, so as to restore it to its former shape and to preserve the features. The nostrils are then carefully stuffed with a piece of fern root; and the lips are generally sewn together; though sometimes they are not closed, but the teeth are allowed to appear. It is finished by hanging it, for a few days, in the sun.

6. Invented in 1808 by Sir William Congreve, these thirty-two-pound sheet iron rockets, fueled by gunpowder, were first used during the Napoleonic Wars by the British Army and Royal Navy. The "rockets' red glare" of "The Star-Spangled Banner" were Congreves. Shore naval surveying parties, by firing the rockets vertically and timing the explosions, could calculate the difference in longitude between two positions. When the surveyors were attacked by hostile natives—yet another hazard of their work—they could use the rockets horizontally. One such brush with hostile natives is described in the *Leven*'s log in vivid detail: "Their appearance was warlike, and had a striking effect as the extensive line moved through the various windings of the path. The grass being wet, they were observed taking particular care to keep their shields above it, as the damp would render them unserviceable; the spears attached to them, being thus elevated, were seen glittering in the sun above the brow of the hill."

Chapter 3

The Sea Surveyors—French

CORVETTES. Flush-decked ships, equipped with one tier of
guns: fine vessels for warm climates, from admitting a free
circulation of air.

COURSET. The paper on which the night's course is set for
the officer in charge of the watch.

Admiral W. H. Smyth, The Sailor's Word-Book, 1867

OASTS, ISLANDS, HARBORS, reefs, shoals, and soundings: the bone and gristle of all charts, all shown on the British
Admiralty Chart 2691 of the Fiji Islands.
  Here is a labyrinth of three hundred islands with outlying
reefs and shoals, all beset with treacherous currents and unpredictable
weather. The notation "heavy breakers" appears with alarming frequency,
and large areas of the chart look as if sprayed with ink drops, coral heads
ready to snare the careless mariner. In short, a naval surveyor's nightmare.
  Sprinkled among the native names appear more manageable ones for
Western tongues. These also give revealing signs of the sailor's contact,
sometimes fatal, with this archipelago, a sort of hydrographic archaeolog-
ical dig. Heemsquerk Reef, Tasman Strait: the reef named after Abel Tasman's flagship when she sailed, in appalling weather, over the coral reef in
1642 and then made her escape through the strait. Turtle Island:[1] named
by James Cook in 1774 after the turtles swimming near the coral reef,
"which in some places extends two Miles from the isle." Bligh Water:
sailed across by Lieutenant William Bligh when he passed through the
middle of the archipelago in 1789 during the thirty-six-hundred-mile voyage in the *Bounty*'s launch. Ever the assiduous surveyor—he had sailed as
the *Resolution*'s master on Cook's last voyage—Bligh made nine rough

sketches of the islands into his notebook. Duff Reef: named by James Wilson after his vessel, which had brought the band of London Missionary Society evangelists and artisans to Tahiti in 1797. Simonoff Island, Bereghis Reef: the island named in 1820 after Ivan Simonoff, the astronomer aboard Bellingshausen's *Vostok,* and the reef meaning "Take care" in Russian. D'Urville Channel, Great Astrolabe Reef: named by Dumont d'Urville in 1827, when his corvette *Astrolabe* narrowly escaped being wrecked. As the ship was sailing at night under courses and reefed topsails, making three knots in a heavy swell, an alert seaman had spotted, in a sudden flash of moonlight, the breakers under their lee. Wilkes Reef, Ringgold Isles, Porpoise Shoals: named in 1840 during the survey by the United States Exploring Expedition and commemorating the commander of the expedition and Lieutenant C. Ringgold and his vessel the *Porpoise.* Belcher Rocks: after Commander Edward Belcher, the brilliant but highly irascible naval hydrographer who passed through the islands in 1840 with HMS *Sulphur* and her tender HMS *Starling* after five years surveying the west coasts of Central and North America.[2]

If one casts a wider net, taking in more than the Fiji Islands, the Pacific Ocean yields a larger catch of Russian, French, and English names. The Russian entry into the Pacific came between 1803 and 1806 with the *Nadezhda* and the *Neva,* commanded by Adam Krusenstern. Krusenstern, a hydrographer of outstanding ability, after service in the British Royal Navy, had written a paper showing the advantages to Russia of a sailing route from the Baltic ports to Russian Alaska via Cape Horn, avoiding the long land journey across Siberia and the Bering Strait. Russian Alaska with its sea otter and fur seal skin trade mightily concerned St. Petersburg. The paper came to the notice of Alexander I. The expedition, virtually at a stroke of the tsar's pen, was set on its way. More expeditions followed. Between 1824 and 1827 Krusenstern published his *Atlas of the Pacific Ocean.* This was an ocean, he thought, where little more could be discovered but one with "many deficiencies to fill up, so many errors to correct."

Some of the deficiencies were filled and the errors corrected by a French expedition. In February 1829 the corvette *Astrolabe,* after a three-year expedition into the Pacific, unloaded at Marseilles a vast collection of natural history specimens, all destined for the Royal Museum at Paris, and the weary commander, Dumont d'Urville, anticipated a fortnight with his wife and children before journeying to Paris to start work on "all the material collected during the course of our long campaign."

The *Astrolabe* had sailed from France with two main purposes: a public one, for science—natural history and hydrography—and a hidden one, to scout the Pacific and find a suitable site for a French penal colony and also to search for harbors and anchorages that could shelter French warships. Without these anchorages, as d'Urville's instructions succinctly noted, any operations against British installations in the Far East would be impossible. The Napoleonic Wars might have ended, but not the age-old Anglo-French rivalry. Strong currents still ran beneath the smooth diplomatic surface.

D'Urville, over the three-year voyage, had surveyed two harbors along Australia's south coast, met with a cool reception from the governor at Sydney (London had warned him of the *Astrolabe*'s hidden agenda), surveyed the east coast of New Zealand's North Island (with the emphasis on harbors), and seen a large fleet of war canoes from the Bay of Islands, some two thousand men, paddling south for a campaign against the Hauraki Gulf tribes. D'Urville admired the Maoris but deplored their incessant tribal warfare. He also had cause to make some comments on the musket economy. As an observer of Maori culture d'Urville thought that the only women offered by the Maoris for prostitution were slave girls or low-class women. Married women were taboo; a husband would never act the pimp for his wife. To test this taboo, the *Astrolabe*'s surgeon and naturalist, the effervescent Dr. Joseph Gaimard, played the devil and tempted a visiting chief with various articles in return for his wife's favors. The chief refused them all until Gaimard offered a rifle. The chief pushed his wife toward Gaimard. D'Urville ruefully conceded the point but thought that these "children of nature" should not be judged too harshly. For them a gun was a greater prize than a "minister's portfolio to a European."

The *Astrolabe* had played with reefs and near shipwreck for months. At Tongatapu, with the *Astrolabe* anchored in a gale, rolling gunwales under, the breakers foaming white on a reef a short distance to leeward, d'Urville had given orders for the men to pack their belongings in preparation for abandoning the ship (d'Urville packed his own sea chest; included were the four chronometers and Krusenstern's and the British East India Company's atlas of charts). The wind eased, the anchor held, and a few days later d'Urville was talking to an elderly *tamaha* (princess) who remembered meeting James Cook.[3]

By December 1827, after a wearisome survey of New Guinea's north coast, the Astrolabes were enjoying the delights of Tasmania's Hobart. The officers, after their warm-water sailing, shivered with cold at an outdoor reception held by the governor for the garrison officers, officials, and ladies of the penal settlement. D'Urville thought the "cold collation" anything but "lavish or delicate," but his younger officers thought the ladies young, well dressed, and pretty. The ebullient Dr. Gaimard, a man not easily cowed by hostile natives or English outdoor meals, thought it the coldest dinner he had ever attended. His English neighbor at table thought it all "very pleasant."

The Astrolabes were also introduced to an English Christmas. "A solemn festival to them," according to d'Urville, "where the people of a certain rank celebrate at home with their families, the common people with drunken orgies and all kinds of excesses." The *Astrolabe*'s common sailors, not to be outdone, also joined in the drinking at the many grogshops. After the inevitable result—insults and then fighting between the two nationals—d'Urville confined his sailors to the ship.

At Hobart d'Urville heard information that dramatically altered the expedition's course. The New Zealand coastal survey, the search for warship anchorages, the sites for penal settlements, all these were shelved. Natural history remained, but it came second to d'Urville's new quest: the solving of a forty-year-old mystery.

In 1788 two French expeditionary ships led by one of France's heroes, Jean-François de La Pérouse, had vanished in the Pacific. Where, no one knew. The where had become, for the French Navy, a search for the Holy Grail.

Cook's three voyages into the Pacific galvanized the French into what Catherine Gaziello, in her *L'Expedition de Lapérouse 1785–1788*, has called a *replique française*—a French riposte in the Anglo-French rivalry. Whether La Pérouse would have seen it in such a combative light is doubtful. La Pérouse regarded Cook as the "first among navigators" and copied Cook's three-watch system (it gave longer periods of rest for the seamen than the two-watch system) and his recipes for salting pigs and the making of spruce beer.[4]

La Pérouse's two expeditionary vessels, with their bemused astronomers, artists, geologists, and naturalists avoiding the cows moored to the masts, sheep in the longboats, pigs along the quarterdeck gangways and hens on the poop deck, had sailed from Brest in 1785.

The expedition collected more than its fair share of tragedies before it ended in its mysterious vanishing. Twenty-one men and two boats from a surveying party were lost in an Alaskan tide race. In Samoa a watering party was attacked by natives and twelve Frenchmen were killed. Not all was gloom, however. Two years out from France, as they were being entertained by some native dancing ladies (the French found the combined smells of sweat and fish oil overpowering) on the Russian Kamchatka Peninsula, a courier burst into the room carrying a large case of mail from France. La Pérouse had been promoted to commodore. All the guns of the port fired a salute in celebration, and the dancing ladies celebrated by drinking vast quantities of brandy.

La Pérouse also received new orders from Paris directing him to sail for Botany Bay in New Holland, where the British were founding a penal settlement. La Pérouse was to report on this new development.

Australia's "First Fleet"—eleven vessels carrying 1,000 people, including more than 500 male and 150 female convicts—sailed into Botany Bay on 18 January 1788. On 26 January, much to the surprise of the British, the French expedition arrived in the bay. The British were in the process of shifting their anchorage to a better harbor, Port Jackson, a few miles north of Botany Bay. For six weeks, except for visits from sociable British officers, escaping convicts, and curious aborigines, the French remained alone at Botany Bay. On 10 March the two vessels were spotted sailing north. They were never seen again by Western eyes.

A Pacific island trader, Peter Dillon,[5] had apparently found evidence of La Pérouse's vanished ships, wrecked on a reef-girdled island in the Santa Cruz group north of the New Hebrides. Dillon, however, was regarded with suspicion in Hobart: little more than an adventurer, according to some people. Nevertheless, d'Urville decided to gamble and sailed for the island. It was after all a quest of medieval legend proportions. And the Astrolabes, as in all quests, from Sir Thomas Malory's *Le Morte d'Arthur* to J. R. R. Tolkien's *The Lord of the Rings*, were to face some fearsome obstacles.

Dillon had not given away the precise location of his island find, only that it was within two days' sailing distance by canoe to leeward of Tikopia. D'Urville knew that the prevailing winds in the area of Tikopia came from the northeast to southeast. He therefore estimated Dillon's island to be "forty or fifty leagues" northwest to southwest of Tikopia.

From Hobart they steered for Tikopia. It was a tedious passage—over three thousand miles—starting with gales in the Tasman Sea, followed by variable winds, calms, tropical rain, and oppressive heat, before they raised the single pointed peak of Tipokia. Hove to offshore, surrounded by the islanders in their canoes, d'Urville learned from a German who had sailed with Dillon that the trader had been speaking the truth. "It is at Vanikoro that Lapérouse was wrecked," wrote a chagrined d'Urville, "and Dillon has forestalled us." Vanikoro, the Tipokians warned him, was deadly. To sleep ashore was death. This was *Mate-moe fenona*—the land that kills. Guided by some Tipokians—who adamantly refused to sleep ashore—the *Astrolabe* sailed for Vanikoro. D'Urville arrived at the island with a healthy crew (only two men with minor complaints) and sailed from it a month later with over three-quarters of his men prostrate with fever and the rest so weak they hardly had the strength to weigh anchor and work the corvette out through the reefs.

But they had found the wreck, brought up coral-encrusted anchors, cannon, a swivel gun, and a blunderbuss. A cenotaph was erected to the memory of La Pérouse and his companions. At the dedication a detachment of ten armed men, spruce in their plumed shakos, white duck trousers, white crossbelts over their blue jackets, discharged three volleys of musket fire, and the *Astrolabe* thundered out a twenty-one-gun salute. D'Urville ruminated that Vanikoro's hills, forty years previously, had perhaps also echoed to the "cries of our countrymen expiring beneath the blows of savages, or succumbing to attacks of fever." The islanders, thought d'Urville, were treacherous, lazy, stupid, savage, greedy, and without any virtues that he could think of. The women, who did all the hard and dirty work, were even less prepossessing than the men. The weather was oppressively hot, wet, and humid. The island reeked of fever. The only plus in this dreary equation of minuses was that he had no worries about his men's deserting. Vanikoro was no Tahiti. Even Dr. Gaimard (who could usually find a rapport with the most intractable of natives) confessed to finding Vanikoro intimidating. He had spent some days ashore living with the natives, collecting information about the loss of the two vessels and the crew's fate (their skulls, it was rumored, were kept in the natives' sacred spirit house) and also collecting a vocabulary of their language. During the language studies he was taught a love song. After writing it down, the irrepressible Gaimard sang it to a different group of islanders who listened to his singing with a frenzied delight. The song apparently was a highly obscene one describing the sexual act in brutally explicit detail. But Gaimard, even though he had established his credentials, still kept his double-barreled percussion gun, three-chambered pistol, and dagger close to hand. He returned to the *Astrolabe* totally exhausted from fever and the constant tension of living at close quarters with the highly volatile and unpredictable natives.

D'Urville, also fever-ridden, with his crew of near corpses sailed from Vanikoro under shortened sail (during squalls not enough men could be mustered to furl the mainsail), and the *Astrolabe* wallowed her way northward to Guam and a Spanish hospital. Most of the crew were carried ashore at Guam into an old, clean, airy convent building. The *Astrolabe* sailed a month later, thirty of her men still not fully recovered. But she was homeward bound.

In the Atlantic, steering for France, the Astrolabes had gazed fondly upon their two prize natural history specimens collected in the East Indies, animals never before seen alive in Europe—and the Royal Museum without even a stuffed specimen—but beasts that ambled out from their specially built cages and snuffled around the *Astrolabe*'s deck under the sailors' admiring eyes. These were babirusas, wild hogs with upturned horns and two long canine teeth that grew upward on either side of the snout and curved backward to near the eyes. Here were animals fit for any medieval bestiary or any questing knight's coat of arms. For d'Urville, however, the Holy Grail had become slightly tarnished. Dillon had arrived in France two months ahead of the *Astrolabe*—and with many more La Pérouse artifacts. Dillon had been presented to the king. Dillon had been given a pension for life. Dillon had been made a chevalier of the Legion of Honor. All this, for d'Urville, a man who nurtured his resentments, was gall and wormwood. The resentments bubbled to the surface in his five-volume history of the voyage.

D'Urville's narrative history never achieved the popularity of his famous eighteenth-century predecessor's, Louis Antoine de Bougainville's *A Voyage round the World*, written and published after his 1766–69 voyage—the first French circumnavigation—with the frigate *Boudeuse* and the storeship *Étoile*. Bougainville's narrative had captivated his readers. Here was a story that held the dreadful overtones of Magellan's harrowing passage across the Pacific: scurvy, fevers, starvation, the eating of rats, and chafing leather gear. In contrast with the horrors were the delights of Tahiti, not only for the French sailors but also for those of Bougainville's readers who knelt before Rousseau's vision of the Noble Savage: the vision of a Garden of Eden, an Arcady, a sylvan, bucolic world of eternal summer where men and women were content, according to Rousseau, to live "in their rustic huts . . . sewing their garments with thorns or fish bones . . . as free, healthy, good and happy men." Rousseau had stood on his philosophic heights, and all he had seen was the beast of emerging capitalism, the tyranny of "iron and wheat": factories and arable farming. Tahiti had suddenly appeared as a vision from across the world proving (to the faithful) that the Noble Savage, the Natural Man, existed.

Bougainville's much-quoted description of the French ships' arrival in Tahiti helped carve in stone the Western world's distorted vision of the South Sea Islands and their inhabitants. The scene opens with the two ships surrounded by canoes loaded with naked young women. "For the men and old women that accompanied them," wrote Bougainville, "had stripped them of the garments which they generally dressed themselves in." The reason for the nakedness soon became apparent:

They pressed us to choose a woman, and to come ashore with her; and their gestures, which were nothing less than equivocal, denoted the manner we should form an acquaintance with her. It was difficult, amidst such a sight, to keep at their work 400 young French sailors, who had seen no woman for six months. In spite of all our precautions, a young girl came on board, and placed herself upon the quarter-deck, near one of the hatchways, which was open, in order to give air to those heaving at the capstan below it. The girl carelessly dropped a cloth, which covered her, and appeared to the eyes of all beholders, such as Venus showed herself to the Phrygian shepherd, having, indeed, the celestial form of the goddess. Both sailors and soldiers endeavoured to come to the hatchway; and the capstan was never hove with more alacrity than on this occasion. At last our cares succeeded in keeping these bewitched fellows in order, though it was no less difficult to keep the command of ourselves.

The canoe welcome was repeated ashore. Some of the Frenchmen were invited into a house where the "civility of their landlords" went far beyond the expectations of young sailors. "They offered them young girls; the hut was immediately filled with a curious crowd of men and women, who made a circle round the guest, and the young victim of hospitality. . . . Here Venus is goddess of hospitality."

Bougainville, wandering ashore among the fruit trees and cool streams, thought this a more populous Garden of Eden. Still in the classical mode, he called Tahiti the *Nouvelle Cythère* after the island off the southern Peloponnese where Aphrodite had emerged from the sea.

Philibert de Commerson, the expedition's naturalist, waxed even more lyrical. Being a devotee of the Noble Savage philosophy, he thought the Tahitians "without vice, without prejudices, without wants, without dissensions," a people whose only God was love. Commerson, however, was highly embarrassed when these perfect specimens of the Natural Man unmasked Commerson's valet, Jeanne Baré (masquerading as a man), as a woman.

Paris society had been captivated by Bougainville's, Commerson's, and Cook's descriptions of Tahitian life. In a society where both the serious and the frivolous had fed upon the romanticism of Rousseau's Noble Savage, the voyages had merely reinforced an intellectual argument. But not only arguments. Bougainville had brought to France a shining example of the Natural Man, Ahutoru, the brother of an island chief, who was made much of by fashionable Paris. Ahutoru in turn took to the rather unnatural and artificial delights of the Paris opera house.

Bougainville's and Cook's voyages, La Pérouse's vanishing turned armchair explorers into Pacific experts. Men who had sailed into the South Seas were lionized in salons and drinking dens. Sailors would show their tattoos—even the young Joseph Banks had a discreet tattoo upon his arm—and tell tales of the islands and their adventures. Curios from the voyaging would be produced and admired: war clubs, canoe paddles, shells, carvings, tapa cloth, preserved heads. The Pacific had become fashionable.

London had its own Ahutoru in the shape of Omai, a native from Huahine who been brought to England by Tobias Furneaux aboard the *Adventure* during Cook's second voyage. Omai, dressed in a newly tailored outfit of brown velvet coat, white silk waistcoat, and gray satin knee breeches, all bought by Joseph Banks, was presented to George III—greeting him with "How do, King Tosh"—and was in turn presented with a sword, an allowance, and London lodgings. Omai became an instant celebrity and hobnobbed with dukes and duchesses, lords and ladies, Joseph Banks, Dr. Solander, Dr. Samuel Johnson. Fanny Burney thought his manners "so extremely graceful . . . you would have thought he came from some foreign Court." He dined with members of the Royal Society at the Mitre in Fleet Street. (The menu consisted of fish, lamb, tongue, udder, greens, stewed beef, pudding, duck, rabbit, brawn, tarts, artichokes. Porter from pewter pots was drunk during the meal, followed by madeira, claret, and port—Omai's favorite—as different cheeses were trundled along the tabletop in mahogany boxes. The scientific gentlemen of the day were serious trenchermen.)

Omai, in return, showed Lord Sandwich, the first lord of the Admiralty and a friend of both Joseph Banks and James Cook, how to cook South Seas style at Sandwich's country house: mutton wrapped in leaves, cooked in a pit filled with heated stones. Banks also took Omai north to Yorkshire for a visit to Constantine Phipps's moldering ancestral home. Although the grouse-shooting season was in full swing, George Colman, another guest, noted that Omai had no idea about the sancitity of domestic birds and shot "dunghill cocks, barndoor geese, and ducks in the pond." Omai returned on Cook's third voyage to the Pacific, where he became cordially disliked by his fellow islanders.

Pacific mania gripped not only society but also literature and the stage. In 1785 *Omai: or a Trip round the World* by John O'Keefe ran to fifty performances at the Theatre Royal, Covent Garden. The stage effects included a storm at sea, hail, icebergs, a red tropical moon in eclipse, dancing girls, and Polynesian costumes. It ended with a chorus of British sailors singing a tribute to James Cook as a massive portrait of their captain was lowered to the stage.

In Paris, three years later, *La Mort du Capitaine Cook* played to packed audiences. Here was another spectacular that included an erupting volcanoe. It was brought over the following year to Convent Garden, where it was billed as "A grand Serious-Pantomimic-Ballet, in Three Parts. As now exhibiting in Paris with uncommon Applause, with the original French Music, New Scenery, Machinery and other Decorations." Not only Londoners watched this extravaganza; separate productions were also staged in Hull, Dublin, and Limerick.

La Pérouse's vanishing with two ships, more than two hundred seamen, and a shoal of well-known savants merely fueled the Pacific infatuation—with the added bonus of mystery. Books, tracts, and plays poured forth. The dramatist August von Kotzbue (father of the Russian Pacific Ocean explorer Otto von Kotzbue) wrote *La Peyrouse: Ein Schauspiel in zwei Aufzugen* in 1797, and it was immediately translated into English, French, Dutch, and Italian. In 1801 John Fawcett presented *Perouse or the Desolate Island* at the Theatre Royal.

The immediate problem for the French in the turbulent closing years of the eighteenth century was to solve the mystery. The Revolutionary National Assembly voted funds to send two ships in search of the missing vessels. Hydrography and science were not forgotten. Aboard the *Recherche* and the *Espérance* sailed two accomplished hydrographers and a naturalist. The expedition ended in disarray and tragedy. The commander of the *Espérance*, Huon de Kermadec, died in New Caledonia, and the expedition's leader, Rear Admiral Bruni d'Entrecasteaux, from scurvy and dysentery off the north coast of New Guinea. (Two visits were made to Van Diemen's Land, and today's Tasmanians are constantly reminded of the French explorations with Bruny Island, D'Entrecasteaux Channel, the Huon River, Huon Gulf, and Huon pine.)

The voyage fell apart at Surabaya, Java. Here the two ships and their scurvy- and dysentery-ridden crew were interned by the Dutch because the Netherlands were at war with revolutionary France. Upon the news that Louis XVI had been guillotined the smoldering political differences among officers, scientifics, and seamen—an inflammable mix of Royalists, Girondins, and Jacobins—burst into flames. After a period of open detention in Batavia the Dutch allowed the French—those who had survived the fever—to return home. Édouard de Rossel, one of the hydrographers escorting the vast natural history collection and the precious draft charts, sailed aboard a ship bound for France. They were captured by the British off St. Helena, and Rossel with his precious collection found himself in England. The "vast Herbarium," as Sir Joseph Banks called it, amounting to ten thousand specimens—over a thousand birds, assorted reptiles, fishes, and insects—at the urging of Banks (now the Royal Society's president) was returned to France. Rossel, since the countries were still at war, was detained in England but given a remarkable amount of freedom and worked on the charts. He and the charts returned to France in 1802 during the short-lived Peace of Amiens.

In June of the same year the British helped a French expeditionary vessel through Sydney Heads and into the harbor. The ship had been wallowing offshore in the Pacific swell, the scurvy-ridden crew incapable of working her into Port Jackson. Here the *Géographe* joined the other half of the expedition, the *Naturaliste,* which had sailed, unaided, into Port Jackson some weeks before. The two ships had sailed from France in 1800 loaded with distillation plants, libraries, twenty-three savants—artists, astronomers, botanists, gardeners, hydrographers, minerologists, zoologists—plus the precious passports[6] issued by the British government.

The expedition's itinerary had been planned by the French Institute of Natural Sciences and sailed with the full approval of the First Consul, Napoleon Bonaparte. The host of savants indicated that hydrography and science were high on the agenda. The hidden agenda, one dear to the First Consul's heart, was the opportunity to disconcert—and also to assess—the fragile, small British settlement in New South Wales.

The deadly mix of civilians, turbulent young officers, and a rigid older commander, Nicolas Baudin, proved a fertile field for the seeds of disunity, and all soon fell to squabbling according to their lights: social, political, and duties. François Peron, the anthropologist-naturalist, blamed Baudin for the scurvy-ridden state of the French. "All know," he wrote, "that it was the inestimable progress of naval hygiene" that enabled the British to maintain their sea power. Louis de Freycinet, a junior officer and naval surveyor, thought far too much time had been spent indulging the naturalists' whims of "picking up shells" on Van Diemen's Land shores.

The *Géographe* and the *Naturaliste* spent five months recuperating at the British settlement. Here they received, according to Peron, "the most delicate and affectionate hospitality." The naturalists went off on expeditions, the artists made drawings, the seamen drank rum in the grogshops, and the officers turned an evaluating eye upon the settlement's defenses.

They sailed in November 1802 with the *Naturaliste,* loaded with the sicker members of the expedition and the precious natural history and coastal surveys, bound for France. She was captured by the British, the short-lived Peace of Amiens over, and carried into Portsmouth. Sir Joseph Banks obtained her release.

The *Géographe* continued her probe of the Australian south coast before sailing to Île de France (Mauritius). Here, after being dogged by ill health for most of the voyage, Baudin died. Peron, the anthropologist-naturalist, now added military strategist to his accomplishments and advised the governor, C.-M. Decaen—a man who loathed the British—that Port Jackson should be destroyed as soon as possible. "Today we could destroy it easily: we shall not be able to do it in twenty-five years time." Freycinet, the naval officer, was of the same mind. "The conquest of Port Jackson would be very easy to accomplish, since the English have neglected every species of defence." Once the governor's house and principal buildings had been taken, "the others would fall naturally into the hands of the conquerors."

The French never took Peron's advice, although their expedition certainly sped the British into making a settlement in Van Diemen's Land. Baudin had shown the governor of New South Wales their draft charts of the Australian south coast with *"Terre Napoleon"* writ large across the land. This was trying Governor Philip Gidley King too high, particularly as Lieutenant Matthew Flinders of the Royal Navy had just completed a survey of the Great Australian Bight coastline. The dreadful vision of French claims and *tricolors* waving in the breeze rose before the governor's eyes. By 1803 the Union Jack was waving over a small settlement on the Derwent River in Van Diemen's Land.

The 1805 British victory at Trafalgar clapped a stopper on any French threats aimed at New South Wales. This was reinforced five years later, when British forces took Île de France (the British gave it back its old name, Mauritius), a hornet's nest of French privateers preying upon the East India Company's ships.

In 1817, with Napoleon safely bottled up on St. Helena—no more *Terre Napoleon*s, *Golfe Bonaparte*s, and *Golfe Joséphine*s to bring a choleric flush to a true-born Briton's face—and the monarchy restored to France, another French Navy expedition sailed for the Pacific.

That a country still smarting in defeat, economically and physically drained, beset by social and political divisions, and with an army of occupation 150,000 strong—British, Russian, Austrian, and Prussian—billeted upon them makes the decision to send out the first French naval expedition for seventeen years is unusual, not remarkable. French prestige was at stake. France might have been defeated on the battlefield, but intellectual fields still remained. Moreover, this was to be a voyage for science with all its wide-ranging disciplines: astronomy, geography, natural history, meteorology, hydrography, terrestrial magnetism. The French authorities, however, had grown tired of the wranglings and endemic feudings of the academics that had been such a part of d'Entrecasteaux's and Baudin's expeditions. The navy officers would serve as astronomers, cartographers, botanists, zoologists. Louis de Freycinet, who had served on Baudin's expedition, had suggested the expedition. The road to advancement in a peacetime navy, reasoned the thirty-eight-year-old Freycinet, was the scientific road.

The expedition left Toulon on 17 September 1817 with Freycinet's corvette *Uranie,* as the winds were light, being towed by a steam tug. A few days later the *Moniteur Officiel* announced the *Uranie*'s sailing on an expedition of which all France could be proud. Weeks later came more electrifying news of the expedition. The *Moniteur* had learned that the captain's wife, the twenty-one-year-old Rose de Freycinet, had been smuggled aboard disguised as a man! All against the regulations that banned women aboard state vessels unless official permission had been given. No permission had been given, but, no matter, the *Moniteur* thought this example of "conjugal devotion" so admirable that it should be made public.

The couple had been married three years, and the uxorious Louis had planned his wife's cruise with care. Permission had been obtained from the navy minister to alter and extend Freycinet's private accommodation aboard the *Uranie.* Provisions included Nicolas Appert's canned meats, vegetables, fruit, and dried milk tablets. Freycinet's officers (most of them southern Frenchmen and the two doctor-naturalists, Dr. Joseph Gaimard and Dr. Jean René Quoy, whose next voyage was to be aboard d'Urville's *Astrolabe*) gallantly went along with Rose's being aboard and never mentioned it in their letters. Also, according to the civilian artist Jacques Arago, there was a remarkable lessening of swearing from the sailors.

To occupy her time on board, Rose spent an hour a day playing a guitar, an hour sewing, an hour studying English, and an hour on her journal. This took the form of letters to an intimate friend in France. What comes across in the journal is not only the charm, vivacity, courage, and humor of this remarkable lady but also the leisurely pace of the expedition, a leisurely, civilized pace that somehow accomplished a remarkable amount of work.

Two months were spent at Rio de Janeiro with Rose and Louis living ashore. Rose was busy with receptions, balls, dinners, and playing the privileged tourist, one with a sharp eye for detail, such as the strange habit of the Portuguese high society men and women who never washed their hands because they, unlike the general populace, never touched anything dirty. The scientific aspects of the expedition, Rose cheerfully admitted, were a closed book to her, men playing at incomprehensible games. The voyage continued its leisurely pace to Cape Town, where she found the English governor at first rather aloof, "a trait that is common to almost all his countrymen." But he soon thawed and became "kind and very gallant." A French merchant invited Rose to stay with his family at their house for the three weeks that the *Uranie* was at Cape Town. He also purchased all her wants and supplies for the next stage of the voyage, claiming, he said, that the business would be too tiring for Rose. The bill, she later found out, was double the normal purchase price.

The voyage continued with stops at Mauritius and Bourbon Island (Réunion Island) followed by a passage across the Indian Ocean to the hot, dry, sandy desert of Australia's west coast at Shark Bay. Here the Uranies set up an observatory and tented camp. They also had their first meeting with naked aborigines armed with spears. Jacques Arago met them playing his castanets.

At Mauritius a seven-year-old boy (an illegitimate mulatto child by a friend of Freycinet's who had left Mauritius) had joined the *Uranie*. Rose, thought Louis, could educate him. An illustration by Alphonse Pellion (published in the 1927 edition of Rose's journal) shows the camp at Shark Bay: men busy about their work, the sand dunes in the background, Louis de Freycinet working at a table, Rose and the boy next to one of the tents. The same illustration appears in the voyage's official record. Rose and the boy have vanished, a portent of Soviet Russia's photographic editing of history.

Rose found it a relief to leave Shark Bay—"a horrible coast"—for the Dutch settlement at Kupang on Timor. But it was only a change from dry heat to humid heat with fever lurking in the background. Louis and Rose drank distilled water (the *Uranie* had been fitted with a fearsome and nearly uncontrollable distillation plant), and Rose promised her husband not to eat fruit—except for mangoes. They escaped the dysentery that felled most of the corvette's crew. Supplies being few at Kupang, the *Uranie* sailed for Dili in Portuguese Timor.

Two illustrations show the reception of the French by the Portuguese governor. The one by Pellion shows a launch, bow onto the sandy shore, being held by seamen knee deep in the water. The seamen are dressed in white with red sashes around their waists and wear glazed hats. A gangway stretches from the bow to the shore. Down this gangway march smartly dressed officers, fore-and-aft cocked hats on head. Two more seamen hold a thin rod, acting as a banister, for the descending officers, who are greeted by the governor, standing under one large blue parasol held by a native. A cannon spurts smoke in the background. This is the official illustration.

Arago's illustration shows a little more confusion. The launch is still bow on to the beach, but the seamen are not so neatly dressed. An officer has tumbled backward in the bow, and his booted feet and legs are high in the air. Louis and Rose, after walking down the gangway, are holding hands as they walk across the beach to the waiting governor and two blue parasols. A cannon spurts smoke in the background. This is the illustration that appears in Rose's journal.

At the reception that followed, in a flower- and foliage-decorated building, and with music playing, the high society ladies of Dili—"rajahs' daughters who had married Portuguese officers"—found themselves entranced by Rose. Her dress was only a light muslin, and her hat had just a few feathers, but she was still, to them, an exotic Parisienne. Their clothes in turn reminded Rose of forty-year-old French fashions. Sensing this, the ladies, with slaves kneeling by their sides holding handkerchiefs and bags containg betel nut, told Rose that a consignment of new fashions had been expected from Macao. Upon their first view of the *Uranie,* their hearts, they said, had beaten the faster, for they thought this the ship that carried their long-awaited precious cargo.

Rose's exotic voyage continued. The darker side also continued. Deaths from dysentery and fever increased, Rose now acting as nurse, and so did the constant danger, for a sailing vessel, of sudden vicious squalls, uncharted reefs, and pirates. These seas, with their numerous islands and straits, provided an ideal location for seagoing brigands. Their well-armed *corocores,* packed with betel-chewing, bandanna-wreathed, bloody-minded cutthroats, oars thrashing the water, streamers and banners flying, drums and gongs beating, snapped up anything that passed their way. Anything, that is, unable to bare its fangs in the way of a row of carronades poking through open gunports.

But the greater danger came from fever. Not until Guam, where Governor Don José de Medinilla (the same generous-hearted Spaniard who was to give the same services to d'Urville's Astrolabes) provided an old convent to act as a hospital, did the men start their slow recovery. Rose and Louis lived ashore, she writing her journal and letters, entertaining and being entertained. She had now become accustomed to the unusual— earthquakes, strange foods, different customs and cultures—but one custom she still found strange: tobacco smoking. Everyone smoked at Guam. Even the women had cigars in their mouths and carried the smoking paraphernalia around in finely wrought gold boxes. Rose was almost tempted to take up the habit just for the boxes. Three months were spent in Guam before the *Uranie* sailed for the Hawaiian Islands.

What did Rose make of these islands? Since Cook had been killed on their shores in 1779, the pace of Western contact had increased with startling speed. Whaleships, fur traders, and sandalwood vessels called in with increasing frequency for provisions, repairs, recreation, and trade. The trader *Fair American,* caught up in the wars between rival chiefs, had had five of her crew beaten to death. One of the crew, Isaac Davis and a crew member from another vessel, John Young, had been protected by one of the fighting chiefs, Kamehameha, and used as gunners aboard the *Fair American* in the war against his rival. George Vancouver, in HMS *Discovery*, had visited the islands three times between 1792 and 1794 and said that Davis and Young had been given wives, land, and every possible comfort. Vancouver had also struck up a great friendship with Kamehameha (who died in 1819 as King Kamehameha I) and provided sails and flags for his largest double-hulled canoe. After sailing it with great delight, the chief had disingenuously observed to Vancouver "that she would make a much better appearance with a few swivels properly mounted; I agreed with him in this opinion but the words 'Taboo King George' were sufficient to prevent a syllable more being urged on that subject."

Vancouver knew he was arguing from a strong position when he invoked King George's taboo, for the Hawaiian kapu system was the chiefs' method of social control. Here were directives coming from the gods through the mouths of priests and chiefs (not much different, in fact, from the methods used in Europe). Everyone lived under kapus, but some lived under more kapus than others. Women and the *maka'ainana*—the common people—happened to live under many kapus, the chief and his administrative nobility under less. The common people lived a life of virtual serfdom. They worked the land, but all the produce belonged to the chief; they were sent by the thousands into the hills to cut down sandalwood for Hawaii's largest trade, and to bring it down from the hills, one to six pieces of sandalwood were strapped to their backs. The carriers were known as *kua leho*—callous backs. The women never ate with the men and were also forbidden to eat pork. Punishments for breaking kapu were swift and terrible. Strangulation and the smashing in of heads, and the breaking of limbs by club were common. Also, blinding. In 1820 missionaries saw a small girl have her eyes plucked out for eating a banana. Jacques Arago, during the *Uranie*'s visit, watched, and drew, a man being held down and beaten to death with a club. He also described a blinding: "The executioner gave . . . a violent blow with his fist over each eye, and almost at the same instant plunged his fore-finger into the lachrymal angle, and pulled out the ball; the other eye was taken out in the same manner."

Rose mentions none of this, only that taboos existed. But then such details would have certainly upset her friends afflicted with Rousseau's Noble Savage philosophy. For Rose there was a touch of the *Thousand and One Nights* about Hawaii. But for the modern reader of Rose's journal the book that springs more readily to mind is *Alice's Adventures in Wonderland* or *Through the Looking-Glass*. This was a world seen through a distorting pane of glass where familiar ceremonies were carried out with a most unfamiliar cast of characters set against a most unfamiliar background. Rose found the Hawaiians large in person and appetites. One chief, after dining aboard the *Uranie*, also wanted the glasses, plates, bottles, napkins, and Freycinet's coat. For a rifle, gunpowder, and a bolt of

"Billy Pitt" being baptized aboard the *Uranie*

"I had a perfect view of the ceremony and the spectators. Abbé de Quélen baptised
Pitt, who appeared quite moved during the entire ceremony." —Rose de Freycinet
(Illustration from Freycinet's *Voyage autour du monde*)

cloth, he was prepared give four coconuts. On deck the same chief asked
Freycinet if his officers were *ali'i*—nobles. Freycinet said yes, and the chief
touched their hands. A seaman standing nearby was presented with the
chief's foot in "a scornful manner." The seaman was not amused—although his companions thought it the best joke in the world. King Kamehameha II (the son of Vancouver's bloodthirsty chief) had a native prime
minister named Billy Pitt after Britain's William Pitt. (A print shows Billy
Pitt being baptized by the *Uranie*'s chaplain on the corvette's quarterdeck. Rose watched the ceremony from her quarters.) The twenty-one-
year-old king was in fact ruled by one of his late father's wives,
Kaahumanu.[7] A vast lady, weighing in at more than four hundred pounds,
she was reported to have said at the young Kamehameha's coronation,
"Behold these chiefs and men of your father, and these your guns, and this
your land, but you and I shall share the realm together." And no one
dared dispute her.

Louis de Freycinet, following protocol, was received by Kamehameha
at his straw hut residence—only twelve feet long and a little less in width—
with the floor covered in mats. Chiefs squatted randomly around the hut,
some wearing long red woolen coats made from cloth presented by Cook

and Vancouver. The king wore a British captain's uniform. Jacques Arago also met Kamehameha this time dressed "like a colonel of hussars wearing a hat like a marshal of France." Arago thought the king "fat, dirty, proud," but the imposing Kaahumanu "prodigiously fat, but her face is interesting. . . . She offered us some beer with much kindness, drank to us, striking her glass against ours."

The *Uranie* sailed from the islands with her deck cluttered with a hundred pigs, some goats and kids, but few vegetables and fewer chickens. They were now two years into the voyage, and Rose found the passage to Sydney interminable. The diet—salt beef, salt pork, boiled pork, cold pork, dried fish, rice, beans—was a "vicious gastronomic circle." She dreamed of tender plump chickens, eggs, and fresh milk. Another fantasy was the picking of fresh flowers—a rose or a carnation. The passage's one pleasure was the discovery of an uncharted island that Louis named after her, an island on which she hoped no future sailors would ever be wrecked. (Fifty years later her hope was shattered. Only three crew members of the San Francisco schooner *Good Templar* survived after she struck the coral reef.)

Sydney was a delight, the welcome generous. Arago found the town handsome with the Government House garden holding a particular magic charm for him. Here black swans stalked sedately along the paths, kangaroos leaped over bushes and hedges, and all the trees and shrubs were new. He was, he said, "a stranger to everything." Arago was particularly impressed with the buildings. Sydney was in the middle of a building boom brought about by the governor. Lachlan Macquarie, the flinty British army officer who had taken office ten years previous to the *Uranie*'s arrival (with orders to clean up the chaos left by the New South Wales Corps's coup d'état against Governor William Bligh), had found Sydney a squalid place. Streets were mere dust tracks in summer, and muddy rivers after rain; the lack of sewage offended the nose, and the rickety wooden shacks the eyes. The convicts' barracks were disgusting, churches were housed in huts, and no proper hospital existed. The economy and most of the inhabitants ran on rum. With a zeal worthy of a John Knox, the new governor and his wife, Elizabeth, set about improving both the physical and moral aspects of the raw and unlovely settlement. The new stone buildings and roads tended to have "Macquarie" attached to their names.[8]

The settlement's social element entertained their visitors with an endless round of dinners, receptions, parties, and balls, although Rose found the heat too oppressive for dancing. Then the social element was terribly embarrassed to hear that the convict element had stolen the *Uranie*'s silverware. Rose struck up a friendship with the wife of Barron Field, a judge who had arrived in the colony in 1816. Field, an intimate friend of Lamb, Coleridge, Wordsworth, Hazlitt, and Leigh Hunt (and a man with literary aspirations of his own), disliked Sydney. To him the finest sight would be the ship whose "wings will bear me from this prose-dull land." His wife,

Rose found, was charming, well educated, and knew French literature. She was also pretty and, as Louis had noticed, swung "a ravishing ankle."

The *Uranie* sailed on Christmas Day, loaded with gifts that included two merino sheep, three cassowaries, eight black swans, two goats, a cow, a calf, and a dozen sheep (the common sheep, goats, and cattle destined for the table). Mrs. Field had given Rose a cornelian ring on which was written "Remember." Also on board, unknown to the officers, were ten stowaway convicts. Christmas Day happened to be a Friday, and Rose was amused to hear the British sailors giving the French dire warnings of the dangers attached to sailing on a Friday: most unlucky.

They were now heading for Cape Horn and the last leg of their voyage. An iceberg was sighted on 21 January, and they doubled Cape Horn on 8 February. The wind was light, the sea calm, and the sun shining. So much for the fearsome cape.

A week later the Uranies were pumping for their lives. The corvette had struck a rock (now Uranie Rock) close to Volunteer Point in the Falkland Islands. Badly holed, near foundering, pumps gushing water, Freycinet managed to sail his sinking vessel ten miles up Berkeley Sound and grounded her, water above the mess decks, on the sandy bottom of what is now Uranie Bay.

Little has changed at Uranie Bay since the corvette drove up on the beach. The wind still whistles across the dunes, spinning itself into sandy whorls; the treeless, rolling, diddle-dee—covered hills look inviting in the sunshine and bleak in the gray overcast. Here is a desert shore, but not the tropical isle desert shore of myth.

Within two weeks a tented village, a village for over a hundred men and one woman, had sprung up on the sandy shore: tents for Louis and Rose (she slept on a plank laid between two chairs with a long cushion for a mattress); officers and midshipmen; sailors; a hospital; a powder magazine with arms and ammunition; equipment; cooks and provisions. The cooks' oven was heated by diddle-dee; men scavenged the wreck for supplies; hunters went out for geese, seals, penguins, and wild horses. Biscuits, ruined by salt water, were still used to thicken soups. After a month with no bread, a sack of flour from Guam, the flour made from the fruit of a tree, was salvaged from the wreck. The chaplain had used the flour as a powder for his hair, finding it better than starch. The cook baked the cleric's flour into rolls. Rose had also bought sago flour at Guam to feed piglets. This was salvaged and also baked into rolls. They were rolls, when cold, of such monstrous hardness they had to be broken with a hammer, but it was bread of a sort, and so the chaplain ate his curling powder and Rose ate her pig food. The indomitable Rose also made beer (they were having to water their wine) from essence bought at Sydney. She followed the instructions given to her and bottled it off. They found it very agreeable.

A month after their shipwreck, as in all desert island stories, the castaways sighted a sail. As in all satisfactory stories, it was also sighted on the day that the *Uranie*'s longboat, being altered to take a small crew to Montevideo for help, was ready for launching. The sails belonged to a sloop from the Salem sealer *General Knox*, anchored a few days' sail away at West Point Island. Within a few weeks Berkeley Sound had a handful of vessels anchored close to the *Uranie*'s wreck and the French camp: a schooner from the *General Knox* with her captain, William Orne (he was asking twenty thousand dollars to transport the castaways to South America); the trader *Mercury* which, taking cannon and passengers from the Plate River to Valparaiso and, having been damaged off Cape Horn in a storm, had run into Berkeley Sound to make repairs; and the British whaler *Sir Andrew Hammond*, homeward bound with a full hold after a very successful two-year voyage in the Pacific. Louis de Freycinet, in long and tedious haggling, had arranged with the *Mercury*'s captain to send his French seamen aboard the trader and make repairs. In return for this, plus a rapacious amount of piastres, the *Mercury* would take the French, plus crates filled with their voyage's collected research, to South America. Freycinet was in no position to bargain (although it did cross his mind to use force).

The interminable haggling with the captains of the *General Knox* and the *Mercury*, the cold, the wet, the constant struggle to find food—they were reduced, wrote Rose, to the eating of "dreadful gulls"—the illness that struck the French camp (both Louis and Rose were ill and in pain) drained away most of Rose's courage. But not all. Rose, even in adversity, gave a dinner for guests from the *Mercury* and the schooner. It was a dinner presented with Gallic style and flair (a dinner that Anthelme Brillat-Savarin, working away on his elegant and witty *Physiology of Taste*, would have approved and understood, as would also the ghost of the admirable Père Labat, who had sailed aboard a French vessel in the West Indies with two cannon but only one cannonball. The cannonball could never be fired as it was kept to grind pepper for their *cochon boucanné*).

Rose thought her menu "quite tolerable" for castaways. The dinner started with soup followed by boiled goose and ham. The four entrées consisted of a hot pâté of snipe and fish, a ragout of goose, and two of pork (one being pork shoulders that Rose had boned and stuffed). Two roasts followed: one of goose and the other of pork. Then came dishes of fresh fish, one with peas and the other with Appert's canned green beans. Dessert was plums, cheese, cherry tart, and a meringue cream (Appert's canned cherries, dried milk tablets, and eggs from the few chickens that had survived the shipwreck). The dinner ended with coffee, tea, and liqueur (the coffee and tea having been rinsed of salt water and then dried, the liqueur being the last bottle).

James Weddell and the *Jane* were in the Falklands at the time of the

Uranie's shipwreck. Although the Americans had tried to keep the news of the shipwreck quiet, Weddell had hitched a ride in the *General Knox*'s schooner to Berkeley Sound. He and *Sir Andrew Hammond*'s captain lunched with the Freycinets a few days before the French sailed in the *Mercury*. Weddell found Louis much worn down and depressed by the shipwreck. But he, as Weddell put it, could enjoy "the sympathising consolation of his lady, who was young and very agreeable." Weddell was obviously enchanted by Rose: "I dined in company with them, and the extreme vivacity of Madame F. seemed well to accord with the character of the French fair: it was reported, that in the midst of the greatest danger and confusion, she retained a most surprising firmness and composure of mind; resembling in this, according to all accounts, the unexampled fortitude of many French ladies during the murderous period of the French Revolution, when their dearest friends and relations were torn from them by merciless assassins." Freycinet gave the sealer his own small rigged rowboat. Weddell named it *Rose*.

Nearly three months after their shipwreck the Uranies, packed tight aboard the *Mercury*, sailed for Rio de Janeiro. A few days out from Berkeley Sound Freycinet bought the trader and altered course for Montevideo to off-load the passengers and crew. The *Mercury* entered the French Navy as the *Physicienne*. By October 1820 a thankful Rose was sailing into Cherbourg. But, as she said, she was no longer the "gay, wild and scatterbrained Rose" who had sailed from Toulon. She had become serious. Freycinet was cleared by a court-martial of the loss of the *Uranie*, and a decent veil was drawn over Rose's presence. Twelve years after their return, during a cholera epidemic sweeping Paris, Rose and Dr. Joseph Gaimard nursed a seriously ill Louis. He recovered, but Rose died. She was thirty-two.

All the French voyages that followed Freycinets' into the Pacific had hidden agendas. The French sea surveyors, in the festering Anglo-French rivalry, allied with the Roman Catholic Church, became gunboat diplomats. Their diplomacy included threatening to bombard Honolulu unless Catholics were given religious freedom (as well as the right for French goods to be imported) and, a few years later, declaring Tahiti a French protectorate (the protection aimed for Catholic missionaries and traders).

Denis Diderot's prediction, voiced some sixty years earlier, would appear to have at last materialized. In his *Supplément au voyage de Bougainville* he had warned the Tahitians—and, by inference, all other Noble Savages—that the Christians would one day come with a crucifix in one hand and a dagger in the other. The Europeans would force their opinions and customs upon the islanders, and "one day under their rule you will be almost as unhappy as they are." But then Diderot was a friend of Rousseau.

NOTES

1. Turtle Island had an evil reputation among American whalers. In 1825 the twenty-one-member crew, save one, of the Nantucket whaler *Oeno*, wrecked on the out-lying reef, were massacred by the natives. In 1840 the Sippican whaler *Shylock* came to grief on the same reef. The captain and seventeen of the crew took to the boats and sailed two hundred miles to a Tongan island. Captain Charles Taber's precipitous bolting left seven men stranded on the wreck. Clinging to the jib boom, they floated to the island, where contrary to expectations, they were kindly treated by the natives.

2. After the Fiji Islands, the *Sulphur* and the *Starling* were ordered to survey the Canton River during the combined operations of the British in the 1840–42 Opium War against the Chinese. Belcher, a surveying officer who liked the smell of gunpowder as much as the complexities of station pointers, sextants, theodolites, and plane trigonometry, was in his element. At one point in the fighting he had himself hoisted to the masthead of a captured junk in order to measure with a sextant the Chinese fortifications. He had forgotten, however, his orders that the junk be burned. The seamen were highly entertained to see their unpopular commander, lowered very hastily, to the smoldering deck. A few minutes later the junk blew up.

3. Cook visited Tongatapu twice: with the *Resolution* for five days in 1773 and for a month in 1777 with the *Resolution* and the *Discovery*. The *Discovery*'s captain, Charles Clerke, captured in his own inimitable style the approaches to Tongatapu: We found this a most confounded navigation. The Bottom, which we too clearly saw a continued bed of Coral Rock, very uneven, with here and there a mischievous rascal towering his head above the rest, almost to the waters Edge; most providentially we had exceeding smooth Water, with just such a breeze as we cou'd wish, and of course took every precaution we coul'd suggest, such as Boats a head, a good look out &c; but these lofty Gentry's heads were so small, that 'twas great odds but you miss'd them with the Lead in the Boats, be cautious as you wou'd. About 10 we gave one of them a rub, but fortunately receiv'd not the least damage.

4. An antiscorbutic concoction made from an extract of spruce leaves, branches, sap, and molasses. Cook added rum. La Pérouse added brandy.

5. Peter Dillon (1788–1847) was one of those larger than life characters that seemed drawn to the adventurous Pacific life. Born of Irish parents in the West Indies, he was taken back to Ireland before sailing, when eighteen years old, for India. A few years later he was among the Pacific islands. A tall, strongly built man, with dangerously red hair (he had a fierce temper), he learned the natives' language. His adventures included being captured by natives on Vanua Levu and then watching his companions being dismembered and roasted before his eyes. He traded throughout the islands with his base at Sydney. It was on one of these trading voyages that he learned about the Vanikoro natives and their articles of French manufacture.

6. Passports were issued by countries at war to the ships of the opposing side if they were engaged on voyages of exploration or science. It was a civilized custom that ended, like many other civilized customs, with Napoleon.

7. Kaahumanu, along with the young king's mother, was pivotal in the abolition of the kapu system.

8. Which is why, a year after Macquarie sailed for home, another Scot produced the following lines:

> 'Twas said of Greece two thousand years ago,
> That every stone i' the land had got a name,
> Of New South Wales too, men will say that too,
> But every stone there seems to get the same.
> "Macquarie" for a name is all *the go;*
> The old Scotch Governor was fond of fame,
> Macquarie Street, Place, Port, Fort, Town, Lake, River;
> "Lachlan Macquarie, Esquire, Governor," for ever!

Chapter 4

The Sea Surveyors— British

DANGER. Perils and hazard of the sea. Any rock or shoal which interferes with navigation.

DIFFICULTY. A word unknown to true salts.

Admiral W. H. Smyth, *The Sailor's Word-Book,* 1867

THE AFT GREAT CABINS of eighteenth-century sailing ships were the most noble interior spaces ever created by shipbuilders. Airy and light, these were no blocky cuboid compartments but ones full of subtle curves from the tumble home of topsides, camber of beams and deck, and dappled with water-reflected light bouncing through the curved sweep of stern windows. In these happy interiors could be heard the reassuring shipboard sounds: the harmony of sail and rigging, the creak of timbers, the grind of rudder pintle and gudgeon, the slap of sailors' feet overhead. In some large ships the captain or admiral— for these were his quarters—could walk out on the balustraded stern gallery, sniff the ocean breeze, contemplate the bubbling wake. So popular were these walkways that the senior officers of the Royal Navy bent naval architects to their will and stern galleries were still a feature of large warships launched during the fourth decade of the nineteenth century.

In 1997 a much humbler great cabin was seen by thousands of men, women, and children. In May of that year a replica of James Cook's *Endeavour,* lovingly built in Australia, sailed into the Yorkshire port of Whitby.[1] It was at Whitby that the original *Endeavour* had been built not as an expeditionary vessel but as a dumpy collier christened the *Earl of Pembroke.* What the carpenters and shipwrights (long moldering in their graves above the harbor) who adzed, sawed, and hammered together the collier would have thought of the huge crowds and buzzing harbor as the replica of their original sailed in is open to speculation.

During their own lifetimes it is certain that they would have been amazed to hear the conversations and discussions and watch the activities that were to take place in a great cabin meant for a skipper carrying coals from Newcastle to London.

In this great cabin, James Cook and Joseph Banks, in a space some fourteen by nineteen feet—but with standing headroom, compared with the crouching, simian four feet of headroom in the officers' cubbyholes—worked, lived, talked, dined, and tolerated each other for three years. Both men were light-years apart in background and attitudes, and both were to influence each other and in turn influence the world they lived in.

Compared with the land-traveling scientific expeditions of the eighteenth century, a sailing ship had incomparable advantages. It was self-sufficient, self-contained, with large storage space, a floating battery with immense firepower when needed. Observatories could be erected on land for astronomical and magnetic measurements; the boats could make detailed surveys of the coast and coastal waters. Miniexpeditions could forage the shores and farther inland to collect unknown flora and fauna, all these to be dissected, drawn, measured, cataloged, preserved, at the great cabin table.

For the keen observer of the animal kingdom, shipboard life could provide its own fauna. Joseph Banks wrote the following into his journal in September 1769, the *Endeavour* rolling her way to New Zealand:

Our bread indeed is but indifferent, occasioned by the quantity of Vermin that are in it, I have seen hundreds nay thousands shaken out of a single biskit. We in the Cabbin have however an easy remedy for this by baking it in an oven, not too hot, which makes them all walk off, but this cannot be allowed to the private people who must find the taste of these animals very disagreeable, as they every one taste as strong as mustard or rather spirits of hartshorn. They are of 5 kinds, 3 *Tenebrios*, 1 *Ptinus* and the *Phalangium cancroides;* this last is however scarce in the common bread but was vastly plentiful in white Deal biskit as long as we had any left.

How Cook reacted to Banks's identification is unknown. Probably with amusement, and Banks would have learned that seamen, demotic speakers all, lumped weevils together as *bargemen*.

It could have been a combustible mixture, this combination of the forty-year-old James Cook and the twenty-five-year-old Joseph Banks. Here, crammed together, living cheek by jowl, were the son of a farm laborer whose whole life had been circumscribed by the sea and whose companions had been, for the most part, rough-and-ready pragmatic men and a privileged, extremely wealthy, willowy dilettante. By a strange alchemy, it worked, and both were the better for it. Cook's inquiring mind was given something to feed on, and Banks learned something of his fellowmen.

A hint of the reason perhaps can be seen in two portraits. The first is the famous one of Cook, commissioned by Banks and hung in his home, after the *Resolution*'s Antarctic circumnavigation (a voyage that Banks, in a fit of pique, had stormed away from in a most mighty huff). Nathaniel Dance's portrait of Cook shows the face of an intelligent man used to command and familiar with being obeyed. A trifle stern perhaps, but the full curved lips give hint of a passionate and generous nature. This is no meanspirited tyrant. Benjamin West's portrait of Banks, painted shortly after the return of the *Endeavour*, shows a smooth-cheeked, personable young man surrounded by Pacific island articles and dressed in a native cloak. A hint of a smile hovers on his lips. The viewer suddenly sees a cheeky small boy peering out from the adult and saying: "Look at all this *stuff!* It's all a bit of a lark, isn't it?"

The *Endeavour* had sailed for Tahiti in 1768. The objective, sponsored by the Royal Society and executed by the Royal Navy, was to observe the transit of Venus across the sun's disk and thereby calculate the distance between the sun and the Earth. Lieutenant James Cook, as well as commanding the expedition, had been chosen by the Royal Society to be the principal observer with Charles Green, a civilian astronomer, as assistant. Also on board was a civilian party, nine in number (plus two dogs), who were sailing at the request of the Royal Society. Banks was their leader.

The young Banks was one of those fortunate beings, eighteenth-century English gentlemen, of large fortune, educated at Harrow, Eton, and Oxford. This was a surefire eighteenth-century recipe for producing arrogant, conceited coxcombs. That it didn't was due to Banks's innate common sense and generous nature. The fortune was considerable. With an annual income of six thousand pounds he could have bought the *Earl of Pembroke* at the Admiralty purchase price, tightened his breeches' waistband, and jogged along for the rest of the year on the remaining thirty-two hundred pounds. Banks, it appears, should have been following Jane Austen's dictum: "It is a truth universally acknowledged, that a single man in possession of a good fortune must be in want of a wife." True, rumor had it that young Mr. Banks, just before he sailed, had become engaged to Miss Harriet Blossom (the ward of James Lee, the Hammersmith nurseryman who had introduced the cultivation of the fuchsia into England and who had also translated part of Linnaeus's work). But Banks—a full-blooded man, no monk—became entangled with various ladies before his 1779 marriage to Dorothea Hugessen.

Banks's true passion was botany. Bewitched when a schoolboy by flowers—as opposed to the dry construe of Latin and Greek—he carried his passion to Oxford, found that university a botanical wasteland, and paid for a tutor to move from Cambridge University to Oxford. Aged twenty-three, with no degree but his passion undiminished, Banks sailed with his friend Lieutenant Constantine Phipps to Newfoundland. Banks spent six months in Newfoundland and Labrador. The richness of the coastal waters, fecund with fish, amazed him. It was cod for the most part, but one gigantic halibut measured by Banks—one inch short of seven feet from nose to tail and weighing 284 pounds, close to the weight of an oxen killed for the ship's company—entered his diary as a fish whose "dimensions I fear will appear incredible in England." He returned to England with the beginnings of his natural history collection. Moreover, the months spent on small boat voyages around the coast, botanizing, fishing, shooting, being pestered with "mosketos and Gadflies in Prodigious abundance," had whetted his appetite for more adventures.

As a member of the Royal Society, Banks was well aware of the voyage into the South Seas to observe the transit of Venus. Here was a chance for a different grand tour from the usual round of Europe with its marbles and ruins, the predictable tour urged on him by his friends. For this suggestion Banks had a ready reply: "Every blockhead does that, my Grand Tour shall be round the whole globe."

On 9 June 1768 the Royal Society wrote to the Admiralty that the recently discovered island of Tahiti—named King George's Island by Captain Samuel Wallis in the *Dolphin*—be selected as the site for the Venus observation. The letter continued with a request that "Joseph Banks Esq, Fellow of the Society, a Gentleman of large fortune, who is well versed in natural history, being Desirous of undertaking the same voyage the Council very earnestly request their Lordships, that in regard to Mr. Banks's great personal merit, and for the Advancement of useful knowledge, He also, together with his Suite, being seven persons more, be received on board of the ship, under command of Captain Cook."

Their lordships had no objection. On 22 July the Admiralty secretary directed Cook to receive "Joseph Banks Esq and his Suite consisting of eight persons with their Baggage." What Cook's personal feelings were on this sudden increase in an already crowded ship is unknown. Philosophical, no doubt. Seamen are adept at living in cramped quarters, and he now had to share his sacrosanct great cabin with two unknown gentlemen plus the draftsmen who would work at the great cabin table. Thirteen years in the Royal Navy had certainly hardened Cook to their lordships' whims. Lumbering him with a "Suite" of nine civilians, unused to navy ways, could be counted among them.

A cursory reading of Banks's party (the four servants and two dogs have always drawn ridicule from many later writers on the voyage) reinforces the picture of Banks as a lightweight dilettante, but a closer study reveals how carefully he had chosen his companions.

The plump and amiable Dr. Daniel Carl Solander provided the well-filled core of the party. The thirty-five-year-old Solander, born and educated in Sweden and an outstanding pupil of Carl von Linné (better known as Linnaeus, whose system of natural history classification had brought some order out of chaos), had settled in England and worked at bringing some order out of the chaos at the British Museum. Herman Spöring, a fellow countryman, acted as clerk. Two artists, Sydney Parkinson and Alexander Buchan, were employed to make the detailed drawings of botanical specimens, landscapes, and figures. Two of the four servants were expert fieldmen and had worked with Banks on botanical expeditions in England, Scotland, and Wales. As for those risible dogs, one was a greyhound to run down game (although it failed with a kangaroo), and the other, a spaniel gundog to flush and retrieve game.

The *Endeavour* returned to England in 1771 after a three-year voyage replete with enough adventures to produce a spate of leather-bound folio and octavo volumes. New Zealand's coastline and the east coast of Australia were placed on world maps and globes, and the thousands of unknown natural history specimens delighted the hearts of philosophical gentlemen. All this, however, had been achieved at an enormous cost in lives. A third of the ship's company had died from the pestilential fevers and diseases of the East Indies. During one terrible week twelve men were buried at sea, and at times the *Endeavour* could muster only four men for the watch.

The voyage set Cook and Banks on their famous careers, Cook as one of the world's greatest navigator-explorers and Banks as the Royal Society's long-lived president, one of the most influential figures in British science, a father figure in the founding of Australia, and the *éminence verte* to future British voyages of exploration.

Cook's statue in London, unveiled in 1914, tricorne-hatted, greatcoated, hand grasping a telescope, gazes across the heads of tourists hurrying down the Mall to Buckingham Palace. Behind him lies the Admiralty. Into that building, over the years following Cook's death, hurried officers who had served with him and were following in his wake. When they too had died, more officers followed, the uniforms changing but not their quest. Cook had become the exemplar for a lineage of naval surveying officers that stretched well into the nineteenth century.

George Vancouver and William Bligh were two of Cook's men. On 1 April 1791 (a sailing date that caused much mirth among the seamen) the thirty-three-year-old Vancouver sailed from England in command of HMS *Discovery* and her much smaller consort, HMS *Chatham*, bound for the northwest coast of North America. Vancouver has gone down in history as a brilliant surveying officer (the ship's boats, the everyday workhorses of coastal survey work, sailed and rowed over ten thousand miles through the racing currents, the wet and the cold, of the labyrinthine North American coast) and as something of a martinet.

The *Discovery*'s naturalist-surgeon was Archibald Menzies, a man selected by Banks for his botanical passion. This passion was not shared by Vancouver, for he and Menzies were often at loggerheads over the care of the seeds and plants painstakingly collected by the surgeon. Toward the end of the voyage Vancouver had Menzies confined to his cabin for insolence and contempt. But among his more famous introductions, Menzies brought back from Chile seeds of the monkey puzzle tree, which Banks started growing in his London garden.

Vancouver also had a midshipman flogged and eventually turned him out of the *Discovery* at Hawaii. Since the midshipman had been the Honourable Thomas Pitt when he joined the *Discovery* and Lord Camelford when he found his own way back to England—where one cousin was the prime minister, another the first lord of the Admiralty, and a brother-in-law the foreign secretary—it would appear that Vancouver was rather imprudent. But Pitt, to go by his later life, was an obviously vicious disrupting influence to have aboard ship, even though his cousins and brother-in-law could have easily wrecked Vancouver's career. Back in England Pitt sought a duel with Vancouver. He later shot a fellow lieutenant over a seniority dispute (and was acquitted), argued with the Admiralty, and, at his own request, was struck off the list of commanders. In London, in the words of the sober *Dictionary of National Biography*, he "achieved extraordinary notoriety by disorderly conduct." By 1804 he was dead, killed in a duel. Vancouver by then had been dead for six years, aged forty-two. He had been a sick man for the last few years of his life, including the last year of his four-and-a-half-year expedition. His *Voyage* was published posthumously.

Being labeled a Captain Bligh has become a cliché of modern times. But the young Bligh, at twenty-two, sailed as a very competent master aboard the *Resolution* during Cook's last voyage. The *Bounty* expedition to Tahiti, the mutiny, the extraordinary thirty-six-hundred-mile voyage in the open launch to Timor happened ten years later. What is not so well known is that Bligh returned to Tahiti in HMS *Providence* and HMS *Assistant* to complete the work thwarted by Fletcher Christian and the mutineers, the bringing of breadfruit to the West Indies as an economical food for the slaves working the sugar and indigo plantations.

The fruit of this tropical plant, when roasted, provides a passing resemblance to bread. (Lord Byron, in *The Island,* let his poetic muse stub a toe when he wrote that the breadfruit "bakes its unadulterated loaves/without a furnace in unpurchased groves.") William Dampier, that exotic mix of hydrographer and buccaneer, was closer to the truth when he wrote in his *Voyages:*

The breadfruit, as we call it, grows on a large tree as big and as tall as our largest apple trees. It hath a spreading head full of branches and dark leaves. The fruit grows on the boughs like apples; it is big as a penny loaf when wheat is at five shillings the bushel. The natives of this island use it for bread. They gather it when full-grown; then they bake it in an oven, which scorcheth the rind and makes it black; but they scrape off the outside black crust and there remains a tender thin crust and the inside is soft, tender and white, like the crumb of a penny loaf. There is neither seed nor stone in the inside, but all is of a pure substance like bread; it must be eaten new, for if it is kept above twenty-four hours it becomes dry and eats harsh and chokey; but 'tis very pleasant before it is too stale.

Alfred Russel Wallace, in his *Malay Archipelago,* is even more lyrical about the culinary delights of breadfruit:

During the time I resided in this place (Amboyna) I enjoyed a luxury I have never met with either before or since—the true breadfruit. . . . It is baked entire in the hot embers, and the inside scooped out with a spoon. I compared it to Yorkshire pudding; Charles Allen said it was like mashed potatoes and milk. It is generally about the size of a melon, a little fibrous towards the centre, but everywhere else quite smooth and puddingy, something in consistence between yeast-dumplings and batter-pudding. We sometimes made curry or stew of it, or fried it in slices; but it is no way so good as simply baked. It may be eaten sweet or savory. With meat and gravy it is a vegetable superior to any I know, either in temperate or tropical countries. With sugar, milk, butter, or treacle, it is a delicious pudding, having a very slight and delicate but characteristic flavour, which, like that of good bread and potatoes, one never gets tired of.

Here was a paragon among vegetables. For its transportation the Admiralty bought the *Providence,* a newly built West Indiaman. As with the *Bounty,* shipwrights made massive changes for the stowage of the thousands of pots to receive the young plants. The only space available with sufficient light, as with the *Bounty,* was the great cabin. A plan of the *Providence* shows that light, airy space converted and named the Garden. In here, to well forward of the mizzenmast, sat the thousands of pots.

Banks—now Sir Joseph Banks and president of the Royal Society—had been the prime mover in the *Bounty's* voyage. On that voyage had sailed two gardener-botanists, David Nelson (who had sailed with Cook on the *Resolution*) and William Brown. The unfortunate Nelson had survived the launch's passage to Timor but died there from fever. Brown was murdered on Pitcairn. Banks was also the prime mover for Bligh's second voyage, which also shipped two gardener-botanists, James Wiles and Christopher Smith, to tend the young plants. The *Providence* carried a serviceable library. Included in this, at the request of Bligh, were the two volumes of the *East India Pilot* with their 108 charts of the oceans and seas between Europe and the East; George Robertson's *Charts of the China Navigation;* Bougainville's *Voyage round the World;* Cook's *Journals* of his three voyages. Bligh's personal copy of Cook's last voyage is now held by the Admiralty Library. On the flyleaf, signed by John Croker, the Admiralty secretary from 1809 to 1830, is a terse inscription: "This copy of Cook's last voyage belonged to William Bligh Master of the *Resolution* who has made some marginal notes, which must be read with grains of allowance for his temper and prejudices. He afterwards became a flag officer."

Bligh's notations became public in 1928, when Lieutenant Commander R. T. Gould published an article in the *Mariner's Mirror.* The seventy-six notations range from the vituperative to the sensible. They reveal a choleric, unhappy man, a man full of bile at his perceived lack of recognition by those above him, contempt for his equals and those below him. Hardly leadership qualities. Here, penned in his own hand, is the lower deck's "Bounty bastard." Bligh died in 1817. His tomb—he shares it with his wife, Elizabeth—is an imposing one in the grounds of St. Mary's Church, Lambeth. The Thames runs close by, and across the river stretch the Houses of Parliament. It is one of life's small ironies that the church is now a Museum of Garden History run by the Tradescant Trust. It seems appropriate for a man so intimately bound up with botany.

The *Providence* and the *Assistant* (commanded by the American-born Lieutenant Nathaniel Portlock, another man who had sailed with Cook) cleared the chops of the English Channel in August 1791. Eight months later they were anchored in Matavai Bay, Tahiti. A quarter of a century had passed since Tahitians had first seen Europeans with the *Dolphin* coming to anchor in the bay.

The islanders had launched an attack in an attempt, as George Robertson, the *Dolphin*'s master, wrote, "to make our Great Canoe their own." The natives, in hundreds of their own canoes, had employed novel diversionary tactics to distract the British sailors' attention: young women standing up in each canoe and making "Lascivious Motions" and playing "all the Wanton Tricks imaginable."

Since that interesting scene many ships and expeditions had visited the island: Bougainville, Cook on all his three voyages, an English privateer with a letter of marque from King Gustavus III of Sweden, Bligh, Vancouver, and, in 1774, a Spanish expedition that had left two Franciscan friars and an assistant, complete with a prefabricated hut, to found the Mission of La Sanctissima Cruz. The friars, terrified for their lives, stayed ten months before being taken off the island. Cook had come across the empty mission in 1777. Near the hut the British found a cross with the inscription "CHRISTUS VINCIT CAROLUS III IMPERAT 1774." This was too much for Cook. A more temporal "GEORGIUS TERTIUS REX ANNIS 1767, 69, 73, 74 & 77" was cut on the cross's back.

(The same day saw an incident that had never happened before and would never happen again. Cook assembled his crew and gave them a choice. The spirits were running low, and ahead of them lay the Arctic cold. Coconuts were readily available at Tahiti. Rather than go on a short allowance in a cold climate they could choose to stop their grog and drink coconut milk. The choice was theirs. They voted for coconut milk. Lieutenant John Williamson was amazed: "the readyness with which they consented to this was a little surprizing, as a Seaman in general would as soon part with his life, as his Grog." It was not, however, total abstinence. Cook allowed the full Saturday night grog allowance: "To drink to their feemale friends in England, lest amongst the pretty girls of Otaheite they should be wholy forgoten.")

Bligh was welcomed back by the Tahitians, but he found much had changed for the worse since his long five-month stay with the *Bounty*. One young midshipman, Matthew Flinders, found the currency for favors received had undergone a subtle change: "The ladies are fond of Shirts or Sheets. Ironwork they will take but do not care much for."

Ten weeks were spent at Matavai Bay before they sailed, two floating arboretums, packed with more than two thousand young breadfruit plants. Some of the seamen sported their newly acquired tattoos, and a quarter of them their newly acquired venereal diseases.[2] Thorns lurked in the blossoms of the Pacific island Garden of Eden.

The passage to the West Indies took them through the Torres Strait north of Australia, the Cape of Good Hope, and St. Helena. Bligh left some plants at St. Helena and in return received a letter from the governor and council thanking him for the gift: "Which had impressed their minds with the warmest gratitude towards His Majesty for his goodness and attention for the welfare of his subjects; while the sight of his ships had raised in them an inexpressible degree of wonder and delight to contemplate a floating garden transported in luxuriance from one extremity of the world to the other."

One of the hardships for the crews of these floating gardens was thirst. Water is always a precious commodity at sea, and the garden required frequent watering. Matthew Flinders at times licked the cans used for watering the breadfruit plants.

In the West Indies Bligh received a more material token of appreciation. The grateful Jamaican House of Assembly voted him a purse of a thousand guineas. Two years after sailing from England the *Providence* and the *Assistant* were paid off, and nearly one thousand different plants, including five breadfruit plants, from the Pacific, St. Helena, and the West Indies were delivered to the royal gardens at Kew. Across the Atlantic the Tahitian breadfruit flourished in the West Indian climate. But the slaves, alas, resolutely refused to eat their fruit.

Matthew Flinders (the *Providence*'s seventeen-year-old midshipman who had found the Tahitian exchange rate subtly altered) years later was sent a questionnaire by the editor of the *Naval Chronicle* as a basis for a biographical sketch. One question ran as follows: "Juvenile or miscellaneous anecdotes illustrative of individual character?" Flinders replied: "Induced to go to sea against wishes of friends from reading *Robinson Crusoe*."

The voyage to Tahiti (where Flinders had found those thorns and was mulcted thirty shillings by the ship's surgeon; as one ship's surgeon noted, Tahitian ladies could leave "warm tokens of their affection") and adventures in the Torres Strait—near shipwreck and attacks by natives—only reinforced Flinders's opinion on the rightness of reading *Robinson Crusoe.*

As a boy growing up in Lincolnshire, his head turned by Defoe's novel and on the advice of a cousin in the Royal Navy, he had extended his reading to books on navigation, geometry, and trigonometry. The cousin, one of those who had warned him against going to sea, had also assured him that influential patrons were an essential for advancement. Flinders found one in Captain Thomas Pasley. Pasley's children's governess happened to be Henrietta Flinders, another of Matthew's cousins. Pasley took Flinders aboard the *Scipio* and then the seventy-four-gun *Bellerophon.* It was also Pasley who recommended Flinders to Bligh and the *Providence.*

On seeing his son after the breadfruit voyage, Flinders's father noted in his diary that he had "come home poorly with the Autumnal fever . . . the warm Climate he has passed makes England chilly and cold to him." Within two years Flinders was back in the Pacific.

But before the Pacific came action aboard his old ship *Bellerophon,* Pasley still in command, in the naval battle known to British history as the Glorious First of June. In this fierce and bloody action, an eighteen-pound French cannonball removed Pasley's leg.[3] In 1795, his mentor out of action, Flinders sailed as master's mate aboard the *Reliance,* bound for New South Wales and the infant penal settlement at Sydney Cove in Port Jackson. On board was the settlement's new governor, Captain John Hunter, and supplies that included a town clock, parts for a windmill, and a peal of bells.

Aboard the *Reliance* Flinders struck up an immediate and lasting friendship with the ship's surgeon, a fellow Lincolnshire man, George Bass. The tall, handsome, energetic surgeon, four years older than Flinders, was fluent in Spanish, a voracious reader, and, like many other naval surgeons, an accomplished botanist and zoologist. He was also a small boat sailor and could navigate as well as any master in the Royal Navy. During the six-month passage to Sydney the two men concocted a plan of exploration. New Holland, as Flinders wrote, "was a new region, in extent equal to Europe. . . . Was it a vast desert? Was it occupied by an immense lake—a second Caspian Sea, or by a Mediterranean to which existed a navigable entrance in some part of the coasts hitherto unexplored? Or was not this new continent rather divided into two or more islands by straits communicating from the unknown parts of the south to the imperfectly examined north-west coast or to the Gulf of Carpentaria, or to both? Such were the questions that excited the interest and divided the opinion of geographers."

The solving of all those questions patently was beyond the resources of a young master's mate and a naval surgeon. Nevertheless, as Flinders recalled, "a determination was found of completing the examination of the east coast of New South Wales by all such opportunities as the duty of the ship and procurable means could admit. Projects of this nature, when originating in the minds of young men, are usually termed romantic; and so far from any good anticipated, even prudence and friendship join in discouraging, if not opposing them."

When the *Reliance* sailed between the sandstone headlands flanking Port Jackson, the Pacific rollers seething at their bases, she entered a body of water that Governor Arthur Phillip had called "the finest harbour in the world in which a thousand sail of the line may ride with the most perfect security." No thousand ships had anchored there—only whalers, trading vessels, and transports bringing their wretched cargo of convicts, male and female, from the prison hulks half the world away in England.

Phillip, an ill man, had sailed for England in 1792, leaving the penal colony under the far from paternalistic care of the officers and men of the New South Wales Corps. This body of men, some three hundred strong and soon to be nicknamed the Botany Bay Rangers, had been raised in England to take over the duties of the marines as convict guards. The officers, for the most part, were brutal men shot through with a strong vein of avarice; the noncommissioned officers and rankers no better.

With Phillip gone, the officers set about turning New South Wales into their personal and private fiefdom. Civil magistrates were replaced by officers. Any member of the corps could have twenty-five acres of free land; the officers, a hundred acres of land plus ten convicts—maintained at government expense—as virtual slave labor.

In 1793 an American trader had arrived at Sydney with a cargo of trade goods including thousands of gallons of rum. The sharp-nosed Yankee skipper stipulated that not one item of goods would be landed unless the colony first bought all the spirits. The New South Wales Corps officers formed a cartel to buy both rum and cargo, with the regimental paymaster, Lieutenant John Macarthur, issuing bills against the regimental funds. The rum and trade goods were then sold at an enormous markup and profit by the cartel. It was, for Macarthur and other officers, the founding of their own personal fortunes and the first Australian family dynasties.

It was with a sense of relief that Flinders and Bass, two months after their arrival, sailed away from this Hogarthian caricature of Georgian England, an antipodean outpost of corruption, disease, thieving, and drunkenness, where rum had become the currency and the New South Wales Corps had earned the soubriquet Rum Corps.

The two men had sailed into Port Jackson aboard a sixteen-gun, 394-ton, three-masted vessel that could set over twenty sails. They sailed out on their first exploratory foray in a ridiculously diminutive craft steered by an oar and setting one lugsail. A modern-day, rather scurrilous aphorism has it that the least practical item to carry aboard a small sailing craft is a wheelbarrow, an umbrella, or a naval officer. The latter would not apply in those days of sail. Flinders and Bass both were superb small boat handlers.

Tom Thumb, the name given to their craft, was owned by Bass and had been brought down aboard the *Reliance.* Measuring eight feet on the keel (about ten feet overall), she carried a small supply of provisions and water. Bass's servant, a boy named William Martin, served as crew. The sailing of *Tom Thumb* fell to Flinders and Bass, one at the steering oar and the other at the mainsheet. Martin bailed.

An air of escapade, of exuberance, of sheer fun and joy surrounds this first venture of Flinders and Bass. *Tom Thumb* took them through the flanking sandstone headlands and out into the Pacific swells, which she rode like a buoyant duckling before slipping into Botany Bay. Here they explored the bay and unknown reaches of George's River. A week later they were back in Sydney and laid their report before Governor Hunter. (The result was the founding of Bankstown, one of Australia's pioneer settlements.)

A few months after the cruise of the *Tom Thumb,* the trio—for it included the boy, Martin—extended their coastal explorations farther south in a three-foot-longer version of the original *Tom Thumb.* On their second voyage they were caught in a "southerly buster," a line squall from the south. It was nighttime, and they ran before it. "The sail," wrote Flinders, "flying away before the mast like a flag, Mr. Bass keeping the end of the sheet in his hand, and hauling aft a few inches occasionally, to keep the boat ahead of those seas, which appeared eagerly following after, to overwhelm us with destruction. I was steering with an oar, and it required the utmost exertion and care to keep her directly before the sea." Over the next five years this unusual partnership—a naval officer with a passion for hydrography and a naval surgeon with a taste for hydrography, natural history, and adventure—unveiled thousands of miles of Australian coastline.

But first came a voyage commanded by Bass alone. In 1797 the surgeon and six seamen sailed from Sydney, with provisions for six weeks, in a twenty-eight-foot whaleboat. Bass was intent upon solving a nagging question: Did a strait or passage exist between New South Wales and Van Diemen's Land? Twelve weeks later the open boat returned after a coastal voyage of twelve hundred miles. Lack of provisions—they had been reduced to eating salted petrels, fish, and seal meat—and a whaleboat whose flexing in a seaway meant constant bailing had forced a return. But Bass was convinced that a passage did exist. The set of the currents, the swell all indicated a strait. One moment of this voyage stands out as pure, unalloyed small boat sailing, the moment that makes the misery worth it, the moment perhaps for Bass being made more significant because it was New

Year's Eve. Here was the whaleboat, Bass at the helm, the water chuckling at her bow, ghosting along an unknown shore, the off watch cocooned and snoring in their blankets, those on watch gazing across a sea dappled silver under "bright moonlight, the sky without a cloud . . . the land low and level. . . ." They could see and hear the surf breaking on the shore. Just before midnight a thickening haze dimmed the shore, and then they heard the sound of "vast flights of petrels and other birds flying about us."

The cedar-planked whaleboat later became a venerated artifact to the colonists. Souvenirs—snuffboxes were a particularly prized item—were made from its timbers—pieces of the true cross—and Governor King, in 1802, presented the French explorer Nicolas Baudin with a silver-framed piece of the keel, a memorial, as Baudin wrote, of an *"audacieuse naviga-tion."*

Bass's supposition that a strait existed was proved within a year. Flinders and Bass with a crew of eight seamen sailed a decked longboat, the sloop *Norfolk*, westward through the strait and made an anticlockwise circumnavigation of Van Diemen's Land. No chronometer was carried—Flinders's superiors thought that article too precious to trust to a decked longboat—and the tools of the surveying trade consisted of a sextant, an azimuth compass, a theodolite with legs, and an artificial horizon. Latitudes were observed ashore with the artificial horizon and longitudes by lunar distance. The *Norfolk* was accompanied for the first stage of the voyage by the fifty-seven-foot trading brig *Nautilus*,[4] partly owned by Charles Bishop, a young merchant adventurer seeking his fortune in the South Seas and now looking for seals among the Furneaux Islands. Bishop's rather swashbuckling approach to life struck a responsive chord in Bass, for the surgeon was a humorous man who tended to find the con-strictions of naval service rather irksome. Adventure rather than duty was the siren song. For Bass the rewards and honors of exploration meant lit-tle. It was the sheer fun of doing it he enjoyed.

Flinders spoke affectionately of the *Norfolk*. This was his first inde-pendent surveying command as a lieutenant. The *Norfolk* might have been ugly, cramped, wet, and uncomfortable, but she still held the lumi-nosity that surrounds all first commands. Plus, as Flinders wrote, she was an admirable seaboat for the stormy waters that surrounded Van Diemen's Land: "Seas that were apparently determined to swallow her up she rode over with all the ease and majesty of an old experienced petrel." Sooty shearwaters, muttonbirds, were creatures they saw in prodigious num-bers. At one point in the Bass Strait Flinders estimated a flight of more than a hundred million birds. This was a river of birds "from fifty to eighty yards in depth and of three hundred yards, or more, in breadth; the birds were not scattered, but flying as compactly as free movement of their wings seemed to allow; and during a full hour and a half this stream of pe-trels continued to pass without interruption at a rate little inferior to the swiftness of a pigeon." This was a flying larder, but with no need to shoot. The sooty shearwater nests in burrows in the ground, and the Norfolks would go ashore in the evening and pluck the birds from out of the ground. When the birds were skinned and smoked, the seamen thought them "passable food."

Black swans provided another source of food. Bass, at Port Dalrymple on Van Diemen's Land, estimated three hundred of them swimming within a small area. But their dying swan song, so celebrated by poets, Bass thought "exactly resembled the creaking of a rusty ale-house sign on a windy day."

The twenty-one-year-old Flinders had sailed to Australia as an obscure master's mate. He returned to England as a twenty-six-year-old lieutenant with a growing reputation as a naval surveying officer. During his passage home on the *Reliance* Flinders busied himself, in his off watch hours, with preparing his draft charts and sailing directions for publication. He also composed a long letter to Sir Joseph Banks.

Thirty years had passed since the young Banks had botanized along New Holland's shores. The years had seen him grow large in bulk and influence. As president of the Royal Society he was listened to with deference, his advice taken with alacrity and his patronage courted. The crimson ribbon and star of the Order of the Bath had been added to his knighthood, and he had the ear of King George III on matters relating to the royal gardens at Kew and on the breeding of sheep, a subject dear to the hearts of both the farmer king and Banks. Moreover, in the ultimate sign of public renown, Banks was a source for cartoonists.

James Gillray, that most barbed of cartoonists, had a lampoon out on the streets within days of Banks's being invested with the Order of the Bath. It shows Banks sprouting butterfly wings, rising from a mud shore, the crimson ribbon and star draped around him. The caption reads: "The Great South Sea Caterpillar, transform'd into a Bath Butterfly—taken from the Philosophical Transactions for 1795—This insect first crawled into notice from among the weeds and Mud of the South Sea; being afterwards placed in a Warm Situation by the Royal Society, was changed by the heat of the Sun into its present form—it is notic'd & Valued Solely on account of the beautiful Red which encircles its Body, & the Shining Spot on its Breast; a Distinction which never fails to render Caterpillars valuable."

New South Wales was dear to Banks's heart. He had after all given advice to the government on the settlement, and he must have had happy memories of those days spent botanizing along its shores. The letter being composed by Flinders aboard the *Reliance* was aimed directly at this interest of Banks. It was a letter soliciting Sir Joseph's patronage and influence with the Admiralty for command of a vessel to circumnavigate and chart the entire New Holland coastline.

For the young lieutenant, Gillray's "Great South Sea Caterpillar" was going to prove very valuable indeed.

NOTES

1. The small steep-sided Yorkshire port of Whitby is today famous for three things: James Cook, Dracula, and kippers. The young James Cook lived and worked here for John Walker, a Quaker shipowner, before joining the Royal Navy. Bram Stoker wrote *Dracula* in Whitby, and this is the port where the count arrives (in the shape of a dog) before leaving in a wooden box on a goods train bound for London. The kippers (oak-smoked herring) come from Fortunes, a company founded in 1872 that used to send its products around the globe to nostalgic Britons. No longer, however. The Brussels bureaucrats have stopped another of life's small joys.

2. The Admiralty ruled that venereal diseases—the "Great Pox" (syphilis) and the "Clap" (gonorrhea)—were the responsibility of the recipients. Seamen were mulcted fifteen shillings—about two weeks' pay—for the surgeon's cure (a mercurial salve), and this was debited against the patient in the ship's paybook. At the end of the commission the mulcts were paid to the surgeon.

3. An event recorded in splendidly dire verse by an anonymous naval rhymster:

   > Bravo, Bowyer, Pasley, Captain Hutt,
   > Each lost a leg, being sorely hurt;
   > Their lives they valued but as dirt
   > When that their country called them!

4. The *Nautilus* had sailed into Sydney from Tahiti carrying eleven men, four women, and four children of the London Missionary Society's evangelicals who had been landed by the *Duff* at Tahiti's Matavai Bay in 1797. A year later the *Nautilus* had called in for supplies, and the missionaries persuaded Bishop not to sell the natives firearms. The islanders, however, soon found out about this stratagem and promptly stripped the missionaries naked, an action that persuaded some of them to sail with Bishop to Sydney.

Chapter 5

Terra Australis

ENTERPRISE. An undertaking of difficulty and danger.

EPAULET. The buillion or mark of distinction worn on the shoulders by officers, now common to many grades, but till recently worn only by captains and commanders, whence the brackish poet—

> "Hail, magic power that fills an epaulet,
> No wonder hundreds for thee daily fret!"

the meaning of which is now pointless.

Admiral W. H. Smyth, *The Sailor's Word-Book,* 1867

HE *RELIANCE* arrived in England on 27 August 1800. On 6 September Flinders sent his letter to Banks's London home. With it went a parcel of flower, shrub, and tree seeds from New South Wales. The letter, as Flinders well knew, also contained the seeds of his bid for fame. Here was outlined his plan for the complete survey of New Holland's coastline, and if—here came the bid for its command—his "late discoveries in that country should so far meet approbation as to induce the execution of it to be committed to me, I should enter upon it with the zeal which I hope has hitherto characterized my services."

The next few weeks were anxious ones for Flinders. No reply came from Banks. The careful sowing appeared to have fallen on barren ground. Not that Flinders was idle. The *Reliance* had to be taken to Deptford, where she was paid off; visits were made to Alexander Dalrymple, the Admiralty hydrographer, and to Aaron Arrowsmith, the engraver and publisher of charts; and, most important, Flinders pursued the wooing by letter of Ann Chappell in Lincolnshire. (The Chappell Isles and Mount Chappell appear on Flinders's chart of Bass Strait.) His great friend Bass was also in London. After the *Norfolk's* voyage Bass had quit the navy, joined Charles Bishop in the *Nautilus,* and then sailed with a full cargo of sealskins for China, where both cargo and *Nautilus* had been sold at a most satisfactory profit. Both men had then sailed for England aboard the East Indiaman *Woodford*, arriving a month before the *Reliance*.

On 8 October 1800 George Bass married Elizabeth Waterhouse at St. James's Church in Piccadilly (Captain Henry Waterhouse, Elizabeth's brother, also happened to be the *Reliance*'s captain). Both Bass and Bishop were busy raising money to purchase the brig *Venus* and fit her out for South Sea trading.

Finally, happily, after nine anxious weeks, Flinders received a letter from Banks. Sir Joseph apologized . . . ill health . . . out of town . . . would be happy to see Flinders at Soho Square. The two men met, and Banks was won over by the young lieutenant.

But Banks, with Flinders sitting in front of him, was placed in a quandary. Ideally Flinders should have been half the world away, still in New South Wales, waiting the arrival of a small surveying vessel that had been marked for his command.

The beginning of this embarrassing situation had started the previous year. On the tenth anniversary of the founding of the colony, Banks and other leading figures in the settlement's development had decided a small surveying vessel was needed to sail up unknown rivers and into the unknown interior. Captain Philip Gidley King, a later governor of the colony, found a suitable, if unusual, vessel building at the Deptford navy yard. Only sixty tons and fifty-two feet on the gundeck, she sported three sliding keels (dagger boards), which gave her a draft of about ten feet for windward sailing and six feet with the boards retracted.

The *Lady Nelson* was the creation, the pride, and the joy of Captain John Schanck,[1] commissioner of the Transport Board, and intended for the use of the board. Schanck, on being approached by King, had thought that a larger *Lady Nelson*, able to carry more stores and provisions but worked with the same number of crew, would be more suitable for survey work. It was a tactical error in the endless games played by government departments. To the fury of Schanck and the other members of the Transport Board, Banks exerted his influence—building another vessel would only cause delay—and their pet *Lady Nelson* was whipped away and transferred to the Colonial Department. The rig was also changed from the designed one-masted fore-and-aft cutter rig to that of a two-masted square-rigged brig, for, according to King, in light of the fact that "few seamen know anything about the management of a cutter, her being constructed into a brig would make her more manageable to the generality of seamen." The change was disastrous. His Majesty's Armed Surveying Brig *Lady Nelson* proved a wretched vessel when, with yards braced around, tacks on board, she attempted her pathetic struggles to claw to windward but succeeded only in sliding away to leeward in a most ignominious, alarming, crablike fashion.

Portrait of Matthew Flinders

"On 19 January a commission was signed by the Lords of the Admiralty for Matthew Flinders, late second lieutenant of His Majesty's ship *Reliance* to be lieutenant of the *Investigator*. . . . Mustered the ship's company and read my commission as lieutenant. Received fresh beef. Snow at times."   —Matthew Flinders

(Illustration from the *Naval Chronicle,* 1814)

Leaking copiously, the *Lady Nelson,* Lieutenant James Grant in command, had long since sailed for New South Wales. The Deptford yard—notorious for corruption—had only puttied the seams rather than use oakum caulking. She had sailed with a convoy of East Indiamen escorted by HMS *Anson* and HMS *Porpoise.* Poor young Grant soon found his command so much of a sluggard in the sea conditions that she had to be taken in tow by the East Indiaman *Brunswick.* It was an episode, what with the seas breaking clean over the little vessel, that caused much amusement to the watchers crowding the *Brunswick*'s stern galleries. Grant, to shorten the ignominy, cut the *Lady Nelson* adrift and watched the convoy sail on.

Banks's grand scheme to place Flinders in command at Sydney had also come adrift. The only course of action was to get another command for Flinders. Lord Spencer, the first lord of the Admiralty, was put into play, and within a week the Admiralty was directing the Navy Board to slip the armed sloop *Xenophon*. Slightly smaller than Cook's *Endeavour*, the *Xenophon* shared a common ancestry: She had been built as a North Sea collier and had the same roomy qualities. Bought into the Royal Navy in 1798 and outfitted with twenty thirty-two-pound carronades and two eighteen-pound carronades, she had been used as a convoy vessel.

A week after the *Xenophon* had been slipped the Admiralty directed the Navy Board to prepare her for foreign service with six months' provisions and stores. By the middle of January 1801 she had been renamed *Investigator* with Flinders commissioned as her commander.

Here at work was the unmistakable influence of Sir Joseph Banks. But the Admiralty was not the only place where Banks was pulling strings and playing the puppet master. He might have been overweight and gout-ridden, but the energy of the younger man still flowed. The civilian scientific staff had to be recruited. Robert Brown, a shy and modest twenty-seven-year-old Scot, son of an Episcopal clergyman and educated at Aberdeen and Edinburgh University, was serving in an army regiment as ensign and assistant surgeon. Like many other medical men, he found his true passion in botany. Banks, who knew him and liked him, had given the young Scot a free run of his collection and library when Brown was on a London visit. The post was offered and accepted. Then Banks had to exert his influence and pry Brown away from a reluctant army colonel and put him aboard the *Investigator* as the naturalist. (Brown never returned to medicine. He became a famous nineteenth-century botanist and friend and adviser to both Banks and Charles Darwin.) The forty-seven-year-old Austrian Ferdinand Bauer, the outstanding botanical draftsman of the age, joined as the botanical artist. The twenty-year-old William Westall found a berth as the topographical painter (his coastal views, from the mariners' point of view, still remain far better than any photograph). John Allen, a miner, was to collect geological specimens; Peter Good, an experienced gardener from Kew, to tend the collected plants (the *Investigator* carried a portable greenhouse to be erected over the great cabin on the poop deck). John Crosley was appointed by the Board of Longitude as astronomer. The six civilians found themselves signed up to sail in a vessel where the shipwrights and carpenters were busy sealing up (not very effectively) gunports, building cubbyhole cabins for the staff and Good's portable greenhouse.

The way matters stood as regards this love feast between Banks and the Admiralty may be seen in an exchange of letters between Sir Joseph and Evan Nepean, the Admiralty secretary. In one letter Banks wrote: "Is my proposal for an alteration in the undertaking in the *Investigator* approved?" Nepean replied: "Any proposal you may make will be approved; the whole is left entirely to your decision."

The Admiralty's benevolence at complying so readily with a civilian's wishes is remarkable. More so when seen in the context of the times. A lone Britain was fighting a frighteningly triumphant France led by General Napoleon Bonaparte—First Consul in name but dictator in practice. With a diplomatic skill equal to his brilliance as a general, he had engineered the revival of the Armed Neutrality among Russia, Prussia, Denmark, and Sweden, all Baltic states. Since hemp, tar, and timber came from the Baltic, this was a direct threat at the essential working fabric of the Royal Navy, the equivalent of a modern threat to oil supplies. The formidable Admiral Lord St. Vincent, under no illusions about this combined Baltic fleet, called it "the present impending storm from the north of Europe . . . a host of foes." The Royal Navy, on convoy duty and blockade duty, was stretched to the limit; every vessel was precious. Seen against this background, depending upon one's bias, the dispatching of two vessels for hydrographic and botanical investigation to New Holland appears either unwarrantable civilian interference in naval concerns at a time of grave peril or an altruistic Admiralty, on the side of the angels, working for science and the general common good.

As with most expeditions, however, the roots were tapped into various sources. At Whitehall the alarm bells had rung when the French representative in London had applied for the Baudin expedition's passport into the South Seas with the *Naturaliste* and the *Géographe*. The passport had been granted. But any move by Bonaparte had to be treated with suspicion. Alarm bells had also rung behind the Ionic columns of East India House. The Honorable East India Company (with many stockholders in the government) suspected the French of having a covetous eye on New Holland; from a suitable base they could threaten the company's trade. Indeed, as a singular mark of its warm approval toward Flinders and the *Investigator*, the company voted £1,200 "to defray the expense of his Table[2] for himself, Officers and the Gentlemen who accompany him." But the taproot, the sturdy nourishment for the expedition, lay with Banks.

In the eight months since his return, Flinders's dream had become a reality. At twenty-six he had been raised to commander, had his own expedition, and, when he arrived in New South Wales, would also have the *Lady Nelson* added to his command. Matters had come a long way since *Tom Thumb*.

Such was his euphoria, so all-consuming, that he now made a move that came close to jeopardizing his career.

On continental Europe, a Bonaparte French army *tirailleur* could pick off his target with ease. In Britain, to the jaundiced eyes of the Admiralty, Cupid and his bow was achieving the same among His Majesty's naval officers. Admiral Lord Nelson appeared to have lost leave of his senses (and his wife, Lady Nelson) and was peacocking around London with the rather déclassée Lady Emma Hamilton, the wife of Sir William Hamilton. London society's tongues wagged behind the flutter of fans. Emma, it was said, had once been the "Goddess of Health" at the suspect Adelphi establishment of a Scottish quack doctor, this being followed by liaisons with various men-about-town until arriving in the aging Sir William's bed, another decorative trophy to add to his collection of Greek vases.

The dilatory Admiral Sir Hyde Parker, commanding the fleet destined for the Baltic to counter St. Vincent's "storm from the north," at sixty-three had just married a nubile nineteen-year-old girl whose overflowing charms—like a "batter pudding," according to St. Vincent—were keeping him (and his fleet) from going about their proper business.

Cupid's darts appeared to be finding more marks.

On being promoted to commander, Flinders had proposed to Ann Chappell. In April 1801 he wrote to her from the Nore:

> My dearest friend,
> Thou hast asked me if there is a *possibility* of our living together. I think I see a *probability* of living with a moderate share of comfort. Till now I was not certain of being able to fit myself out clear of the world. I have now done it, and have accommodation on board the *Investigator*, in which as my wife a woman may, with love to assist her, make herself happy.
> P.S. It will be much better to keep this matter entirely secret. There are many reasons for it yet, and I have also a powerful one: I do not know how my great friends might like it.

It was a prescient postscript. One great friend was to be profoundly annoyed.

Eleven days after he wrote his letter, Matthew and Ann were married in Lincolnshire. Stuffing a roll of banknotes in his boot for safekeeping, Flinders and his bride rode for London (but not before visiting his surprised father, who wrote in his diary: "Matthew's Marriage—with concern I note that my Son Mattw. came upon us suddenly & unexpectedly with a Wife on Sat. April 18 & left us next day—it is Miss Chapple of Partney. We had known of the acquaintance, but had no Idea of Marriage taking place until the completion of his ensuing Voyage. I wish he may not repent his hasty step").

Ann was installed aboard the *Investigator*, fondly hoping to sail to New South Wales with her husband. The Admiralty soon got wind of Flinders's plan. An inspecting officer found Ann in Flinders's cabin making herself comfortable "without her bonnet," as did an irritated Banks, who dashed off a letter to Flinders on 21 May:

> I have but time to tell you that news of your marriage, which was published in the Lincoln paper has reached me. The Lords of the Admiralty have heard also that Mrs. Flinders is on board the *Investigator*, and that you have some thought of Carrying her to sea with you. This I am very sorry to hear, and if that is the Case I beg to give you

my advice by no means to adventure measures so Contrary to the regulations and discipline of the Navy; for I am convinced by language I have heard, that their Lordships will, if they hear of her being in New South Wales, immediately order you to be superseded, whatever may be the Consequences, and in all Liklyhood order Mr. Grant to Finish the survey.

A shot across his bows from such a big gun forced a change of plan upon Flinders. A few days later he was writing to Banks: "Mrs. Flinders will return to her friends immediately our sailing orders arrive." His troubles, however, were not over. Sailing from the Thames to Portsmouth, the *Investigator* ran aground on a sandbank off Dungeness. That the sandbank didn't appear on the chart supplied by the Admiralty was of no consequence; the Mrs. Flinders episode still rankled with a testy Admiralty.

In late June a short paragraph appeared in the *Times* of London: "The *Investigator* (late *Xenophon*), ordered to Botany Bay on a voyage of discovery, is expected to sail from Portsmouth with the first fair wind. She is admirably fitted out for the intended service, and is manned by picked men, who are distinguished by a glazed hat decorated with a globe, and the name of the ship in letters of gold."

The fair winds came and the fair winds went. But no sailing orders came from the Admiralty. Flinders chafed at the delay; the gentlemen botanized on the Isle of Wight; and the seamen, flush with two months' advance pay—but not allowed ashore in case they ran—enjoyed the mercenary charms of Portsmouth's notorious bawds, come aboard by bumboat and carrying smuggled rum in their petticoats.

But the delay ensured that Flinders gained an experienced master, John Thistle, back in England for only three weeks after six years in New South Wales. His career in the Royal Navy had been seaman, midshipman, master. He had volunteered from the *Reliance* to sail with Bass on the whaleboat voyage and then with Flinders and Bass on the *Norfolk*. These sorts of voyages appealed to him. One day, still kicking their heels at Spithead, Thistle and some Investigators went to a Portsmouth fortune teller. Not surprisingly, they were told they were going on a long voyage and that Thistle would be lost at sea and the others shipwrecked.

At last, on 17 July, Flinders received his sailing orders from the Admiralty and also the precious passports from the French. The *Investigator* sailed next day, eighty-eight men on board, with eighteen months of salt meat, twelve months of dry provisions, seven months of bread, and fifty-eight tons of fresh water. Cooped in their pens were sheep, goats, pigs, barnyard fowl, and, tethered closely during the weighing of the anchors, hunting dogs for land game. At least two cats—one of them belonging to Flinders—prowled below deck looking for rats. Yet another Royal Navy vessel—with more than a passing resemblance to a floating farmyard, complete with noises and smells—was off on her long voyage halfway around the world. As an exploration vessel she also carried the usual bartering goods for trade with the natives: pocketknives, looking glasses, combs, beads, earrings, finger rings, blankets, baize cloth, linen, needles, thread, files, scissors, hammers, axes, hatchets, and King George's head medals. Also aboard were a library for the scientific staff and a copy of the *Encyclopaedia Britannica* provided by Banks.

Ann Flinders, the bride of three months, was home in Lincolnshire when the *Investigator* sailed. Lincolnshire men were well represented among the officers: Robert Fowler (an officer from the *Xenophon*) as first lieutenant and Samuel Flinders (Matthew's younger brother) as second lieutenant. John Franklin, a relation by marriage to Matthew Flinders, a round-faced, jolly, fifteen-year-old—"all fun and mischief to the backbone," according to a contemporary—was one of the midshipmen. Franklin had just returned from the Battle of Copenhagen and the sixty-four-gun *Polyphemus*. This voyage aboard the *Investigator* was to give the young Franklin his taste for exploration.

Bass, Bishop, & Co.'s 142-ton brig *Venus* had sailed for Sydney six months before the *Investigator* cleared the English Channel. The syndicate had raised the money, bought the *Venus*—seventy-six feet long, teak-built, copper-sheathed, "very sound and tight," according to Bass—and loaded her "as deep as she can swim and as full as an egg" with a general cargo to be sold at Sydney.

On the long haul to Simon's Town at the Cape of Good Hope, Flinders, modeling himself on James Cook, instituted a regimen under which, on fine days, the cockpits and decks below were cleared, swept, scrubbed, flogged dry, aired with stoves and then sprinkled with vinegar. On wet and dull days they were just swept and aired. Care was taken that the seamen, careless creatures when it came to their own welfare, did not sleep on wet decks and in wet clothes. All their bedding, clothes, sea chests, and seabags were aired once a fortnight. Every Sunday and Thursday the ship's company was mustered with every man clean-shaved and clean-dressed. Three months after sailing the *Investigator* had not a single man on the sick list. At Simon's Town, however, John Crosley, the astronomer, did fall ill. Too sick to continue the voyage, he did manage to set up his tents, observatory, and instruments and taught Samuel Flinders, selected to take his place, his new duties.

Flinders's orders from the Admiralty had been to start the New Holland survey at the southwest and work eastward along the south coast, looking for any straits or rivers that might lead to the unknown interior. If nothing was found, Flinders was to sail through the Bass Strait to Sydney, where he would take the *Lady Nelson* under his command. Both vessels would then continue the coastal survey northward along the west coast; the reef-strewn Torres Strait; the Gulf of Carpentaria; and, finally, the east coast. It was a massive anticlockwise sweep around New Holland, which might prove to be two or more large islands. Having done all this, he was then to sail for survey work among the Fiji Islands before returning with all possible speed to England.

After leaving Simon's Town—and its inhabitants, whose curiosity had been piqued by the observatory with its telescopes and the magnificent Ramsden theodolite—the Investigators raised Cape Leeuwin at the southwest of New Holland on 6 December 1801.

Thousands of miles farther east his friend George Bass, aboard the *Venus*, was sailing for Tahiti to load salt pork for Sydney. The *Venus* had arrived at Sydney in August but found the market glutted and Governor King running a tightfisted economic policy for the settlement. "Our wings are clipped with a vengeance," wrote a rueful Bass, "but we shall endeavour to fall on our feet somehow or other." The result was a contract to supply salt pork for the colony.

Salt pork is hardly the stuff of romance and adventure, but pork-trading voyages to Tahiti always had added spice. King Pomare I supplied pigs to the traders for muskets and ammunition. One visitor, John Turnbull, wrote that "nothing was so acceptable to them as fire-arms for they consider everything else as useless trifles." Pomare also relied upon the well-armed sailors from the traders to fight on his side in the intertribal wars. Indeed in 1801 Pomare had written to Governor King (in a letter obviously drafted by the missionaries): "I love King George and his subjects, and will, while I live, be a protector to those who put themselves under my care . . . and therefore I wish your excellency to present me with a few fire-arms, whereby my authority may be maintained, and the peace of my kingdom preserved." Governor King obliged. The colony needed salt pork, Pomare needed muskets, and the missionaries, who needed Pomare's protection, found their scruples over musket trading had vanished.

Far from Tahiti's tropical forest–covered mountains; the groves of coconut and breadfruit trees; the girls with hibiscus-, jasmine-, and frangipani-decorated hair; the black sand beach of Matavai Bay with the long Pacific rollers booming on the reef, far from all this lushness, the Investigators started their survey of New Holland's south coast, a coastline that could have come from another planet.

A long, lonely, desiccated coast where the huge Southern Ocean rollers still hurl themselves at high sandstone cliffs or sweep far inland over the saltwater flats. Inland stretches the ominous-sounding Nullarbor Plain, a treeless, flat scrub desert where the dreadful heat can kill the unwary traveler in hours. (Today, on the three-day Indian Pacific Railway journey from Sydney to Perth, the passenger doors are locked when crossing the Nullarbor. The train pulls into a siding to allow a freight train to pass, and the intercom warns passengers that being left behind means certain death.)

Some forty years after Flinders surveyed this coast a tough thirty-five-year-old Englishman, Edward John Eyre, perhaps the colonies' most experienced bush traveler, with thousands of miles of overlanding (the driving of cattle and stock to market) behind him, set off (carrying Flinders's charts) on a march along this awful coast in an attempt to establish a stock route. He set off from Port Lincoln (a harbor discovered by Flinders that was then used by American and French whalers) in October 1840. At Fowler's Bay (named after the *Investigator*'s first lieutenant) the struggle started in earnest. Eyre left the bay with another Englishman, John Baxter, three natives, sheep, and horses. Only Eyre, one native, and some horses arrived at the small settlement of Albany on King George Sound. The nine months and more than a thousand miles of dreadful plodding had seen Eyre and Baxter go down with dysentery, waterholes dug every night, the sheep and horses killed, their meat dipped into the sea and then hung out to dry. Two of the natives, seeing no point in this journey, shot and killed Baxter and stole some rations along with the only working firearms. Eyre and Wylie (the remaining aborigine) struggled on along this dreadful coastline with a rifle, a round jammed in the chamber, that Eyre had fixed by holding the barrel over a fire until the round fired. Eyre peered over the cliffs and saw carcasses of whales, shells of giant turtles, and wrecks of unknown ships. He was fascinated by Wylie's gargantuan gorging. When a horse was killed, Wylie sat up all night eating; a dead penguin was consumed whole; only the bones of a shot kangaroo remained after Wylie had set to work, flesh, tail, hind legs, entrails, and skin having gone down Wylie's gullet. Some three hundred miles from Albany, at Lucky Bay, one of Flinders's old anchorages, the two men came across a French whaleship, the *Mississippi*, commanded by an English captain. They were welcomed aboard, and Captain Rossiter explained to Eyre that the French ship was anchored here because he feared war had broken out between France and Britain. The generosity of the whaler was as great as Wylie's appetite (which astonished the French crew), and Eyre found himself reading old English newspapers and feeding on the produce of a small island where Rossiter kept a stock of sheep and pigs, vegetables from a small garden on the shore, fish from the sea, duck and kangaroo, and the *Mississippi*'s wine. As Eyre wrote, this was "a change in our circumstances so great, so sudden and so unexpected it seemed more like a dream than reality."

After two weeks Eyre and Wylie set off on the last stretch to Albany. The horses—shod with horseshoes fashioned from old harpoons—carried flour, biscuit, rice, beef, pork, sugar, tea, cheese, butter, salt, brandy, tobacco, and pipes. Eyre wore clothes from Rossiter's sea chest. Rossiter saw Eyre off after breakfast aboard ship and added six bottles of wine and a tin of sardines. Eyre promised, if war had broken out, to say nothing of the *Mississippi*'s presence. It was obvious to Eyre that any stock route along this dreadful coast, with no watercourse for fifteen hundred miles, was impossible.

Eyre's epic journey had been made slightly easier by Flinders's charts. The same air of dogged perseverance that surrounds Eyre's journey also collects around Flinders's narrative. For Eyre the perseverance was for simple survival; at one time, in the hallucinatory state that comes with total physical and mental exhaustion, he felt that he "could have sat quietly and contentedly, and let the glass of life slide away to its last stand. There was a kind of dreamy pleasure which made me forgetful or careless of the circumstances and difficulties by which I was surrounded."

For Flinders the perseverance was in the unromantic work with sextant, theodolite, azimuth compass, chronometer, and nautical tables. Flinders, during the coastline running survey, established a routine. During the daylight hours the *Investigator* would sail as close to the shore as possible, the leadsman calling soundings from the chains, Flinders taking bearings and notes, testing the water salinity and temperature, Westall making his unsurpassed coastal views. The ship would then haul offshore for the night, and Thistle and Flinders, by guttering candlelight, would work on the first-draft charts. The next morning, at first light, the *Investigator* would work her way back to the precise position she had left the previous evening, and the daily round of bearings, soundings, sketching would start again. Landings were made where possible, safe anchorages and harbors being sought and charted; the botanists made their collections; birds, seals, and kangaroos were shot for the pot, and their hides turned into shoes and hats.

Three months after starting their survey one of the Portsmouth fortune teller's predications came true. The invaluable John Thistle, a young midshipman, and six seamen, returning from searching for water, were lost in a tide rip. Cape Catastrophe in South Australia memorializes the collective tragedy, and the names of the offshore islands the individual drowned men.

A few days after the tragedy the Investigators were setting up tents and an observatory at a harbor that Flinders named Port Lincoln. Pits had to be dug for water, the botanists scoured the countryside, Westall painted a view of the harbor, Flinders with his officers made a harbor survey (naming many features with Lincolnshire names), and Samuel Flinders worked in his observatory. Port Lincoln's position was to be established with the utmost precision: the latitude from the mean of four observations; the longitude by thirty sets of lunar distances and the chronometer. The chronometers had to be checked for their gain or loss and then compared with that calculated fifty-seven days previously and over a thousand miles away at King George Sound. All longitudes for the coastal features observed between the sound and Port Lincoln were then recalculated. A solar eclipse was observed (another aid to pinpointing Port Lincoln), and the magnetic variation and dip of the compass needle were noted, as were the flow and tidal range. In short, the humdrum, daily routine of survey work from which all future seamen would benefit.

Flinders sprinkled more than a hundred names in what is now the state of South Australia, and the *Investigator*'s spoor is easy to follow with such names as Point Westall, Franklin Harbour, Investigator Group, Investigator Strait, Cape Donington (Flinders's birthplace), Partney Isles (the village where Ann Flinders lived and where they were married), Spilsby Island (the town where the Franklins lived), Spencer Gulf, St. Vincent Gulf, Yorke Peninsula (the last three all Admiralty first lords), Sir Joseph Banks Group, Cape Bauer, Point Brown, Fowler's Bay, Backstairs Passage, Encounter Bay.

At the last, in April, a strange encounter did occur. After the *Investigator* landed at Kangaroo Island, which supplied much welcome fresh meat after months of salt meat, and navigated through Backstairs Passage at the island's east end, a sail was sighted. The men were sent to quarters as the two vessels closed. The newcomer proved to be Nicolas Baudin's *Géographe* on the French exploratory voyage that had sailed some months before the *Investigator*. As far as both captains knew, their countries were still at war. Flinders lowered a boat and, with his boat's crew wearing kangaroo-skin hats, went alongside the French ship. The precious passports were shown, and with Brown translating, Baudin gave Flinders a tale of woe. He had lost touch with a boat's crew (they were picked up by a sealing brig) and also his consort, the *Naturaliste*. His supplies were running low, and his crew was far from healthy. The two ships parted with Flinders promising to keep an eye open for the boat's crew and the *Naturaliste*.

The *Investigator* came to anchor off Sydney in May with a fit and able crew, not a sick man on board. Also in the harbor was the *Naturaliste* with the French officers and men enjoying the colony's rather restricted social life among the Rum Corps officers, their ladies, the shantytown grogshops, and the hoydenish, brawling prostitutes at the Rocks. Six weeks after the *Investigator* had come to anchor the *Géographe* was sighted wallowing off the coast, unable to work her way into Port Jackson. Ship's crews, including a boat from the *Investigator*, went to help the stricken French ship through the heads and into the Port Jackson anchorage. The Géographes were in a dreadful condition with every man of the 170 crew scurvy-ridden, some with open sores and ulcers, and only 4 men, according to Baudin, capable of working the deck. News of the peace between France and Britain had been received in the settlement, and Governor King, on seeing the condition of the French crew, had them brought ashore to the hospital. The French pitched their tents close to those of the *Investigator*.

The Investigators spent ten weeks at Sydney before sailing on the second part of their coastal survey. A new eight-oared boat had been built on the same lines as Bass's whaleboat, now hauled out on the shore, to replace the one lost off Cape Catastrophe. Moreover, nine convicts "of good character" and a new master, John Aken, replaced the lost boat's crew.

Aken, "an easy, good natured man," according to Flinders in a letter to his wife, had volunteered from the convict transport *Hercules*. And was thankful to do so. The convicts had attempted to take over the transport on her passage to Sydney. Fourteen had been shot, and before the *Hercules* arrived in Sydney, another thirty had died from disease. The convict transports had an evil reputation.

With the *Investigator* sailed the *Lady Nelson*, Lieutenant John Murray in command. The unusual triple-sliding-keel brig, contrary to most seamen's predictions, had managed the long passage to Sydney and been the first vessel to sail west to east through the Bass Strait. But a wayward, clownish aura hovers over the *Lady Nelson*. Her long voyage from England had started with the ignominious towing and ended with her sailing into Port Jackson carrying an eccentric ship's surgeon who had been shipwrecked at Delagoa Bay and then traveled in South Africa with a dog and pet baboon. At Cape Town Grant had persuaded him, complete with pets, to sail to Sydney. There the doctor was installed on an island in the harbor given over to the Lady Nelsons as a vegetable garden. His job, with his dog and baboon: to guard the produce from thieving convicts.

After three months of the *Lady Nelson*'s wayward ways—crablike sailing and a habit of finding coral reefs with her keels—an irritated Flinders ordered her back to Sydney. At Shoalwater Bay, a thousand miles north of Sydney, Murray managed to lose his anchors. A search of the shore found stands of ironbark tree, and the carpenter, after a week of laborious work, made a massive and primitive anchor some twenty feet long (about one-third of the *Lady Nelson*'s length). At its first test it floated. But when waterlogged and weighted with a couple of swivel guns, it sank and served its purpose. This magnificent construction later became a standing joke at Sydney. Upon the arrival of the *Lady Nelson* at her anchorage off Governor's Wharf, the carpenter's creation was let go. Much to the embarrassment of the Lady Nelsons and the hilarity of the shoreside watchers, it floated. The days spent sailing down the coast had dried out this unique anchor. To add to the wharfside mirth, Murray then had to sail his small brig onto a mudbank.

A floating anchor in Port Jackson might be cause for comedy, but a leaking ship in the Gulf of Carpentaria was cause for concern. Since the *Investigator* had entered the Torres Strait, her pumps had been manned hourly, with the carpenter reporting the hull making twelve to fourteen inches of water an hour. Flinders had her beached—one of the advantages of the flat-bottomed collier's hull—and the carpenter reported a dire catalog of rotten frames and planks and leaking seams. Given fair weather, she might last six to twelve months. Given gales, she would founder.

Flinders, calculating the odds, spent three more months on the coast survey before steering for Kupang on Dutch Timor. But Kupang could

His Majesty's brig *Lady Nelson*

"The Admiralty . . . proceeded to make a bold experiment, and built a 60-ton brig, the
'Lady Nelson,' with three sliding keels, designed to perform a voyage of discovery to
New South Wales."   —R. T. Pritchett

(Illustration from *Yachting,* 1894)

supply nothing for ship repair and little in the way of provisions—only
fever and dysentery that killed eight men. The west coast survey had to be
abandoned, and Flinders made an anticlockwise sweep around New Holland before anchoring in Port Jackson eleven months after sailing from it.
The *Investigator* proved so rotten—a cane could be thrust through some
of the starboard side planks—that she was condemned as unfit for service.
She was, as Flinders wrote, "decayed both in skin and bone."

Flinders's long odyssey now began. Like the adventures of Homer's
hero, it was to last for years and included shipwreck, captivity on an island,
and a waiting wife.

Because Sydney had no suitable vessel to complete the survey, Governor King and Flinders pitched upon the plan to sail the *Porpoise* back to
England, Fowler in command, with Flinders as a passenger working on his
charts and journals. In England Flinders would petition the Admiralty for
another ship to complete the survey. The *Porpoise* accompanied by the East
Indiaman *Bridgewater* and the merchantman *Cato,* sailed in August. Before sailing, Flinders left a letter for George Bass—still Pacific trading in
the *Venus*—with Governor King. A prophetic phrase reads: "Should these
three ships go through safely [the Torres Strait], and I do not fear the contrary. . . ."

Seven days out from Sydney, during the night, the *Porpoise* and the

Cato struck upon a reef and became total losses. Three men were drowned, including a young seaman who had been shipwrecked upon every one of his four previous voyages. The *Bridgewater*,[3] well aware of the disaster, happily ignored it and sailed on to Batavia. Wreck Reef, as it soon became named, lies some eight hundred miles from Sydney and two hundred miles off the east coast. It consists of a chain of reefs extending some eighteen miles and includes five small coral sand cays. One of these, only three feet above sea level, lay a half mile from the wrecked ships. By boats, rafts, spars, hen coops, and swimming, ninety-four men found themselves stumbling around what one of them called this "small uncertainty." The wind easing and the sea diminishing, stores, provisions, water, gunpowder, swivel guns, muskets, canvas, and even a few sheep were landed. (One of the sheep, driven ashore by the young Franklin, trampled over some of Westall's drawings; the hoofmarks can still be seen on one of the originals.) Within days the cay was a tidy encampment with tents made from the ship's canvas and enough stores landed for three months (including 225 gallons of spirits, 113 gallons of wine, and 60 gallons of porter—forty-nine days' worth at full rations). Over their fragile stronghold, perched feet above the water, flew an upside-down blue ensign as a distress signal. But the chances of being saved by a passing vessel were so remote as to be laughable. Relief would have to be found at Sydney.

Nine days after the shipwreck Flinders, the *Cato*'s captain, and twelve seamen sailed from Wreck Reef—it happened to be a Friday, and some of the sailors thought this most unlucky—in one of the *Porpoise*'s six-oared cutters. They were provisioned for three weeks, and the cutter had been named the *Hope*. Flinders also carried a letter from John Franklin to his father. The superscription reads: "Providential Bank, August 26th, 1803, Lat. 22° 12′ Long. 155° 13′ (nearly) E" and continues: "Dear Father, Great will be your surprise and sorrow to find by this that the late Investigators are cast away in a sandy patch of about 300 yards long and 200 broad." A brief history follows of the *Investigator*'s adventures since she had left Sydney, her being condemned, the shipwreck, and the *Bridgewater*'s "shameful and inhuman" conduct. It ends with a query about prize money (Franklin obviously had no worries about surviving): "Have you got the prize money? I see it is due, and may be had by applying at No. 21 Milbank St., Westminster; due July 22, 1802. If you do not, it will go to Greenwich Hospital. I had occasion to draw for necessaries at Sydney this last time £24 from Capt'n. F."

As the *Hope* punched into the seas on its way south to Sydney, the men on Wreck Reef set about building another vessel from the two wrecks, an insurance against the cutter's being lost. Within six weeks one of the sailors was scribbling into his diary that they had launched "a rakish schooner" and were about to start a second vessel. The schooner was christened the *Resource*. The sailors then set about making charcoal for the blacksmith to forge the second vessel's ironwork.

Three days after the *Resource*'s launching, and six weeks to the day that the *Hope* had left on her rescue mission, one of the sailors, out in a boat with Fowler, saw something. It was a white object, clear against the blue of the sky and low on the horizon. At first he thought it a seabird, but then, gazing harder, jumped to his feet and yelled: "Damn my blood, what's that?" The "that" proved to be one of the topgallants of a three-vessel rescue flotilla. Within hours Flinders was ashore, men crowding around him, all of them trying to shake his hand.

The *Hope* had arrived at Sydney two weeks after sailing from Wreck Reef. Flinders and Park from the *Cato*, both weary, burned brick red from the sun, unshaved, clothed in salt-stained breeches and jackets, went straight to Governor's House. They startled Governor King and his family at dinner. To an anxious Flinders the arrangements for getting the men off the cay took an interminable time: "every day seemed a week." It was decided that a three-vessel fleet would sail to the rescue. The merchant-man *Rolla*, bound for Canton, would pick up some of the men; the smaller *Francis* would bring some men back to Sydney; and the even smaller *Cumberland*, a twenty-nine-ton schooner, locally built, only forty-feet on deck with a twelve-foot beam, would then sail for England with Flinders in command. A most inadequate vessel—but the only one King could spare. The *Cumberland* proved cranky, wet, and verminous. Flinders could not work on his charts, and his journal was written as he sat on a locker, his knees forming a desk, while water swirled across the cabin sole and seas came through the skylight and companionway hatch. The only crew member unperturbed by all this was Flinders's constant companion, Trim, his seagoing cat, hunting for vermin.

The *Cumberland* sailed from Wreck Reef, steering for the Torres Strait on 11 October 1803. Crammed on board were seven seamen from the *Investigator*, the boatswain, the master, John Aken, Flinders's servant, Flinders, and Trim. The leaks worsened, and a quarter of the day was spent pumping with defective pumps. Kupang at Timor again proved of little use with no means of repairing the pumps or stopping the leaking seams. Ahead lay the seven-thousand-mile passage to the Cape of Good Hope. The conditions twenty-three days out from Kupang, with a vile cross sea running, the seams squirting water, and the one effective pump working twenty-four hours a day, forced a decision upon Flinders.

The *Cumberland*'s seams had to be re-caulked and her pumps repaired. The nearest place for this was the French island of Île de France. In case war had started again between Britain and France, Flinders carried the insurance of the precious passport issued by the French government. It was admittedly made out to the *Investigator*. But, thought Flinders, it must still be valid "to protect the voyage and not the *Investigator* only." Flinders changed course for the island. On the morning of 15 December the island's peaks stood jagged against the horizon. Two days later Flinders was under arrest, and his charts and journals were impounded.

Britain and France were at war, and Flinders had sailed to an island controlled by a man who loathed the British.

General Decaen, a man who had trained for the law but joined the army, had taken over Île de France just four months before Flinders's arrival. He knew of Flinders from the *Géographe*'s officers (they had sailed from Île de France one day before the *Cumberland*'s appearance). Decaen, a brusque, quarrelsome man—he spoke of himself as being "of a petulant character and too free with my tongue"—considered Flinders a spy and believed (the lawyer creeping in) that the passport covered only the *Investigator*. Flinders, thinking himself shabbily treated, his nose out of joint, then made the mistake of refusing an invitation to dine with Decaen and his wife. The two men's posture of mutual hostility was molded and cast. Decaen, no loving Calypso, kept Flinders bottled up on the island for more than six years. Flinders, no cunning Ulysses (he had also given his parole), could find no way off it. Release finally came in 1810, when Flinders's sword was given back to him and he went aboard the cartel vessel *Harriet* bound for Bengal. Flinders could then write: "After a captivity of six years five months and twenty-seven days I at length had the inexpressible pleasure of being out of the reach of General Decaen."

The British had a blockading fleet off Île de France and Flinders changed to the sloop *Otter* sailing to Cape Town with dispatches. By the end of October Flinders was back in England and reunited with his wife. John Franklin came to see him, as did Brown and Bauer. Banks took him to a meeting of the Royal Society and gave him a dinner in his honor. The Duke of Clarence, later William IV, himself a sailor, met him and inspected his charts. Over the next four years Flinders worked on his charts, the text for his *A Voyage to Terra Australis,* and a nagging problem associated with the marine magnetic compass. He was a very ill man during those years— aged thirty-nine, he looked seventy, "worn to a skeleton," according to Ann in a letter to a friend—and the Admiralty did little to help his circumstances.

The bureaucratic mantra of "no precedence" was the response from John Barrow, the Admiralty secretary, when Flinders asked that his promotion to post captain be antedated to 1804 (when, if he had made it back to England, he would have been made post captain) and, when this was refused, that he should be paid full rather than half pay, while working on the narrative and charts. A friend advised him to reconsider working on his projects and not get "in debt to gratify persons who seem to have no feeling." The first copies of the *Voyage* came from the press on 18 July 1814. Flinders never saw it. He was then in a coma and died a day later. Efforts were made by friends, including Sir Joseph Banks, that Ann Flinders, with her two-year-old daughter, be given a state pension—as with James Cook's widow. (Elizabeth Cook was still alive; the tough-minded old lady lived into 1835.) The Admiralty turned a convenient deaf ear, and nothing was done even though this time there was a precedence.

Australia was not so meanspirited. In 1853 the colonies of New South Wales and Victoria each voted a pension of one hundred pounds to Ann Flinders with reversion to her daughter. As with Flinders's never seeing his *Voyage,* so it was with Ann Flinders's never seeing her pension. News of it arrived in England after her death. But the daughter did benefit: "Could my beloved mother have lived to receive this announcement it would indeed have cheered her last days to know that my father's long-neglected services were at length appreciated . . . and the handsome amount of the pension granted will enable me to educate my young son in a manner worthy of the name he bears, Matthew Flinders."[4]

Playing such a large part in defining Australia on the world's map—including the country's name—Flinders stands large in Australian hagiography. Three cities boast statues: Sydney, Melbourne, Adelaide. The first statue, with Flinders bare-headed and holding a sextant, was unveiled at Sydney in 1925. A recent addition nearby is a bronze statue of Trim, Flinders's faithful cat, prowling a windowsill of the State Library of New South Wales. Here was a cat to rival T. S. Eliot's Growltiger (a mere river cat sailing the Thames). Trim had been born at sea on the *Reliance* in the Southern Ocean. A constant companion through storm and shipwreck, Trim ended his days at Île de France with Flinders believing him killed and eaten by starving slaves. "Thus perished my faithful intelligent Trim!" wrote Flinders in a tribute. "The sporting, affectionate and useful companion of my voyages during four years . . . never wilt thou cease to be regretted by all who had the pleasure of knowing thee."

More pertinent memorials, particularly for nineteenth- and twentieth-century seamen, were Flinders's magnificent charts (two of them, with corrections, were only withdrawn from service in 1912) and the Flinders bar.

The mariners' magnetic compass has to be corrected for two variables: *variation* from true north because of the Earth's magnetic field and *deviation* owing to the ship's own magnetic field and brought about by iron fittings. Variation has been solved by kindly hydrographers who incorporate the compass variation upon their charts. It is not a constant. It changes annually across the surface of every part of the globe. Deviation is another matter and can be added to the headaches that bedevil sailors. First noted in the sixteenth century, it became a particular concern to Flinders during his coast surveys. He had noted the difference between readings of the azimuth compass taken at the binnacle (the ship's steering compass) and those taken at other positions. Plus an even more puzzling anomaly: These differences altered when the ship's heading changed. In 1805 Flinders's paper on the problem, "Concerning the Differences in the Magnetic Needle, on Board the *Investigator,* arising from an Alteration in the Direction of the Ship's Head," was read before the Royal Society. On his return to England experiments were carried out by the Royal Navy at Sheerness and Portsmouth. To correct these strange variations, Flinders suggested placing an "upright stanchion or bars of iron" at a selected spot. In 1837 the Admiralty formed a Compass Committee, and in 1855 worried merchant ship owners set up the Liverpool Compass Committee. Sir William Thomson (later Lord Kelvin) became interested. Aboard his yacht *Lalla Rookh* he perfected, and patented in 1879, a compass and binnacle. It used a vertical bar of soft iron. In an article in *Good Words for 1879* he named it a Flinders bar. The patented Kelvin binnacle became the standard marine magnetic compass. For close to a hundred years, on thousands of ships, thousands of seamen spent countless hours polishing the shining brass container housing the Flinders bar.

George Bass never received the letter written to him by Flinders in 1803. The pork voyages with the *Venus* had proved profitable—enough money to send his wife in England some funds "to stop a few holes in my debts"—and the *Venus* was still the apple of his eye: "She is just the same vessel as when we left England, never complains or cries, though we loaded her with pork most unmercifully." In February 1803 Governor King gave Bass a most imposing-looking certificate. It stated that "Mr. George Bass, of the brigantine *Venus,* has been employed since the first day of November, 1801, upon His Britannic Majesty's service in procuring provisions for the subsistence of His Majesty's colony." It continued that if Bass came to any Spanish port on America's west coast, "this instrument is intended to declare my full belief that his sole object in going there will be to procure food, without any view to private commerce or any other view whatsoever." Bass, in other words, was not smuggling goods into South America.

The Spanish official policy was to restrict trading to Spanish ships and merchants. It was a policy constantly broken through the media of corrupt officials, a ready market, and an immense coastline. With King's certificate safely tucked away aboard the *Venus,* Bass wrote a final letter to his brother-in-law: "In a few hours I will sail again on another pork voyage, but it combines circumstances of a different nature. . . ." The letter ends with "Speak not of South America to anyone out of your family, for there is treason in the very name." Since Spain regarded Sydney as a safe harbor, a wasps' nest, for British smugglers and privateers, Bass's warning and certificate from King reflected his worries.

After sailing from Sydney, the *Venus* and Bass vanished. Later that year the brig *Harrington,* another smuggling vessel, reported that the *Venus* had been confiscated in Peru, and Bass with the mate of the brig sent to slave labor in the silver mines. But the report was all hearsay with no hard-and-fast evidence.

Reading Bass's letters, one wants to have met him. He shares the same qualities as the *Astrolabe*'s Joseph Gaimard and Charles Clerke of Cook's voyages. It is an adventurous, unbuttoned, humorous, relaxed, and amiable quality. All three men, one knows, would have made the best of ship-mates and the most entertaining of dinner companions.

John Franklin's adventures were not over. He, with other officers and men from the *Investigator,* sailed from Wreck Reef to Canton aboard the *Rolla.* In January 1804 they all took passage with a fleet of East Indiamen bound for India and England, close to thirty sail. Waiting for them, off the Malay Peninsula in the South China Sea, lay a squadron of French warships. The fifty-eight-year-old Nathaniel Dance, commodore by seniority of the homeward-bound fleet and captain of the *Earl Camden,* organized his fleet into a passing resemblance of a convoy under escort by the Royal Navy and also used the Investigators in key positions: Fowler ran the lower gundeck on the *Earl Camden* and Franklin the signals. The French made one attack but, feeling outnumbered, hauled their wind and disengaged. Dance, chock-full of impudence, bluff, and chutzpa, gave the signal for a general chase. The merchantmen had the sheer undiluted joy of seeing a powerful squadron of warships fleeing before them. Dance was knighted, presented with £5,000 by the Bombay Insurance Company and a pension by the East India Company; Lieutenant Fowler was presented with a sword valued at fifty guineas; and the eighteen-year-old Franklin added another anecdote to go with the nuts and the circulation of the port decanter.

Governor King had noticed Franklin's enthusiasm at working in the *Investigator*'s observatory at Sydney and invariably called him Mr. Tycho Brahe. It was Flinders's example that fired Franklin's enthusiasm for exploration that later took him into the Arctic. Flinders also proved an example for Philip Parker King, Governor King's son. Only a ten-year-old at the time, he never forgot the unshaved and weather-beaten Flinders's startling entrance during the family dinner after the *Hope*'s voyage from Wreck Reef. Within a decade King was a Royal Navy lieutenant, and by 1822, following Flinders's example, he had filled in more blanks of Australia's coastline.

The 1820s were the start of the Pax Britannica years and the Royal Navy's extraordinary, almost evangelical zeal in stamping out piracy and the slave trade—and surveying the world's oceans and seas. Philip Parker King, now a captain, with the *Adventure* and the *Beagle* went on to survey thousands of miles of South America's maze of waterways around Tierra del Fuego, and Franklin thousands of miles of North America's coastline. Captain William Owen with the *Barracouta* and the *Leven* started and completed the deadly African coast survey. (Owen, like Flinders, had also fallen into Decaen's clutches and spent two years on Île de France. He was released in the same cartel as Flinders and wrote to him from Madras with a letter that breathes the spirit of the times: "You cannot doubt how much our society misses you. We toasted you, Sir, like Englishmen . . . and women too . . . three times three loud and manly cheers . . . and the ladies did each take an extra glass to you.")

In 1837 Sir John Franklin, now the famous Arctic explorer, returned to the Southern Hemisphere as the lieutenant governor of Van Diemen's Land. The round-faced, amiable youth was now a round-faced, amiable, stoutish middle-aged man with a round-faced, alarmingly energetic wife, Lady Jane Franklin. Sir John, during his seven-year tenure, must have looked back with wistfulness to the relative simplicities of dealing with his Arctic privations compared with the Machiavellian bureaucratic backstabbings, the seething bitter politics, and the sheer load of human misery of his island penal colony. Two of his pleasanter episodes were welcoming a French expedition led by Dumont d'Urville with the *Astrolabe* and the *Zélée*—the French officers thought Lady Jane *très charmante*—and a fellow countryman and Arctic explorer, Captain James Clark Ross, with HMS *Erebus* and HMS *Terror*. At Hobart, Ross heard of the discoveries made in the high southern latitudes by d'Urville as well as those of an American expedition led by Lieutenant Charles Wilkes. The American expedition, the largest of all three, had also been the longest in gestation and birth.

Its conception was also curious.

NOTES

1. John Schanck (1740–1823) was a remarkably inventive Royal Navy officer. In 1774, stationed at Boston, he designed and built a small boat with a sliding keel that extended some two-thirds the length of the boat. Later, in 1790, came a sixty-five-foot cutter with three sliding keels. She was bought by the Admiralty, considered a great success, and the Admiralty went on to build more sliding keel vessels. Schanck, nicknamed Old Purchase after another invention, a lowering, tilting sea cot, died an admiral.

2. Table money was an allowance paid to admirals and senior officers, in addition to their pay, to meet the expenses of entertaining official guests. The East India Company often paid table money to the officers of escorting Royal Navy vessels. The directors voted the *Investigator* twelve hundred pounds, but only six hundred was paid at the voyage's start.

3. The *Bridgewater* completed her passage to India, where her captain claimed that any rescue attempt would have been impossible. One officer, in protest at these lies, left the ship. The *Bridgewater* sailed for London from Bombay and was never heard of again.

4. Sir William Matthew Flinders Petrie (1853–1942), the famous archaeologist and Egyptologist.

Chapter 6

Holes at the Poles

FANTODS. A name given to the fidgets of officers, who are
styled jib-and-staysail Jacks.

FITTING OUT OF A SHIP. The act of providing a ship
with sufficient masts, sails, yards, ammunition, artillery,
cordage, anchors, provisions, stores, and men, so that she is
in proper condition for the voyage or purpose to which she
is appointed.

Admiral W. H. Smyth, *The Sailor's Word-Book*, 1867

EW EXPEDITIONS have sprung from so bizarre a concept.
A reminder of this quirky origin sits in the Philadelphia Academy of Natural Sciences. It is a wooden globe that, to the observant eye, has unusual characteristics. True, like the globe of
schoolroom memories, it is tilted with a spindle running through its axis,
enabling the observer to play God while idly spinning this shrunken world.
But this world has been cruelly topped and tailed at the poles and exhibits
a hollow interior. This curious globe was used during the 1820s to demonstrate, with iron filings, magnet, and sand, a closely reasoned theory that
the actual world inhabited by the watching American audiences, some
skeptical, some believing, was also hollow and contained at least five hollow concentric spheres with air space between and all the surfaces habitable.

The apostle and demonstrator of this intriguing theory, diligently
working his props, was a man of impeccable American ancestry. John
Cleves Symmes's forebears had sailed to New England in 1634 aboard the
same vessel as Anne Hutchinson, that sweet-tempered and clever lady
whose theological theories had drawn the ire of the Massachusetts Bay settlement's ministers, leading to her banishment, the founding of
Portsmouth, Rhode Island, her moving to what is now Pelham Bay Park

in New York City, and the massacre of her and all her family, save one, by Indians. Symmes's theories brought no such tragic end.

Symmes, born in New Jersey in 1780, had the usual common school education—the physical sciences particularly interested him—before joining the army as an ensign in 1802. Later in life he said that he had joined "to merit and obtain distinction, and accumulate knowledge, which I had seldom tasted but in borrowed books." After service in the War of 1812 he resigned from the army, moved with his family to St. Louis, and spent two years as a supplier to troops on the Mississippi and as a trader with the Sac and Fox Indians. He also busied himself with his pet theory.

There is something likable about Symmes. Here is a rather naive, wrongheaded, harmless eccentric riding his hobbyhorse, another Barrington with an equally strong Magpie factor, but a Barrington without the influence. John James Audubon made a drawing of Symmes for the Western Museum (the penniless Audubon, a more flamboyant eccentric, working on *his* particular hobbyhorse, also stuffed fish for the museum). The drawing shows Symmes sitting at a table with a globe behind him; the forehead and thinning hair look vaguely Napoleonic.

By 1818 Symmes was ready to unleash upon the world his "New Theory," and he issued his *Circular Number 1* with copies to "each notable foreign government, reigning prince, legislature, city, college, and philosophical society, quite around the earth."

LIGHT GIVES LIGHT, TO LIGHT DISCOVER—"AD INFINITUM."
ST. LOUIS, (Missouri Territory.)
North America, April 10, A.D. 1818
TO ALL THE WORLD!

I declare the earth is hollow, and habitable within; containing a number of solid concentrick spheres, one within the other; and that it is open at the poles 12 or 16 degrees; I pledge my life in support of this truth, and am ready to explore the hollow, if the world will support and aid me in the undertaking.

Jno. Cleves Symmes
Of Ohio, late Captain of Infantry.

N.B.—I have ready for the press, a Treatise on the principles of matter, wherein I show proofs of the above positions, account for various phenomena, and disclose *Doctor Darwin's Golden Secret.*

My terms, are the patronage of this and the new worlds.

I dedicate to my Wife and her ten Children.

I select *Doctor S. L. Mitchell, Sir H. Davy* and *Baron Alex. de Humboldt*, as my protectors.

I ask one hundred brave companions, well equipped, to start from Siberia in the fall season, with Reindeer and slays, on the ice of the frozen sea; I engage we find warm and rich land, stocked with thrifty vegetables and animals if not men, on reaching one degree northward of latitude 82; we will return in the succeeding spring.

J. C. S

A prudent thought crossing Symmes's mind led to his attaching a certificate attesting to his sanity.

This rather eccentric document, as might be expected, met with a mixed reception. The western press was enthusiastic; the eastern skeptical, while the silence from the scientific establishment only reinforced the westerners' views that Symmes would be proved right, a most satisfactory David and Goliath prospect with their self-taught David humbling the scholastic Goliath. For nothing, as one newspaper wrote, was more "mortifying to the pride of science that more discoveries have been made by *untaught geniuses* than by regular *savans.*"

Over the next few years the pros and cons fought a spasmodic and vituperative war of words in the newspaper columns. The Bible inevitably was consulted for use as a crutch for support or an ax to demolish. One correspondent argued that the theory flew in the face of Mosaic creation as given in Genesis. Another argued that the second verse of Chapter 1 of Genesis—"the earth was without form and void"—had been translated from the Greek *beos* for "void," but this could also mean "hollow." If, wrote another, the openings at the poles were so large—Symmes estimated about four thousand miles in diameter in the north and six thousand miles in the south—why was this enormous flattening at the poles not seen in the Earth's shadow cast on the moon? Indian mythology buttressed the arguments of the Symmesonites. A Mohawk legend told of ancestors who had lived in the interior regions. One of these ancestors, finding a hole leading to the outside surface, emerged and discovered fat deer and rich earth. He had returned to lead some of his tribe to this new land, and they began a new life with the planting of corn and hunting.

But the ultimate acknowledgment of the infatuation with Symmes's theory came in 1820 with the publication of a satire, *Symzonia: Voyage of Discovery* by Adam Seaborn. The author had sailed to the south polar opening in a steam-driven vessel remarkably like a trireme of the classic world. In the internal world the explorers discovered an island that they named Symzonia. It was inhabited by a friendly race only five feet tall; its system of government had a bicameral legislature whose chief held the title Best Man; there were no taxes; and anyone in political life accused of intrigue or backstairs influence was banished to the North Pole. Seaborn was sorry to leave. The satire drew enough attention to warrant an article in the *North American Review.* The reviewer, entering the spirit of things, concluded that Symmes was right. Everything good "carries its merits within" while everything external "is transitory and worthless." He himself thought the world could be seen as a huge fig with an unappetizing skin but a nutritious pulp: Symmes's name, with the passing of time, would come to overshadow that of Christopher Columbus.

Ridicule and satire, however, were hardly the attention courted by Symmes. But the fanciful expedition in the steam-driven trireme did reflect that final paragraph in *Circular Number 1,* the baited hook to entice his fellow countrymen: an expedition. Symmes now labored to set the hook. He enlisted the support of Senator William A. Trimble of Ohio to petition President James Monroe and Congress for an expedition of three vessels (one of them a steam vessel) to sail for the northern opening. That two British Royal Navy expeditions had returned from the Arctic and found no opening was of small account. Captain John Ross's 1818 voyage into the northern reaches of Baffin Bay with the *Isabella* and the *Alexander,* and Lieutenant William Parry's overwintering with the *Hecla* and the *Griper* in 1819–20 on Melville Island left Symmes unworried. It only meant that an American expedition, rather than British, would establish trade with the inner world. Trimble was not so sanguine. The United States Treasury was empty . . . Congress about to adjourn . . . his canvassing had produced little support for an expedition.

Symmes, undeterred, battled on. A circular letter urging its readers to petition Congress for an expedition went out to newspapers. Enough signatures came from the citizens of Kentucky, Ohio, Pennsylvania, and South Carolina for the consideration of the Republic's elected representatives; the more facetious suggested the matter be sent to the Committee on Foreign Relations or the Committee on Commerce. The memorials were tabled.

Ailing from a long illness, impoverished by the costs of his quixotic quest, Symmes moved with his family—a large and loyal family—to a few acres of land near Hamilton, Ohio. From here he set out on lecture tours of western towns. In 1824 the citizens of Cincinnati (dense bear brake at Symmes's birth but now a thriving town that boasted one paved street, one theater, churches, and chapels. Fanny Trollope later called it a "triste little town" and one she would have "liked much better if the people had not dealt so very largely in hogs") gave a benefit for Symmes in the one theater with a five-act melodrama and a local bard reciting a composition in praise of Symmes. The whole evening ended with whoops, hurrahs, and stamping of booted feet (another American practice frowned on by Mrs. Trollope) as the bard came to the final verse:

> Has not Columbia *one* aspiring son,
> By whom th' unfading laurel may be won?
> Yes! history's pen may yet inscribe the name
> Of SYMMES to grace her future scroll of fame.

A young newspaper editor, converted to Symmes's theory, now joined the cause as a fervent apostle. Jeremiah N. Reynolds, a burly, energetic man, some twenty years younger than Symmes, had been born in Pennsylvania and then moved as a child to Ohio. His stepfather, a frontier farmer with a contempt for learning—handling a plow, a swill bucket, and an ax was all a child need learn—had refused to send the young Jeremiah to common school. Reynolds, however, as he later wrote, felt no calling for the land. Instead he "imbibed a relish . . . for books of voyages and travels, when I had not as yet seen the ocean." He also had ambition. He left home before he was fourteen, worked his way through school; then taught in school; spent three years at Ohio University; went back to teaching; and finally became editor of the *Wilmington Spectator*. But listening to Symmes and the "Theory" was the road to Damascus; here was the opportunity to escape small western towns and make his mark in a larger world than that contained by Clinton County, Ohio.

In the fall of 1825 Symmes and Reynolds, this most unlikely pair—one the western Don Quixote, his head turned by books on the cosmos, the other a Sancho Panza eager for fame (if not an island's governorship)—set off to cross the Appalachians and convince the eastern doubters of the truth of their cause. But before wooing the Atlantic states came lectures in Ohio and western Pennsylvania. The Reverend Andrew Wylie, president of Washington College, thought the theory "in strictest accordance with the economy of Nature." A writer in the *Pittsburgh Mercury* considered every intelligent man in town converted and urged Reynolds to lobby Washington for an expedition.

But in Philadelphia an almighty row developed between the two men, Symmes even threatening a duel. The pair had split forces for the lecture tour, and Reynolds, testing the winds of opinion, had trimmed his sails to suit. He was also throwing overboard the more cumbersome and embarrassing baggage of the theory. An opportunist himself, he recognized the American antipathy toward theory and preference for action—particularly when the action held out profit. Both men wanted an expedition. Symmes wanted one to the north, but Reynolds wanted one to the south; there lay the seals and whales. Symmes was furious. Word of this dispute became public, and a waggish editor of the *New York National Advocate* suggested Congress finance two expeditions, one to the south with Reynolds and the other to the north with Symmes. The duel would be fought with cannon firing snowballs through the holes in the poles.

The pair separated, Symmes to lecture in Washington, Maryland, New York (where a reporter thought his language "far from being correct" but that Symmes had "as fine a high, philosophical forehead as a phrenologist could wish"), and New England. Later, back home in Ohio, Symmes admitted to his wife that he had made a grave mistake by taking Reynolds into his confidence, but "the lesson has been learned too late."

After that acrimonious parting in Philadelphia Reynolds ranged the eastern seaboard states, lecturing, campaigning, cajoling, honing his skills as a lobbyist and propagandist—and researching. The research was a quest for the nuts and bolts, the nails and lumber, on which to build his platform for a polar expedition. It led him to books on expeditions to the polar seas, the *Philosophical Transactions* of the Royal Society, a new edition of Daines Barrington's writings on open polar seas, the *Encyclopaedia Britannica*. In the latter Professor John Leslie of Edinburgh University stated that "at the Pole itself, during the complete circuit of the sun in midsummer's day, the measure of heat would be greater than at the Equator, by about 1/4th, or 797 thousand parts. The continued endurance of the sun above the horizon more than compensates for the feebleness of his oblique rays." Such weighty pronouncements from a famous professor could only give more credence to the possibility of open polar seas.

James Cook and Thaddeus Bellingshausen might have been halted by ice, but James Weddell had sailed to 74° 15′S in an open polar sea. Also, an open polar sea held attractions denied to one packed solid with ice.

Reynolds published his great plan in 1827. His lectures had convinced him that the tide of public opinion was running in favor of an expedition funded by Congress. Not, he hastened to add, in the style of those costly Royal Navy expeditions to the Arctic in large vessels equipped with printing presses[1] but one based on "plain Republican" principles. Two small, strongly reinforced vessels, provisioned for two years, would suffice.

Reynolds, his antennae acutely tuned to the equalitarian sentiments of his countrymen, knew he was treading a dangerous path with calls for a federal government expedition. Here was a morass into which he could sink and vanish. States' rights, the power of the federal government, taxes, the different interests of the country's three main areas: the North with its manufacture, trade, and shipping; the South with its agriculture; the West looking west. All the thorny constitutional problems of an infant democracy working out is freedoms (a freedom that was "enjoyed solely by the disorderly at the expense of the orderly," according to the acerbic Fanny Trollope). This quintessential American problem is encapsulated in thirteen words that passed between Alexis de Tocqueville, the French political commentator, and Joel Poinsett, the American politician. DE TOCQUEVILLE: "How are roads made and repaired in America?" POINSETT: "It's a great constitutional question. . . ."

During his lectures Reynolds, the canny campaigner, would end with a graceful compliment: "To the ladies who have honoured us with their attendance." America, said Reynolds, "with all its boasted privileges and high destinies, owes its discovery to the patronage of a single female, Isabella, queen of Spain; who, to the imperishable honour of her sex, even pledged her jewels to sustain the expense of an adventure, which . . . gave us the happy land in which we live." A patriotic Charleston Isabella donated fifty dollars, and two others stitched together an American flag to wave above the southern ice floes.

The groundswell for an exploring expedition increased, and Washington was flooded with memorials and petitions, most of them from New England. A typical one came from Nantucket:

The subscribers, citizens of Nantucket in Massachusetts, respectfully represent the intercourse maintained between this place and different parts of the world, especially the islands and countries of the Pacific Ocean, has become a matter deserving of the protecting care of national legislation.

Besides the employment of energy and enterprise by our seamen and merchants, they would represent that they have sixty whaleships, representing 20,000 tons of shipping, requiring $1,000,000 to maintain with attendant industries, and some two thousand seamen. Whether viewed as a valuable nursery for bold and hardy seamen or as employment of capital, or furnishing an article of indispensable necessity to human comfort (whale oil), it seems to your petitioners to be deserving of public care.

Increased extent of voyages now pursued by whaling and trading vessels, in seas but little explored, has increased continual dangers and losses to our mariners and merchants. Within a few years their cruisings have extended from Peru and Chile to the northwest coast of this continent and to New Zealand and the islands of Japan. Several vessels have been wrecked on islands and reefs not laid down on any charts; many ships have gone into these seas and no soul returned to tell their fate.

Your petitioners consider it a matter of earnest importance that these seas be explored, and that they should be surveyed in an accurate and authentic manner, with the positions of new islands recently discovered and shoals ascertained.

The advancement of science, and not private interests, but the general interests of the nation, seem to imperiously demand it. They therefore, pray that an expedition be fitted out under the sanction of the government to explore and survey the islands and coasts of the Pacific sea.

The campaigning by Reynolds, the fostering of friendships with men of influence, the bombardment of Washington with memorials and petitions finally, most satisfactorily, produced results. The grand plan, having moved with glacial slowness, gathered momentum. The chairman of the Committee on Naval Affairs requested Reynolds to submit his views for the reasons why an exploratory expedition would promote overseas trade. The timing, for Reynolds, was perfect. He had just returned from New England's whaling ports, had talked with men whose livelihood depended upon whaling, sealing, the China trade. All the facts, the opinions, the concerns, the advice of these men were at his fingertips. Reynolds reeled off the whaling statistics, the decline in the fur seal trade and the sandalwood trade. An expedition was essential to discover more whaling grounds, more seal rookeries, more islands bearing sandalwood. With the increasing use of whale oil for conversion into gas for lighting, islands and shoals should be explored for elephant seal and porpoise; both produced oil. The valuable sea otter fur trade of the north could perhaps be repeated in the south. Mackerel fishing could be expanded, and the market opened up in South America, provided Latin Americans could be persuaded to eat fish rather than vegetables on fast days. Not even birds escaped Reynolds's far-flung net. Seabirds could supply feathers "nearly equal in quality to the eider-down beds of Russia." Feathers would also supply quills, "and instead of paying near half a million of dollars a year to

Holland and Russia, and other countries, for quills, we could by this trade, supply our own market and others." Moreover, the exchange articles required for this Pacific trade were all available in the United States: "Rice, tobacco, rum, whiskey, blankets, coarse woollens, cottons, calicoes, the ordinary kinds of cutlery, and trivial jewellery, and agricultural utensils, and some articles of household furniture, will soon find a market. . . ." Reynolds was astute enough not to list firearms. Washington had problems enough with continental armed natives.

The committee chairman, on reading Reynolds's letter, asked the navy secretary, Samuel Southard, to give his opinion. Southard—a friend of Reynolds's—was enthusiastic (as was President Adams) but thought that any expedition should be small and recommended that the House appropriate fifty thousand dollars for the enterprise.

The House later heard an impassioned speech from Congressman John Reed, whose district included Nantucket and New Bedford. In full rhetorical flow, brandishing a chart showing American whalers' voyages and a copy of the *Nantucket Inquirer* listing their discoveries in the Pacific, Reed invoked the shade of Edmund Burke, who had "looked across the Atlantic with astonishment and admiration upon the inhabitants of the little island of Nantucket." The island, Reed continued, "still remains a proud monument of the same perseverance, activity, dexterity, sagacity, and enterprise. They not only pursue their gigantic game, the whale, as in the time Burke spoke, but have since doubled Cape Horn, and traversed the Pacific six thousand miles, north to California, and westerly across the mighty ocean to Asia, on the coast of Japan and New Holland." Reed, reaching the finale of his bravura performance, asked: "What peculiar attention have they received? What favours? I am aware that they have participated in the common blessings of our common country, which I do not consider few or small; but, extraordinary and exclusive favours, they have never received." Whalemen, ended Reed, had no time for surveying or the means. This was a job for the government.

In May 1828 the House of Representatives passed a resolution calling on the Navy Department to send one of its smaller vessels "to the Pacific Ocean and the South Sea to examine the coasts, islands, harbors, shoals and reefs." It would, however, have to be accomplished by the department with its allotted funds. No $50,000 allocations; this was to be a shoestring operation. Frugality was the watchword.

Southard, now able to act, found himself in the embarrassing position of being unable to find a suitable vessel. A few days after the House had passed its resolution, the navy secretary (with feelings of envy of his counterpart in London, who could conjure vessels from the air) wrote that "there was no vessel belonging to our navy which in its then condition was proper to send upon this expedition." But he could send his friend Reynolds, appointed as a special agent to the Navy Department, out into

New England to gather as much information as possible on American activities in the Pacific.

First came a meeting with the fifty-nine-year-old Edmund Fanning. The younger man listened to him like a small boy entranced with tales of derring-do upon the high seas. Here was a man wise in the ways of ships, seamen, sealing, and the China trade. Born in the village of Stonington, Connecticut, he had gone to sea as a fourteen-year-old cabin boy. Over the years he had made sealing voyages to the Falkland Islands, the Patagonian coast, South Georgia (where a whaleboat, lying astern of the anchored mother ship by a single painter, had been picked up by one of the island's vicious squalls and spun in the air like a feather attached to a thread), and the Juan Fernández Islands. He had anchored in Pacific lagoons and atolls where the crew had hung up boarding nets, posted sentries, and fabricated "quakers" (dummy cannon made from wood), all to give the appearance of a warship in the pious hope of fooling hostile islanders. He had fought off natives in canoes at the Marquesas Islands and pirates in proas in the Sunda Strait; dealt with mandarins and hong merchants in Macao and Canton; discovered islands; rescued shipwrecked seamen; been imprisoned by the Spanish and had his ship impounded in Chile; entertained the court ladies of Nuku Hiva aboard his ship (he thought the ladies, coated with a mixture of coconut and sandalwood oil, an "anti-fragrant company"). His voyages had made him an expert trader in sealing, sandalwood, mother-of-pearl, tortoiseshell, bêche-de-mer, coral moss (the Chinese considered this a great delicacy; Fanning thought it tasted like bilge water), and birds' nests (another Chinese delicacy). He had also made a personal fortune.

Fanning had not been to sea for ten years, but those years had been filled with giving advice, organizing, investing, and acting as agent for New England sealing fleets (Reynolds dubbed him the "father of all sealers"). The fleets had sailed south of Cape Horn to the South Shetland Islands off the Antarctic Peninsula, where in three short summers the vast fur seal rookeries had been virtually exterminated. Fanning's keen Yankee nose had twitched at the thought of a government-funded expedition to find more rookeries. In addition, Fanning, in a disinterested way, more than most sealers, had an interest in geographical discovery. He recommended an old friend, business partner, shipowner, captain, and sealer, Benjamin Pendleton, to act as a pilot for the expedition. Naval officers, the old sealer suspected, would be at a loss in Antarctic waters.

The whole expedition was now gaining speed. Southard had found a vessel, the sloop of war *Peacock*,[2] building in New York, and the navy secretary was being whipped along by President Adams, anxious to see this expedition on its way during his term of office. An election was looming with America's hero, General Andrew Jackson, waiting in the wings, Adams had no illusions about who would be bowing to the hootin' and hollerin' audience when the curtain came down on the electioneering and the votes were counted. (Adams's instinct was right. On Jackson's inauguration day a whiskey-soaked jubilant mob burst into the White House, snatched the celebratory punch meant for the more sedate Jacksonians, and left only when tubs of punch were put on the lawn.) Southard, the bit between his teeth, looked for an escort vessel. Pendleton's brig *Seraph,* loading cargo for Málaga, would serve admirably. She was unloaded. Scientists, keen to go on the expedition, were interviewed and selected. Naval officers with a bent for science, keen to go on the expedition, were interviewed but—here came the problem—there were so few of them. American naval officers with scientific interests, in the felicitous phrase of William Stanton, "could virtually be counted by the ears on one's head. . . ."

Such a one was a twenty-seven-year-old lieutenant, almost at the bottom of the naval officers' pecking order in terms of seniority, who had spent the last few years officially on leave waiting for orders. The thin-faced, bony-nosed Charles Wilkes came from New York society and had married into the same circle. During his years of leave Wilkes had picked up the triangulation methods of survey from Ferdinand Hassler[3] and geomagnetism from his brother-in-law James Renwick, a professor at Columbia College. Wilkes wanted to be the astronomer—and perhaps even more. Southard, curious about his reply, asked his opinions on a suitable commander for a scientific exploring expedition. Wilkes went through the Navy List and, for various reasons, eliminated them all. As for officers of his own rank, the younger and lowest in seniority were most eligible. They at least could still remember what they had learned for their exams. Wilkes, in all modesty, thought he should be appointed to the command of the expedition's escort vessel and second-in-command to the expedition. There was no possible way he could take orders from a civilian scientist. Wilkes was sent off as assistant astronomer (to a civilian astronomer) to buy instruments. And Master Commandant Thomas ap Catesby Jones was appointed to command the expedition (Wilkes, in his cool assessment of potential commanders, had said that Jones would be nothing remarkable). Reynolds was appointed historiographer. He was to write the expedition's story and complete his research into American commerce in the Pacific and South Seas. Wilkes worried him; he thought him "exceedingly vain and conceited" and that the Wilkes-Renwick clan, with their smooth, condescending eastern ways, had something up their sleeve. Indeed they did. Wilkes dragged his feet in collecting the scientific instruments so that navy officers, as he told Jones, could be trained for the limited science— except for the pendulum experiments, of which only two men in America were capable, his brother-in-law and himself. No need for civilians to destroy the harmony of a well-run ship.

Then a senator from South Carolina, an ardent Jacksonian and states' rights senator and, unfortunately, chairman of the Committee on Naval Affairs, hove over the horizon and blew the expedition out of the water. Huffing and puffing, in a fine senatorial lather, Robert Y. Haynes fulminated away on secretaries of the navy who stepped out of line and wasted citizens' money. Haynes's essence ran that Southard had not been given proper authority. Article 1, Section 7 of the Constitution required both houses to approve resolution . . . this not done . . . whole matter unconstitutional . . . overseas exploration unnecessary . . . could tempt Americans away to form colony . . . surveying of reefs and islands too expensive . . . thousands of dollars on this expedition . . . millions on next . . . plenty enough exploration left in North America. Jackson was in, and Adams was out. Reynolds's rejoicing had proved premature; his "first American Expedition of discovery, the first to go to the South Pole, and the first from any Republican Government" bubbled to the bottom. Sunk. Haynes steamed away, leaving only flotsam bobbing on the surface.

Wilkes had spent over a thousand dollars of his own money and promised three thousand more on instruments. His bill was refused by the new secretary of the navy. Wilkes would have to apply to Congress for "relief." The *Seraph* was returned to Pendleton "as is and where is." Pendleton asked recompense for the lost Málaga voyage and the money and time spent in fitting out for the expedition. He too was told to seek "relief" from Congress.

Tidewater New England was incensed, claiming that this was spiteful, dirty politics at work (as was true), and set about forming its own private exploratory expedition. A "South Sea Fur Company and Exploring Expedition" rose, like a phoenix, from the ashes. Funds came from money donated at Reynolds's lectures and from eastern Yankees seething at western and southern Jacksonites. In October 1829, seven months after Jackson's inauguration, a reporter from the *New York Enquirer* went aboard one of the expedition's three vessels berthed at New York:

THE SOUTH SEA EXPEDITION. The brig *Annawan*, the flagship of the expedition, dropped down to the lower bay, yesterday, and will proceed to sea this morning. Thus, after three years of perseverance and industry Mr. Reynolds finds himself upon the ocean, in search of the undiscovered islands of the south. In addition to the commercial importance of this expedition it is highly important in a national point of view. . . . The stores of science will be increased by the products of far-distant islands, as yet unknown to civilized man, and curiosity may, perchance, be gratified by something new.

We visited the *Annawan* on Thursday. She is a fine vessel and a very fast sailer. She is furnished with an excellent library, and all the instruments necessary for such an expedition. She has a stout and hardy crew, an experienced captain, and first rate officers. After the commercial objects of the expedition shall have been accomplished, Mr. Reynolds intends to sail round the icy circle, and push through the first openings that he finds. Success to him.

Mr. R. is accompanied by Dr. Eights, of Albany, a gentleman of talents and scientific accomplishments.

The *Annawan*'s captain was indeed experienced. Nathaniel Palmer, an accomplished seaman, had made three seailing voyages to the Antarctic. His younger brother, Alexander, commanded a small schooner, the *Penguin,* and Pendleton the *Seraph.* The "stout and hardy crew" had all, like whalemen, signed up for the voyage on the lay system of payments. All three vessels sailed separately, and all three returned separately.

Little can be said about the South Sea Fur Company and Exploring Expedition except to draw a decent shroud over its corpse. But why did it die so quickly? The South Shetlands produced few fur seals (what else was to be expected?), no geographical discoveries were made, and after arriving in Chile, where the three vessels were gathered together for the first time, the crews, suffering from scurvy, with no lay to their names, mutinied. Some deserted. Nathaniel Palmer was forced to sail north to Valparaiso and hand over a large part of his crew to the U.S. consul. Reynolds, the grand mover in the enterprise, left the expedition to wander among the Araucanian Indians. With barely enough hands to work the vessels, Pendleton and the Palmers sailed for home. By August 1831 all three shorthanded vessels were back in New England. Pendleton, after this dreary experience, wrote "that an exploring expedition, under private means, never can produce any great or important national benefits, the same must be under authority from the government, and the officers and men under regular pay and discipline, as in the navy."

Reynolds stayed in Chile. In 1832 he joined the U.S. frigate *Potomac*[4] as private secretary to her commander. James Eights, the only man with any pretensions to science on the expedition, did return. He provided some crumbs of comfort to the trustees of New York City's Lyceum for Natural History, who had given five hundred dollars to the expedition. Eights had found some strange creatures from the cold seas that had never been seen before. He had also seen boulders embedded in icebergs and deduced that icebergs could transport the "erratics" that were so exercising geologists of the time. But ten-legged sea spiders and chunks of rock in an iceberg rated nothing with the popular press.

Reynolds returned in 1834 to write the narrative of the *Potomac*'s expedition. He also had the draft for a story, a story common among whalemen. Reynolds entitled it *Mocha Dick; or, The White Whale of the Pacific* and had it published in the *Knickerbocker,* a New York literary magazine.

As for Symmes, that bewildered western Don Quixote, he had died a few months before the *Seraph,* the *Penguin,* and the *Annawan* sailed south.

His grave in Ohio was marked by a hollow globe.

NOTES

1. An obvious reference to the printing press carried on the Arctic expedition of the *Hecla* and the *Griper* and the weekly printing, during the winter months, of the *North Georgia Gazette and Winter Chronicle*.
2. The *Peacock*, although a new vessel, was entered on the naval register as a "rebuilt" ship by incorporating some of the old USS *Peacock*'s timbers in her construction. It was all sleight of hand accounting by the Navy Department.
3. Ferdinand Hassler (1770–1843), the brilliant Swiss-born geodesist, came to America in 1805. With Jefferson's help he was a prime mover in the organizing of the U.S. Coast and Geodetic Survey and led the Atlantic coast survey from 1816 to 1818. He was then effectively dismissed by Congress through a law that required that only naval and military men be employed in the service.
4. The USS *Potomac*, Commander John Downes, had been ordered to Sumatra by President Jackson on a reprisal expedition. Downes's handling of the situation, with the slaughter of men and women by marines and sailors, at Kuala Batu, followed by the town's being bombarded, caused much concern in the United States. The *Peacock*'s first commission, launched with much fanfare as an expeditionary vessel, was to sail on a secret diplomatic mission to Vietnam, Thailand, and Oman and as a backup vessel for the *Potomac*.

Chapter 7

Infinite Confusion

GATHER WAY, To. To begin to feel the impulse of the wind on the sails, so as to obey the helm.

GUNNER'S DAUGHTER. The name of the gun to which boys were *married,* or lashed, to be punished.

Admiral W. H. Smyth, *The Sailor's Word-Book,* 1867

HE AUGUST of 1831 was a busy one for Pendleton. The *Seraph's* small cargo of sealskins went up for auction, and Pendleton reported to the customhouse that six of his men had deserted during the voyage. A report was written to Fanning on the expedition's lamentable failure, and in it Pendleton called for a government-sponsored expedition to search for new sealing grounds. The report was forwarded to Congress by Fanning. The scientific community sourly noted, as it had suspected, that the expedition had little to do with science or discovery but a lot to do with sealing.

Fanning continued lobbying for a government-sponsored expedition and tried—but failed—to claw back the expedition's losses from the public coffer. In 1833 he published a book on his voyages and those on which he had acted as agent. *Voyages round the World* was an instant success. One of the chapters called for an expedition to the South Pole. Fanning was an open polar sea advocate and suggested two places as the jumping-off point for the dive south. One was a South Atlantic approach from a base in the Falkland Islands and one, Fanning advised, that should sail south on a course between South Georgia and the South Shetland Islands, a virtual carbon copy of Weddell's farthest south of 1823. The other was a Pacific Ocean approach from a base in Chile down the 120°W line of longitude, an approach close to Cook's farthest south of 1774. Pendleton and Fanning might have preached to the wind for all the notice taken by Washington.

Reynolds, a far better propagandist than Fanning, returned from his *Potomac* voyage in 1834. America had changed during his years of absence. He had left in the days of the stagecoach and returned to railroads. Jackson had been returned for another term of office, and the talk was of nothing but dollars. The eastern patricians deplored the new America, and foreign visitors tended to agree with them. Tocqueville, that most perceptive of observers, wrote that "love of money is either the chief or secondary motive at the bottom of everything the Americans do. This gives a family likeness to all their passions and soon makes them wearisome to contemplate." Washington Irving and James Fenimore Cooper, after their years in Europe, returned home and were appalled at the changes in their country. Irving wrote of the chase after the "almighty dollar, that great object of universal devotion throughout our land." Cooper was struck by the vulgarity of the New York streets lined with glaring red-brick buildings decked out with bright green shutters, the greediness of the "gulpers" in the eating houses, the unpleasantness of the pigs foraging along the streets. The rabid nationalism and braggadacio he found distasteful. When he commented on the bad sidewalks, roads, and street lighting, his friends took him aside and warned him that it was unpatriotic to criticize anything American, even the scenery. The one freedom not found in the new Jacksonian America was the freedom to criticize.

David Crockett's "Go Ahead" was the country's slogan but one that usually omitted his "Be sure you're right." John O'Sullivan had yet to write that it was America's "manifest destiny to overspread the continent allotted by Providence" and Horace Greeley his "Go west, young man, and grow up with the country." But the young man in the street could hear the beating of the slogans' wings. And the wings belonged to a bald-headed eagle.

It was to this atmosphere of "breathless cupidity," as Tocqueville called it, that Reynolds returned. But keen observers of the political climate could detect a slight shift in the Jacksonian position on federal funds for what the president called "the diffusion of knowledge," and Reynolds was a man with a sharp political nose. After publishing his narrative of the *Potomac*'s voyage—it achieved instant popularity and Reynolds a literary reputation—he joined the propagandists in their lobbying for a government exploring expedition. The lobbyists were a remarkably diverse group. In it were numbered John Quincy Adams and Samuel Southard (the former president now in the House of Representatives and the former navy secretary in the Senate), Edmund Fanning, the East India Marine Society of Salem (every member had to have doubled either Cape Horn or the Cape of Good Hope), the Boston Society of Natural History, Commodore John Downes of the *Potomac,* and Passed Midshipman Matthew F. Maury, who had just returned from a Pacific cruise aboard the USS *Vincennes.* Here, collected together, were advocates for commercial interests, science, and hydrography. Helping them in their propaganda came news from across the Atlantic: John Biscoe's discoveries in the Antarctic; the hydrographic work of the Royal Navy in South and North America; the sailing of HMS *Beagle* (with a young naturalist by the name of Charles Darwin on board) to establish a worldwide range of meridian distances; the latest Admiralty Chart Catalogue[1] listing more than a thousand charts that could be bought across the counter from any Admiralty chart agent; and the arrival in Washington of Dumont d'Urville's magnificent volumes entitled *Voyage de la corvette l'Astrolabe.* (A welcome departure from Washington was the Jacksonian senator Robert Hayne, who had sunk the *Peacock* expedition before it had even sailed.)

Reynolds, two years after stepping ashore from the *Potomac,* now reached the zenith of his influence as a propagandist for a government-sponsored exploring expedition. Years before, after being mocked by his schoolfellows, he had replied that one day they would feel proud that they had known Jeremiah N. Reynolds. On the evening of 3 April 1836 that came true. At the invitation of the House of Representatives he gave an address before the assembled congressmen on the benefits of a government expedition to the Pacific and South Seas.

After a preliminary reminder of his western credentials—"though a dweller in western forests"—to disarm the men who would, he knew, form the core of skeptical opposition, Reynolds launched into his address. It was a remarkable performance. For too long America had benefited from the explorations, both geographic and scientific, of other countries: "By us no step has been taken to add even to the science of navigation. The great improvements in mathematical instruments . . . of which we daily and hourly reap the advantages, were brought to light by the liberality of foreign governments, and we still continue to sail by charts we have no hand in the making." More to the point, "our government, from which alone any extended assistance can proceed, has done absolutely nothing."

Warming to his theme, Reynolds said that any expedition should not slavishly follow European examples but should be bigger and better. It should "collect, preserve, and arrange everything valuable in the whole range of natural history, from the minute madrepore to the huge spermaceti, and accurately describe which cannot be preserved; to secure whatever may be hoped for in natural philosophy; to examine vegetation, from the hundred mosses of the rocks, throughout all the classes of shrub, flower, and tree, up to the monarch of the forest; to study man in his physical and mental powers, and his manners, habits, and disposition, and social and political relations . . . to examine the phenomena of winds and tides, of heat and cold, of light and darkness," and amid this prodigy of scientific effort: "Cast anchor on that point where all the meridians terminate, where our eagle and star-spangled banner may be unfurled and planted, and left to wave on the axis of the earth itself!"

To achieve all this, Reynolds suggested a fleet of five vessels plus a frigate. Aboard this flotilla would sail a group of dedicated officers and a large corps of civilian scientists all working in harmony. They would, "like stars in the milky-way, shed lustre on each other, and on all their country!" This was all rousing, boot-stamping, flag-waving oratory pitched for his patriotic audience, particularly so after sailing rather close to the wind in some of his criticisms of his country's attitude to "intellectual labours." But the address, stripped of its flag-waving (Reynolds was something of a cynic. He held that a nation, like children, should have playthings; an expedition would do as well as anything else), held for its time an insight into the role of science and scientist in a rapidly changing world. Science should be judged by the same standards as geographic discovery. The result of scientific research, the "utility," as Reynolds called it, could never be computed in advance. Geographic discoveries had proved their utility. England's search for a Northwest Passage had shown the limits of the North American continent but had also brought wealth through the fur trade, the cod fishing off Newfoundland, the whale fishing in the Davis Strait: "Yet not one of these rewards of enterprise was anticipated, or formed an element in the calculation, when her Cabot, her Davis, her Hudson and Baffin, were dispatched on their perilous voyages."

Within six weeks of Reynolds's address both houses had voted in favor of sending out "a surveying and exploring expedition to the Pacific Ocean and the South Seas." Funding for the enterprise was set at three hundred thousand dollars.

Opposition to the expedition had been fierce, particularly in the House of Representatives where Congressman Richard Hawes from Kentucky fumed that the idea was "chimerical and harebrained" and that dollars should not be "wrested from the hands of the American people" just to take "the vessels and seamen of the United States, and send them to the South Seas, exposing them to all the diseases, hurricanes, and mishaps of that climate." Hawes and his cohorts were defeated, 79 to 65, and the organization of the enterprise handed over to the secretary of the navy, Mahlon Dickerson.

He promptly set about stifling the expedition at its birth. Dickerson, a wealthy New Jersey ex-governor and ex-senator, a fussy sixty-six-year-old bachelor keen on gardening, happiest socializing around a dinner table, held strong views on the federal government's role in the Republic: The less the better. The idea that his department should be part of this harebrained scheme was anathema. As the scheme was dear to his archenemy, Samuel Southard, he suggested to Jackson (no friend to Southard) that it would be a brilliant political stroke, chopping Southard off at the knees, to cancel the whole enterprise. But by that strange alchemy that happens in the *Alice in Wonderland* world of politics, Jackson was now full of enthusiasm for the expedition.

Dickerson makes a most satisfying White Rabbit in this *Wonderland* world. One can almost hear, "Oh dear! Oh dear! I shall be too late!" and "Oh my furs and whiskers!" as he enters up his diary for the months of 1836. Here he records forgetting a Cabinet meeting (he had two men working in his garden); being "plagued" by Reynolds; being "plagued" by the expedition; being "plagued with the correspondence of Capt. Jones & J. N. Reynolds." His final entry for 1836 is pure White Rabbit: "End of the most perplexing and busy year of my life."

The Jones in his diary entry was the same Thomas ap Catesby Jones who had been given the command of the aborted 1828 *Peacock* expedition. Jones, the old comrade-in-arms of Jackson at the Battle of New Orleans, still hunched and nursing a British musket ball in his shoulder, had returned from a tour of duty in the Pacific and been appointed—on Jackson's suggestion—to command the new exploring expedition. The enterprise had received Jackson's benediction, and he wanted the fleet off and sailing by October 1836 before his last term in office came to an end. He was, ironically, repeating Adams's wishes of 1828, and, ironically, it was Jackson's own navy secretary who was attempting to sabotage the new expedition. Jones, in Dickerson's eyes, wanted too big, too expensive an expedition. The navy secretary, in White Rabbit mode, scurried over to the White House carrying Dumont d'Urville's volumes on the French expedition, which had achieved much with only one vessel. Dickerson's gambit failed. Jackson thought that a bigger expedition could only harvest more and better results.

Jones had been appointed to his command at the end of June. A few days later, before escaping the dreadful sweltering heat of Washington, Jackson scribbled a note to Dickerson appointing Reynolds Jones's secretary with powers to "condense the reports made to the Commander, by the scientific members of the expedition." Knowing Dickerson's deep dislike of Reynolds and having a shrewd idea of Dickerson's mulish propensities, Jackson thought it prudent to add a postscript: "It will be proper that Mr. Reynolds go with the expedition—this the publick expects—A. J."

The navy secretary's mantra of plagued, perplexed, and busy, mouthed so many times, was repeated by others during the last months of 1836. Jones had requested the frigate *Macedonian*,[2] building at Norfolk, as his flagship, plus two brigs, two schooners, and a storeship. Jones saw the expedition as both military and scientific. The large frigate would house the corps of civilian scientists with all their paraphernalia, while the frigate's immense firepower—the big stick—would overawe and, in times of need, be used in self-defense against the "barbarous and some times ferocious natives." (He also casually suggested to Dickerson that the Bonin and Hawaiian Islands be annexed and occupied.) The brigs and schooners would operate in pairs. The bellicose Jones, however, was allowed only the *Macedonian*, two brigs, one schooner, and a storeship. The building yards selected were spread the length of the eastern seaboard from Boston (brigs), New York (schooner), Philadelphia (storeship), to Norfolk (frigate). Supervision became a nightmare. The navy yard commandants' were perplexed at building and outfitting expedition vessels rather than warships; the navy agents perplexed at allocating funds for what and why. Dickerson and Jones argued over the selection of officers, and Dickerson, the Sunday botanist, was surprised to find a virtual desert when it came to finding navy officers with even a Sunday interest in any form of science.

But Lieutenant Charles Wilkes, appointed in 1833 as head of the Washington-based Depot of Charts and Instruments, was one of the few bright flowers in this desert. In July he was ordered to England and the Continent, sailing by fast packet boat, twenty thousand dollars at his disposal, to buy all the scientific instruments and charts. He had a time limit of three months.

The long, hot summer and fall of 1836 trickled away with Jones and Dickerson locked in acrimonious battle over the selection of officers. Jones urged the navy yard commandants, past masters at the art of stalling and raising objections, to speed up construction. Dickerson looked in vain for naval scientific officers so that he could prune, or even eliminate, any civilian corps of scientists. Reynolds canvassed the small group of civilians who could lay claim to any science and would be willing to sail with the expedition.

During the fall and into the winter, as the trees were stripped of their glorious colors, the various vessels were launched. Jackson's desire that the expedition be off by October had withered along with the fallen leaves. Wilkes was still abroad; no scientific staff had been selected (one of Dickerson's diary entries reads: "Must be cautious not to attempt too much business"); and the Jones v. Dickerson squabbling was made public in the press. Dickerson had promised Wilkes (brother-in-law to Professor James Renwick, a Dickerson crony) the command of one vessel and the command of another to Lieutenant Alexander Slidell, an officer with literary aspirations who had just published a book on Spain. Slidell, said Dickerson, would also write the expedition's history (and cut out any chance that Reynolds, who thirsted after the appointment, would become the chronicler). Jones, however, would have none of this. The two lieutenants lacked seagoing experience and stood close to the bottom of the seniority list, which was an article of faith with Jones.

By the end of the year all the vessels had been launched, and Jones ordered them to Norfolk. The brigs, rerigged as barques and sailing from Boston in January, proved to have a fiendish motion in a seaway—as prophesied by Edmund Fanning—and leaked like sieves. The new anthracite-fired galley stoves proved difficult to light, but when alight and roaring away, they melted the pitch in the deck seams, burned the food, and, much to the alarm of the crews, also threatened to incinerate their vessels.

If 1836 had proved a turbulent year for Dickerson, the next twelve months were to prove even more chaotic. One almost feels sorry for the bewildered secretary, sighing for the peace of his garden, as he was swept by vicious currents into a maelstrom of clashing egos and perplexing problems.

In the fall of 1836 he had asked various societies to suggest the science to be studied and those scientific gentlemen who would be willing to join the expedition. Only one society, the Brooklyn-based United States Naval Lyceum, showed any interest in the Antarctic. The lyceum's report noted that Captain James Cook had thought the intense Antarctic cold was caused by a great landmass stretching to the pole and that Charles Lyell, the eminent British geologist, estimated the unexplored area below the Antarctic Circle to be at least twice the size of Europe. Here was an area well worth exploring for science. The lyceum recommended the expedition sail "south on a meridian much further westward than that followed by Captain Weddell."

Wilkes returned at the end of January with his harvest of instruments and charts. The London manufacturers, although snowed under with work—they thought it due to the popularity of private scientific observations—had made the American instruments their priority. Wilkes had met with the leading lights in the British scientific world; been instructed in the use of the pendulums by Francis Bailey, vice-president of the Royal Society; been helped by Professor Peter Barlow and Commander James Clark Ross on the workings of the magnetic instruments and the taking of observations; and visited Captain Francis Beaufort of the Admiralty Hydrographic Office and collected all the required charts. Paris and Munich had provided more instruments and charts. All the precious chronometers—more than forty of them—came from England. Wilkes, in a letter to Dickerson, wrote: "It is impossible for me to give you an adequate idea of the enthusiasm which prevails on the subject of the expedition in England."

Back home in North America the enthusiasm was more muted. The civilian corps, at first enthusiastic, was bewildered at the delays and annoyed at the uncertainties; some of them, having resigned their bread-and-butter posts, were feeling the pinch, adrift in a payless limbo. Officers and men had to be recruited, the barques modified.

Wilkes, expecting a command, found nothing. But his keen nose sniffed out the turmoil and what one officer called the atmosphere of an enterprise filled with intrigue and rife with discord. It reeked of disaster.

He took himself off to survey Georges Bank, an important cod fishing ground, some hundred miles east of Cape Cod, in the U.S. brig *Porpoise.* News came in the spring of a French expedition with the corvettes *Astrolabe* and *Zélée,* commanded by the experienced Dumont d'Urville, preparing at Toulon for a scientific expedition into the Pacific and the Antarctic. King Louis Philippe had signed an order promising a bounty for all men on the expedition if they reached 75°S latitude, plus a smaller bounty for every degree closer to the South Pole. James Cook and James Weddell, with their farthest souths, had turned into potent totemic figures.

Before handing over the presidency to Martin Van Buren, Jackson wrote a curt letter to Dickerson. The scientific corps had to be appointed "forthwith" and the expedition sail as soon as possible. "This done, no blame can attach to the Executive department on the score of supineness or neglect. Please attend to this." But the victor of New Orleans, when he retired to his estate in Tennessee, retired defeated. Supineness still ruled. The scientific corps was not appointed and put on the payroll until 4 July.

Much of the spadework in the selection had been done by Reynolds, eager to see a group of young men dedicated to their disciplines aboard the expedition rather than the Sunday dilettantes beloved by the navy secretary. The list was impressive: four zoologists, a botanist, a geologist, a naturalist, a philologist, a conchologist, a "natural philosopher,"[3] three natural history draftsmen, a taxidermist; and two artists.

Many of them had already resigned from their positions and had spent their own money on books and instruments. Wilkes, no naturalist, had failed to buy microscopes. Eighteen thirty-seven, with its depression and financial panic gripping the country, was no time to fall into debt. This was a time when dollars were hoarded. In New York, at hotels and oyster cellars, a dollar handed over for a glass of brandy and water brought change in a ticket "Good for one glass of brandy and water." Barbers gave change with tickets "Good for one shave." A conversation overhead on Wall Street ran as follows:

"Tom, do you want any oysters for lunch today?"

"Yes!"

"Then here's a ticket; and give me two *shaves* in return."

July also saw an exchange of broadsides in the letters columns of the newspapers between "Citizen" (Reynolds) and "Friend of the Navy" (Dickerson). Reynolds was convinced that Dickerson, with Machiavellian cunning, was attempting to sink the expedition. The correspondence succeeded only in sinking any chance that Reynolds had of sailing with the expedition. Jackson may have wanted Reynolds aboard, but Jackson was no longer in the White House.

Perhaps the matter of the instruments reflects the shambles into which the expedition was falling. After arriving from Europe, the chronometers, sextants, pendulums, dip compasses, transits, and theodolites spread out from the Depot of Charts and Instruments like oil on the water. Walter Johnson, the physicist who had resigned as professor at Philadelphia's Franklin Institute to join the expedition, eager to inventory, check, and calibrate the instruments, found complete instruments missing, parts missing, the chronometers unchecked. An irritated Johnson wrote an acid letter to Dickerson that delicate instruments were not "muskets or cutlasses, which, after undergoing a rough and hasty proof, may be put into the hands of any soldier or marine, sure of fulfilling their purpose." Jones asked Dickerson to appoint officers to track down all the missing items. The exploring expedition was turning into what wags were soon to call the Deplorable Expedition.

In the fall Jones ordered the fleet from Norfolk to New York to have complicated heating systems installed. Many of the crew, signed up for a three-year period, were already more than a third of the way through their service. The problem of replacing crew and shipping them home in the middle of an expedition was bound to be complicated. Jones offered a bonus payment to those who cared to sign for another three years. Many did. And more than 150 seamen promptly deserted, carrying their bounty with them.

The New York into which some of the deserting seamen fled was the most water-oriented city in the United States. This was a city, as now, best approached from the sea. Like Venice, it was built on an island, and like Venice, it was a city of merchants. "All the world over," wrote James Mc-Cabe in his *Lights and Shadows of New York Life,* "poverty is a misfortune. In New York it is a crime."

A walker, strolling Manhattan's main artery, the poplar-lined Broadway, could turn left or right at any point and soon come to the Hudson River or the East River. River shores lined with a forest of masts, of bowsprits and jibbooms stretching over jostling crowds of spitting, bristle-chinned roustabouts and longshoremen, cursing draymen, drunken sailors, stall owners pushing wheelbarrows loaded with bags of oysters and clams, luggage-laden porters shouting a way for elegantly dressed gentlemen fastidiously flicking canes at the more noisome objects in their path, loungers on bollards, clerks and bookkeepers gulping gin and oysters, pickpockets, and thieves. Along the wharves and piers lay the steamboats, smoke belching, whistles blowing, that could take you to Boston in fifteen hours, the two hundred miles through Long Island Sound to Providence in thirteen hours and then two hours by railroad to Boston. Side-wheel steam ferryboats shuttled every few minutes between Manhattan, Brooklyn, and New Jersey. Shipyards building the fast packet boats that sailed to Liverpool and Le Havre lined the East River. Officered by hard-boiled, hard-driving Yankees and crewed by "packet rats," the scum of the Liverpool waterfront, the packet boats sailed on a regular timetable and could take you across to England in sixteen to eighteen days. Travel first class, and you had fresh eggs from the hen coops, fresh milk from the cow stabled over the main hatch, fresh meat from the pigs and sheep penned on deck under the longboat. Travel steerage, and you brought aboard your own bedding, food, utensils.

The harbor swarmed with the equivalent of Venice's gondola: the white-painted cedar-planked lapstrake Whitehall rowing boat. Steered with rudder and yoke, two men rowing double banked oars, these water taxis, along with the New England whaleboat, were the world's first stock-built boat. Originally made on New York's Whitehall Street, they were soon being constructed in every American port. They carried passengers, chandlers, and boardinghouse crimps to arriving ships and shanghaied sailors, given doped drinks in those same boardinghouses, to departing ships.

Heeling to the wind, slipping along on the current, sailed the Hudson River sloops, some seventy-five feet long, with masts and topmasts towering a hundred feet above their beamy hulls, eighty-five-foot booms reaching far beyond their transoms. With such rigs the sloops carried an enormous amount of canvas, and their sails dappled the harbor like a pointillist painting. These river workboats carried passengers, produce, lumber, and stone. Given favorable conditions, they could sail the 150 miles upstream to Albany in three days. Steamboats churned upriver in half the time.

To foreign visitors and the sober citizens of Boston, Baltimore, and Philadelphia, the pace of life in New York appeared brasher, cruder, and faster than in their own cities: the babble of foreign tongues and shades of skin along South Street; the "Bowery B'hoys," dressed in flaming red shirts tied at the collar with extravagant cravats, black breeches tucked into boots, hats cocked at rakish angles over hair plastered to skulls, cigars clamped in mouth corners, escorting their girls, decorated like parakeets, in a blaze of colors, bonnets strung with ribbons, parasols twirling on shoulders. The Bowery, once a farming area, was now a street of cheap shops, pawnbrokers, suspect boardinghouses, brothels, saloons, and dance halls. Respectable folk did not walk the Bowery. Even worse was the Five Points district, a filthy rat-infested warren of buildings and alleyways filled with scavenging pigs, dogs, and vagrants; the home to criminals, prostitutes, and the absolute destitute. Police avoided the place.

Battery Park and Broadway were the parading grounds for the more genteel New Yorkers and those wishing to show off their new carriages. The hurrying pedestrians, dodging the pigs, made an easy mark for the street vendors, men, women, and children, who patrolled Broadway's sidewalks with their trays and boxes. Anything easily portable could be found for sale: watches, cheap jewelry, newspapers, fruits, tobacco, cigars, taffy apples, cakes, ice cream, lemonade, flowers, stockings and socks, cotton yarns, wool, pins, gloves, hats, even dogs and birds. Irishwomen in quilted bonnets and shawls with a strong line of blarney sold apples, ice cream, coffee, soups, and oysters from stands. Little girls sold toothpicks, newspapers, song sheets, and flowers. Fanny Trollope, that most acerbic critic of all things American, approved of New York City. Contrary to Cooper, she thought the red-painted brick buildings, with their white pointing and green shutters, attractive. Pigs are not mentioned. Perhaps her experience in Cincinnati had hardened her to the porcine aspects of America.

Captain Frederick Marryat, in the United States at the time the expedition was gathered at New York (his play *The Ocean Wolf* opened at the Bowery Theatre in October 1837), also approved of New York. On the evening of 3 July he noticed the police putting up placards warning that anyone setting off fireworks would be arrested. They were followed by a troupe of small boys firing off squibs, crackers, and small cannon made from shinbones. The next morning the more decorous New Yorkers, riding on wagons, coaches, and carriages, set off north, away from the center of celebrations and smell of gunpowder. American flags hung from windows and flew at mastheads. Broadway was lined with booths and stands selling plates of oysters, clams, pineapples, boiled hams, roasted pig, pies, puddings, barley sugar, porter, ale, cider, brandy, whiskey, rum, punch, gin slings, cocktails, mint juleps. Bands played; the militia and volunteers marched; artillery rolled; officers in regimentals, long white feathers in hats, tried to control their mounts as the rougher element tossed squibs and firecrackers. The Declaration of Independence was read at City Hall, hats were tossed in the air, and gallons more punch went down patriotic throats. The fireworks, thought Marryat, were the best he had ever witnessed, as were the handsome girls and women parading on Broadway.[4]

It was in this bustling, greedy, flamboyant, cosmopolitan, endlessly entertaining city that the men of the United States Surveying and Exploring Expedition found themselves. New Yorkers, being curious about anything that floated in their harbor, came to see the black painted ships with their broad white bands at the gunports, their snowy decks and neatly furled sails. Patriotic articles appeared in the newspapers. In October, at one of the city's three theaters, the daily playbill announced the attendance of a group of the expedition's officers. They were greeted with cheers, foot stamping, and applause. They were cheered again at the intermission, and words like *Honor* and *Glory* rang from the pit. One of the officers, Lieutenant James Glynn, wrote that he felt rather foolish at receiving all this adulation when they had done nothing to deserve it. "We certainly are the Lions of the day; but popular opinion is notoriously fickle, and it may be the fashion to sneer at us in a month."

It was to take longer than a month. But not much longer. At the end of November, claiming ill health, Jones handed in his resignation. On the advice of the fleet surgeon he returned to his Virginia home. On 6 December Dickerson accepted the resignation and scribbled into his diary remarks on the "infinite confusion" and lamented that "no one will take the command in such vessels as he [Jones] has had constructed, or such arrangements as he has made." This was rather unfair considering that Dickerson was equally to blame for the general chaos. But it was obvious to most officers that the expedition's command had turned into the navy's poisoned chalice.

NOTES

1. The catalog first appeared in 1821 and listed all the charts that could be bought by the public. By 1829 close to a thousand charts were listed. Admiral Sir Francis Beaufort, the brilliant head of the Admiralty Hydrographic Office from 1829 to 1855 (he took office when aged fifty-five, the age when today's hydrographer of the navy retires), added new charts at the extraordinary rate of fifty to sixty a year. The Beaufort wind scale, still in use, was his creation.
2. The name *Macedonian* had a particular resonance for Americans. In 1812 HMS *Macedonian,* a British frigate, had been captured by Stephen Decatur's *United States.* The *Macedonian* on the stocks at Norfolk was a completely new vessel.
3. The word *scientist* was not coined until 1840. Today's *physicist* would be the closest to the pleasant-sounding *natural philosopher.*
4. The captain had a sailor's roving eye when it came to the ladies. During a visit to the Albany Female Academy, and present at their French examination, he whispered answers into the young ladies' ears. After New York and the Albany visit he decided that American girls were the prettiest in the world. But at a Louisville hotel the gallant captain found himself in grave trouble with a phrenologist, Dr. Collyer, whose wife had a bump of amativeness considerably larger than her bumps of cautiousness and conjugality. The episode is pure French farce. Having a suspicious mind, Collyer told his wife he would be absent that night. He then hid himself, in classic fashion, under the hotel bed. At one o'clock his suspicions were confirmed. Leaping from under and crying, "Treason, fire, rape," he grappled with the scantily clad captain, while his wife, equally scantily clad, collapsed weeping on the bed. Within minutes the room was filled with startled guests and the hotel manager. For one of the few times in his life, Marryat's powers of invention deserted him, and he stammered that he had heard of Mrs. Collyer's expertise at easing sprains, and, suffering from one himself, had come for treatment.

Chapter 8

Wilkes Takes Charge

HALF-LAUGHS AND PURSER'S GRINS. Hypocritical
and satirical sneers.

HEAVE AND A-WASH. An encouraging call when the ring
of the anchor rises to the surface, and the stock stirs the
water.

Admiral W. H. Smyth, *The Sailor's Word-Book,* 1867

ICKERSON'S SECOND WINTER of discontent was upon
him. It was not made brighter by the news from across the Atlantic that Dumont d'Urville, with his two corvettes, had sailed
from Toulon in early September. The French had put their expedition together in six months and would be attempting to pass Weddell's farthest south during the short Antarctic 1837–38 summer.

The Navy secretary's critics were not slow in pointing out that the
American expedition, still in New York in December, would now have to
wait for the 1838–39 Antarctic summer season in order to attempt any exploration, a year behind the French. As the kinder critics pointed out,
such a state of affairs was a matter of acute embarrassment to the Republic because the Americans had started their preparations a year ahead of the
French. (Less generous critics, pointing to 1828, said a decade.)

The poisoned chalice of the expedition's command was promptly refused by the first three of Dickerson's choices: the first because he considered the *Macedonian* too big and the two barques unseaworthy; the
second because the *Macedonian* had been dropped from the expedition on
the advice of a navy review board of three commodores, a board commissioned by Dickerson; the third because he was attempting to marry the
incompatible—engineers and sailors aboard the navy's first steamship.

From Congress came a request for all the papers relating to the expedition's delay, a request that worried both Dickerson and President Martin Van Buren. The activity in getting together the papers and writing a report brought on Dickerson's headaches, an affliction not soothed by one congressman's claiming that Dickerson's "imbecilities" had made America the laughingstock of the world.

His headaches, all the problems, all the *bother* of the expedition brought Dickerson to the brink of resigning. But not a single person could be found to take over as secretary of the navy. Here was another poisoned chalice.[1] The urbane, dandyish Van Buren, the political "Little Magician," who rowed to his objectives with muffled oars, came up with the political answer. Dickerson would remain in office, but the organization of the expedition would be taken over by the secretary of war, Joel Poinsett. Poinsett (another amateur botanist; the poinsettia is named after him), something of a diplomat, said that his position was merely to aid Dickerson with advice "whenever he may think proper to request it."

Poinsett immediately took off the velvet gloves. The exploring expedition, now the butt of cartoons and lampoons, had become the Deplorable Expedition. All that old John Quincy Adams wanted to hear about it was that it had sailed.

Lieutenant Francis Gregory was ordered to take command and promoted to captain. But Poinsett had not reckoned with Gregory's wife. She was desolated at the thought of his going, said Gregory. The new captain pleaded to be released from the appointment. Poinsett agreed. But so graceful was Poinsett's letter, so full of patriotic feelings, that Mrs. Gregory urged her husband to reconsider and take the command. He did. Then, about to set off for the squadron, Gregory realized that his wife's "unspoken words" on his sailing would leave him with "endless regrets." He begged to be relieved for the second time. Poinsett, gritting his teeth, realizing that a commander of this caliber could only be a liability, agreed for the second time.

The expedition appeared to be dying of sheer inertia. Officers were resigning. The seamen, young, energetic men who had signed on for the sheer adventure, being confined to dull harbor duties, were bored and avid listeners of the latest rumors and scuttlebutt, the perfect recipe, in a military service, for low morale and a breakdown in discipline. The adulation from the public and the pride of belonging to the exploring expedition had vanished. The cheers had changed to sneers.

Poinsett set about feeling the pulse of the demoralized squadron by interviewing Lieutenant Matthew Maury, who had been appointed, much to the chagrin of Wilkes, the expedition's astronomer. Aged thirty-two, a southerner of mixed French Huguenot and English stock, Maury had just published a treatise on navigation that had been adopted as a textbook for midshipmen. Poinsett eventually arrived at the heart of the interview.

Whom would Maury recommend, regardless of rank, as a suitable commander for the expedition? An unusual question for a secretary of war to ask of a very junior lieutenant half his age. Maury "gave him a list of the officers belonging to the expedition; myself, the youngest lieutenant in the navy, at the bottom of the list." It was a list that obviously held small appeal for Poinsett.

The secretary, baffled by so many naval officers' reluctance to command the first United States exploration voyage, finally pitched upon Captain Joseph Smith to take the poisoned chalice. Smith warily agreed, provided that certain lieutenants known to him, three in number, consented to command the smaller vessels. One of the lieutenants was Charles Wilkes. Summoned to Washington—he was about to start a survey of the Savannah River—Wilkes refused any position with the expedition. The civilian corps of scientists, he claimed, would make the navy's officers mere "hewers of wood and drawers of water."

Another lieutenant also declined to sail, and Smith, his conditions unfulfilled, joined the ranks of officers who had refused the poisoned chalice. Poinsett's record—two refusals—was fast approaching Dickerson's three refusals. (The more cynical expedition watchers, counting Gregory's refusals as two, claimed Poinsett and Dickerson were running neck and neck.)

Poinsett, however, still had hopes of nailing down a commander. Professor Renwick thought his brother-in-law Charles Wilkes an extremely capable surveyor, an excellent astronomer, and well versed in magnetism. In short, he was the most capable scientific officer in the navy. He could, hinted Renwick, be approached to take a larger position than that of commanding one of the expedition's smaller vessels. In other words, the expedition itself. Poinsett offered the command, and Wilkes accepted. On certain conditions, however. The expedition would have to be changed. Naval officers would take over all the physical sciences and surveying. Botany, zoology, geology, conchology, philology (barely sciences, according to Wilkes) would be taken over by naval surgeons.

The appointment of Wilkes brought roars of outrage from certain quarters in the navy. Wilkes was a junior officer with very little time at sea, thundered the complainers. Obvious collusion, with Smith as the stalking-horse, cried others. The sacred seniority system of the lieutenants' list was being attacked, said those at the top of the list. Poinsett weathered the storm and stayed with his choice.

Wilkes, who had celebrated his fortieth birthday on 3 April, also seemed undaunted by the storm. Slim, energetic, with close-set eyes bracketing a long, bony nose, Wilkes looked like the typical Yankee. Later in his life the archetypical Yankee look increased. Sketch a wispy white goatee on the chin, slap a top hat on the head, and any photograph of an older Wilkes looks remarkably like Uncle Sam. It's a transformation that would

Portrait of Charles Wilkes

"The originating, getting up, and getting off a first National Expedition, is a work of no small difficulty, and this is much increased by the public thinking, talking of, and interfering too much with it. I felt this myself, although it did not cause me much difficulty." —Charles Wilkes

(Illustration from Wilkes's *Narrative*, vol. I)

have appealed to the navy officer. For Wilkes was a patriot—a northern patriot—to his fingertips.

He was born in New York City, and his family was well connected, wealthy, with roots that stretched across the Atlantic to France and England. His great-grandfather Israel Wilkes had been a prosperous London distiller, and John Wilkes, the turbulent political figure of eighteenth-century England, his great-uncle. John Wilkes was a family phantom to be reckoned with: member of Parliament, lord mayor of London, a most damnable thorn in the flesh for King George III and his ministers, darling of the London mob, supporter of the American colonists in their contretemps with the crown, friend of Benjamin Franklin, rake, and wit. His great-nephew, from the time he took over the expedition and in his subsequent naval career, took on some of his great-uncle's stormy petrel attributes, but without the wit and charm of his squint-eyed relative, immortalized by William Hogarth. It was said of John Wilkes that it was impossible for him to walk from his London house to Guildhall without leaving at least one Londoner chuckling in his wake.[2] This was the Wilkes of the famous meeting and dinner, arranged by Boswell, with Samuel Johnson, a dinner at which the two political enemies (united only by a mutual dislike of the Scots) met face-to-face for the first time and which ended with this incongruous pair's hugely enjoying each other's company and parting the best of friends. Johnson later confided to Boswell that "Jack has great variety of talk, Jack is a scholar, and Jack has the manners of a gentleman. . . . I would do Jack a kindness, rather than not."

Another totally different strand ran through Wilkes's genetic heritage. An aunt, on his mother's side, was Elizabeth Seton, who had converted to Roman Catholicism in 1805, set up Catholic schools and colleges, and died as the mother superior, Mother Seton, of the Sisters of Charity.[3] Here, in the young New Yorker, was a volatile mixture of the sacred and the profane.

It was an unlikely choice, a sailor's life, for a morbidly religious and priggish young boy whose small study next to the family parlor was schoolroom and prayer closet. But New York was a sea-oriented city, and the romance of the wharves packed with schooners, sloops, brigs, and full-rigged ships rocking gently to the harbor's surge within their cat's cradle of mooring lines, the wheeling, screeching, scavenging gulls, the rumble of barrels rolling across the cobblestones, the creak of tackles as cargo was hoisted out from holds, the cries of seamen and longshoremen, the smells of spices, fish, tar, and hemp, all the sounds, sights, and smells of a seaport hinted at excitements far beyond those contained by a cramped schoolroom and tedious tutors.

But it was not the merchant service that Wilkes had set his heart on joining. Nothing less than a warrant as a midshipman[4] in the U.S. Navy would do. His father, a banker and no adventurer (except with capital), with financial interests in shipping and the China trade, had few illusions about the sailor's romantic life. James Fenimore Cooper, a family friend who had served as a midshipman, only reinforced them.

Charles Wilkes then showed his determination—a lifelong characteristic—and broke down his father's resistance. The Navy Department, on being approached by the banker about a midshipman's warrant for his son, suggested the son be shipped off in the merchant service for practical seagoing experience. With some sea miles behind him the Navy Department would look more favorably at his application. (This came as a surprise to Cooper. Wilkes, he had prophesied, not being of the right political party, would be refused outright.)

For a banker with shipping interests, the practicalities of finding a berth for his son presented few problems. In 1815, aged seventeen, the young Charles Wilkes, rated as ship's boy in the books, was sailing across the Atlantic to Le Havre in the cramped fo'c'sle of a packet boat. Stowed carefully in his sea chest was a sextant, an unusual item for a ship's boy. This, plus his bumptious conceit—or his "high idea of my consequence," as he later wrote—led to his being unmercifully bullyragged by the packet rat crew, having his cheeks daubed with tar, and becoming the butt of endless practical jokes to such an extent that he thought of jumping ship in France. (Not that he would have ended up in some seedy doss-house; he was met at Le Havre by his father's agent and then traveled to see relatives in Paris, where the talk was all about the return of the Bourbons after the Battle of Waterloo.)

Two years later, with one more voyage to France under his belt and the help of the French minister to Washington, he received his coveted midshipman's warrant. His first naval orders came on 26 January 1818. He was to report to Captain William Bainbridge of the two-decker USS *Independence,* lying at winter quarters in Boston, and serving as a school ship for some fifty midshipmen. The next six months were to be spent learning the strange customs, unwritten laws, and unspoken transgressions that a young man has to be aware of when serving in any military or naval service. By the summer he was aboard the USS *Guerriere* sailing to the Baltic, carrying diplomats with their families to Sweden and Russia.

By 1838 Wilkes could look back on twenty years of naval life, of which only a small proportion had been spent at sea. His seagoing experience consisted of the voyage to the Baltic and Mediterranean, a second voyage around Cape Horn to South America, and a third voyage to the Mediterranean. Only two other lieutenants in the U.S. Navy had less time at sea. Indeed some of the passed midshipmen had more sailing experience than their commander. But Wilkes had been chosen for his scientific and surveying capabilities rather than his seamanship. The years ashore on extended leave had not been wasted, and Wilkes had immersed himself in the intricacies of mathematics, pendulum experiments, magnetism, astronomy, and the triangulation method of coastal survey work with the Swiss-born head of the U.S. Coastal Survey, Ferdinand Hassler. In 1826 Wilkes had taken and passed the examination for promotion to lieutenant. The same year, in a very important move, he had married Jane Renwick,[5] sister of the Columbia College professor James Renwick, a man with influence in Washington.

In 1833, after some months working on a survey of Narragansett Bay, Wilkes had been appointed to head the Washington-based Depot of

Charts and Instruments, where his primary work consisted of rating and testing chronometers. He also established, at his own expense, an observatory with an English-made transit. In 1836 he had left for Europe to collect instruments and charts for the expedition, followed by the Georges Bank survey in the *Porpoise*.

So far nothing in this recital suggests any outstanding ability for the command of one of the largest sailing exploration expeditions ever mounted. His qualities as a seaman were virtually untested, and his scientific background, perhaps unusual in a navy that despised science, would have been found unremarkable in other navies.

What he did have was energy, determination, ruthlessness, ambition, and an even greater sense of his "consequence" than that of his youth. With these went a suspicious nature, almost to the point of paranoia, an unhealthy tendency to discount the efforts of others, and a petty martinet approach to discipline. More Bligh than Cook. But what mattered now was energy, determination, and ruthlessness.

Wilkes, with all those qualities working at full throttle, set about knocking the Deplorable Expedition into shape. Much had to be done if the expedition was to sail south in time for the looming 1838–39 Antarctic summer. Except for the storeship all the expedition's vessels had been declared useless. In their place came a new squadron, but all the vessels required modifications for their new duties, and the modifications had to carried out in short order. Wilkes's flagship was the 127-foot *Vincennes,* a sloop of war built in 1826 and the first U.S. naval ship to circumnavigate the world. Remarkably beamy for her length, she was considered fast and seaworthy. Seamen liked her. For the expedition another deck was added; it also added a modicum of extra room for the *Vincennes'*s complement of 190 men. Next came the smaller 118-foot *Peacock*, the ship launched for the aborted 1828 expedition. She had just returned from a cruise, needed repairs, and also had to have a second deck added. Next in size came the 109-foot storeship, the *Relief,* a handsome vessel for such a calling and one with snug accommodations for her seventy-five-man crew. Specially built for the expedition, she had been afloat for eight months and had grown a vast amount of weed and barnacles. Slipping was required. Wilkes's old command, the 88-foot brig *Porpoise,* with a crew of sixty-five crammed into her spartan quarters, had to have a poop cabin and forecastle added on her flush deck, additions that Wilkes hoped would not compromise her speed and seaworthiness. At surprisingly short notice, just two weeks before the expedition sailed, two New York pilot boats were added as tenders. Schooner-rigged, the seventy-three-foot *Sea Gull* and the seventy-foot *Flying Fish,* although their masts and rigs were shortened for ocean sailing, promised to provide exciting, if uncomfortable, sport for their young officers and seamen.

The selection of officers for the fleet had brought minor problems, which Poinsett had solved. Commanding the *Peacock* and second-in-command of the expedition was the amiable mutton chop–whiskered Lieutenant William Hudson. A seaman to his fingertips, but with no surveying experience, the forty-four-year-old Hudson had at first refused the appointment. Wilkes was below him on the sacred naval register and also had far less sea time. Poinsett suavely assured him that the expedition was civil, not military, and pointed out that such an expedition, mounted "to promote science, and extend the bounds of human knowledge, ought to command the services of all who can contribute to its success." Hudson capitulated. Plus, from Wilkes, came hints of promotions to captain for both of them.

The remaining officers, including the six naval surgeons, numbered over fifty. They were unmarried for the most part, in their twenties, eager to be off on the great adventure that under Wilkes was gaining momentum, and their names told of old, established American families and regional roots: Samuel Lee of Virginia, James Alden of Massachusetts, Henry Gansevoort of New York, Robert Pinkney of Maryland, James Blair of Washington. One who decided to resign from the expedition was Matthew Maury. Appointed astronomer to the expedition under Jones, Maury considered Wilkes an officer whose career had been spent mostly ashore and who was totally unfitted to command such a large enterprise. Maury had also locked horns with Wilkes over the locating of the missing instruments. It was obvious to the southerner that he and Wilkes were incompatible.

The close confines of shipboard life are an inevitable breeder of cliques and discord. Particularly aboard the *Vincennes,* the various factions were soon collecting into their groups: southerners and northerners (seven officers were to join the Confederate navy); officers who still held allegiance to Jones rather than to Wilkes; officers with no surveying experience (the vast majority) and those with; officers with contempt for science and the civilian corps of "oyster and clam catchers," as Dickerson had called them, and those officers eager to help.

The eliminating of the civilian corps had proved a problem to Wilkes as he contemplated the remolding of the expedition to his own vision. He had banked on the naval medical corps to provide the expertise, but according to one naval surgeon he consulted, the corps was incapable of providing a single naturalist or botanist. The civilians, however, if they could not be eliminated, could be reduced in number from what Wilkes called "this ridiculously overgrown corps."

In a letter to Poinsett Wilkes outlined his plan to accomplish his ends. The plan, devious and shabby, left Poinsett's conscience unruffled. Wilkes suggested that those civilians selected for dismissal should have their "pay continue until the sailing of the Expedition, which will keep them quite quiet, as that has undoubtedly been the motive which has induced many of them to get employment in the expedition." They would of course not be told that they were superfluous until the expedition had sailed. Their letters of inquiry on their status, the fleets intended sailing date, etc., were to be dropped into a bureaucratic black hole.

Since most of these men had spent months preparing and giving advice to the expedition, had resigned from other employment, had spent their own money on the tools of their various callings and on outfitting themselves for the long voyage—many of them were feeling the financial pinch—Wilkes's sly plan and its support by the Navy Department seen against this background leaves an unpleasant stench in the nostrils.

On 26 July President Van Buren, Poinsett, and the newly appointed secretary of the navy, James Kirke Paulding, arrived at Norfolk to give the government's benediction to the expedition. Swinging to their anchors in Hampton Roads lay the *Relief, Peacock, Macedonian* (being used as a receiving ship for seamen), and *Vincennes*. The fleet was dressed overall with flags and bunting, yards were manned, cannon fired their twenty-one-gun salutes, the crews cheered, and sixty people sat down aboard the *Vincennes* for lunch and numberless toasts to the expedition's success. Wilkes eagerly awaited the announcement of his promotion to captain. But nothing was announced. For Wilkes this amounted to nothing short of betrayal, and he seethed with self-righteous anger. In a letter to Poinsett it all bubbled to the surface: "I hope you will never feel the mortification that I do . . . at being left now to grapple with things the Govt. might have put under my entire control by the one act of giving Mr. Hudson and myself temporary acting appts for this service and which I consider was fully pledged to us." Wilkes, however, had a contingency plan. At some future opportune date he would promote Hudson to captain and himself, as leader of the squadron, to captain and commodore.

Three weeks after Van Buren's visit all the vessels of the squadron were riding at anchor in Hampton Roads, collected together for the first time. From the black-hulled rakish schooners with their predatory grace to the matronly *Vincennes* with her apple cheek bows and domestic-looking stern and quarter windows hinting at comfort within, the reconstituted United States Exploring Expedition vessels, with their Stars and Stripes waving in the soft Virginia air, made an impressive and soul-stirring spectacle for both boat and shoreside Sunday sightseers.

Packed aboard the vessels were the usual casks of salt meat, flour, molasses, dried beans, whiskey, and rum. On a higher intellectual level the twenty-nine English chronometers ticked away in their padded mahogany boxes, and the remainder of the English, German, and French scientific instruments, gleaming bronze and brass works of craftsmanship, lay nestled in their boxes. In the flagship's library sat rows of books on Pacific exploration covering three centuries, among them Louis de Freycinet's narrative of the *Uranie*'s voyage, Dumont d'Urville's voyage in the *Astrolabe* with its atlas of charts, Vancouver's *A Voyage of Discovery* with its atlas and ten foldout charts, a memorandum from Admiral Krusenstern on the Pacific Ocean and South Seas with its listing of doubtful island sightings and positions, and, most important, the large collection of Russian, English, and French charts.

The heavy firepower of the two principal vessels, no longer warships in the proper sense, had been reduced. The flagship now carried only eight twenty-four-pound carronades compared with her usual twenty-four. The *Peacock* was reduced from her twenty thirty-two-pound carronades to eight twenty-four-pounders. The armory for small arms included breech-loading rifles, pistols, cutlass pistols, plus the more traditional cutlasses and swords. English-made twenty-four-pound Congreve rockets provided an exotic extra. Like the British in their African coast survey, the American could use these from their launching frames for survey work or for defense.

On a sultry and close August Saturday afternoon, with the ebb starting to make and a light southwest wind beginning to fill in, a signal gun boomed out, and the code flag to weigh anchor broke out from the *Vincennes*'s signal halyard. Bosuns' pipes shrilled, lieutenants shouted through trumpets, seamen's bare feet slapped the deck, capstan bars were swifted and manned, more seamen raced aloft, the capstan pawls began to click, the anchor hawses squirted water, sails dropped, sheets and guys were trimmed, yards swung around, and after all the years of indecision, incompetence, lobbying, and politics the United States Exploring Expedition stood out from Hampton Roads and into Chesapeake Bay. The five vessels, in line ahead, their sails barely filling as they slipped down on the ebb, ghosted past Old Point Comfort and its fort crowded with sightseers waving flags, scarves, and bonnets. A few hours later the wind had died, the flood was making, and the squadron came to anchor.

John Meiny, a master-at-arms, began his journal with a somber note on this "long and perilous voyage" and wrote that though the seaman's hearts were "brimming with patriotism," their faces "did not bear the impress of smiles and mirth." Before midnight the capstan pawls were clicking again, and by dawn the squadron was standing out of the bay. At nine o'clock on the Sunday morning of 19 August the Norfolk pilot was scrambling down into the pilot boat off Cape Henry with its tall lighthouse marking the southern entrance to Chesapeake Bay. Back in Norfolk he told a reporter from the *Norfolk Beacon* that he had never seen men more "bent on accomplishing all within their power for the honor and glory of the Navy and of the country, and full of life and zeal." The United States Exploring Expedition, the country's first and last under sail, had received its final benediction.

Four months previous to the expedition's sailing, the world's largest ship, the 212-foot-long SS *Great Western,* the creation of Isambard Kingdom Brunel, had docked at New York after a two-week passage, paddle wheels churning, smoke belching, from Bristol. Brunel's dream of steam-powered oceangoing vessels running on a regular schedule had arrived. Although it proved to have a lingering death, oceangoing sail was doomed.

NOTES
1. Washington Irving was offered the post but refused.
2. John Wilkes, with his lightning wit, delivered the ultimate stinging repartee to Lord Sandwich, rake, libertine, politician, gambler. "I am convinced, Mr. Wilkes," said Sandwich, "that you will die either of a pox or on the gallows." Wilkes's reply was instant. "That depends, my Lord, whether I embrace your mistress or your principles."
3. The first native-born saint of the United States, she was canonized in 1975.
4. Midshipmen, according to one American foremasthand, were "usually the progeny of naval captains and members of naval bureaus, of United States senators, of members and ex-members of congress, and of other great men. . . . The consequence of this is that midshipmen commonly look upon themselves as being somebody. . . . They are at sea something near what constables are on land—the summoners, reporters and informers, while their superiors may be styled the executioners of the law. Though in general they are looked upon with contempt by the men, yet the laws protect them from insult." After five years' service and passing an examination these creatures became passed midshipmen.
5. Jane Renwick's mother was born Jean Jeffrey of Lochmaben in Scotland. Robert Burns's roving eye lighted upon the pretty fourteen-year-old girl in 1788 and was so bowled over by "fair Jeanie's face" that he wrote verse about her.

Chapter 9

Hurrah! for the Exploring Expedition

ICE-BLINK. A streak or stratum of lucid whiteness which appears over the ice in that part of the atmosphere adjoining the horizon, and proceeds from an extensive aggregation of ice reflecting the rays of light into the circumambient air.

IMPOSSIBLE. A hateful word, generally supplanted among good seamen by "we'll try." A thing which is impossible in law, is pronounced to be all one with a thing impossible in nature.

Admiral W. H. Smyth, *The Sailor's Word-Book,* 1867

T WAS PERHAPS just as well for stomachs that had been ashore for far too long that the first day at sea for the men of the United States Exploring Expedition was one of light winds and smooth seas. It was also a Sunday. At six bells in the forenoon watch—11:00 A.M.—the close to five hundred men of the expedition mustered aboard their vessels for divine service. Aboard the *Vincennes,* leading the fleet strung out in line ahead formation, Chaplain Jarred Elliott, with the flag-draped capstan as his lectern and standing on a grating raised by shot boxes, addressed the blank-faced officers who sat to starboard and the equally blank-faced men who stood to port, swaying to the gentle movement of the deck.

Behind the blank faces lurked various emotions. Wilkes felt an intense feeling of responsibility that he compared with "that of one doomed to destruction." Passed Midshipman William Reynolds, four months short of his twenty-third birthday, would have been shocked at Wilkes's disquiet. This engaging young man—eager, enthusiastic, intensely patriotic—in his private journal and letters to his sister opens up a perspective to the expedition totally missing from Wilkes's official *Narrative.*

Reynolds, at the voyage's beginning, admired Wilkes with a touching fervor. By the voyage's end he had come to hate and despise his commander. Wilkes, according to Reynolds, merited "hanging, only that he deserved impaling, long ago." But on this first Sunday, in the moving shadows cast by sails curved to the warm breeze, listening to the creak of rigging and the raised voice of the chaplain, Reynolds felt completely "wedded to the Expedition and its fate, sink or swim." Also, below was a most superior cabin, which he shared with an old friend, Passed Midshipman William May. A cabin where blue damask-covered couches served for bunks at night and white and crimson curtains hung at the bulkheads. A cabin that sported a handsome bureau and mirror and an elegant white, green, and gilt washstand. A cabin where plated candlesticks gleamed like silver, where a Brussels carpet and soft mats hid the deck. A cabin where the bulkheads were decorated with "Bowie knives, pistols, cutlasses etc," just to give "the man of war finish to the whole." A cabin, a stateroom in fact, far better than any he could have met with in the normal course of duty. "Hurrah! for the Exploring Expedition," as he wrote to his sister, perfectly summed up his feelings in August 1838.

A young seaman living in far less luxury was a mizzen-top man by the name of Charles Erskine. His mess of twelve men had a sheet of canvas that formed a tablecloth when spread on the deck. Food was dished out from a tin pail and two brass-hooped wooden kids. Each man had a tin pot, plate, and spoon. Erskine had sailed with Wilkes aboard the *Porpoise* and nursed a deep hatred for his pockmarked commander.

At Boston, after the Georges Bank survey, Erskine had been ordered to collect the *Porpoise*'s mail from the navy agent, mail that he had stowed away in his tarpaulin hat. On the way back to the brig the hat had been knocked off into the water, and the letters soaked. Wilkes was furious and had Erskine seized to the breech of a sixty-two-pound Paxon gun—"the gunner's daughter"—and whipped with a rope colt.[1] Erskine's only thought, sailing once more with "his worst enemy," was revenge.

The Sunday scene aboard the *Peacock* mirrored that of the *Vincennes,* but with Hudson taking the service. The thirty-eight-year-old Titian Ramsay Peale, one of the civilian corps, thought that Hudson read the service and prayers in a most impressive manner. Six weeks later Peale was complaining of Hudson's lengthy sermons. These were homilies intended for a seated congregation, not for unfortunate recipients who had to stand and balance themselves against the *Peacock*'s heaving deck. (On one memorable Sunday, a day of vile weather, men were flung and washed against the bulwarks.)

Before sailing, Peale had written a farewell letter to his two young daughters describing his accommodation:

The little stateroom in which I live is just about as large as your mother's bedstead; in it I have a little bed over and under which is packed clothes, furs, guns, Books and boxes without number, all of which have to be tied to keep them from rolling and tumbling about, and kept off the floor as it is sometimes covered with water. I eat with the Lieutenants and Surgeons in the *Ward room* down underneath the surface of the sea, where we have to have candles burning in the day time, the water we drink is kept in barrels and Iron tanks, it is very warm and now smells very bad, but as we do not come on board ship to be comfortable we content ourselves with anything we can get.

After two weeks at sea Peale came to the sorry conclusion that the expedition's vessels were totally unfit for their service. The scientific corps's cabins were wet and dark, places where no drawings or specimens could be made or prepared. The *Relief,* Peale concluded, was the only vessel in the squadron fit for the expedition (at least from the point of view) of the "scientifics", but she had the disadvantage of being a miserably poor sailer.

The civilian scientific corps had been pared away to nine men, about half the size of the one envisioned by Jeremiah Reynolds. Included in those dismissed from the expedition were Reynolds and James Eights. The naval ax, hefted by Wilkes and guided in part by Peale and other Philadelphian cronies of Dickerson and Poinsett, had chopped off the two men familiar with the Antarctic.

Peale's fellow "scientifics" (including two artists) were spread among three vessels. Aboard the *Vincennes* berthed Charles Pickering (naturalist), Joseph Couthouy (conchologist), William Brackenridge (assistant botanist), Alfred Agate (artist). Sailing aboard the *Peacock* were Peale (naturalist), James Dwight Dana (geologist), Horatio Hale (philologist). The slow-moving but comfortable *Relief* had William Rich (botanist) and Joseph Drayton (artist). Drayton, Peale, and Pickering were the corps's elder statesmen with Hale, a twenty-one-year-old Harvard graduate, the youngster. Hale had, like Reynolds and Eights, been listed for dismissal. But vigorous lobbying by influential friends and, more to the point, his mother, Sarah Hale (editor of the influential *Ladies' Magazine* and *Godey's Lady's Book* and author of "Mary Had a Little Lamb"), had won the day. Poinsett had capitulated and reinstated Hale among the chosen.

The civilians, unused to naval ways, unsure how to deal with men over whom they held no authority, found themselves in a difficult position. Peale understood their anomalous standing in the authoritarian naval hierarchy. He thought the government should have assigned a nominal rank to the civilians. It was of course an idea that would have had short shrift with the navy. Only one civilian, the twenty-five-year-old Dana, was familiar with the arcane rituals of a man-of-war. After his graduation from Yale he had spent a year in the Mediterranean aboard the USS *Delaware* and the USS *United States* attempting to drum the rudiments of mathematics and navigation into the skulls of young midshipmen.

The other civilian familiar with the sea was the thirty-year-old Joseph Couthouy. A Boston merchant, master in the merchant marine, and passionate shell collector, he had been placed in the civilian corps by President

Jackson. The story ran that the exuberant, heavily bearded Couthouy had met with Jackson and won him over—after being told that all the expedition's appointments had been filled—by exclaiming: "Well, General, I'll be hanged if I don't go, even if I have to go before the mast." Pure animosity, however, was the only feeling between the extrovert, cheerful Couthouy and the secretive, paranoid Wilkes. The festering relationship was destined to come to a head in the Pacific. But on this first leg across the Atlantic, Couthouy, the merchant marine captain, could only stare in wonder as Wilkes, acting the petty martinet, had the two schooners range alongside the *Vincennes* with their crews in rank, toeing the line of a deck seam, balancing themselves to the heave of the sea, while the squadron's commander inspected them through his spyglass and shouted out the deficiencies in their appearance across the narrow band of sea.

Six months after sailing out of from Chesapeake Bay and into the Atlantic, the squadron was anchored in Orange Harbor, Tierra del Fuego, a safe and protected anchorage some forty nautical miles northwest of Cape Horn. This particular anchorage had been chosen as the springboard into the Antarctic from the sailing directions given by Captain Philip Parker King. The Royal Navy surveying officer had spent five years, 1826 to 1830, with HMS *Adventure* and HMS *Beagle* surveying the South American coast and the dreadful maze of waterways that splits Tierra del Fuego into a seaman's nightmare. (This was the same King who in 1803 had been eating at the dinner table when Matthew Flinders, weather-beaten and near crackling in salt-encrusted clothes after his open boat voyage from Wreck Reef, had walked in and startled Philip's father, the governor of New South Wales, and his family at dinner.)

Little has changed at Orange Harbor since the American squadron swung to their anchors dug deep in sand and hard mud. The fierce winds—the williwaws—still sweep down from the bare-boned mountains of the Hardy Peninsula to bend the stunted trees—Winter's bark and false beech for the most part—that form an almost impenetrable scrub on the lower slopes. Kelp, the seaweed underwater forest, undulates in the slight swell. Mussels and limpets cover the rocks close to shore. Commerson's dolphins, sporting their beautiful black and white livery, flash through the clear, cold waters. Predatory Dominican gulls wheel and soar in the air, cold yellow eyes looking for prey. White kelp geese patrol their shoreline territory while their chocolate brown mates, marvelously camouflaged, meld into the background. The only life missing in this primordial scene are the Yahgans, the nomadic canoe natives.

Here was a race, the southernmost people in the world, who lived in a vile climate where it rained or snowed on most days of the year, whose clothing consisted of a scrap of seal or otter skin that was draped around one shoulder and that was shifted according to wind direction. The Yahgans were a small—just over five feet tall—deep-chested people with long, strong arms but sticklike legs brought about by sitting in their canoes and shelters. The canoes were double-ended and made from beech bark sewn together with bone needles and animal sinew over a framework of split saplings. More saplings kept the hull apart. The canoes leaked abominably. A small fire, bedded on clay or sand and stones, smoldered amidships and was carefully tended. The women paddled the canoes, the children sat huddled near the fire, and the men, when not bailing, crouched in the bows, watching for animals to spear: otter, seals, and fish. Only the women were able to swim, and their job was to moor the canoe among the kelp and then swim to shore. Mussels, limpets, fish, crabs, birds, and seal meat formed their diet, and the shell mounds, covered in bright green vegetation, may be seen to this day. Except for a fungus growing on trees and small berries they ate no vegetables, not even the wild celery and scurvy grass that grew upon old shell mounds. Blubber from stranded whales was buried for use during the starvation times. Ashore they lived in hastily built shelters made from branches, twigs, and grass. Slings and snares were used to catch birds. They covered themselves in grease, paint, and ashes, their hair was long and matted, and they smelled, at least to Western nostrils, foul. The women, under the dictates of femininity, wore necklaces of polished shells and bones. Clubs and stones—the stones hurled with unerring accuracy—were the men's fighting weapons. In more domestic fights, usually over a woman, a man could break his rival's neck with a grasp and a twist. (Robert FitzRoy of the *Beagle* forbade his seamen from wrestling with the Yahgans; the puny-looking natives usually won.) They lived in fear, never venturing north, because of another tribe, the Ona. Here was a tribe, physically bigger and technologically more advanced—they had better bows and arrows—that hunted the guanaco, ate its meat, clothed themselves in its skins, and lived in guanaco skin tents. Luckily for the Yahgan they built no canoes.

Westerners were always amazed at the Yahgans' extraordinary ability not just in managing to exist in this desolate part of the world but also as mimics. Some forty years after the Americans had come to anchor in Orange Harbor, a French scientific expedition arrived in the bay to photograph the transit of Venus. The French, brought down by a gunboat, carried with them prefabricated wooden huts. Soon, much to the amazement of the natives, a scientific base arose upon the shores of the bay. E. Lucas Bridges, when a small boy, met the French scientists at work. In his *Uttermost Part of the Earth* he tells of walking to their hut across duckboards laid over the boggy ground. The Frenchmen, brainy fellows, wearing colored spectacles and beards of different shapes and hues, filled Bridge's "boyish mind with awe." He was also amused by one Yahgan who had sailed aboard American sealing vessels and spoke a vile mixture of Yahgan, English, and Spanish. Spicy French exclamations plus body language had now been added to the mix. When talking, he would spread his hands, palms upward and tilted toward his listener, and then shrug his shoulders with a Gallic gesture "a comedian might well have envied." This mimicry could be exasperating. A diligent philologist, eager to learn this new language, would point to his own nose, ear, or eye and, speaking slowly and clearly, pronounce the English or French word. The Fuegian, gazing fondly at this strange Westerner, would then point to his own nose, ear, or eye and repeat the word. Joseph Drayton, the earnest American artist, this time on a religious tack, once placed his hands together in prayer and pointed skyward. The Fuegians did the same, and Drayton contentedly assumed that they had some knowledge "of a supreme being."

Running neck and neck with their ability to mimic was their masterly pilfering. One such act had been the theft, in 1830, of one of the *Beagle's* whaleboats when out on survey. It led to some young Fuegians' being taken to England by FitzRoy in the evangelistic and fervent hope that they could be educated and returned to spread the Gospel. Three years later the Fuegians were back in their homeland, having sailed from England in the *Beagle*. FitzRoy was again in command, and the young Charles Darwin sailed as naturalist. It was a five-year circumnavigation that determined, as Darwin said, his whole future career. The natives of Tierra del Fuego, particularly the Yahgans, were to haunt his imagination for the rest of his life. The returning natives, the rather sullen York Minster, the fat little girl Fuegia Basket, and the dandy Jemmy Button with his carefully parted hair, gloves, and polished shoes, had lulled Darwin into a frame of mind that was severely jolted on his introduction to the canoe people in their habitat, a habitat where he thought "death and decay prevail" and whose inhabitants were the "most abject and miserable creatures I anywhere beheld." Darwin could only suppose that the Fuegians enjoyed "a sufficient share of happiness, of whatever kind it may be, to render life worth having." Nature, it was obvious, "has fitted the Fuegians to the climate and the productions of his miserable country." But—and it was a big *but*—how did it happen that the serious, learned, sherry-sipping dons of Cambridge, Darwin's friends, were of the same species?

Darwin's distaste, almost horror, when it comes to the Fuegians, had not been matched by Sir Francis Drake's chaplain, Francis Fletcher. On the passage of the *Golden Hind* through the Magellan Strait in 1578 the Englishmen had come across another tribe of Fuegian canoe natives, the Alacalufs, whom Fletcher thought "a comely and harmless people . . . gentle and familiar to strangers." But those long-dead Elizabethans had stronger stomachs and more robust views on life than the nineteenth-century middle class.

Comely, harmless, and *gentle* were not adjectives that sprang to Wilkes's mind. "It is impossible," he wrote, "to fancy any thing in human nature more filthy. They are an ill-shapen and ugly race." Wilkes, however, had more pressing problems to worry about.

The expedition had arrived late, dangerously late, at Orange Harbor. Any approach under sail to Antarctica has to be timed. The summer is short and unpredictable, and the end of February is not the best of times to be sailing south toward the continent. The American and British sealers who had stripped the South Shetlands and South Orkneys of their elephant and fur seals in the 1820s had been sailing north, not south, at that time of year. Wilkes's orders read that he was to explore, with the two schooners and the *Porpoise,* "the southern Antarctic, to the southward of Powell's Group [South Orkneys], and between it and Sandwich Land, following the track of Weddell as closely as practicable, and endeavouring to reach a high southern latitude." After reaching this high southern latitude (south of Weddell's would be most satisfactory), he was to return to Orange Harbor and then, with the whole squadron, "stretch towards . . . the Ne Plus Ultra of Cook . . . and return northward to Valparaiso, where a store-ship will meet you in the month of March, 1839." Weddell and Cook were to be toppled from their Antarctic plinths.

The orders, signed by Paulding, the secretary of the navy, bear the same unreality (if not the final reckoning in human suffering) as First World War staff officers' battle plans to their frontline soldiers, the same perverse ignorance of terrain, conditions, and timing. (Hugh Quigley, in his *Passchendaele and the Somme,* describes Lieutenant General Sir Launcelot Kiggell, Field Marshal Sir Douglas Haig's chief of staff, paying his first visit to the mud and horrors of the fighting zone: "As his staff car lurched through the swampland and neared the battleground he became more and more agitated. Finally he burst into tears and muttered, 'Good God, did we really send men to fight in that?' The man beside him, who had been through the campaign, replied tonelessly, 'It's worse further on up.' ")

But although Paulding had signed the instructions, Wilkes had written them. He had, he said, "organized the whole out of the wreck, if I may so call it, of the first attempts and had drawn up my instructions in full." The instructions directed the squadron to sail first to Rio de Janeiro and then to the mouth of the Río Negro, some five hundred miles south of Buenos Aires, to investigate trading possibilities, then to sail for Tierra del Fuego. Wilkes, however, had chosen to call first at Madeira and Pôrto Praia in the Cape Verde Islands—the clock ticking away and the austral summer slipping by—before calling at Rio.

On that first leg to Madeira Charles Erskine had seen an opportunity to take revenge for his flogging across the gunner's daughter. One midnight, having just relieved the lookout on the lee quarter, he had glanced down the open skylight and noticed Wilkes bent over the cabin table. On deck, close by, were heavy iron belaying pins in their racks. Erskine grabbed a pin, held it over the hated head, and waited for the ship's weather roll before dropping it. But then, true to a sentimental Victorian melodrama, "At that instant I saw, or fancied I saw, the upturned face of my mother." The mother won over the devil, and Erskine replaced the pin in its rack.

Another seaman, George Porter, a maintopman, had also come close to death. As he loosened the main topgallant sail, a buntline had caught him around the neck and thrown him over the yard. He was seen from the *Vincennes's* deck, hanging by the neck, swinging to and fro against the clear sky. Two men raced aloft and brought him down. With his livid face and protruding tongue they thought him dead. But Porter miraculously revived. His messmates, wrote Reynolds, said "he was not born to be hung, or he would not have missed so good a chance." Porter himself, in typical sailor fashion, was furious when his grog was stopped by the ship's surgeon just because he had come near to "Braking his Neck."

The passage to Tierra del Fuego had proved to be a shakedown cruise for both men and ships. The heavily laden *Relief,* ploutering through the Atlantic swells with much fuss and bother, had been detached from the squadron and ordered to make her own way to Rio de Janeiro. The *Peacock's* refitting by the navy yard had been found shoddy and slapdash. Beneath the fresh paint lurked rot, poor caulking, rotten and rusty pumps, defective spars and masts (one split in the mizzenmast had been packed with rope yarn and putty and then painted over). In a seaway the berth deck was awash with water. Even Hudson's cabin was flooded—knee deep, according to the rueful Hudson—with his "carpet floated up, and myself almost floated out." The *Peacock,* he wrote, "has been fitted out, (so far as the navy-yard was concerned,) with less regard to safety and convenience, than any vessel I have ever had anything to do with."

The cold-weather clothing issued to the men (fishermen's boots, guernsey frocks and drawers, kersey trousers, pea jackets, mackinaw blankets, and buckskin mitts) was found to be poor stuff. Surgeon Silas Holmes thought the boots had been made on the "sieve principle." Peale blamed the dreadful quality on the "swindling propensities of the contractors."

The six-month shakedown had also given the officers and men time to assess their commander, and a growing unease was seeping through the squadron. Wilkes's capricious and arbitrary disciplinary methods were bubbling to the surface. He was getting the reputation for punishing first and asking questions after.

At Rio he had demonstrated a maturing ability to offend and annoy; the *American Dictionary of Biography* circumspectly calls it his "limitations of temperament." One of the men to receive a flash of this temperament was Commodore John Nicholson of the USS *Independence,* the tubby bachelor commander of the American Brazil Squadron and wooer of Rio's society ladies. Their rather acrimonious dealings came to a head when

Wilkes lectured Nicholson for not addressing him as Captain Wilkes, a title that Wilkes thought his due. The thunderstruck Nicholson ironically wished Wilkes success on any future promotion. Another side of the temperament had been shown in the affair of Sugar Loaf Mountain. Lieutenant George Emmons of the *Peacock* and Lieutenant Joseph Underwood of the *Relief*, friends from previous voyages, having heard that no American, only Englishmen, had climbed the mountain that overlooked Rio's harbor, set off to even the balance. Arriving at the summit, scraped and breathless, they found a glass bottle containing a message and the names of some Royal Navy officers who had scrambled to the top the previous May. The two Americans added their names, drank a toast from their wine flasks to the success of the exploring expedition, and then plunged off downward, gathering plants on their way for the botanists, feeling rather proud of themselves at this little jaunt and hoping they would earn "the silent approbation of the Commander of the Expedition." They were proved wrong. Wilkes heard of their outing and was annoyed. A curt letter soon arrived for Hudson:

Sir
      I learn with surprise & regret that an officer of your ship made an excursion to an important height in this vicinity without obtaining the necessary instruments for its correct admeasurement; as it results only in the idle and boastful saying that its summit has been reached, instead of an excursion which might have been useful to the Expedition.
      I am Sir
      Very Respectfully
      Your most Obt Servant
      Chas Wilkes

Wilkes had suspected that Hudson was far too easygoing with his officers. This excursion was proof.
      Another incident at Rio *had* met with Wilkes's approval. This was the affair of the singing competition. Anchored in the harbor was HMS *Thunderer*, mounting ninety guns and carrying a crew of more than a thousand men. Every night the crew sang a medley of songs and, the Americans having arrived in the harbor, wound up their evening's entertainment with the first or last part of "The Chesapeake and Shannon." The sound of that song from a thousand throats echoing across the waters, telling as it did, of an American defeat in the War of 1812, riled the Americans to stage their own riposte. Fifty men from the *Vincennes* rehearsed "The Parliaments of England," a song listing American victories over the Royal Navy. The Thunderers having rounded off their evening's entertainment with the usual irritating song, the Americans burst into *theirs*. A moment's silence filled the harbor after the final lines had been bellowed out. Then the

Americans heard, according to Erskine, "the call of the boatswain followed by his mates, calling all hands to cheer ship, and then we were given three times three, from the one thousand voices on board the ninety-gun ship."

It was a competition from which both sides had retired with honors. Not so pleasing was the loss of 125 gallons of whiskey from one of the flagship's casks, an infestation of cockroaches and rats aboard all vessels, and finding most of the bread taken off the *Relief* full of worms and weevils. The lumbering storeship had taken one hundred days to reach Rio—she had arrived three days after the squadron—which her officers cheerfully admitted must have been a record for slowness. (Wilkes blamed Long for not finding the trade winds. He then went to the time and trouble in his *Narrative* to list the fastest and slowest passages from the United States to Rio. The shortest was twenty-nine days and longest, until the *Relief*'s, ninety days.) The Reliefs were given very little time ashore. Wilkes ordered them to sail for Tierra del Fuego three weeks before the squadron's departure.

The squadron had spent a lengthy time at Rio—almost seven weeks. Some of the time had been spent working on the *Peacock,* but she had been ready by 16 December and had then been ordered to spend Christmas at sea, with the two schooners, to perform a faintly unnecessary survey at Cape Frio, some seventy miles east of Rio. The squadron, at last, had sailed from Rio on 6 January 1839, sailed from a harbor where, according to Wilkes, "there is no difficulty in beating out. . . ." Reynolds's journal tells a different story. Both the *Vincennes* and the *Peacock* managed to fall aboard an anchored brig. "We were much mortified," wrote Reynolds, "because the thing looked lubberly and right in the very face of every body, among all the men of war. It was the first mishap of that kind that I ever witnessed occur to an American man of war."

The sail down the coast to the Río Negro had taken nearly three weeks. And the nine days spent there could only be described—even by the most enthusiastic members of the expedition—as unproductive. Only the wandering course of the river's mouth through its treacherous sandbanks had changed in the five years since Charles Darwin had landed there from the *Beagle.* FitzRoy had learned the virtual impossibility of surveying this coast in the deep-draft *Beagle.* So he had hired two small sealing schooners from a Mr. Harris, an English trader. The schooners were rancid with oil and disgustingly dirty, but Fitzroy's men soon had them cleaned and dapper. Aboard the fifteen-ton *Paz* went Lieutenant John Wickham with Harris as pilot, and aboard the nine-ton *Liebre* (she was a frigate's barge with a deck added) went Assistant Surveyor John Stokes[2] with a Mr. Roberts, another Englishman, as pilot. Roberts happened to be a very large man, and FitzRoy later expressed some concern to Wickham on his large bulk aboard a vessel that looked "no bigger than a coffin."

Wickham cheerfully assured Fitzroy that his worries were misplaced—even though Roberts had once broken the mast when going aloft as a lookout. He also made admirable movable ballast, and when they ran aground, he always jumped overboard and heaved the *Liebre* off. Darwin's concerns centered more on finding fossil bones to add to those he had found at Punta Alta, some 150 miles north of the Río Negro. His chapters in *The Voyage of the Beagle* on his travels between the Río Negro and Buenos Aires breathe a sense of delight and joy.

No such joy invests any of the journals from the exploring expedition on its brief stay at the Río Negro. A telling point is that no seamen deserted. The Río Negro and its settlement of El Carmen, with its rows of mud and brick huts, its one near empty, dusty store, its ramshackle fort, its unpaid government officials, its listless natives and violent gauchos, had the air of having been deposited, a rotting pieceof flotsam, on the river's shore by the tide of Spanish colonialism. Such a place held few charms.

Only the schooners had managed to navigate the bar across the Río Negro's mouth. Both, in the process, struck upon the shifting sands, the *Sea Gull* being pounded so fiercely and for so long that Peale thought the masts would go by the board. The remainder of the squadron had anchored in the exposed and uncomfortable roadstead.

The days at the Río Negro had proved wasted. Little, except acrimony between Wilkes and some of his officers and the scientifics and officers, had been achieved. The squadron had narrowly avoided being caught on a lee shore when a gale sprang up from the east. The ships had been forced to slip their cables and barely weathered the breakers before hauling offshore until the wind eased and they could return to retrieve their anchors. The *Peacock* never found hers. Reynolds hoped that he would never see the Río Negro ever again. Wilkes felt only relief at leaving such a dangerous anchorage.

Why, pondered the squadron's officers and men, were they anchored at Orange Harbor? The expedition's first six months had been carried out in an annoying veil of secrecy. No one, not even Hudson, had known their first port of call when sailing from the Chesapeake Bay. The same from Madeira, Rio de Janeiro, the Río Negro. Reynolds had heard about Orange Harbor only with the *Vincennes* bucketing through the Le Maire Strait, four days out from the anchorage. In a letter to his sister he groused at Wilkes's excessive, almost paranoid secrecy, a secrecy that extended to their letters home, in which they had been ordered not to reveal "even *where we have been.*" Reynolds begged his sister not to show his letters to anyone; he feared it could lead to trouble and disgrace.

As for Orange Harbor, Reynolds thought it a mere stopping place for wood and water. Then they would be off to yet another unknown destination. "Just as if," he wrote, "some terrible enemy was lying in wait to destroy us." All very rum. But Reynolds was soon put right. After the *Vincennes* had come to anchor, Wilkes went into overdrive and and began shifting his officers around the fleet in a frenetic game of nautical chess. Wilkes's twitching nose smelled cabals and sedition among his officers, particularly among those appointed by Thomas ap Catesby Jones. Eleven officers were moved in this unsettling game.

For the next few days Orange Harbor, surrounded by its snow-covered peaks, was a hive of activity. The *Relief* disgorged ten months' provisions into the *Peacock*, the *Porpoise*, and the two schooners; all vessels were wooded and watered; the civilian corps collected plants and shells, shot birds, chipped at rocks; the seamen kitted out the Yahgans with old clothing, gave them strips of red flannel (much prized by the natives and usually wound around the head) and swore at them for stealing; flags were hoisted on 22 February and the seamen drank a hasty tot of grog to George Washington. Chaplain Elliott's text for his Sunday sermon, two days later, came from Daniel, Chapter 5—Belshazzar's feast with its bibulous princes, wives, and concubines—with the chaplain giving a warning on the "sin and danger of intemperate revelry," while the listening men, poker-faced, gazed across the bleak waters to the thin fires of the Yahgans. The same day Wilkes signed his orders for the ships' commanders.

The two-pronged attack on the Antarctic would start in less than a week. The Weddell objective would be taken by the *Porpoise* (commanded by Wilkes) and the *Sea Gull* (commanded by Lieutenant Robert Johnson, late of the *Vincennes*). Weddell's record south lay more than fifteen hundred nautical miles away, which had been reached on 20 February 1823. But on the basis of his years of Antarctic experience, Weddell had turned north, fearing the lateness of the season and being trapped by ice.

The *Peacock* (commanded by Hudson) and the *Flying Fish* (commanded by Lieutenant William Walker, late of the *Peacock*) would go for Cook's "Ne Plus Ultra," also more than fifteen hundred nautical miles away. (One has the feeling that Elliott would have been better employed using Daniel, Chapter 6 as his text: the delivery of Daniel from the lions' den resulting from his faith in God.)

The *Vincennes* would stay anchored in the harbor, and the crew would busy themselves with fishing, dredging, taking astronomical observations, and noting tides. A launch, provisioned for twenty days and with a crew of ten men and two officers, would be sent off to survey some nearby islands.

Wilkes ordered the *Relief*, the squadron's sailing disaster with not one discernible good seagoing quality except the ability to float, into the tortuous maze of Tierra del Fuego's channels, channels that the British had surveyed with whaleboats. Long was to take the storeship into the channels at Brecknock Passage some 170 miles west of Cape Horn. He was then to take the Cockburn Channel and Magdalene Sound into the Magellan Strait. Once in the strait the *Relief* would sail east and make a clockwise circuit around Tierra del Fuego back to Orange Harbor. The "scientific gentlemen" would sail with Long. Wilkes recommended King's charts and sailing directions to Long's "attentive examination." King's comments, read today, on the coastline into which Wilkes had blithely ordered the *Relief* are not encouraging: "No vessel out to entangle herself in these labyrinths. . . ." Darwin, having seen the seas exploding in great gouts of foaming white among the shoals and rocks, thought it a coast "to make a landsman dream for a week about shipwrecks, peril, and death."

By the evening of 26 February Orange Harbor was empty except for the *Vincennes*. With her topmasts sent down, the ship eerily quiet after the noise and bustle of the squadron's departure, her reduced crew of officers and men wandering the decks, she felt like a regiment taking its ease far from the front lines.

The *Porpoise* and the *Sea Gull* had sailed that morning, slipping slowly out from the anchorage with a light northerly breeze and the cheers of the squadron echoing around the bay. They were soon followed by the *Peacock* and the *Flying Fish*. The *Relief*, with all the scientists except for Couthouy and Peale, sailed the following day. Couthouy had elected to stay with the *Vincennes*, and Peale with the *Peacock*.

The next day, clear of Cape Horn and heading south, the *Porpoise* spotted a sail. It proved to be a whaleship, the *America*, thirty-five days out from New Zealand and homeward bound for New York with thirty-eight hundred barrels of oil. Wilkes handed over hastily written letters to the whaling skipper and—the white-gloved naval officer coming to the fore—thought he had never seen "a more uncombed and dirty set of mariners" than these whalemen, "the ravages of scurvy" being the only possible result for all this squalor.

An air of inevitable futility, like that of so many western front offensives, hangs over the expedition's first Antarctic attempt: the crossing of the no-man's-land of the Southern Ocean; the same discomforts and terror; the same meeting with an impregnable defense; the same collapse into ruin of all the detailed orders.

Two days out, with the sea temperature down to 32°F and the two vessels followed by albatrosses, Cape pigeons, and giant petrels, Wilkes decided to adopt a cautious approach to the South Shetlands and hove to during the hours of darkness. These were iceberg waters. The two vessels were now below the Convergence, the point where the comparatively warm waters of the subAntarctic meet the cold Antarctic waters. They were now, as defined by the *Antarctic Pilot*, in the Antarctic. On 1 March, in the early-morning light and with frequent snow flurries sweeping around them, they sighted their first icebergs, and at noon they made their landfall at King George Island in the South Shetlands.

The South Shetland Islands lie some sixty miles off the Antarctic Peninsula's tip. During the early 1820s, on the islands' rocky beaches, thousands of American and British sealers had slaughtered elephant seals and fur seals close to the point of extermination. Only the rare and hopeful sealer now visited the islands, the last one being an American schooner for the 1836–37 summer. The 1837–38 season had seen Dumont d'Urville with the *Astrolabe* and the *Zélée* make their attempt on Weddell's farthest south. Now here was Wilkes, a year later, following in the Frenchmen's wake on the same quest. D'Urville had retreated after two months fighting the ice. Wilkes, arriving later in the season, was to retreat after four days.

The day after sighting King George Island the brig and schooner, cloaked in mist and fog, were creeping across the Bransfield Strait, which separates the South Shetlands from the Antarctic Peninsula. They hove to at night, fearful of running into icebergs. The next day, 3 March, they raised the mountains at the peninsula's tip. The mist and fog cleared, and they were rewarded with the sight of sea crowded with icebergs that sported every conceivable architectural shape and ranged in color, not only in the expected white but from emerald green to opal. Cape pigeons flirted in the air currents off the sails; albatrosses wheeled and soared in their wake; penguins burst out of the water like rockets and made their harsh croaking calls. But Antarctica's enchantment lasted only a few hours. Ahead lay solid pack ice and icebergs. Fog and mist blew in on a wind that by the next day was blowing a gale. The decks turned into ice-covered skating rinks; the standing and running rigging became encased in such a thickness of snow and ice that the sheets, guys, and braces barely moved through the blocks. Matters were not helped by the men's shoddy clothing and, more worrying to Wilkes, signs of scurvy in the overcrowded *Porpoise*.

On 5 March Wilkes admitted defeat. He ordered the schooner to sail for Deception Island some sixty miles to the east in the Bransfield Strait. Once there she was to look for a maximum-minimum thermometer left by HMS *Chanticleer* on a scientific expedition in 1829.[3] The *Porpoise* with her dispirited crew headed north and came close to shipwreck on Elephant Island. The one thing that saved her was a sudden lifting of the fog that revealed the island's cliffs looming dead ahead. The crew were fifty miles out from their dead reckoning position.

As the *Porpoise* retreated north across the Drake Passage to Tierra del Fuego, the *Sea Gull*, after a grim and dreary beat to windward, came to anchor at Deception Island. A search failed to find the thermometer, but Johnson left a bottle containing his report tied to a flagstaff.[4] Gales kept them pinned fast in the anchorage, and the men entertained themselves by attacking the molting penguins with oars and boathooks and, to vary their diet, by making a stew of penguins and sheathbills, curious and faintly comic pigeonlike birds that scavenge among the penguin colonies. Before the schooner arrived back at Orange Harbor on 22 March, half the crew had fallen ill from eating their new dish.

On 30 March the *Porpoise*, her men tired and grim, came to anchor close to the *Vincennes*. They had been battered by gales, had lost a launch—but no lives—in the surf at Good Success Bay in the Le Maire Strait, and *pour encourager les autres*, Wilkes had suspended Lieutenant John Dale (another tainted Jones officer) from duty for not showing enough zeal in getting his launch off the beach through the wicked surf. In addition, Wilkes had nearly run the brig ashore a few miles from Orange Harbor.

Officers and men swapped sea stories. Those who had spent the few days below the Convergence told of icebergs, pack ice, the fogs, the biting cold, the sheer misery of handling frozen canvas, the frostbitten fingers. The Orange Harbor men spoke of the tremendous squalls that roared down from the mountains and one hurricane-force gale (the same one that had struck the *Porpoise* at Good Success Bay) during which the *Vincennes* had started dragging her anchors and which had kept the surveying launch pinned in a secure anchorage for eight days.

The launch's two officers, Lieutenant James Alden and the letter-writing Reynolds, had eased the hardships of living aboard a half-decked boat with ten seamen by taking along champagne and madeira. During the eight days tucked away in their secure anchorage they had feasted on limpet and mussel stew, fish, duck, and geese. They had also amused themselves with songs and listening to the seamen tell their yarns. "Pleasant times," Reynolds told his sister.

The *Sea Gull*, on her return, had been sent out to search for the survey party. She had found them and brought them aboard—Reynolds, after two weeks aboard the cramped launch with its light rigging and sails, thought everything so *big* aboard the schooner—and the launch was towed astern. A few days later, with the schooner hove to in a gale, the launch filled with water and was lost. There, as Reynolds ruefully told his sister, was the end of his first lieutenancy. No matter, being aboard the *Sea Gull* was a wonderful experience. Here was a glorious craft, easily handled with magical sea-keeping qualities, enough to give a "sailor's heart a charm, an ecstasy that cannot be told."

The other schooner, the *Flying Fish*, sailed into Orange Harbor on 11 April. Her crew had a tale to tell that eclipsed any of those told by a *Porpoise*, a *Sea Gull*, or a *Vincennes*.

Hudson, unlike the secretive Wilkes, as soon as the *Peacock* and her small consort were offshore, had told his officers the main objectives, one of which was to beat Cook's farthest south in longitude 105°W. Hudson had also given Walker four rendezvous positions, all on the way to Cook's "ne plus ultra," in case the vessels became separated by bad weather. Two

At the tiller of the *Flying Fish*
"It was almost impossible to stand on deck, without danger of being carried overboard;
and below, everything was afloat."   —J. C. Palmer
(Illustration from *Thulia: A Tale of the Antarctic*)

days out from Orange Harbor, in the inevitable gale, the separation happened. Walker then put the *Flying Fish* to a wet and tedious thrash to
windward in the teeth of westerly gales. So began days of utter misery as
each rendezvous position was reached with no sight of the *Peacock*. The
hull and deck of the lightly built pilot schooner leaked at every seam, reducing the spartan accommodation to a sodden and stinking slum; the
men wrapped their feet in blankets, so useless were their boots; waves
breached right across the schooner, reducing her boats to matchwood; one
breaking Southern Ocean monster swept away the port binnacle—the
schooner was tiller-steered and had two compasses—injured the helmsman
and lookout, swept away the companionway hatch, and half filled the
cabin with water. Sails were split, lowered, sewn, rehoisted, painful work
for men with ulcerated hands covered in saltwater boils. Three of the crew
were unable to work; one had a broken rib that his companions bound
with the sailor's plaster of paris, a woolding of canvas and pitch. Their thermometers broken, they hung up a tin mug filled with water and headed
south "till it froze." The first iceberg was seen on 13 March, and a week
later, booming south in a thick mist, they suddenly came across a solid line
of pack stretching across their course. The next two days had been spent
threading their way through pack ice and icebergs. At night they hove to,
and in the gray early-morning light, the mist wreathing through the frozen
white rigging, spars, and sails, they would find themselves surrounded by
the menacing pack ice and icebergs. The men on watch, their clothes covered with ice and hoarfrost, looked like ghosts.
    At Orange Harbor Walker's brother officers had congratulated him on
his new command and jokingly said that "she would at least make him an

honourable coffin." Looking at the pack ice and icebergs, Walker could only think they had been right. On two occasions all had looked lost. Once, on going below to "stick my toes in the stove," he was suddenly called on deck to find the schooner encircled by floes and icebergs. But like putting a horse to a high fence, he had put the *Flying Fish*, booming along at over six knots, at the narrow leads (he called them sutures) and drove her through, much to the anguish of the carpenter, who claimed the schooner would break apart. She survived. On the second occasion there had been less wind with the snow lying unmelted upon a sea that could be heard freezing with the ticking sound of a deathwatch beetle. Walker had wriggled the schooner through the hardening slush until she was clear. Their farthest south, "about 70°S., longitude 101°16′W.," was more than a degree short of Cook's. But on 24 March, running short of fuel and acknowledging the "general unfitness of the vessel, and want of preparations," Walker, much to the relief of his men, particularly the carpenter, had turned the schooner's head north. The next day they had sighted the *Peacock*.

Walker, going aboard the *Peacock,* found that their experiences had mirrored those aboard the schooner. The same gales, icebergs—the Peacocks had seen their first iceberg on 11 March, and it had caused enough excitement to bring the men from their breakfast—and pack ice. One experienced seaman, the captain of the maintop, had fallen from the yard and bounced off the rigging into the sea. There he had floated, feet up, until a running bowline was flung around his legs and he was hauled aboard. He had died, two days later, from internal injuries. The Peacocks had found the cold intense: 21°F air temperature and 28°F sea temperature. During the gales the ship became sheathed in ice. Hudson, in a grimly humorous mood, thought the "Antarctic Caulker" had made his ship watertight for the first time. Not all that watertight, however. Peale wrote that the gundeck was a constant slimy film of water, making his cabin almost untenable.

On Sundays, wrote Peale, Hudson looked after the spiritual life of his men by "reading us a long and salutary sermon, the men meanwhile sitting or laying on the deck to prevent their being thrown from side to side by the sundry heavy lurches of the ship." The temporal side was taken care of on a daily basis. Hudson had given much-appreciated orders that hot coffee be issued at the change of watch.

On 25 March the *Peacock* managed to take a noon sight—the first for six days—and found herself at 68°S. That evening she had fallen in with the *Flying Fish*. His own experience, and those told him by Walker, had persuaded Hudson—and his officers agreed—that the winter was upon them and any more time spent in the high latitudes would be foolish. Both vessels put their heads to the north and, under a pale moon, threaded their way through the floes into clear water. On 1 April, north of the

Convergence, Hudson had given dispatches to Walker and ordered him to Orange Harbor. The *Peacock* headed for Valparaiso.

All this (or most of it) was listened to by the squadron's officers and men. The only vessel now missing was the *Relief*. Wilkes had given Long an absolute maximum of fifty days for his surveying work in the channels and Magellan Strait. On April 20 an impatient Wilkes, with the *Vincennes* and the *Porpoise*, weighed anchor and sailed for Valparaiso, leaving behind the two schooners, the *Flying Fish*, commanded by Passed Midshipman Samuel Knox, and the *Sea Gull*, commanded by Passed Midshipman James Reid. They were to wait at Orange Harbor for the laggard storeship. She never appeared during the waiting period ordered by Wilkes. On 28 April the two schooners slipped out from Orange Harbor straight into vicious squalls that lengthened into a full-blown gale. Knox ran back for shelter at Orange Harbor and caught a glimpse through the scud of the *Sea Gull*, hove to, close to False Cape Horn.[5] It was the last ever seen of the schooner that had so enchanted Reynolds. Also of her two officers and eleven seamen.

Not until 1 May was the *Flying Fish* able to poke a cautious bowsprit out from Orange Harbor. Later that day she spoke to an American whale-ship whose skipper bellowed out his surprise at seeing a New York pilot boat so far off station. Knox, not wanting to be outdone by a mere blubber hunter, asked if he was in "want of a Cape pilot."

With that very satisfying riposte the schooner's sheets were hauled in, she put her shoulder to the Pacific swells, her tiller came alive, the wake fanned out astern, and Knox set her head for Valparaiso some two thousand miles away. The exploring expedition's first attempt at the Antarctic was over.

NOTES

1. Smyth, in his *Word-Book*, defines *colt* as "a short piece of rope with a large knot at one end, kept in the pocket for starting skulkers." Erskine was beaten with a knotted colt, three feet long and half an inch in diameter. American boatswains and their mates kept their colts coiled inside their hats.

2. Both Wickham and Stokes, during the years that the United States Exploring Expedition was at sea, ended up commanding the *Beagle* on the survey of the Australian coast started by Flinders. In the Gulf of Carpentaria Stokes found a tree with the word *Investigator* cut into the bark by Flinders some forty years previous. Stokes had *Beagle* cut into the other side of the tree. The tree was uprooted by a cyclone in in 1887, but part of the tree, with some letters of the ships' names, was retrieved and given to the Queensland Museum. Stokes went on to command HMS *Acheron*, a five-gun paddle-wheel sloop, between 1847 and 1851 in a survey of New Zealand's coastline. It was the first use of an auxiliary-powered survey vessel in Australasian waters.

3. HMS *Chanticleer* (the same class of gun brig as the *Beagle*), commanded by Cap-

tain Henry Foster, perhaps the Royal Navy's most brilliant scientific officer and mathematician—or any other navy's for that matter—was sent out by the Admiralty at the suggestion of the Royal Society on what became known as the Pendulum Voyage. By setting up measurement stations around the earth and measuring, by pendulums, the infinitesimal changes in the forces of gravity, the scientists could calculate the true shape of the earth. Deception Island was one of the chosen measurement points. In 1829 the *Chanticleer* spent two months at the island. The scientists carried out their recondite experiments, surveyed the island, ate more than seven thousand penguins, and left the maximum-minimum thermometer, and all were heartily glad when the brig sailed out from the caldera of this curious volcanic island. Cruise ships now sail into the caldera, anchor in Port Foster, and visit Pendulum Cove, where the tourists take a dip in the hot waters that seep out from the black shores of this volcanic island. They also walk between traffic cones to keep them off a small area that today's scientists have decided is a Site of Special Scientific Interest. The thirty-five-year-old Foster, two years after sailing from Deception Island and still working on the Pendulum Voyage, was tragically drowned in the Chagres River while surveying the Isthmus of Panama.

4. The *Chanticleer's* thermometer was found in 1842 by William Smyley of Newport, Rhode Island, an American sealer. On picking it up, he moved the maximum indicator but was more careful with the minimum. It registered –5°F. Smyley brought the thermometer back to the United States and in a letter to Wilkes, dated 15 August 1842, he wrote: "When I left the Isle of Deception the South Side of the Isle was all on fire there being 13 volcanoes and many other places where you might pick up the Sinders the water was boiling hot in many places in the harbour."

5. False Cape Horn lies some thirty miles northwest of Cape Horn. A vessel approaching Cape Horn from the west and mistaken in its latitude can be fooled into thinking it has rounded the true Cape, a mistake that almost guarantees shipwreck on the Woolaston Islands.

Chapter 10

South Pacific Prelude

JAMMED IN A CLINCH. The same as *hard up in a clinch* (which see).—*Jammed in a clinch like Jackson,* involved in difficulty of a secondary degree, as when Jackson, after feeding for a week in the bread-room, could not escape through the scuttle.

JIB AND STAYSAIL JACK. A designation of inexperienced officers, who are troublesome to the watch by constantly calling it unnecessarily to trim, make, or shorten sail.

Admiral W. H. Smyth, *The Sailor's Word-Book,* 1867

HE PEACOCK had been anchored in Valparaiso's exposed anchorage for close to two weeks on the day that the *Flying Fish* quit Orange Harbor. Except for a scare over a fire the *Peacock's* passage north had been uneventful. On smoke's being discovered the crew had been drummed to quarters, and the source quickly located: a bag of freshly roasted coffee smoldering in the hold. Plus, and it was a big plus, the men had had the rare entertainment—the alarm being raised at midnight—of seeing their commander dashing around in his underwear.

A week out from Valparaiso the gunports had been opened to air the ship for the first time in months. The warm air and sunshine, like a spring or fall day at home, according to Peale, brought a smile to all faces and a discarding of their heavy, stiff, salt-laden clothing. The slime that had grown on Peale's cabin deck could be scrubbed off.

Much to the *Peacocks's* surprise they had found the *Relief* anchored in Valparaiso's harbor. And Long told the following story to Hudson.

On sailing from Orange Harbor, he had decided to take an offshore course to avoid the strong east-flowing current that runs along the Fuegian shore. It had proved to be a mistake. It had taken the *Relief,* no oceangoing greyhound, three weeks to thump her way, against persistent westerly gales and the east-going current, the 170 miles to the entrance of the Brecknock Passage. On 18 March, close to the coast, with a gentle breeze flicking between south and east, and with the Reliefs anticipating what one officer called their haven of rest, all their dreams fell apart. Within hours the gentle breeze had developed into a storm (the same storm that caused the *Vincennes* to drag her anchors and kept the survey launch in its protected anchorage) of dreadful proportions. Dana described the wind howling through the rigging "with almost deafening violence." A few hours after the storm had struck, breakers were spotted under the bow, and looming through the murk of driving hail, sleet, scud, and foaming waves appeared the Tower Rocks, more than a hundred feet high, with spray and foam whipping across their tops. More breakers had appeared, and Long had put about the ungainly *Relief* in an attempt to struggle away from what appeared certain shipwreck. But they had made little headway with such a sea running, and their slide to the rocks continued. Long put the *Relief* about once more and crabbed toward a nearby anchorage, mentioned by King, under the lee of Noir Island.

The anchorage had been found, both bower anchors let go, and the chain cables run out to their bitter ends. Topgallant masts had been sent down, and the yards pointed into the howling storm-force winds. By morning the wind had lessened its eldritch screaming. By noon it had returned with more violence and shifted into the south, making the anchorage even more exposed, with the *Relief* snapping, jerking, and rolling at her anchor chains like a demented animal. A third anchor was dropped. During the night the three anchors had started to drag, and all on board had heard the terrifying rumble of anchor chains grinding across the bottom. Dana, giving little for their chances of survival and in a philosphical mood, thought "his the happiest lot who was soonest dead" and then committed himself "to the care of our Heavenly Father and retired to rest. It was a night, however, of broken slumber." The next morning they found one of the chains had parted. They dropped their fourth anchor. It did nothing. The slow rumbling continued into the next night. Just after midnight, with Long on the foreyard grasping his trumpet to shout orders, all the men on deck, their ship close to a reef, the bows had been hit by a massive wave that then swept across the deck, bowling men over like ninepins with the boatswain being carried from the fo'c'sle to the gangway. All the anchor chains had then snapped. The *Relief*, dragging her anchorless chains, had then cleared, within the proverbial biscuit toss, the point of Noir Island. Long had yelled his orders, the cables were slipped, scraps of sail appeared, and they headed offshore, having escaped certain death, away from this awful coast. The whole crew had nothing but praise for Long and his seamanship.

With all the anchors lost—except for a very small stream anchor—it was plainly impossible for Long to obey any of Wilkes's orders. But Valparaiso was mentioned in the orders as being the next port of call. Long, heaving a sigh of relief at their escape, scribbled a heartfelt "I hope I shall never be unmindful that 'A sweet little cherub sits up aloft / Who keeps a good look out for poor Jack.' " He set a course for Valparaiso, where the Royal Navy had come to their aid with HMS *Fly* giving them an anchor. This was the essence of the *Relief*'s story, suitably embellished, that circulated among the *Peacock*'s officers and crew.

The *Vincennes* arrived at Valparaiso three weeks after the *Peacock*, followed, a day later, by the *Porpoise*. Both vessels had had a rough and wet passage from Orange Harbor, Wilkes driving his ship unmercifully hard in order to get to port as dysentery was sweeping through the ship's company and scurvy had made an unwelcome appearance. Even Reynolds, the gloss long gone from his adoration of Wilkes, admired the way he drove their ship until "the poor craft's frame shook like an aspen leaf in the violent encounters with the Seas." At Valparaiso Wilkes heard about the *Relief* and the reasons for her nonappearance at Orange Harbor. Not from Long, however. Hudson had ordered her to Callao in Peru to collect more anchors and anchor chain, unavailable at Valparaiso. In addition, the seasonal northers were due to arrive, and these winds with the accompanying swell and sea could cause mayhem in the exposed anchorage. (In June 1822 eighteen vessels had been lost.)

What was available at Valparaiso was the expedition's mail. The supply ship *Mariposa*, with stores and letters, had arrived from the United States. Americans might beat the egalitarian drum in the presence of less enlightened Europeans, but the distribution of mail from the letter bags showed that some expedition members were more equal than others. All the officers, as Erskine noted, had letters from home when the letter bags were opened on the quarterdeck, but only a "dog-watch of the crew" received any, "all the rest of us being left out in the cold." For the letterless seaman, however, Valparaiso had other compensations to offer with its lowlife district: the Fore, Main and Mizzen Top, named after a row of hills. This was the place for grogshops and black-eyed women wearing the red *bayetas,* the mark of their trade. Here was where a sailor could drown his sorrows, have his pocket picked, or collect a dose of the clap or the pox with equal facility.

Reynolds became enchanted with the ladies belonging to Valparaiso's less seamy side, and in a rather undiplomatic letter to his sister he waxed lyrical on their charms: "Oh! their very walk has an indescribable grace; even the common class of females have a bewitching gate that our *belles* would give the world to possess."

By the end of June, except for the missing *Sea Gull,* the expedition's vessels were gathered together at the flea-plagued Peruvian port of Callao. The rat-plagued *Relief* was fumigated, producing three barrels chock-full of dead rodents. Here Wilkes displayed his fast-maturing abilities at alienating his officers, men, and scientific staff. Long was reprimanded for not returning to Orange Harbor, blamed for all the *Relief*'s problems since sailing from Norfolk, and also held responsible for the possible loss of the *Sea Gull*. So intemperate was Wilkes's language that Long requested a formal court-martial. Not enough time, replied Wilkes, who promptly packed off all the correspondence to Washington. The *Relief* and Long would be detached from the expedition, be sent to Hawaii and Sydney to drop off stores, and then sail for the United States via Cape Horn. The plan also enabled Wilkes to rid himself of the sick, the incompetent, and those troublesome officers who had failed to show their commander sufficient deference.

The seamen, in their usual way, caused problems by deserting and getting drunk at every possible opportunity. Whiskey was broached from casks being unloaded from the *Relief*, and whiskey, with brilliant ingenuity, was smuggled aboard in pumpkins floated down on the current. The culprits were flogged. The remaining officers were rotated around the squadron with such bewildering speed that Reynolds feared he would be shifted from his "elegant and comfortable room."

The expedition, now reduced to four vessels, sailed from Callao on 13 July. The Reliefs watched them sail with pleasure, one lieutenant scribbling into his journal a heartfelt "Thank God! They are off." Erskine, aboard the *Vincennes*, noted that all hands wished they were sailing with Long and the *Relief*.

Two days out from Callao the coach whip flying from the *Vincennes*'s masthead, indicating a lieutenant commanding, was lowered to be replaced by a broad blue pennant indicating the *Vincennes* a flagship and her commanding officer a captain. From the *Porpoise*'s deck, Lieutenant Robert Johnson, peering through his spyglass, could make out Wilkes on his quarterdeck sporting the epaulets of a captain. Johnson was too far away to see the added buttons. Wilkes, with his squadron headed out into the Pacific and with little chance of meeting with another U.S. Navy vessel, had promoted himself and Hudson to the highest rank in the U.S. Navy.

Thirty days and more than three thousand miles from Callao the expedition sighted, to great collective excitement, its first coral island, Clermont-Tonnerre (Reao) in the Tuamotu archipelago, a sprinkling of low-lying islands and reefs (Bougainville's "Dangerous Islands") that epitomized the fabled Pacific coral atoll islands. It was so low-lying that the Americans' first sighting was of the coconut and pandanus trees standing above the horizon like the masts of a fleet at anchor, followed by the strip of white beach with the surf creaming upon an outer reef. Within the white and green belt of beach and trees lay an impossibly blue and quiet lagoon. Reynolds, perched on the royal yard, was seduced by this view of the "tempting Edens of the South Pacific" and entranced by the "singular and picturesque loveliness of the scene."

Not so entranced was Peale. Wilkes, now in his surveying element, started a running survey of the island. But no boat was allocated to the civilian staff for a landing. An acerbic entry went into Peale's journal: "It is a sorry business that our government should have sent a Scientific Corps to collect information and make a 'survey' (in the present day this term includes all the Nat*l* Sciences) of the countries we may visit, when the officer under whose charge it has been placed should consider it quite unnecessary to appropriate a single boat out of the whole squadron for their use. . . ." This was to be a recurring refrain in Peale's journal. It reached a peak days later at the island of Raraka: "We have been close to this island all day, could see it abounded in Scientific riches, & boats were swinging idly in their davits, men were looking as to paradise, but no, a survey is made, *nothing more* is requisite, and time flies.

"WHAT WAS A SCIENTIFIC CORPS SENT FOR?"

The angry Peale considered the civilian corps at the mercy of a "petty tyrant" and that the English and French did their explorations, scientific and hydrographic, in a far better manner. (But then the English and French had been doing it for far longer; this was the first American attempt.)

A month was spent sailing through the Tuamotus. The officers and men soon became expert at the tedious details of running surveys along island shores and taking boats through the surf to make landings on the pink and white beaches. The Americans wore India rubber life vests, items that caused bewilderment to natives whose life centered on swimming.

The scientific staff fumed at Wilkes for the few paltry hours they were let loose onshore and with his orders that they always remain in sight of the boats and watch for the signal to return, with all the staff back on board by sunset. Pickering and Couthouy were slow on one occasion, and Wilkes threatened to keep all the civilians confined to their vessels. Peale, loathing Wilkes as he did, held Hudson in high esteem. The amiable *Peacock*'s commander, a Pickwick compared with Wilkes's Gradgrind, had once allowed three boats for the staff to make a landing, an episode that drew a censorious letter from Wilkes and a few lines in Peale's journal on this "literary curiosity coming from the commander of a Scientific expedition, and wholly unworthy of that branch of our government which allowed him to have the command."

The ebullient Couthouy, a man who would dive through the surf to make an approach to hesitant natives, a man with a zest for life and a passion for shells, became a special target for Wilkes. Couthouy's collection of shells offended him. The commander gave orders that "no specimens of coral, live shells, or anything else that may produce a bad smell, will be taken below the spar-deck, or into any of the rooms." He also told Couthouy that only one example of a shell or coral was allowed, and these were to be stored on deck. On Couthouy's pointing out that other expeditions had had no problem in the collection and storing of large and numerous specimens, Wilkes had replied that "he did not care a d——n for what had been done in previous expeditions, or consider himself in any way to be governed by it, and that he should take the responsibility of deciding all matters relative to our collection according to his own views." For Wilkes science came a poor second to survey. Also, the scientists were proving as touchy to handle as some of the natives on the inhabited islands. Benjamin Vanderford, a master mariner from Salem, the expedition's interpreter and pilot, a man of vast South Sea experience who had traded in sandalwood and bêche-de-mer, pronounced that any island with coconut palms indicated natives.

The reception given to the Americans on the inhabited islands varied from the outright hostile to the friendly. On one island the young philologist Hale sat under a coconut tree surrounded by girls teaching him the names of certain items; when he pronounced them correctly, they rewarded him with a hug. This might sound a pleasant way to learn vocabulary, but it had its drawbacks: The girls were coated in rancid and foul-smelling coconut oil, acting as a fly repellent. (Peale noticed the absence of flies on the uninhabited islands.) Three seamen, lured by the islands' attractions and unworried by rancid oil and flies, deserted. Other seamen found the women offering their bodies for three feet of calico or an ax. But the closer the expedition approached Tahiti, the stronger became the missionary influence.

On 10 September the *Vincennes,* piloted by the smiling native "English Jim," dressed in a white suit, black shoes, and a blue cap with a gold band, glided into Tahiti's Matavai Bay. Here was the fabled island of philosophers and sailors, pregnant with deep significance for both their callings. True to all the legends the *Vincennes* was welcomed by a fleet of canoes. But showing the changes since the days of legend, they were only soliciting business to wash the squadron's laundry.

Seventy-two years had passed since Wallis and the *Dolphin* had come to anchor, followed over the years by Bougainville, Cook, and Bligh. Forty-two years since the *Duff* had landed its load of evangelical artisan missionaries from the London Missionary Society. Forty-one years since Bishop and the *Nautilus* had carried off some of the disillusioned evangelicals to Sydney. Thirty-seven years since Bishop and Bass had arrived in the *Venus* on their pork collection voyage. Four years since Charles Darwin had arrived in the *Beagle* and scrambled three thousand feet up into the heights where the small ferns and coarse grass reminded him of the Welsh hills. Not so Welsh, a day later, had been a longer trek into the interior with Darwin's servant, two native guides, and a coil of rope. The guides had built shelters at night from bamboo stems roofed with banana leaves. They had taught Darwin to light a fire by rubbing together two pieces of the soft hibiscus wood and dined that night on beef, fish, banana, and arum tops wrapped in leaves and cooked between hot stones. They had drunk cool stream water from coconut shells. Darwin had also brought a flask of spirits and offered a tot to the guides. Before taking a sip, they would, as a propitiary gesture, put their fingers before their mouths and say the word *missionary*. Drinking spirits, including the making and drinking of the mouth- and mind-numbing native kava, had been forbidden by the missionaries.

Just one year before the arrival of the *Vincennes* the French frigate *Vénus*, commanded by Abel Dupetit-Thouars on a Pacific voyage to protect French whaleships, promote French trade, and help the proselytizing aims of French Roman Catholic priests, had anchored at Papeete in a show of gunboat diplomacy. A decade earlier Pope Pius, modeling himself on his fifteenth-century predecessor Pope Alexander, who had split the world into Spanish and Portuguese spheres of influence, split the Pacific into two with the *Mission d'Océanie* and designated two French orders as the frontline troops in the battle with the Protestant missionaries: the Société de Picpus in the eastern islands and the Société de Marie in the western.

In 1836 two French priests from the Picpus order had made their beachhead landing on Tahiti. George Pritchard, the gaunt English missionary and power behind the throne of the young Queen Pomare IV, had persuaded her to issue an expulsion order. The Protestant Pritchard was going to have no Romish priests and incense tainting the pure Tahitian air. The French were furious. Dupetit-Thouars's orders required him to obtain from "the Queen of the island full reparations for the insult France has sustained." Within hours of the *Vénus's* anchoring an ultimatum was on its way to the queen. She must write a letter of apology to King Louis Philippe in French and Polynesian and sign both texts as well as pay two thousand Spanish dollars as compensation for the insult. Also, the French flag had to be raised on a small island that lay opposite Papeete and the flag given a twenty-one-gun salute. Failure to comply within twenty-four hours would mean that he would be obliged to "commence hostilities against the States under your dominion and that such hostilities will continue by all ships of war that will successively visit these Islands until France has received satisfactory reparations."

Pritchard and other missionaries raised the money and organized the letter. The Tahitians had no gunpowder or French flag. Dupetit-Thouars provided both. French honor was satisfied. (A South Pacific comic opera, one may think, played out against a backdrop of breadfruit, banana, orange and coconut trees, red hibiscus, frangipani, tiare, and yellow jasmine flowers. But Dupetit-Thouars, a few years later, was to return with a French squadron and troops to declare Tahiti and the Society Islands a French possession. Pritchard was expelled, and Queen Pomare fled to a nearby island. Sporadic rebellion flared on the island for a number of years until it was finally snuffed out by the French. The islands had become pawns in the Oceania Game played by the Great Powers.)

Dumont d'Urville had been at the island at the same time as the *Vénus*. After his first bout with the Antarctic he had sailed, like Wilkes, to Chile and then into the South Pacific. He and Dupetit-Thouars had gone together to browbeat Queen Pomare. Poor Pomare. One has a sneaking sympathy for her. Manipulated by the Cromwellian Pritchard, threatened by autocratic French naval officers, she was shortly to be lectured (fortunately by letter; she happened to be pregnant) by the flinty-faced Wilkes on the treatment of American citizens and seamen. He also thought it an absolute necessity to provide a jail for deserters from the whaleships, plus a police force to watch over and "secure any offenders." So was born the Calabooza Beretanee, a lockup that came to hold, three years after Wilkes's suggestion, the whaleship deserter Herman Melville. (Now a must on every tourist's sightseeing visit.)

Wilkes's letter also contained a veiled threat: "The President will order vessels of war to visit these islands frequently, for the protection of American citizens and commerce." The commerce, with more than seventy American whaleships calling at the island annually, was considerable. Although a law, missionary-inspired, prohibited the sale of spirits, Hudson found his men getting drunk on gin priced at three dollars a jug. They were getting it from the American consul, S. R. Blackler, a rogue who had imported seventy cases for the use of the squadron. (Another enterprising Yankee whaler from New Bedford, Tobias Tobey, had once set up a "Floating Grog Shop" aboard his whaleship *Swift* and sold thirty barrels of whiskey for a profit of two thousand dollars.)

Although he thought the attractions of the Tahitian scenery and the fabled womenfolk overrated—the women's only attribute being their cheerfulness and the "soft sleepiness" about their eyes; otherwise he found them dumpy, parrot-toed, and prone to prattling—the generally censorious Wilkes approved of Tahiti. The missionaries, he concluded, were "fulfilling the laudable object for which they were sent." Moreover, even though the island was "proverbial for its licentiousness," the "vice, at any rate, does not stalk abroad in the open day, as it did in some places we had lately visited upon the American continent." Wilkes, warming to his theme on the missionaries' efforts to bring the blessings of civilization to the Tahitians, found one sad lack. Although they had done an admirable job of running the schools and turning the population into a literate society, stamping out infanticide and human sacrifice, they had made no attempts to introduce "the mechanic arts" or make improvements in agriculture. A cotton factory, alas, had failed on Mooréa (the neighboring island) because "the natives were not prepared to pass at once from habits of desultory exertion, to the regular and stated occupation of the mill." Wilkes, a product of Jacksonian America with its watchword of "Go ahead!" and

Protestant work ethic, thought that the spinning wheel, the hand loom, and the plow should have been introduced solely to serve as a "preparation for more continuous industry." These were sentiments echoed by Reynolds (for once agreeing with his commander), who had expected to see an island where factories flourished and the rest of the population tilled the land, an enlightened community of "sober, decent & religious people." The reality was something different. Over their sexual morals it was also best to draw a veil. But in a moment of insight Reynolds added a rider: "Who can judge one nation by another?"

The scientific staff, like Darwin, headed into the interior; the officers surveyed the harbors; the *Peacock*'s carpenters, blacksmiths, and seamen carried out extensive repairs on the *Flying Fish*'s mainmast and hull; and the seamen, in the early hours of the morning, snoring in their hammocks, would be woken by sweet-voiced girls serenading them from the beach. The girls would then swim out and beg to be taken aboard. Old Tahiti still lived on. But Wilkes had given strict orders regarding natives aboard the squadron's vessels. None was allowed on board before seven o'clock in the morning or, unless a white flag flew from the mizzenmast, and all had to be ashore half an hour before sunset.

It was inevitable, under these circumstances, that a handful of seamen would judge South Sea island life preferable to one in the Antarctic. Lured by the cheerfulness and the soft, sleepy eyes, they deserted. Just as inevitable, Wilkes offered a large reward of thirty dollars to the natives for every seaman rounded up—two were brought back slung on poles like carcasses—followed by thirty-six lashes for the deserters.

On 29 September, with a favorable southeast wind, the men of the *Vincennes* watched the peaks of Tahiti and Mooréa slip below the horizon. Ahead to the west lay more islands. By 7 October, after a hasty visit to Bellingshausen Island, they raised the low-lying Rose Island, the smallest and easternmost of the Samoan group. This was Rose de Freycinet's island, little more than an overgrown coral reef, but Rose had been proud of it. The Americans, after a landing, found it waterless and uninhabited except for vast numbers of breeding terns, frigate birds, boobies, and some inedible turtles.

Wilkes's instructions had expected him to reach the Samoan Islands by June, carry out a survey, and then sail for a Fiji Island survey before heading for Sydney, the springboard for the second Antarctic investigation. Such a plan was now laughable. The Fiji survey was patently impossible, and the Samoan was going to be rushed. A bare month, a month marked by rapidly deteriorating relations between Wilkes and the harried officers, civilians, and men, was spent in the Samoas.

For Reynolds it was the watershed in his feelings for Wilkes. In his personal journal and a long letter to his sister he poured out all his accumulated frustrations with a commander who had lost the respect of his officers and civilian staff. Wilkes, wrote Reynolds, had started the expedition holding the officers' admiration and devotion in the palms of his hands. He had thrown it all away by his wildly intransigent and unpredictable behavior. Reynolds now thought him a "malignant *villain*" and even questioned his sanity. The passion of Reynolds's outpouring could perhaps have been caused by two incidents. One was Wilkes's suspending Reynolds from duty and confining him to his sweltering cabin for six days, a punishment for appearing on deck improperly dressed. The other was Reynolds's transfer to the *Peacock*. Reynolds's waterproof jacket, worn by someone else while he was away an survey duty, had been found on deck. Although marked as owned by Reynolds, Lieutenant Overton Carr (a Wilkes sycophant) stowed it away in the ship's "lucky bag" to be auctioned off. It was the way of things that any of the crew's discarded clothing might find its way into the bag—but never the officers'. Reynolds protested. His transfer to the *Peacock* was virtually instantaneous. A stiff-faced William May, Reynolds's cabin mate, asked to be transferred with Reynolds. Wilkes obliged but sent him to the *Flying Fish.*

Reynolds's questioning of Wilkes's mental state was more than a wild accusation by a romantic-minded and disillusioned young man. Wilkes's conduct as a seaman, over the months, had been causing comment. His excitability and rudeness were cause enough for comment, but it was increasingly obvious to the officers and men that Wilkes under stress, when decisive orders and calmness were called for, showed neither. Two incidents loomed large in their memories, the first after a collision between the *Vincennes* and the *Porpoise*. Wilkes had rushed on deck, shouting the most inappropriate orders, until a lieutenant, taking over, had managed to sort out the whole sorry mess and disentangle the two vessels. Wilkes had followed this by insults bellowed through his speaking trumpet at the *Porpoise*'s watch officer, accusing him and all the watch of being asleep—a most serious accusation calling for a court-martial. (The fault in fact lay with the *Vincennes*'s watch officer, who seemed to have some confusion about port and starboard tack.) The second incident occurred when tacking out of Pago Pago in the Samoas. The *Vincennes* had missed stays, fallen back, and very narrowly escaped being wrecked on a reef. Wilkes in his *Narrative* says that he had "no very precise recollection" of the crisis until it had passed. Others did. Wilkes had buried his face in his hands, unable to speak, a broken reed as a commander. The wind had shifted, the Pago Pago pilot, calculating the odds, had given his orders, and the *Vincennes* had crept by the breakers marking the reef. Wilkes then refused to heave to in order to drop off the pilot until well out to sea. The pilot got his revenge. Once aboard his boat he had called up to Wilkes a sarcastic "You may fill away now, *Sir!* Fill away as soon as you like." Wilkes, as Reynolds noted, went incandescent with rage. Wilkes later suggested to Ringgold that if the pilot ever came aboard the *Porpoise,* he be given a good flogging. In short, a classic performance of the insecure, incompetent commander held up to public ridicule, his leadership found wanting.

In his mordant *On the Psychology of Military Incompetence* Norman Dixon has suggested that many people are attracted to the armed services because the military feeds the needs their personalities hunger for: authority, obedience, approval, orderliness, hostility. These are the qualities that lead to quick advancement, but rigidity, overcontrol, fear of failure, and inflexibility are not qualities likely to inspire confidence in subordinates or make for quick and accurate decision making in times of stress—the fog of war. Another analyst of military incompetence was Colonel General Baron Kurt von Hammerstein. He divided his officers into four classes: the clever, the stupid, the industrious, the lazy. Each officer tended to combine at least two of these qualities. The clever and lazy were suited for the highest command, the clever and industrious for staff appointments, use could even be made of the stupid and lazy, but the stupid and industrious should be removed at once: "nothing is more frightening than ignorance in action."

No one on the expedition was more industrious than Wilkes. From his great cabin gushed a constant stream of written orders (even one "Relative to the Want of Conformity to Orders"). One order in particular greatly antagonized his officers. Seeing cabals and cliques huddled in every cabin, he issued an edict that the officers, contrary to regulations that gave them separate quarters according to their grade in order "to secure good order, discipline, proper respect and efficiency," had converted their quarters into a "lounge" leading to "familiarity" and a thwarting of the said regulations. The familiarity had to stop. From this time on, as Reynolds noted, between Wilkes and most of his officers, it was "war to the knife."

Joseph Conrad claimed that the language of seamen was the most "flawless thing for its purpose." And an esoteric vocabulary surrounds everything connected with square-rigged sailing ships, the most complicated artifact of the nineteenth century. But *clubhauling, fouling a hawse, buntline legs, servicing and parceling, mousing a hook, grafting a block strop, doubling a futtock, clenching, keckling, nippering, cat-harpins, puddening, whipping, laying boards, Turk's heads on a monkey tail* all are terms that tend to produce slack-jawed gapes in landlubbers along with visions of unspeakable practices on the tween deck.

"You know a Man of War . . . here's too much damning of Eyes & Limbs. . . ." So wrote the admirable Charles Clerke to Joseph Banks as the *Resolution* sailed up channel after the Antarctic circumnavigation. Seamen used and abused intemperate language, both on deck and in the fo'c'sle. Along with the bosun's starter or colt it was an accepted part of a discipline that rested on violence. Wilkes's intemperate language riled his officers and civilian staff; violent, insulting, offensive, incoherent, and rude were some of their opinions. When he was excited, his language became more insulting, and even the loyal Hudson admitted that Wilkes became easily excited.

A parallel exists between Wilkes and Bligh. Both men thought they should have been promoted to captain's rank for their respective expeditions. Both went before a clutch of courts-martial investigating their conduct. Both retired as admirals. Both had a reputation for violent (but not obscene) language. Both grew excited and tended to dance around when provoked. Both suffered from severe headaches. Both disparaged other men's work, harbored grudges, and complained that their own work was not sufficiently recognized. And both were very competent surveyors, although Bligh was the better seaman.

Reynolds, writing to his sister on his few weeks in Samoa, presents a picture of the salty sailor straight out of Robert Ballantyne's *Coral Island*. (Ballantyne, then but fourteen years old, based his stories on narratives written by men such as Reynolds.) Those weeks, despite Wilkes, were the happiest of times, perhaps the happiest of the four-year expedition. This was a coastal survey in a whaleboat, away from what he called the irksome restraints of the ship, sleeping ashore at night among the villagers, who gave them hospitality and who were amazed at the vast wealth of the Americans with their fishhooks, hatchets, knives, scissors, and needles. He taught a chief's young daughter—"the image of faultless beauty, & the pearl of pure and natural innocence"—to sew and play the Jew's harp. Here was a different freedom, he thought, from that of the United States with its consumer-oriented society. Here he was, the very image of the sailor: bronzed, bearded, barefooted, wearing faded duck trousers, a knife belted around his waist, an open-necked shirt, all topped off with an old white hat that had been ridiculed by his family. No matter, he had worn it on all occasions, "rain or shine, and it has always been a comfort and protection." He would bring it home and "sport it among the Hills."

Reynolds's letter to his sister—number 11—was dated 1 December 1839 and headed "US Ship *Peacock*!!!, Sydney, New South Wales, *near to* Botany Bay." The change from the usual "US Ship *Vincennes*" heading plus the exclamation marks warned his sister and family that he had lost that comfortable and elegant cabin described in his letter number 1.

The *Vincennes* and the *Peacock* had sailed into Sydney's harbor, Port Jackson, just two days previous. They had sailed in at night, causing Hudson, following in Wilkes's wake, acute anxiety. Come the morning it astounded, and annoyed, the British to find two foreign warships anchored among the shipping. The *Porpoise* and the *Flying Fish,* brought in by a pilot, arrived later that same morning. Wilkes's reputation went up a notch in the squadron—giving one in the eye to John Bull was always satisfying for Americans—as well as his ego. But he was careful to keep secret the information that he had the latest charts and that the *Vincennes* had been piloted in by a quartermaster who had traded out of Sydney and knew the channel. No mention of the quartermaster is made in his *Narrative*. (Indeed he claimed that "we were all unacquainted with the channel.")

The Americans were just as bewildered by Sydney as the locals were by the Americans. One woman was overheard to express surprise that the Americans were not all Indians and Negroes, and nothing had prepared the ex-colonials for a colonial penal settlement where ex-convicts and their children lived in palatial sandstone mansions and where police, soldiers, and convict chain gangs were an everyday sight. The rapidly growing town, brash and new, had the same feeling as many an American town, and the inhabitants had the same single-minded pursuit of money. Where Sydney differed was in the numbers of drunks who reeled along the streets, day and night. What was truly shocking were the brawling, drunken, termagant women. The "fair sex" was being thrust upon its Victorian pedestals by the evangelical middle class, but these dreadful shrews appeared more suited to the gutter. This was Hogarth come to life. They gave meaning to Governor Lachlan Macquarie's comment: "There are but two classes of persons in New South Wales, those who have been convicted, and those who ought to be."

The expedition's officers were made honorary members of the Australian Club and started a long round of balls, dinners, and parties. They also met (with the exception of Wilkes, who made a feeble excuse) Captain Philip Parker King, whose charts and sailing directions had been used in Tierra del Fuego and the South Pacific. Wilkes, however, did meet with John Biscoe, who had made the third circumnavigation of Antarctica, discovered Enderby Land, and thought that a continent lay to the south. Wilkes, as with the piloting quartermaster, makes no mention of the meeting.

The seamen's pleasures were simpler. Sydney had an extraordinary number of taverns, grogshops, and drinking dens, more than one for each hundred of the population, according to Wilkes, among them the Jolly Sailors' Inn, Sailors' Inn, Soldiers' Inn, Ladies' Inn, Punch-Bowl Inn, Shamrock Inn, Thistle Inn, Ship's Inn, King's Arms Inn, not forgetting the inevitable Dew Drop Inn. Erskine and a boat's crew from the *Vincennes* visited the Jolly Sailors' Inn and found it to be a large, square room with national flags hung over large tables. Under the Russian flag sat homesick Russian sailors singing national songs. They were followed by a chorus of British sailors, sitting under the Union Jack, who belted out "Rule Britannia." Then some French sailors, sitting under the tricolor, gave a spirited performance of the "Marseillaise." Erskine and the boat's crew, under the Stars and Stripes, rounded it all off with "Yankee Doodle." In this atmosphere of multinational goodwill they toasted one another: the British drinking half-and-half[1] from pewter tankards, the French claret from thin glasses, and the Russians and Americans "something harder" from thick glasses.

The camaraderie at the Jolly Sailors was not shared by the expedition. Relations between Wilkes and his officers were now plunging to new lows. Reynolds estimated that only three officers supported Wilkes, and the commander's bony nose was sniffing out "cabals" and disrespect on every vessel.

The physical state of the expedition's vessels mirrored that of the expedition's morale. The *Peacock*'s sheer strake, bulwark stanchions, gun and berth deck waterways were decayed and rotten,[2] and the deck, because of overcaulking, leaked like a sieve. But Hudson thought it his duty "to contend" with his decaying ship, and Wilkes felt it "absolutely necessary for the credit of the Expedition and the country" that the *Peacock* sail for Antarctica. The *Flying Fish*'s masts were replaced with New Zealand kauri pine masts, slightly larger in diameter and three feet shorter. The other vessels were overhauled and loaded with ten months of provisions but only seven months' worth of fuel.

The vessels were also visited by the curious, who, being well aware of the changes that had been made to HMS *Erebus* and HMS *Terror* for their upcoming Antarctic voyage, were amazed to find no watertight compartments, no adequate heating system, no ice saws, no double-laid decks with canvas sandwiched between to ensure watertightness. The deficiencies, to the listening Americans, seemed dismayingly long, so dismaying that five seamen from the *Flying Fish* deserted, soon followed by others from the rest of the expedition. "Run" against a seaman's name became an all too familiar entry.

Wilkes saw one gleam of sunshine in the gloom. Here was an opportunity to rid himself of the civilian corps—at least for the Antarctic voyage. Suggesting that there would be little of interest among the ice, he gave them permission to rejoin the ship at New Zealand, in the Bay of Islands, on 1 March 1840. The two months would give them time—the tempting carrot that they all gobbled—to travel in New South Wales and New Zealand. The civilian corps, equally pleased to be away from Wilkes's louring presence, happily agreed.

The day after Christmas the expedition weighed anchor and stood down the bay. Between Sydney Heads the last guests departed, and the *Vincennes*, in light winds, missed stays and was forced to anchor while the *Peacock* and the *Porpoise* forged ahead into the Pacific.

Before they set sail, a lugubrious entry had gone into the journal of George Sinclair aboard the *Flying Fish:* "I do not suppose that a vessel ever sailed under the U.S. Pendant with such a miserable crew as we have now. We have no cook and only 7 men, four of them are not in my opinion worth their salt, but they are all we can get. It will be a great wonder to me if we return from the southern cruise." The tone was repeated by Reynolds in a letter to his sister: "We shall have a dreary time among the Ice, and God send us safe out of it. When this is over, the rest of the cruise will go more easily and every move we make will be bringing us nearer Home. If we should fail to come back! I cannot write more, my heart is full; Good bye and may God bless you all."

Such feelings gripped most of the crews. In the eighteen months since sailing from Norfolk they had seen nothing but seas and lands familiar to countless seamen. They were now about to sail into a little-known and terrifying ocean.

As the Americans sailed from Sydney, more than five hundred miles away in Hobart, the *Astrolabe* and the *Zélée* were making ready to sail south. Dumont d'Urville had talked with John Biscoe, who told him of his long conversation with Wilkes. D'Urville also learned that Biscoe had once sailed south along the meridian of New Zealand but had been stopped by ice at 63°S latitude. Sealers, however, were convinced that land lay to the south. Thousands of miles away in the Atlantic the *Erebus* and the *Terror* were also sailing south to Kerguelen Island. James Clark Ross carried a trump card in the shape of a copy of John Balleny's *Eliza Scott* log, for Balleny *had* discovered islands and land to the south of Australia.

Twenty years after the sealers a flotilla of government ships were zeroing in on Antarctica.

NOTES

1. Equal amounts of beer and ale or beer and porter.
2. The channels or chain plates were bolted to the sheer strake. The shrouds, supporting the mast, were attached to the channels. A rotten sheer strake could lead to the loss of a mast.

Chapter 11

The Everlasting Expedition

KEEPING A GOOD OFFING. To keep well off shore while
under sail, so as to be clear of danger should the wind suddenly shift and blow towards the shore.

KEGGED. Feeling affronted or jeered at.

Admiral W. H. Smyth, *The Sailor's Word-Book,* 1867

HE FOUR VESSELS of the United States Exploring Expedition had ideal sailing conditions for their first week sailing
south. It was just as well. Few nineteenth-century sailing vessels
have been so poorly prepared and so unsuited for polar exploration, even though the crow's nest,[1] the insignia of ice navigation, would
soon be rigged at the *Vincennes*'s fore-topmast. As they sailed south in reg-
imented line, the preparations for the polar conditions started. Gunports—
always a constant source of leaks but also a source of fresh air into the usual
fetid below-deck atmosphere—were caulked and covered with tarred canvas; protective housings were built over companionway hatches; charcoal
stoves on lead sheets were slung belowdecks, as were thermometers.
Wilkes had given orders that the temperature belowdecks should never ex-
ceed 50°F. Such a temperature, thought Wilkes, "would have the effect of
inducing the men to take exercise for the purpose of exciting their animal
heat." The poor-quality cold-weather clothing was issued with the addition of Sydney-made boots (just as bad as their American-made boots). All
unessential items were stowed away, and the guns doubly secured.

Wilkes's instructions for the second Antarctic probe had ordered him
to sail south from Tasmania and then, having reached the ice—or land—
to sail west to "longitude 45°E., or to Enderby's Land." The squadron

should then rendezvous at Kerguelen Island. His own instructions to the various commanders—Hudson of the *Peacock*, Ringgold of the *Porpoise*, Pinkney of the *Flying Fish*—reduced the sweep west to 105°E, followed by a rendezvous at the Bay of Islands in New Zealand.

Wilkes's instructions to his commanders also urged upon them the necessity "to use every means in your power to avoid a separation, as the lives of those entrusted to your particular care, and those comprising the squadron, may be jeoparded by it." Rendezvous points, in case of separation before reaching the pack ice, were set at Macquarie Island (remaining for forty-eight hours) and the coordinates for the suspect Emerald Isle (remaining for thirty-six hours).

Separation came within a week.

On New Year's Day, eight hundred miles south of Sydney, with the wind increasing from the north and a nasty cross sea running across the westerly swells, the overburdened *Flying Fish* dropped her mainsail and ran under topsail, foresail, and jib. The topsail suddenly blew apart. Then, as is the way of things at sea, there followed a series of disasters. The schooner continued running before the stiffening gale under foresail and jib. The foresail, after a number of heavy jibes, carried away the gaff jaws, and the sail was manhandled to the deck. They were now reduced to the jib. But this was soon carried away. In this sorry condition with no sails to steady her, wallowing rail under, the seas swirling across her deck, the *Vincennes* bore down close enough for the schooner's struggling seamen to distinguish Wilkes and other officers on the quarterdeck. The *Vincennes* then hoisted the signal to "make sail" and forged ahead, deliberately leaving them, as Sinclair bitterly wrote, "to whatever fate the gods of the Winds might have in store." But, with cathartic satisfaction, the *Vincennes* was followed by "a few deep toned curses."

Ten days later, having made her lonely repairs, the *Flying Fish* arrived off Macquarie Island.[2] To their joy the crew caught a glimpse of the *Peacock,* but fog rolled in, and she was lost to sight. The next morning revealed an empty horizon. Only the dull green flanks of the island lay nearby. Sinclair and a boat's crew made a difficult landing through the surf to leave a signal pole and letters. Apart from the penguins and elephant seals they thought the island "dreary and inhospitable." Three days later they arrived at the second rendezvous point and found nothing. The Emerald Isle did not exist, nor, for that matter, might have any of the squadron's vessels.

The schooner headed off south, and by 21 January, some seventy miles north of the Antarctic Circle, she had reached solid pack ice. She then started her slow, wet, uncomfortable passage west. Pinkney was ill with fever, and only four of the crew were able to stand a watch. The compass, close to the south magnetic pole, was virtually useless, and during times of thick fog they steered by the sounds of waves breaking on the pack ice to port and the deep, booming noise of waves entering iceberg caverns to starboard. Sinclair, who had been aboard the *Relief* during those terrifying nights anchored off Noir Island with the sound of anchor chains rumbling across the bottom, thought the booming caverns equally "blood chilling." The hull and deck of the lightly built schooner leaked abominably in any seaway, and at times the bilgewater was level with the cabin sole. Conditions for the seamen in the fo'c'sle were so wet that Pinkney had the men moved aft into the twelve-by-nine-foot officers' cabin, which also held the stove. Not that it was alight all the time; seas would swirl across the deck and gurgle down the flue pipe, ending the warmth with a hiss. One man, his feet so swollen that he was unable to wear boots, stood his four-hour watch in stocking feet. By the end of January the crew was so reduced that it was unable to reef the foresail and hove to during a gale with the full sail—a dangerous procedure because the schooner would fly up into the wind and take a stern board into the high seas. On 5 February the seamen signed a petition saying that they had had no dry clothing for seven days, most were ill, and any continuation of these conditions "must terminate in our death," the "death" being written in large capital letters. Pinkney in turn, getting everything down on paper to absorb Wilkes's bile, asked his officers for their opinion. They, also in turn and also getting it down on paper, thought "an immediate return to milder climates" imperative. The formality of the letters (headed "U.S. Schooner Flying-Fish, Lat. 66°S., Long. 143°E., Feb. 5th, 1840") is curious when one thinks of the cramped and awful conditions in which they were written—and written in obviously mutual, if damp, collaboration. Pinkney put the schooner's head north, away from the pack ice and icebergs. Their modest, but uncomfortable, four-hundred-mile sweep had produced no positive sighting of land.

Unknown to Pinkney his schooner had followed close in the 1839 wake of another schooner, the similar-size *Eliza Scott,* and her much smaller fifty-six-foot consort, the Solent-built cutter *Sabrina.* Looking for new sealing grounds, the British schooner and cutter had found, instead of fur seal–breeding colonies, the Balleny Islands and the Sabrina Coast. It was a copy of the *Eliza Scott*'s log and journal that had been given to James Ross. There was no log from the *Sabrina.* A few days after sighting the coast named after her she was lost with all hands in a Southern Ocean storm.

North of the Convergence, with sea and air temperatures rising, Sinclair noted that the sick men came crawling out on deck "like Galápagos Terrapins" to sun themselves in the warmth. A week later this sorry band of sailors was sufficiently recovered to start fighting among themselves. On 10 March the schooner came to anchor in the Bay of Islands to find a bored and waiting civilian corps.

The scientists had sailed from Sydney aboard an overcrowded passenger brig and had been kicking their heels at the Bay of Islands since 24 February. Peale groused that they had "gathered all the plants, shot all the Birds, caught all the fish, and got heartily sick of the Natives." They had also been plagued by mosquitoes, sand flies, fleas, and, worst of all, meat flies, which deposited "their young in our blankets & stockings, and on our food while we are eating."

Wilkes was the only card lacking for Peale to hold a royal flush of irritants.

The *Peacock,* glimpsed by the *Flying Fish* for those few tantalizing minutes off Macquarie Island, had also become separated. Four days after Wilkes had left the schooner rolling in the Southern Ocean seas, Hudson had lost contact with the *Vincennes* and the *Porpoise* in a thick fog. Reynolds wrote an exultant valedictory into his journal: "Captain & all hands happy to be clear of her." Reynolds might still hanker after that comfortable cabin he had shared with May, but he was now aboard a cheerful ship with a captain whose seamanship everyone trusted.

Hudson, after the separation, made for the rendezvous at Macquarie and lay to off the southeast corner. The island, twenty-one miles long, three miles wide, rising to a green, humped plateau of a thousand feet, rimmed by steep cliffs and slopes, lies north and south athwart the prevailing westerly winds and Southern Ocean swells. Kelp in certain places provides a breakwater against the constant surf that pounds on the island's shores. It's a diabolical place for a boat landing.

Hudson sent in Passed Midshipman Henry Eld, a bearlike Connecticut Yankee, with a boat's crew to attempt one. The boat searched for a reasonable landing beach and eventually anchored off, just beyond the breakers, until Eld and a quartermaster, seeing an opportunity in a lull, leaped overboard and made a very wet landing. The quartermaster set up the signal flag and post while Eld booted his way into a royal penguin colony. "As we wanted a number of specimens," wrote the nonchalant Eld, "I commenced kicking them down the precipice, and knocked on the head those which had the temerity to attack me." Alas for science, the specimens were lost in the surf—and Eld was knocked into the kelp— when the two men attempted to get off the shores of an island that they thought "affords no inducement for a visit."

The *Peacock* passed so far to the east of the second rendezvous point that Hudson considered the beat to windward a waste of precious time. On 13 January, at 61°30'S, they sighted their first iceberg. The first tabular iceberg is always a memorable experience, and few people ever forget it. It's like seeing the first elephant in the wild. Reynolds—this was his first iceberg—came on deck to admire and wonder.

That midnight, coming on deck for the middle watch, he found it so light that no binnacle lamp was needed; there was light enough for the men to read *Pickwick* and the doctor his Bible. The latitudes of the sixties, much to their surprise, were proving almost pleasant. The temperature rarely fell below freezing, the sea was smooth, the winds were mild, and except for the occasional snow flurry, the skies were clear blue. The fogs, sleet, rain, and gales of the fifties had been left behind. Moreover, their captain, the expedition's very own Mr. Pickwick, had ordered a pint of hot coffee served out to every man at each watch, and it was so appreciated that there came little growling from the men about the loss of their usual grog.

By 15 January they were sixty miles north of the Antarctic Circle with no pack ice in sight, only scattered icebergs. An excited Reynolds, visions of fame dancing in his head, wrote that "we would pass 70°—Eclipse Cook, & distance the pretender Weddell." The visions were short-lived. Later that day scattered ice floes appeared, and then a long white streak in the sky, low across the horizon: ice blink, the sure sign of great quantities of pack ice stretched across their course. Reynolds's dream, as he ruefully admitted, was destroyed.

By late afternoon they had been stopped by the barricade of pack ice. In a calm sea consolidated pack ice presents an inanimate barrier, but given wind and swell, it takes on sinister life. With its seaward front heaving in snakelike movements, smoothing out to the ominously quiet and treacherous floes lying behind, the whole white expanse studded with icebergs looking like fortresses, pack ice suddenly becomes actively hostile.

This barrier was inanimate. But it still barred any progress south. The *Peacock* turned west, keeping a good offing from the pack, and threaded her way through the floes in a sea and sky full of life: surfacing whales, soaring albatrosses, petrels, and flocks of Cape pigeons, the dark chocolate brown and speckled white petrels much loved by sailors.

More life was soon seen in the shape of the *Porpoise*'s topsails. Ringgold rounded to under the *Peacock*'s stern and gave his news. The *Vincennes* and the *Porpoise* had reached the pack ice on 11 January and then hove to. The next day, in thick fog, they had lost contact with the *Vincennes*, and Ringgold had started to work his way west. All that he could report was the shooting of two elephant seals hauled out on an ice floe. The carcasses had been saved. They were taken aboard the *Peacock* for preservation. The two vessels then filled away on opposite tacks (the wind had turned against them) and worked their separate ways to the west.

The next day, 16 January, both the burly Eld and the enthusiastic Reynolds were aloft, gazing south across the pack ice. The visibility was good, and both were entranced with the day (smooth sea, mild air, sunshine) and the scenery (much purple prose in their journals). Then both saw what they thought was land. They had come aloft without a spyglass and sent down to the deck for one. After peering south for half an hour, they became even more convinced that they were seeing land in the form of three peaks, one conical and two domed. Bursting with their news, Reynolds reported to the watch officer, and Eld to Hudson in his cabin. Then, unexplainably since it was land they were searching for, a vast inertia descended upon the Peacocks. Nothing went into the logbook; no one else went aloft; Hudson seemed unexcited, not even bothering to come on deck, and fobbed off Eld with the casual statement that they would probably see more land in two or three days. The *Peacock* was put about and stood away from the pack ice. Reynolds could hardly contain his "disappointment and mortification." Both he and Eld thought this a most remarkable way to receive a report of land in these high latitudes. (Doubts must have crossed Reynolds's mind. He made no entry of the sighting into his own journal until three months later—when a page was added and the day's events were revised.)

The next day, a Friday, they fell in with the *Vincennes*. Wilkes had nothing to report. The two vessels split on opposite tacks to continue their separate searches. For the next two days the three vessels zigzagged through the ice floes, catching fleeting glimpses of one another through the passing parade of icebergs, snow flurries, and mists. On Sunday, 19 January, just north of the Antarctic Circle the *Peacock* came across a large bay in the pack and headed into it across a mirror-smooth sea spread with floes looking like white rugs scattered across a polished floor. The sailing conditions were so unusual, almost magical, that the deck became crowded with men. Just before the change of the afternoon watch the watchers sighted a hint of land at the bay's head. The indefatigable Reynolds, aloft once more, was certain it was land. A midshipman perched nearby agreed. Both reported to the deck, and this time, much to Reynolds's satisfaction, the rigging was soon crowded with men, including Hudson. Nearly all agreed that it was land at the head of the bay.

By midnight they had arrived at the bay's head and estimated the land to be twenty-five miles away.[3] Then doubts crossed Hudson's mind. The land was only an iceberg held in the pack, he remarked to the watch officer, who changed the entry in the logbook. The *Peacock* stood out of the bay, through ice floes and the sound of spouting whales that reminded one officer of high-pressure steamboats on the Ohio. Reynolds's blood pressure on finding the amended logbook, his land changed to an iceberg, rivaled any Ohio steamboat's.

The next few days gave the Peacocks lumpy head seas, squalls, reefed topsails, icebergs, snow, and a glimpse of the *Porpoise*. The magnetic compass, in these high latitudes close to the south magnetic pole, took on a life of its own. Steering by one compass, the *Peacock* was heading south while by another she was heading north. One afternoon every man came on deck to watch a killer whale, living up to its name, clamped fast to the lower jaw of a doomed whale.

The men, even though they felt personally thwarted by the barrier of ice, remained cheerful, found new games to play, danced and sang in their off watch hours. On 23 January Hudson's happy ship was rewarded. Standing into a bay with a light wind from the southwest and good visibility, the men spotted the *Porpoise* sailing out. The *Peacock* then lay to and lowered boats to make magnetic observations on nearby ice floes and to collect ice from icebergs to melt into fresh water. The sea being an olive green color—an indication of shallower water than the usual deepwater blue—Hudson decided to take soundings. They found bottom at 320 fathoms, the lead line men shouting with joy. The armed lead brought up pebbles and slate-colored mud. At the same time the visibility cleared, and they saw land. The delighted crew cheered, the lead line men coiled away, singing and hurrahing, to the music of a fiddle, and the whole wonderful afternoon was topped off with the traditional splicing of the main brace—an issue of extra grog as celebration.

Eld, one of the officers sent away in the boats, returned with an emperor penguin stunned by a boathook (it's obvious that no penguin was safe near Eld). The bird proved such a tough fellow to handle that they had been forced to lash its beak. Its life once aboard the *Peacock* was short. Opened up, it produced five pebbles. The enterprising cook found twenty-seven more and promptly sold them to the crew as "South Pole stones."

The euphoria of that day was short-lived. Within hours of the unfortunate penguin's delivering up its stones, Eld and the rest of the crew were fighting for their lives.

The following morning, a Friday, Hudson took the *Peacock* south for another approach to the land. Eld was at breakfast when he was nearly pitched out of his seat by a tremendous crash. His first thought was that the bow must have been stove in. On deck he found that the *Peacock*, working her way through large floes, bergy bits, brash, and growlers[4] in attempting to tack, had struck a large growler, come head to wind, and then been driven stern first into another large chunk of ice (probably a bergy bit), which had split her rudderhead and jammed the rudder askew and immovable. The wheel ropes, running from tiller to steering wheel, had also snapped. The ship still had her masts and sails but no means of steering. All hands were called on deck, and their struggles began.

The wind was now driving them deeper into the pack ice. Attempts to steer by sail alone proved useless. If she did gather way, an ice floe would knock her off course. She was like a billiard ball caroming around a table. But the cushions were damnably hard, and she was striking them port and starboard, from bow to stern. Hudson tried to bring her around to a more favorable tack with the aid of an ice anchor. Boats were lowered, and the ice anchor was taken out to a large floe. Just as the cable was brought aboard, but before it could be put around the bitts, the *Peacock* charged astern, and the cable was dragged from the men's hands.

Still charging astern, the ship struck another bergy bit. This one finished off the rudder. Sails were furled, and spars put over the side as fenders, boats, and men struggled through the fast-closing ice to put out more ice anchors. The anchors dragged. The *Peacock,* the fenders chewed to splinters by the ice, was whirled on her way to a huge tabular iceberg with an overhanging top like the eaves of a roof. Hudson had more spars readied as fenders and the main yards cockbilled.[5] She struck on her port quarter. The force of the collision broke the spanker boom, ripped off the port stern davit, and smashed the stern boat to matchwood. The starboard stern davit was then ripped away, followed by the starboard bulwarks. They were now under the overhanging ice. But the sheer momentum of the collision drove the *Peacock* forward on a rebound. Her head was now pointed to clear the end of the iceberg. Jibs were set, and she slowly gathered way. A few seconds later the overhanging ice broke off and thundered into the sea a few feet astern. They had escaped death by the proverbial whisker.

Their fight for life continued. They might have survived that battle, but the sky had taken an ominous look, and they were still trapped in an ice-filled bay. Dinner was piped as usual, a welcome interlude before the battle resumed. After the interlude the nautical marionette performance of steering a rudderless ship began. Sails and yards were constantly trimmed and dropped with the marionette strings of halyards, braces, guys, sheets, lifts, and downhauls. Ice anchors were set, and their cables hauled in to bring her head around. All this in a heavy swell among floes that smashed against the hull, ripping away stays, shrouds, and bowsprit. Even the anchors worked loose, carrying away eyebolts and lashings. Working in the boats, carrying out ice anchors, was hellish. It was nearly impossible to row in such an ice-cluttered sea, and one crew came close to extinction between two large, rolling bergy bits.

That afternoon, the ice clearing away from the stern, they hauled aboard the shattered rudder, and the carpenters started their work. It now began to snow. The struggles with ice anchors continued in a rising sea. By midnight the bergy bits, floes, and growlers were pressing in. Hudson, giving up on finesse, adopted a more brutal approach with the gathering ice. The *Peacock* was set at the ice under full sail in an attempt to smash her way through. Pumps worked overtime; men were knocked to their knees; chronometers were flung from their beds of sawdust. The smashing progress continued until all on board were wondering how much longer their ship could take this dreadful punishment. Through all this the carpenters worked nonstop. By late Saturday morning they declared the rudder ready for shipping. The *Peacock* was hove to, rolling in the swells, and the dangerous and tricky business began. All knew that this was their one hope of survival, and everyone carefully watched the handling of the precious lifeline. By noon it was shipped and working. They could steer.

The *Peacock* smashing into the iceberg
"She went nearly stern foremost, and struck with her larboard quarter upon the ice-island with a tremendous crash."   —Charles Wilkes
(Illustration from Wilkes's *Narrative,* vol. II)

But they were still in the bay and surrounded by floes. A view from the masthead also showed that the bay opening appeared shut fast by ice. But at midnight they found a small opening, and by Sunday morning they had crept out into an open sea.

The relief was palpable. All had thought themselves doomed to a nasty death. Some saw the hand of God in their survival. But the majority, discounting divine intervention, thought their survival the result of the surprising strength of their decaying ship and Hudson's seamanship.

They were not completely safe, however. Their ship, as Hudson put it, "with a rudder hanging by the eyelids—the poor Peacock's feathers ruffled," was in no shape to continue her battle with Antarctica's ice. Sydney was the closest port for repairs, and these, estimated Hudson, would take a month. The squadron was due to leave the Bay of Islands on 1 March to start a survey in the Fiji Islands. At a meeting with all his officers he put his case for Sydney and repairs. Only two held out for continuing in the Antarctic—provided they could avoid meeting ice.

Nearly a month later, on the night of 21 February, after a rough passage nursing her delicate rudder across the Southern Ocean, the *Peacock* anchored between Sydney Heads. The next day Hudson sailed into Sydney Cove and anchored off the government wharf. The railway for hauling out, used by merchant ships, was considered too fragile for the *Peacock*, and she sailed across to Mosman Bay, on the harbor's north shore, for repairs. Today Mosman Bay is a fashionable Sydney suburban address, thickly wooded and exclusive, with no reminders—except for a small sandstone building—of its stench-filled days as Archibald Mosman's whaling station. The advantages for Hudson of Mosman Bay were twofold. The men were distanced from the temptations of Sydney's brothels and grogshops, and the inlet made an ideal, totally sheltered, wet basin for repairs. A man in a "diving machine"—an India rubber suit with a metal helmet fitted with glass eyes, according to one officer—inspected and reported on hull damage. Mostly up forward at the stem was his verdict. The *Peacock* was beached at high tide, and her hull inspected. The stem piece (or cutwater, in more evocative nautical parlance) had been ground down by the ice to within an inch and a half of the plank ends. Another few hours of battering through the ice would have sprung the planks apart, followed, no doubt about this, by a dramatic increase of widows and grieving mothers in the Republic.

On 11 March the *Peacock* survivors, much to their surprise, heard that the *Vincennes* (she should have been on her way to the Fiji Islands after calling in at the Bay of Islands) was anchored in the harbor.

Before sailing from Sydney the previous December, the *Vincennes* had been searched by the master-at-arms for convict stowaways. Even sailing into the Antarctic aboard an American warship was considered preferable to a convict's life in New South Wales. Ten days out Wilkes was surprised to hear that three stowaways, one of them a youngster, were on board. They had obviously been hidden with the crew's help. At a crew muster they had been rigged out in seamen's dress: blue trousers, blue flannel shirts, black silk handkerchiefs, and black tarpaulin hats. By their bearing and appearance Wilkes thought them soldiers rather than convicts. He entered them on the books for provisions only and warned them that they would be returned to Sydney after the Antarctic cruise. The youngster, a drummer boy but at one time a London pickpocket, soon became a favorite with the crew. Under the inevitable nickname of Oliver Twist he came to entertain them with stories of his days working for the Fagins of London.

Wilkes, after leaving the *Flying Fish* floundering in his wake on New Year's Day, followed by the *Peacock*'s going astray, on coming into Macquarie Island's latitude found his ship so far downwind of the rendezvous that he decided not to attempt the thrash to windward. No time was spent at the second rendezvous, the coordinates for the Emerald Isle.

The *Vincennes*'s and the *Porpoise*'s southerly course, after seeing their first iceberg on 10 January, came to a halt late next evening. In front of them stretched the pack ice—Wilkes's "icy barrier"—and the two vessels hove to and waited for sunrise, while the watch admired the night sky and listened to the soft rustling of floes. Fog rolled in at sunrise, and the *Porpoise* was lost to sight, not to be seen for a number of days. For the first week Wilkes adopted a cautious approach in the confrontation with his icy barrier. (One of his orders to the watch officers was that they should avoid sailing through brash ice, an unworkable instruction that was quietly forgotten.)

On his blank chart Wilkes started laying down the edge of the pack ice and the *Vincennes's* zigzag course as she worked her way west through icebergs, mists, and freezing fog, groping her way along the curb of ice like a blind man. On 16 January—the clear day on which Reynolds and Eld were convinced they had seen land—all three vessels were in sight of one another. The following day the *Vincennes* and the *Peacock* were close enough for Wilkes and Hudson to talk. By now Wilkes had given up all ideas of the squadron's sailing in company, and he gave Hudson free rein to explore independently.

On 19 January the *Vincennes* sailed past the bay entered by the *Peacock,* the bay where Reynolds was convinced that he had seen land for the second time. These two dates, in a few months' time, were to take on patriotic importance. In three years' time they were to be the center of some confusing and contradictory evidence at Wilkes's court-martial.

Wilkes, in his *Narrative,* claims that he saw land on the morning of 19 January. Although no mention of this was made in the logbook, Wilkes, much later, showed land on his chart some 40 miles away from the southernmost point of the *Vincennes's* track for the nineteenth. (The closest land in fact lay 120 miles away.)

For the next month Wilkes, loosing his cautious approach of the first week's tapping along the ice edge, sailed west. The *Vincennes's* switchback, zigzag track moved across the draft chart, with the edge of the pack ice and even individual icebergs carefully shown. Relations between Wilkes and his officers plunged to new frigid depths with the paranoid commander seeing malignant enemies on every side, enemies who "would be as sorry to find land here because it may add some degree of eclat to the Expedition and myself . . . no I must be patient, altho' I cannot help feeling how disgusting it is to be with such a set of officers (one or two I must except) who are endevouring to do all in their powers to make my exertions go for nothing."

But the unhappy ship, as she sailed west through icebergs, brilliant crystal days and foggy days, snowstorms and gales, was sighting land with increasing frequency, and Wilkes was adding considerable lengths of hachuring, indicating land, behind the barrier of ice. At one bay, which he named after Thomas Piner, the signal quartermaster, the snow- and ice-covered land was estimated to rise to three thousand feet, and a sounding in the bay gave a depth of thirty fathoms. Unknown to Wilkes he was in the same bay discovered by d'Urville.

By the end of January Wilkes was convinced that the sightings added up to a continent. But it was also obvious, with the lengthening sick list, that his crew was becoming weaker. A series of gales had all hands on deck and aloft, struggling to reduce sail with frozen reef points. Men working out on the yards were so stricken with cold they had to be lowered to the deck, rheumatism and frostbitten fingers and toes became the norm, nearly every man broke out in boils, and the smallest scratch became ulcerated and refused to heal. The two assistant surgeons, aghast at what they were dealing with, submitted a report to Wilkes stating that if these conditions continued, the crew would be so reduced as to hazard the safety of the ship. Surgeon Edward Gilchrist, suspended in Sydney for writing a "disrespectful letter" to Wilkes, was reinstated, and backed up his assistants. Wilkes disagreed, and the *Vincennes* continued west, the sick list increasing.

By 12 February they had traced the edge of the pack ice for close to a thousand miles. Wilkes was even more convinced that behind the barrier lay an Antarctic continent. As a celebration for the continent a champagne party was held in his cabin for a small group of the more respectful officers.

Two days later the seamen landed on a large iceberg (three times the size of Boston Common, according to Erskine) to collect fresh water in leather bags. The men, released from the ship's confines, stumbled around on the snow, slid down slopes, collected stones and pebbles frozen into the surface, dragged seals by the tail, chased penguins, snowballed one another, and generally cavorted around like schoolboys during break. A number of emperor penguins were caught, their legs tied, and bundled into a boat. Halfway to the *Vincennes* the captives let loose with such a cacophany of squalling and cackling that the boat was invaded by penguins swimming nearby. Bursting out of the water like submarine missiles, the emperor penguins nipped with their bills, pummeled with their wings, and defeated the republican Americans. Even the tied penguins managed to escape.

By 21 February, after tracing close to fifteen hundred miles of "icy barrier" and reaching 100°E, now running short of water, the winter season advancing, Wilkes made the decision to call a halt to his westward progress and head for New Zealand.

The *Porpoise* had been the last contact with any of the squadron. On 26 January Wilkes had shouted across to Ringgold the rate of the *Vincennes*'s standard chronometer, and the two vessels had then gone their separate ways.

Four days later the *Porpoise* sighted two vessels standing north under

The men of the *Vincennes* at play

"We remained upon this iceberg several hours, and the men amused themselves to their hearts' content in sliding." —Charles Wilkes

With the *Vincennes* in the background and Wilkes's Newfoundland dog, Sydney, in the foreground.

(Illustration from Wilkes's *Narrative*, vol. II)

easy sail. Knowing that James Clark Ross was Antarctic bound, Ringgold thought them the *Erebus* and the *Terror.* Hoisting the American colors, he bore down on them, "ready to cheer the discoverer of the North Magnetic Pole." Suddenly the two strangers hoisted French colors, one with a broad pennant. Ringgold realized that this was Dumont d'Urville's expedition.

He headed for the flagship's stern, aiming to pass within hail. The French suddenly piled on sail, as if to avoid the brig. Ringgold saw this as an insult, hauled down his colors, and bore away. The whole extraordinary incident later caused Wilkes to fulminate that d'Urville had "not only committed a wanton violation of all proper feeling, but a breach of the courtesy due from one nation to another." D'Urville saw the incident in a different light. Noting the speed of the approaching brig, he had ordered more sail to keep pace and was baffled by the American hauling down of colors and change of course.

Two weeks after sighting the French the *Porpoise* was heading for New Zealand. On the way Ringgold stopped at the Auckland Islands and anchored in the seductively named haven of Sarah's Bosom. The islands, since their discovery in 1806, had provided an anchorage for sealers and whalers. The Americans found a small hut built by a French whaler, a grave with a wooden cross, and a small garden of turnips, carrots, and potatoes. The brig's doctor added some onions. On the passage from the Auckland Islands to the Bay of Islands Ringgold spoke with an American whaleship that said that more than a hundred vessels were whaling off New Zealand's east coast. The brig anchored in the Bay of Islands on 26 March and began her exchange of news with the *Flying Fish*.

The *Vincennes* arrived at Sydney—the ship was running low on water, and Wilkes also thought Sydney a better port from which to send Washington his report—as the *Porpoise* was leaving the delights of Sarah's Bosom. With the *Vincennes* and the *Peacock* at Sydney, the *Porpoise* and the *Flying Fish* at the Bay of Islands, the squadron was now safe out from the Antarctic. Against all the predictions of the officers, it looked as if Wilkes had brought it off and made a major discovery. The only vessel with no discovery claims was the small *Flying Fish*. It was as if she had collected all *her* honors during the first Antarctic season in the chase after Cook's "Ne Plus Ultra."

Discovery honors, dear to the hearts of all patriots, stood as follows: Cook and Weddell still held their record souths; the Americans lay second in the discovery of land in Antarctica's Pacific and Indian ocean sectors— that done by Biscoe, Balleny, and, unknown to the Americans, the sealer Peter Kemp in the *Magnet*. Both Biscoe and Balleny had spent more time south of the Convergence, but neither had discovered such a vast length of coastline as the Americans.

At Sydney Wilkes talked with Biscoe and heard of Balleny's island discoveries. But worse news came from Hobart. Dumont d'Urville had discovered land on the afternoon of 19 January[6] and also landed on a small offshore island. The French, in short, had managed to find land before any discoveries had been entered into any American logbook.

Wilkes put a stop to that by claiming, in the 13 March issue of the *Sydney Herald*, that he had discovered land "on the morning of the 19th of January, in latitude 66°20′south, longitude 154°18′east." He had then run down the coast for some seventeen hundred miles and "completed the discovery." The paper was loud in its praise for the Americans. The editor thought that the land would be of little benefit to commerce, but the whole expedition was a noble "commencement in the cause of science and discovery."

Reynolds sent a copy of the article with a letter to his mother. The letter, with much underlining for emphasis, reinforced the claim that he and Eld had seen land days before the French and again on the afternoon of the nineteenth. He was also very dismissive of the French and their first Antarctic season and equally so of this one: "They only ran 150 miles along the ice and then put back. They could not wait longer, when to have preserved might have enabled them at least to say that *'they had done all they could'* and *'accomplished all that was practicable or necessary';* but no! Frenchmen like, they must run away to *tell* of their success." This was all terribly unfair of Reynolds but perhaps only to be expected.

Wilkes's claim to the morning discovery of 19 January—"a deliberate and wilful falsehood," in the words of the charge—was to form the basis of one of the many charges brought against him at his court-martial. But Wilkes, in his *Narrative,* making sure that the French were put right out of the picture, claimed 16 January as the Americans' first sighting. For this date Reynolds and Eld were brought into play. No sightings had been recorded in the logbooks, but memories were refreshed and massaged, personal journals consulted and modified. National honor was at stake, and Wilkes was being driven by its demon.

More seamen deserted before the *Vincennes* sailed for the Bay of Islands. Making Sydney their port of choice for desertion, a total of forty-one men from the expedition jumped ship and vanished into the town's crimps and dives. Three of the *Vincennes*'s officers attempted a more formal desertion by requesting transfer to the *Peacock.* Wilkes refused.

The Sydney stowaways were handed over to the authorities, with young Oliver Twist being gathered up by a sergeant of the 56th Regiment, given a court-martial, and sentenced to 105 lashes at the triangle. The last 5 cuts were laid across his dead body. Erskine, who had listened to his tales of London lowlife, hoped his soul rested in peace.

The *Vincennes* sailed from Sydney, bound for the Bay of Islands, on 19 March. The *Peacock,* still working on her repairs, remained at Sydney until the end of the month before she sailed to join the squadron in the Tonga Islands.

Reynolds took a few days off from the *Peacock* and traveled, for a change of scene, the fifteen miles to Parramatta, where, like most visitors to New South Wales, he went to look at the notorious Female Factory housing more than a thousand women convicts (a sightseeing trip, according to contemporary accounts, equivalent to a modern-day visit to a zoo). Reynolds was told the women worked at sewing and outside labor. All this under man-of-war discipline. The women were dressed in mob-caps, short gowns, and petticoats. Some, the hard-core reprobates, were in solitary confinement; others in confinement for childbirth.

The prison, over its sad and terrible years, also served as a lonely hearts marriage bureau for male "dungaree settlers" and "stringybarks" from the bush; as a whorehouse with the women working at the "buttock-and-twang" for money; as a nursing home for convict women made pregnant when working as assigned servants. (They usually claimed the Reverend Samuel Marsden, the hated "flogging parson," as the father.)

Reynolds thought the whole "assemblage and their conditions very curious to see." Wilkes, who had visited the prison before sailing for the Antarctic, thought it an "assemblage of ugly creatures . . . where the countenance now indicates only the prevalence of the baser passions." On being shown into their workrooms, with the women sitting on benches sewing clothes for Sydney's shopkeepers, coarse clothing for convicts, or picking oakum, Wilkes had been taken aback by "their disgusting leering faces, staring at us with a malignity and hatred that were not soon forgotten."

At the Bay of Islands Wilkes found the *Flying Fish*, the *Porpoise*, and the waiting scientific staff. Peale now had his royal flush with the "unpleasant intelligence" that he would be sailing aboard the *Vincennes* until the squadron was reunited with the *Peacock* at the Tonga Islands.

Pinkney was also due for some unpleasant intelligence. He had spent his time at the Bay of Islands making repairs to his schooner. Wilkes, however, was not pleased with the schooner's new signal topmasts. Far too "flashy." He made Pinkney pay five hundred dollars from his own pocket for the three-thousand-dollar total repair bill. Pinkney, never a Wilkes favorite, was also reprimanded for promoting one of the crew without permission. The result was more acrimony, followed by Pinkney's suspension, yet another officer added to the expedition's exclusive club.

Although the trade in preserved heads had been banned for some years, the Americans were somewhat disconcerted to find it still flourishing aboard a missionary brig. The steward, swearing them to secrecy, took some officers forward to his small storeroom and offered for sale two "beautiful specimens." They were promptly bought and added to the expedition's curio collection.

Another item of business for Wilkes was to make a copy of his Antarctic discoveries. It showed the *Vincennes's* track, the edge of the "icy barrier," and, most important, the hachuring showing land. This, with a covering letter, was sent to Hobart to await the arrival of James Clark Ross and the *Erebus* and the *Terror*.

It was a generous gesture—and one in disobedience of orders that required him to keep all his discoveries secret. But Ross and other Royal Navy officers had been helpful when Wilkes had been collecting the expedition's charts and instruments in England. Wilkes, with a lawyer's eye for a loophole, had made his own interpretation of the instruction's wording to escape the secrecy hook. Also, and it must have been most gratifying, it gave him a chance to give Ross, the world's most experienced polar navigator, a few tips on polar sailing.

This generous gesture, however, was to lead to a mighty clashing of egos.

The United States Exploring Expedition, by March 1840, was not halfway through what was to become close to a four-year odyssey. Their three months of Antarctic adventures and horrors were now over. Ahead of them lay the Pacific and warmer, if no less dangerous, work.

Before arriving at the Fiji Islands, the officers settled their wills. These were the infamous cannibal islands, and the survey work was going to be done in the ships' boats.

The boats, open whaleboats, cutters, and launches, worked in pairs and were sometimes out for three weeks at a stretch. About half a dozen men crewed a boat crammed with masts, sails, oars, tents, and anchors. Provisions consisted of hardtack, salt pork, two breakers of water, and one of whiskey. Along with the normal boat equipment went the surveying equipment: watches, notepads, pencils, spyglasses, sextants, flags, and poles. Every man had a pistol, musket, and cutlass. Blunderbusses were mounted on pivots, and some of the boats carried Congreve rockets. Reynolds armed himself with a Hall breech-loading rifle fitted with a yard-long bayonet. Wilkes, when going ashore, put his trust in an armed guard, two pistols holstered at his belt, and his faithful companion Sydney, a massive Newfoundland dog. Sydney would sit in the bow of Wilkes's launch, leap ashore on the beach, and chase off any natives—a Newfoundland dog was beyond their comprehension—and then act as a guard dog as the seamen set up the temporary survey position. Sydney had slid down Antarctic icebergs and terrified penguins. At the Fiji Islands he took on a doggy pathological dislike of the natives and terrified them. A word from his master and he would have ripped out their throats. The Fijians, being keen observers of animal nature, knew it.

The islands also gave proof of the wardroom and fo'c'sle tales, often discounted by the skeptical as Munchausen rubbish, that these were the Cannibal Islands. The Americans were shown the sacred cooking pots only used for human flesh and heard eyewitness stories from the missionaries and beachcombers who had lived for years among the natives. Finally they also became eyewitnesses.

Some canoes carrying men and women had come alongside the *Peacock,* and the horrified Americans noticed that one of the canoes carried a cooked and partly eaten man's body. One of the canoeists was gnawing at a thighbone, and another at an eye muscle (a Fijian epicurean delight, equal to the flesh of the upper arm and thigh). One of Reynolds's native friends still "had his chops all greasy from . . . the repast." The skull (purchased for a fathom of cloth) was added to the expedition's collection.

The Fijian survey took four months. Two officers, one of them Wilkes's nephew, were killed by natives, and Wilkes extracted his revenge by burning to the ground two villages with Congreve rockets—the natives called them fiery spirits—laying waste the crops, and killing about a hundred Fijians in the villages and canoes.

Reynolds was eager to quit these islands, which had brought so much sorrow. He hoped that he would never see them again. In a letter to his family he wrote that the Antarctic, the Fiji Islands, and the Columbia River in Oregon had loomed large among the expedition's "bugbears." And they all dreaded the Columbia River more than most would admit. Reynolds was to be proved right.

The tedious passage across the Pacific to Honolulu, with the men on short rations, forced to drink putrid water, eat salt beef that could take a polish, plagued by rats and swarms of three-inch-long cockroaches that shared their plates of lobscouse, ate the horn buttons off their jackets, and their toenails as they slept at night, mirrored thousands of other passages across this vast ocean.

By October, more than halfway through their odyssey, the four expedition vessels were gathered together for the last time. The Hawaiian Islands were to act as the center of a spider's web as Wilkes ordered his vessels on separate surveying voyages into the North Pacific and the American northwest coast. The feared Columbia River levied its toll by wrecking the *Porpoise* on its bar. Reynolds, shifted by Wilkes to the *Flying Fish* at Honolulu, watched the shipwreck from seaward of the breakers. No lives were lost, and the *Peacock* was replaced with a brig bought by Wilkes and renamed the *Oregon*.

Wilkes continued his familiar leadership style by shifting his officers around in a game of nautical musical chairs. More joined the list of those suspended, dismissed, and arrested. Reynolds, in a letter to his father, thought his commander's leadership so tyrannous, so extreme that insanity could be the only excuse.

The squadron, bound home, sailed from Honolulu for the last time at the end of November 1841. Wilkes carried with him some disturbing news. James Clark Ross's two ships had sailed beyond Weddell's farthest south and reached 78°04′S. But worse was the information that Ross had sailed over the land marked down by Wilkes.

At Singapore the *Flying Fish*—"The Daughter of the Squadron" to the sentimental sailors—was sold to an Englishman who thought it would make a beautiful yacht. (She ended up as the *Spec*, a notorious smuggler, running opium into China.)

The squadron, reduced to three vessels, sailed from Singapore at the end of February. A few days later Wilkes gave out his last orders to his little fleet, orders that caused seething resentment. The *Porpoise* and the *Oregon* would sail for St. Helena and then Rio de Janeiro before heading for New York. The call at Rio was to pick up some scientific specimens. On their passage, every day, they were to heave to and take the water temperature at a depth of one hundred fathoms (a proceeding, as Reynolds noted, that had been performed but a half dozen times throughout the cruise). Everyone knew what was behind this. Wilkes wanted to be first home to reap all the glory. Reynolds thought the orders to be pure persecution. Other believed the orders diabolical, even more so when the specimens collected at Rio proved to be only five small boxes of minerals, shells, plants, and birds, each box capable of being lifted by hand. The *Vincennes* arrived in New York weeks ahead of the two brigs. Towed in by a steamer from Sandy Hook, the *Vincennes* dropped her commander off at the Battery, leaving Hudson to take her into the navy yard and the seamen, as soon as they were ashore, to head for the attractions of New York's Hook and Five Points districts.

When Wilkes stepped ashore at the Battery, Reynolds in the *Porpoise*, still sailing for New York, thought that the eager boys and men who had sailed from Norfolk all those years ago much changed. The boys had grown into men. The men had become wrinkled and gray. But, no matter, he hoped that the experiences and memories of what had started as the Deplorable Expedition—now changed into the Everlasting Expedition— would last "in all their freshness, as long as I have life."

For many, the voyage's experiences and memories were to be overshadowed by the climacteric of war. In two decades officers and men who had worked together for four years, would be fighting each other. But that was all in the distant future. For the immediate future the United States Exploring Expedition, strangely conceived, born in turmoil, lived in acrimony, was to end in rancor and bitterness.

Within days of landing Wilkes was filing charges against four of his officers. They responded by filing charges against him. One of the charges was the "wilful falsehood" of the 19 January sighting of land in the Antarctic all to forestall the French. An Antarctic avalanche, triggered by James Clark Ross and Dumont d'Urville, was about to engulf Wilkes.

NOTES

1. The crow's nest was a small shelter, usually a cask, for the masthead lookout when looking for whales or leads in the ice. It is an invention credited to William Scoresby (1789–1829) of Whitby, the famous Greenland whaling master.

2. Macquarie, at 54°30'S, lies just over eight hundred miles southeast of Tasmania and just north of the Convergence. Its climate can be summed up as dreary: cold, wet, windy with low cloud cover and mists. Discovered in 1810 by Frederick Hasselborough in the sealing brig *Perseverance,* it proved a sealing bonanza. Within a decade the fur seal population (estimated at between two and four hundred thousands) was wiped out. The sealers then turned to elephant seals for oil.

3. The nearest land in fact lay over a hundred miles away.

4. Sea ice has its own glossary. The *Mariner's Handbook* defines a *floe* as a flat piece of sea ice twenty meters or more across. A *bergy bit* is a large piece of glacier ice, generally showing less than five meters above sea level and about one hundred to three hundred square meters in area. A *growler* is smaller than a bergy bit, often transparent but appearing green or almost black in color, extending less than one

meter above the sea surface. *Brash ice* is an accumulation of floating ice made up of fragments not more than two meters across; it is the wreckage of other forms of ice.

5. A cockbilled yard is one topped up by one lift so that it is angled from the horizontal. A well-cockbilled yard would not extend beyond the ship's deck. It was also a symbol of mourning.

6. D'Urville, claiming 19 January for the sighting, was a day off in his reckoning. The true date, with a nice touch of irony, should have been 20 January. He had not changed the date when crossing the 180° meridian.

Chapter 12

Haunted by Cook

LAND-BLINK. On Arctic voyages, a peculiar atmospheric brightness on approaching land covered with snow; usually more yellow than ice-blink.

LET FALL! The order to drop a sail loosed from its gaskets, in order to set it.

Admiral W. H. Smyth, The Sailor's Word-Book, 1867

HEN DUMONT D'URVILLE gave his order to let fall the mainsail to keep pace with Ringgold's fast-approaching *Porpoise*, he gave it in a polar sea that he cordially disliked. Although born in Normandy, d'Urville favored the south of France, the Mediterranean, and the Pacific. As he freely admitted, he would prefer to spend three years under burning equatorial skies than two months in the polar regions.

Jules Sebastien César Dumont d'Urville had been born in 1790. His father, a senior judge and minor aristocrat, had been lucky to escape the guillotine. His mother, domineering, rigid, cold, came from a very old, very poor Norman family with pretensions to nobility. This formidable lady was adamant that her children addressed her with the formal *vous*. The young Jules, being a sickly boy, was sent out in the worst of weathers, hatless, lightly clothed, in order to toughen him up. The one humanizing influence in this stunting family atmosphere was his mother's brother, the Abbé de Croisilles. He instilled in Jules a love of languages and reading. In the Caen library the young boy came across the writings on voyages of discovery. Here, far removed from the dull, pedestrian Normandy world, were revealed the exotic, adventurous worlds of Bougainville, Cook, and Anson.

Portrait of Dumont d'Urville

"In accepting the perilous mission that the King had entrusted to me, I had considered solely my own strength and the desire to pay tribute to scientific progress for the last time." —Dumont d'Urville

(Portrait from d'Urville's *Voyage to the South Pole*)

From all accounts d'Urville was an aloof, serious, clever young man. But at seventeen, swayed by his reading and having failed at physics for entry into Napoleon's new École Polytechnique, he made the curious decision—his only knowledge of the sea coming from books—to join the French Navy. This was 1807, two years after Trafalgar, with the French Navy a very poor and despised cousin to Napoleon's Grand Armée. Continental Europe might have been a marching ground for Napoleon's soldiers, but the seas, from the Baltic to the Dardanelles, were dominated by the British Royal Navy, none more so than the waters lapping the French shores. Here Napoleon's ships were bottled up in their ports under close blockade. Privateers and smugglers might slip in and out, but rarely the ships of the French Navy. Alfred Mahan, the American naval historian, has summed it up in naval history's most romantic, Churchillian paragraph: "The world has never seen a more impressive demonstration of the influence of sea-power upon its history. Those far distant, storm-beaten ships, upon which the Grand Army never looked, stood between it and the dominion of the world."

A bottled-up navy meant bottled-up officers. D'Urville's first years of navy life were spent at the Channel port of Le Havre, where he spent most of his time learning languages. Bored with dull harbor duties, which included ferrying the commandant's mistress and her dog from ship to shore, and disliking his fellow officers, who had grown idle and dissolute under their forced inactivity, d'Urville asked for a transfer. In 1810 he was posted to the *Suffren* at Toulon. But out in the Mediterranean, with their frigates' topsails nicking the horizon, lay the Royal Navy's blockading fleet. So, scrambling about the hills of Provence, d'Urville added botany to his language interests.

It was not until 1814, with Napoleon exiled to Elba, a fat[1] and gouty Bourbon king back on the French throne, the tricolor replaced by the Bourbon fleur-de-lis, the blockade lifted, that d'Urville went to sea for a short cruise in the Mediterranean. Two years later he married Adèle Pepin, the daughter of a Toulon watchmaker. The marriage to the attractive, vivacious brunette, a Provençale to her fingertips, infuriated d'Urville's mother. Her son, she thought, had married below his class. The implacable beldam refused to meet Adèle or, in the years ahead, her grandchildren.

Three years after his marriage d'Urville sailed as an *enseigne* aboard the *Chevrette* for a surveying voyage of Mediterranean islands. D'Urville's concerns, displayed in published papers on the subjects, were to be botany, insects, and archaeology. At Milos in the Cyclades, on a botanizing expedition, d'Urville came across a marble statue recently unearthed by a Greek peasant. The statue, in two pieces joined by iron tenons, was close to six feet in height. D'Urville was struck by its beauty and grace. Here was a bare-breasted women with her raised left arm holding an apple. Her right arm held a draped sash that fell from hips to feet. The hair was drawn back and held by a thin headband. The face was beautiful except for a damaged nose. The ears were pierced for earrings. The young *enseigne* drew the only conclusion, the apple being the clue, that here was a statue of Aphrodite/Venus holding the golden apple awarded to her by the shepherd Paris.

The Greek peasant, smelling a buyer, offered to sell the statue. But d'Urville's captain refused to buy it, claiming there was no room aboard the *Chevrette*. At Constantinople the thwarted d'Urville showed his sketches of the statue to the French ambassador and persuaded him that here was a great work of art. The ambassador ordered his secretary to sail for Milos and buy the Venus for France. But the peasant had sold the statue to a priest, who was about to ship it off to a rich Turk. Priests, however, have their price; the secretary outbid the Turk. Lugging the statue back to their ship, the French sailors were attacked by Greek brigands, and in the fracas d'Urville's Venus lost her arms. The sailors refused to return to pick them up, the result being the *Légion d'Honneur* for d'Urville, the Venus de Milo in the Louvre, and some lyrics for a song.

The Venus de Milo might have lost her arms, but d'Urville gained an epaulett and promotion to lieutenant. A few years previous, as an unknown *enseigne*, he had applied to join Freycinet's voyage in the *Uranie*. Over d'Urville's shoulder hung the shades of Anson, Cook, and Bougainville. Exploration, the search for knowledge, not war, was going to be his path to fame. But his application was refused. The refusal rankled. D'Urville, like his mother, had a prickly side to his character, and the refusal was taken as a personal slight. He never forgot that refusal and always disparaged Freycinet's voyage as of little account.

One of Freycinet's officers, Louis Isidore Duperrey, four years older and senior to d'Urville, saw unfinished work in the Pacific. Duperrey and d'Urville were friends, and both put their heads together and drafted a plan for further exploration. It was heard by receptive ears. The French were looking to the Pacific, where, in the words of the *Moniteur*, the French "could transplant civilization and its benefits."

In 1822 the corvette *Coquille* sailed from Toulon on a voyage—like today's space probes—to investigate everything that politicians and the Paris savants could scrape together. France had been boxed out of the Pacific during the Napoleonic Wars; now was the time to move in. It was also thought that the novel experiment of the New South Wales penal settlement could perhaps be repeated with a French penal settlement in western Australia or New Zealand. The corvette sailed with Duperrey commanding and in charge of hydrography, meterology, and magnetism. D'Urville was his first lieutenant and in charge of natural history. The *Coquille* returned to France in March 1825. D'Urville was now thirty-five years old, and the puny youth had turned into a tall, strong, heavily built man, rather brusque, aloof, with little small talk. His fellow officers admired his stamina and capacity for hard work, but his coldness and air of superiority they found less than amiable. Strangely at odds with his heavy arrogance went a total lack of concern about his clothing. On the *Coquille*'s deck and below he looked shabbier than the scruffiest sailor. Torn duck trousers, unbuttoned threadbare jacket, open-necked shirt, no socks, the whole hobo outfit topped off by an old straw hat full of holes were his normal dress. R.-P. Lesson, one of the ship's surgeons and naturalists, wrote that d'Urville combined the stern sobriety of a Spanish hidalgo with a tramplike appearance. It was an image that confounded the punctilious and smartly dressed British Royal Navy officers when they visited the corvette. But since d'Urville and Lesson—driven from their cabins by voracious cockroaches that ate leather and skin from feet and even drank the inkwells dry—slept for ten months on mats laid on deck, even during tropical rainstorms, perhaps smartness of dress would have been a lost battle.

D'Urville's attitude to food, contrary to the received opinion that all the French are gastronomes, was a mirror image of his approach to dress. A love of highly spiced foods and a preference for salt or smoked meat to fresh went along with a disdain for hygiene and doctors' opinions. A specific known as Leroy's purgative was d'Urville's panacea for all ills.

Within two months of the *Coquille*'s return d'Urville had presented the minister of marine with a proposal for another Pacific voyage. The years aboard the corvette had soured his friendship with Duperrey, and d'Urville wanted his own command. The minister was persuaded; d'Urville was promoted to *capitaine de frégate* (commander), and the *Coquille*, renamed *Astrolabe* in honor of La Pérouse's lost ship, sailed from Toulon in April 1826.[2]

The *Astrolabe* returned with its huge natural history collection and draft charts in February 1829. But the d'Urville who returned was no longer the tough, indestructible man of the *Coquille* voyage. The years of salt meat and tropical fevers had taken their toll. Gout, severe stomach pains, and kidney[3] infections were to afflict him for the rest of his life.

D'Urville spent two weeks with his family at Toulon before traveling to Paris and the minister of marine. The d'Urvilles had now been married for thirteen years, and more than half those years had been spent apart. Their first child, a boy, had died when d'Urville had been at sea in the *Coquille*, but another boy, Jules, was a healthy four-year-old.

The next five years were spent by d'Urville, now promoted to *capitaine de vaisseau* (post captain), working on the *Astrolabe*'s narrative. The five volumes were published between 1832 and 1834. He also wrote a two-volume best seller, *Voyage pittoresque autor du monde*, describing famous voyages of exploration. In it was a compressed version of his voyage in the *Astrolabe*.

D'Urville was no diplomat, and his brusque manner, goaded by gout, made him few friends in high places. The epilogue to the five volumes did nothing to improve matters. In tactless, incendiary prose he mounted an attack on the Ministry of Marine, fellow officers, the Academy of Sciences, and the administration of King Louis Philippe. The *Astrolabe*'s arduous and dangerous voyage had not been given enough recognition; his officers had been neglected for promotion; the ministry and some naval officers were narrow-minded and blind to the benefits of exploratory voy-

ages; he himself had failed to be elected to the Academy of Sciences because of the machinations of a powerful clique; and the government—
d'Urville had strong republican sympathies—was returning France to the
bad old days.

By 1835, the narrative completed, the naval hierarchy alienated,
d'Urville found himself returned to the humdrum activities of port duties
at Toulon. That same year the d'Urvilles' two-year-old daughter—"the
apple of our eyes," wrote her father—died in a cholera epidemic sweeping
through Provence. But Jules, their other child, escaped the nineteenth
century's killer disease. Moreover, Jules, much to his father's satisfaction,
was turning into a very clever young boy with a talent for languages.

Another son was born; the dull port duties continued; the attacks of
gout came and went. D'Urville was now forty-seven. Homelife was comfortable with his cherished Adèle; he had two sons, one of them with outstanding intellectual potential. But during his years working on the
Astrolabe's narrative he had come across gaps in the knowledge of the
languages and races of Oceania. Through his blood, like Cook's and
Flinders's, ran the exploration virus. Oceania still beckoned. Tennyson's
later line from *Ulysses* "Some work of noble note, may yet be done" would
have struck a receptive chord.

In addition, d'Urville was being haunted by the example of Cook's
three great voyages. At night he was tormented by dreams in which he was
making his own third great voyage. This dream third voyage often took
him into the polar regions. (Although he freely admitted his admiration
for the polar voyages of Cook, Ross, and Parry, these were voyages that
held few charms for d'Urville.) The dreams included running aground in
narrow channels, on reefs, even trying to sail across dry riverbeds. The
"Ulysses factor," the Ulysses virus, could not be ignored.

In January 1837 d'Urville wrote to the minister of marine outlining his
suggestions for a third voyage into Oceania.

King Louis Philippe was shown the plan and suggested an addition: a
probe to the South Pole—or at least farther south than Weddell. The
Americans were still (interminably) preparing their expedition. The British,
having located the north magnetic pole, were thinking of making it a
brace and bagging the south magnetic pole. Here was a chance for France
to join the southern race and perhaps beat at the post both their old
enemy and the younger commercial rival from across the Atlantic. Substi-
tute polar regions for space, and the nineteenth-century equivalent to the
twentieth-century space race was off and running.

D'Urville was at first taken aback by the proposal. Polar voyages came
low on his list. But he could hardly back out from uninterest or dislike, and
the more he examined the idea, the more he warmed to it. Napoleon,
wrote d'Urville, had said "that people like to be astonished." A voyage to
the South Pole would certainly astonish them. It was novel and would

focus their attention. In the new age of literacy and newspapers, the new, the unusual, the unique were bound to draw attention to the expedition. Oddly enough, after he accepted the new proposals, his dreams of sailing in polar waters ended.

The French preparations gathered speed, but not as quickly as d'Urville would have liked. The latest date for sailing from Toulon was set at 15 August. Later than that would cut the expedition's polar time in the short Antarctic summer. But compared with the American expedition and its bungling preparations, the French were performing prodigies of efficiency. Two vessels were chosen in March: d'Urville's familiar and faithful *Astrolabe* and the slightly smaller *Zélée*. Both vessels had been built as storeships, and their titles as corvettes may be considered almost honorary. Slow but seaworthy with great carrying capacity, they were very close in size and type to Cook's ex-colliers—ideal exploration vessels. To command the *Zélée*, d'Urville picked Charles Hector Jacquinot, an old friend and shipmate who had sailed with d'Urville aboard the *Coquille* and the *Astrolabe*.

D'Urville, with the two corvettes being refitted at Toulon, set about collecting all the equipment, instruments, books, and charts. Not all these could be found in France, and he spent a week in London on a buying expedition. He also met with Captain Francis Beaufort, the Admiralty hydrographer, and with Captain John Washington, the secretary of the Royal Geographical Society. Both men—but Washington in particular—were fervent apostles for a British expedition into the Antarctic and the scientific search for the south magnetic pole. D'Urville sensed their regret that they might be forestalled by the French.

Dining at the Raleigh Club, he asked his fellow diners, travelers all, their opinion of James Weddell. D'Urville thought him "a simple seal hunter" and had reservations about his navigational competence and truthfulness. In other words, d'Urville, in his tactless way, was asking if they thought Weddell a liar. Shocked, his dining companions replied that Weddell was "a true gentleman" and they all had complete faith in the truth of his voyage.

Another, stranger visit was made to a London phrenologist. D'Urville had become a firm believer in this faddish nineteenth-century pseudoscience, the feng shui of the day. Needless to say, the reading of d'Urville's character from his skull bumps by the "cranioscopist" was so true to d'Urville's own perception of himself (love of travel, autocratic, took risks to attain lofty goals, love of languages, classics, history, the sciences, etc., etc.) that he was amazed. All this served only to reinforce d'Urville's belief in his new faith to such an extent that he appointed Pierre Dumoutier phrenologist aboard the *Astrolabe,* the first "cranioscopist" to sail on an exploring expedition. (Later in the voyage, when d'Urville was so ill he thought he was about to die, he drew up a a new will in which he left his head to Dumoutier, who was required to prepare and preserve it for phrenological study. Dumoutier was also required to cut out and preserve his heart, this to be delivered back to Toulon and given to Adèle.)

A month after his return from London d'Urville was back in the blazing sunshine and heat of Toulon. On the day that the *Astrolabe* was commissioned, a day of brilliant sun and airless heat, the harbor stinking of rotting fish and open sewers, a tired, gout-ridden, hobbling d'Urville was grimly amused to hear a new seaman mutter to his companion: "Oh! This old boy won't get us very far!"[4] It was a comment that determined him to show them how far he could, and would, lead.

To tempt the expedition's sailors, d'Urville had suggested to the minister of marine a financial carrot: one hundred gold francs for every member of the expedition if the corvettes reached 75°S latitude, and then an extra twenty francs for each degree south of this latitude. (Weddell's farthest south had been 74°15′S latitude.)

On 7 September 1837 the two corvettes, three weeks later than planned by d'Urville, sailed from Toulon. The decks were loud with the noise of livestock on the hoof and cackling of hens in the hen coops. Much equipment and stores still cluttered the ship, all to be stowed and secured. D'Urville's instructions directed him first into what is now the Weddell Sea and as far south as ice would permit, then north to the Magellan Strait and Chile, and then Oceania, his true love. The new British colony in western Australia was to be inspected, followed by a visit to Hobart, then to New Zealand and the search for facilities for the French whaling fleet. New Zealand also sorely tempted the French as a site for a penal colony along the lines of New South Wales. This was to be followed by a cruise through the East Indies and a return to France via the Cape of Good Hope. Science, commerce, hydrography, and power politics: the usual mix.

Across the Atlantic, as the two corvettes and their 165 officers and men sailed south, the American expedition was stumbling from crisis to crisis under Mahlon Dickerson and the increasingly disillusioned Thomas ap Catesby Jones. The French, not knowing the almost farcical state of affairs, thought the Americans were just being very careful and conscientious in their preparations.

In England an influential scientific lobby was trying to persuade the government to send a Royal Navy expedition to the snow and ice of the south magnetic pole.

D'Urville's expedition had a clear field and was off to a flying start.

After a call at Tenerife, where the seamen disgraced themselves by getting drunk, fighting with the locals, and being slammed in jail, the two corvettes headed down the long stretch of the Atlantic Ocean. They anchored for a few hours off Rio de Janeiro to send ashore a young officer who had been suffering severe chest pains since Toulon. It's surprising that more men were not bundled ashore when one reads of the Noel and Taboureau canned meats served out to the crew. When the first thirty-kilogram can was opened, it had given off a foul smell. It was still cooked and eaten. But the seamen disliked it, claiming the saltpeter gave them toothache. After three drums (drum seems more appropriate to describe sixty-six pounds of rotting beef) had exploded, nothing more was heard about dishing out Noel and Taboureau's preserved meat.

By the end of November the corvettes were approaching the Strait of Magellan. D'Urville, after rereading his collected library of Antarctic exploration accounts, decided he had time to explore before heading south. More than three weeks were spent in the strait (with d'Urville very approving of Captain Philip Parker King's accurate charts) before the French expedition headed back into the Atlantic and then south in the attempt to knock Weddell off his perch and collect the hundred gold francs for each man.

The fabled Patagonians had proved a disappointment. D'Urville thought the men lazy and dirty and the women "extremely lascivious." New Year's Day 1838 had been spent by a Patagonian river with the officers eating lunch on the sandy beach. The commander handed out expedition medals to his officers, relaxed a little, and tucked into a "merry feast" of sausage, salt pork, roast chicken, and goose, washed down with white wine followed by champagne.

Two weeks later the Frenchmen were gazing at their first iceberg. By 20 January, at 62°S, they were threading their way through a line of icebergs, close to Weddell's track of 1823. Even the most pessimistic were talking of reaching at least 80°S latitude. But the next night d'Urville was woken by shouts and went on deck to find a vast field of pack ice stretching across their course. The corvettes could only turn northeast and coast slowly along what d'Urville called *la banquise*—the ice barrier.

Here, thought d'Urville, was a new, terrible world: silent, mournful, eerie. Ghostly petrels gliding around the snow-drifted corvettes were the only movement, spouting whales the only sound to break the "sad monotony." Heaven help anyone, he thought, abandoned here.

The Frenchmen's two-month battle with the Antarctic pack ice and weather had started. D'Urville likened it to a battle with a formidable enemy. Furthermore, at one point, during five days in February, it looked as if the enemy were set to defeat and destroy them.

In an attack similar to the reckless philosophy that gripped French generals during the early months of the First World War, that almost mystical belief in "will" and the *offensive à outrance*, d'Urville set his corvettes at what appeared to be a thinly held channel in the pack and forced his vessels into a small and relatively clear basin. There they anchored to a large and stable floe as if moored at Toulon. The officers were so elated that a

The *Astrolabe* trapped in the ice

"The only way out was the way we had come in."   —Dumont d'Urville

(Illustration from d'Urville's *Voyage to the South Pole*)

group walked over from the *Zélée* to the *Astrolabe* and celebrated with punch. D'Urville was not quite so sanguine.

The wind changed; the channel filled in; ice closed around; the corvettes were held fast, beset. The only escape lay in cutting the ice and hauling their way through the pack. Men struggled on the ice to set ice anchors, to pry apart floes with picks and mattocks. Ten hours of effort produced less than a mile of progress to freedom. After five days of labor they were in clear water. The ice saws bolted to the corvette's stems were torn away; the hulls were battered. Long ice stalactites hung from the spars. Halyards, guys, braces, and sheets had to be chipped clear of ice and snow. The men were exhausted, and the sick list was growing. D'Urville vowed in future to treat the pack ice with more respect.

Toward the end of February d'Urville gave up any more ideas of breaking through the pack and reaching Weddell's south. The gentlemen of the Raleigh Club might consider Weddell's account truthful, but d'Urville still had his doubts.

After a visit to the South Orkney Islands to collect geological specimens plus penguin meat for the cooking pot—the seamen thought it tasted like chicken—the corvettes headed west for the South Shetland Islands and Bransfield Strait.

Through the fogs and drifting snow the French caught glimpses of land not shown, or shown only sketchily, on any of their charts. D'Urville, for once being diplomatic and also knowing who was providing the butter on his bread, named the dimly seen coasts Louis Philippe Land, Joinville Land, Rosamel Island.[5]

But after weeks of sailing through fogs and snow d'Urville decided to quit what he called "these gloomy regions." Living conditions aboard the corvettes were deteriorating, and the crews were showing alarming signs of scurvy with sore mouths and aching limbs. The berth decks, with only crouching headroom, were becoming foul-smelling underworlds, where forty to sixty men ate, drank, spit, and slept. The berth decks also held the galleys and storerooms, and they was shut tight against waves, air, and light. In this murk the steam from the galley cookers coated every partition and bulkhead with a film of water. Cooking smells mixed with the smells from the storerooms, holds, and unwashed bodies. It was a brave man who went to the "heads" at the bow to relieve himself in the middle of a blizzard. The bilges became their toilets.

By the end of the first week in March the corvettes were heading north. D'Urville admitted that their attempt had been a complete failure. The goal had been to follow in Weddell's track, but *la banquise* had blocked them off.

The passage north to Talcahuano in Chile was painfully slow. Scurvy was decimating the crews of both vessels with the *Zélée*'s men so scurvy-ridden that the officers had to help in shortening sail. A month after sail-

The corvettes at anchor in Nuku Hiva
"A swarm of black heads above the water . . . all the young beauties of the island are coming to board the ships. To avoid the moment of chaos that would follow such an extraordinary invasion, I gave the order to raise the boarding nets."

—Dumont d'Urville

(Illustration by Louis Le Breton from d'Urville's *Voyage to the South Pole*)

ing from the South Shetlands they came to anchor at Talcahuano close to a British frigate. The *Zélée* was a virtual hospital ship with thirty-eight men down with scurvy. Jacquinot, as the sick men were carried on deck and put into boats to be taken ashore into a temporary hospital, found his men so changed by sickness that he failed to recognize familiar faces. The *Astrolabe* was little different with twenty scurvy cases.

The vision of this line of sick men reminds one piercingly of First World War photographs showing gassed soldiers with bandaged eyes, arms outstretched to touch the man ahead, stumbling back from the front lines. But even before surveying the shambles of his expedition as they went ashore, d'Urville had made up his mind to make a second attempt at Antarctica from Hobart.

It was, however, a venture to be kept secret until the time came to reveal it.

Twenty months were spent in the Pacific and East Indies before the corvettes came to anchor at Hobart on 12 December 1839.

For the seamen the best of times had been the week spent at Nuku

Hiva in the Marquesas. Here the island's young women had swum out to the corvettes—canoes were taboo for women—and d'Urville, knowing full well their intentions, had had the boarding nets raised. The naked girls had clambered aboard and formed, according to d'Urville, a somewhat novel living, chattering cordon around the decks. At six o'clock the evening gun had been fired, and the nets lowered. D'Urville dryly noted that what followed held some truly comic scenes. The rest he left to the reader's imagination.

The worst of times came when sailing from the East Indies to Hobart: Fourteen men and three officers had died from dysentery and been buried at sea. Another six were to die at Hobart.

For d'Urville, at the personal level, the worst of times had come at Valparaiso. In a letter from his wife he had learned that their young son Emile had died from cholera. The distraught Adèle had begged d'Urville to give up his sailing and return home. She cursed all the glory and honor that might come his way from the voyage. The price of his absence was too high. Clément Dumoulin, the *Astrolabe's* talented hydrographer and a close friend of d'Urville's, had watched the tears running down his commander's cheeks as he read Adèle's letter. Running a close second must have been the hours spent in physical agony. At times only lying in a tub of hot water could ease the agony of gout and stomach pains.

As for the best of times, they probably came when he looked over the draft charts made by Dumoulin and the exquisite drawings of Ernest Goupil[6] and Louis Le Breton.

For one officer, Barlatier Demas, perhaps the most surprising time had come at Raffles Bay in northern Australia. He had been ashore with a party to shoot kangaroos, parrots, and doves. One of the party, seeing a movement in the long grass, was about to shoot when two aborigines burst out from the grass, crying "Waterloo! Wellington!" "What a recommendation!" wrote Demas with a touch of irony. "These were the names the English had given them. But we never expected to have these two words shouted at us by two wretched savages in the middle of the Australian desert."

The French were made very welcome at Hobart. A building was provided as a hospital for the sick and dying. Fresh vegetables were sent on board. The officers looked for lodgings ashore. The foul-smelling corvettes were scrubbed clean from the detritus of dysentery and repainted. Masts, spars, rigging, and sails were overhauled and repaired.

Both d'Urville and Jacquinot found Hobart much changed in the twelve years since their last visit in the *Astrolabe*. The population had tripled to twelve thousand; what were once dirt pathways were now streets laid out at right angles with military precision and lined with small, clean, pleasant houses; tall windmills, blades turning in the wind like giant automatons, dotted the hills; the distinctive aroma of breweries and the one distillery drifted across the town; grogshops and taverns had multiplied, as had the government buildings and the smart-looking equipages of the prospering business class. The anchorage was full of ships, many of them whaleships, and bustle and activity spread out from the waterfront. All this affluence, as the French noted, had been built with convict slave labor on land given by the government. Rum, slaves, free land and whaling. Many observers of the time had also noted the remarkable similarity between this new British colony in the Southern Hemisphere and the United States, the old colony in the north.

Sir John Franklin, the Arctic explorer and now lieutenant governor of Tasmania, inspected the French corvettes and invited their officers to dinner at Government House. The officers were charmed by the good-natured Franklin and his equally amiable wife, Lady Jane Franklin. D'Urville heard that Wilkes's vessels were in Sydney, making ready for their venture south and that Wilkes had draped a cloak of secrecy over the expedition's activities.

A few days later d'Urville met with John Biscoe, the discoverer of Enderby Land and now master of a brig trading between Hobart and Sydney. Biscoe had met with Wilkes in Sydney but could add nothing to d'Urville's limited information on the American's intentions. But he did give d'Urville the information that he, Biscoe, had recently made a venture south of New Zealand and had been stopped by ice at 63°S latitude.

D'Urville had set his sights on 1 January 1840 as the date for sailing south. But the expedition's crew losses from dysentery set him to toying with the idea of sailing with only one vessel, the *Astrolabe*. Her crew losses would be made good with volunteers from the *Zélée*. Jacquinot's corvette would stay in Hobart until the sick had recovered and then rendezvous with d'Urville at the Auckland Islands or New Zealand.

During a walk along Hobart's streets d'Urville unfolded the plan to his faithful second-in-command. Jacquinot was so upset, argued so passionately to share the venture south that d'Urville capitulated and agreed that the corvettes would sail together—provided that Jacquinot could find replacements for his vessel from Hobart's pool of suspect seamen, deserters from French whaleships and what d'Urville called English "rogues." Enough deserters and rogues were persuaded to sign on, and the two corvettes sailed from Hobart on 1 January 1840.[7]

The day before they sailed the Franklins had given a party and ball in honor of the French. Aboard the corvettes were officers with aching heads, enough live pigs and sheep to provide fresh meat for three weeks, and gallons of lime juice, taken aboard on the advice of the English, to stave off scurvy.

D'Urville's plan was simple: to sail south from Tasmania until he came to the ice and to take magnetic observations to aid in the location of the south magnetic pole. Then the *Astrolabe* would sail to the Auckland Islands or New Zealand and the *Zélée* to Hobart to pick up the sick.

A Gallic insouciance surrounds d'Urville's plan. It's the last scene in *Casablanca* with Bogart and Rains sauntering off into the mists bound for Brazzaville.

The simple plan required a simple course order for the watch: south. Or as close to south as the wind would allow. But the wind, to d'Urville's dismay, did not allow. It hung in from the south and was accompanied by a big swell from the west that made life aboard the rolling corvettes acutely uncomfortable. Worse, however, was the return of dysentery, which claimed one life and put sixteen men on the sick list. But as the vessels worked their way south, the sick list shortened.

A gale forced them to heave to for two days among monstrous seas, and the albatrosses that had followed them since Tasmania vanished at 50°S latitude. A day later came a sudden drop in air and water temperature. The vanished albatrosses were replaced by thousands of petrels; the expedition had crossed the Convergence into the Antarctic. At 60°S latitude, on 16 January, they sailed by their first iceberg. Two days later, at 64°S latitude, they were sailing in thick snow past enormous tabular icebergs. Ahead lay the Antarctic Circle, for which the sailors had been preparing a ceremony equivalent to the traditional crossing of the equator. D'Urville, knowing that the costume making, the buffoonery, and the practical jokes were ways his men could let off steam, agreed to the ceremony. He also told the men that he would be the first initiate—with the one proviso that no water be involved. Water and duckings might be all very well when crossing the tropical line but not at the frozen circle.

On 19 January, after a rain of rice and beans from the topmast, d'Urville was officially informed by a messenger mounted on a seal that Father Antarctic would board the corvette the following day. The announcement was well timed. Land had been sighted in the afternoon. That evening, the vessels surrounded by massive tabular icebergs perfectly reflected in a calm and windless sea, the men watched in a profound silence as the sun set behind their new discovery.

Early the next morning they saw the snow-covered land even more clearly. It stretched from east to west, uniform, no peaks showing through the snow cover, and sloped down to the sea. The corvettes lay reflected in a flat, calm sea as Father Antarctic came aboard. Sailors in outlandish dress paraded around the deck; there were mimes, sermons, a banquet, dancing, and singing. No splashing of water, only the pouring of wine.

A wind picked up the following day, and d'Urville took his vessels through a massive concentration of icebergs to close with the land. At times they were so hemmed in that the officers' shouted orders echoed off the icebergs as if they were sailing through the depths of a white-walled canyon. By noon of 21 January they were three miles off the land that d'Urville estimated to be between one thousand to twelve hundred meters high. It ended at an ice-covered sea in a vertical cliff of ice. Here, thought d'Urville, was the source of all the surrounding icebergs. All day they slowly sailed westward, coasting by the ice cliffs, unable to get closer because of the loose pack ice. That evening outcrops of rock were seen in the snow-covered land. The corvettes hove to, boats were lowered, and after a hard row the French landed on a rocky islet, one of about ten, that lay a quarter mile offshore from the cliffs of ice. A lieutenant from the *Zélée,* Joseph Dubouzet, recorded in his diary the landing:

> It was nearly 9 o'clock when, to our great joy, we landed on the western part of the most westerly and loftiest islet. The *Astrolabe*'s boat had arrived a moment before, and already the men had climbed up the steep sides of this rock. They hurled down the penguins, who were much astonished to find themselves so brutally dispossessed of the island, to which they were the sole inhabitants. . . . I then immediately sent one of our men to unfurl the tricolour flag on this land, which no human creature had either seen or stepped on before. Following the ancient custom, faithfully kept up by the English, we took possession of it in the name of France, as well as of the adjacent coast. . . . The ceremony ended, as it should, with a libation. To the glory of France, which concerned us deeply just then, we emptied a bottle of the most generous of her wines . . . never was Bordeaux wine called on to play a more worthy part; never was a bottle emptied more fitly.

Loaded with their trophies, rocks and penguins, and with a bitterly cold wind filling in from the east, the boats sailed back to the corvettes. They arrived at nearly midnight with the boats covered in a thin skin of ice.

D'Urville named their new discovery Terre Adélie and the rock and penguin hunting island Pointe Géologie.[8] The naming of the land after his wife he considered an obligation, a small token of his thanks to the devoted wife who had consented to three "long and painful separations" during his years of exploration. The memory of her distraught letter at Valparaiso, that cry from the heart, still haunted him.

Two days later, after a slow sail westward tracing the coastline in good visibility and a light easterly winds, they came across pack ice stretching across their course. They were now in a cul-de-sac bounded by the coast to port, ice ahead, and ice reaching out to starboard toward the northeast. D'Urville put his corvettes about and, with yards braced up, tacks on board, started a wearisome thrash to windward to escape from the trap of a lee shore. For days the weather had been magnificent with good visibility and light winds. But now an ominous swell was building from the east, as were dark and threatening skies. Within hours the corvettes, hidden from each other by thick, swirling snow, were struggling to claw away from the pack ice in storm-force winds. The *Astrolabe* lost her mainsail, torn to ribbons when clewed up. The compasses, so close to the south magnetic pole, were useless; ice built up on hulls, decks, spars, and rigging. At one point, heeled over by the press of a vicious squall, the *Astrolabe*'s leeward battery of guns was underwater. The storm lasted twenty-four hours with everyone, including d'Urville, thinking that these were their last hours. By the afternoon of 25 January, after a last ferocious squall, the wind died away, and by evening the two corvettes were sailing side by side as if nothing had happened. Except that both vessels were busy repairing damage and bending new sails to replace those torn from their bolt ropes. Four days later the French had their brief sighting of Ringgold's *Porpoise*. Standing southwest in poor visibility, the corvettes had sighted a line of ice and promptly clewed up their mainsails to reduce sail and speed. A few minutes later, the fog clearing, they sighted a vessel bearing down on them under full sail. D'Urville, noting the American flag and pennant at her masthead indicating a man-of-war, knew she must be one of Wilkes's squadron. With the American approaching so fast d'Urville gave the order to let fall the mainsail to pick up speed and stay alongside the racing brig, which immediately, much to the mystification of the French, promptly bore away and vanished in the mists.

D'Urville later heard of Wilkes's interpretation of the meeting and his remarks. The Frenchman skewered Wilkes to the wall with his riposte.

We had no object in keeping secret the result of our operations. . . . Besides these are no longer the days when navigators, impelled by the interests of commerce, think themselves obliged to hide carefully their route and their discoveries in order to avoid the concurrence of rival nations. On the contrary, I should have been glad to give our co-explorers the result of our researches. . . . If I can believe what was told me in Hobart Town, it seems the Americans were far from sharing these feelings. They have always maintained the greatest secrecy concerning their operations at all the points where they landed, and have refrained from giving the slightest indication of the work which they have accomplished.

The following day the corvettes were sailing along sheer ice cliffs some 100 to 150 feet high. Opinions were divided. Was this a huge mass of ice independent of land? Or a massive crust of ice covering a solid base of rock? D'Urville was of the latter opinion and named it Côte Clarie after Jacquinot's wife.

On 1 February d'Urville made the decision to turn north for Hobart. The magnetic observations had been taken; land had been discovered. It would have been possible to sail farther west, but he and his crew were tired. D'Urville believed, after his short passage of arms with the Antarctic, that "the greater part of the polar circle is surrounded by land, and that in the end it will be found by some navigator sufficiently fortunate and bold enough to break through the masses of accumulated ice which ordinarily surround it." Also, of course, the news of their discovery had to be made public, preferably before news of any American discovery. Seventeen days later they were back at Hobart, and on 21 February the *Hobart Advertiser* carried a report of the French discovery.

At Hobart d'Urville learned that three more of his men had died in the hospital and that two were close to death. He also learned that a dozen French whalers had visited Hobart, that three remained, and that a handful of deserters could be persuaded to make up his crew numbers. Sir John Franklin told him that James Ross with the *Erebus* and the *Terror* were expected shortly, that nothing had been heard from the American expedition, and that he, Franklin, was eager to hear of the French discoveries and their adventures.

The corvettes sailed from Hobart in the early hours of 25 February bound for the Auckland Islands. Here Dumoulin would play the magnetician before they continued on to New Zealand. On 11 March they dropped anchor at Sarah's Bosom, the favored anchorage of sealers and whaleships. But only one Portuguese whaleship rode at anchor off the rocky and kelp-lined shore.

An anchorage with such a name suggests maternal warmth and plenitude. Anchored in Sarah's Bosom on a clear and sunny summer day, the gentle slopes of Mount Eden cloaked in the crimson blossoms of the rata tree forest, melodious bellbirds calling in the forest's shade, red-crowned parakeets flickering along the shore, a weary seaman might think himself in paradise. But the Auckland Islands are a paradise only for the ornithologist, the botanist, the Hooker's sea lion lover. Uninhabited and lying 250 miles south of New Zealand, they are set squarely across the face of the prevailing westerlies and the Southern Ocean swells. *Wet* and *windy* sum up the climate. Discovered in 1806 by Abraham Bristow of the *Ocean,* a whaleship owned by the Enderby Brothers of London, the Aucklands were soon stripped of their fur seals and then became a base for whaleship's working the New Zealand waters. Within a hundred years they collected an evil reputation as the Southern Ocean's maritime graveyard. Nearly a dozen vessels and over a hundred lives were lost in the seas foaming at the base of the west coast craggy cliffs: a thirty-mile-long ambuscade, two hundred feet high, set across the great circle course of sailing ships running their easting down from Australia to Cape Horn. In 1886 the *General Grant,* carrying twenty-five crew, fifty-eight passengers, and a cargo that contained a large amount of gold, ground into the cliffs. Unlike most of the island's catastrophic shipwrecks, it happened in a calm while drifting on the swells into a large cavern on the west coast. Sixty-three drowned and five more died on the island before the fifteen survivors, eighteen months later, were rescued.

The captain of the whaleship showed d'Urville an almost indecipherable letter left by Ringgold. Ashore the French inspected a conspicuous pole with a black board and freshly painted lettering: "U.S. brig Porpoise, 73 days out from Sydney, New Holland, on her return from an exploring cruize along the antarctic circle, all well; arrived the 7th, and sailed again on the 10th March, for the Bay of Islands, New Zealand."

The *Porpoise* had sailed just one day before the French arrival. The French spent their few days at Sarah's Bosom in pouring rain. The crews wooded and watered, fished—the fish were found full of worms—and inspected the newly dug grave of a French whaleship captain who had committed suicide in a fit of depression. Before sailing for New Zealand, following Ringgold's example, they left a painted board with the following message: *"Les corvettes Françoises l'*Astrolabe *et la* Zélée, *parties de Hobart Town le 25 Février, 1840, mouillées ici le 11 Mars, et réparties le 20 du did pour la New Zéland. Du 19 Janvier au 1 Février, 1840, découverte de la Terre Adélie et détermination du pôle magnétique Austral!"*

D'Urville and Jacquinot were now sailing into familiar waters. They anchored at three harbors on New Zealand's South Island and met with French whalers, who told them that whales were getting hard to find off South America but still appeared plentiful in New Zealand and Australian waters.

On 26 April they were anchored at the familiar Bay of Islands among a dozen whaleships, a British warship, and a transport bringing settlers. An irascible d'Urville, suffering from gout and severe stomach pains, gloomily noted the moral deterioration of the Maoris since his last visit. Drink, tobacco, and prostitution had destroyed a culture. His Anglophobia, fanned by gout, colic, and the signing of the Treaty of Waitanga by the Maori chiefs, which had turned New Zealand into a British colony, set him to railing against the "sordid avarice" of the Protestant missionaries, the dissolute deserters, and the runaway convicts and to sorrowing on another lost opportunity by the French to establish a Pacific colony.

He also learned that Wilkes with his expeditionary ships had sailed from the Bay of Islands just three weeks before the corvettes' arrival. His informant told him that the Americans had been very closemouthed about their Antarctic venture, giving nothing away.

The French expedition was now entering into its final phase, the last homing trajectory across half the world's face before touchdown at Toulon.

Sailing from the Bay of Islands, the corvettes headed for the Torres Strait, that reef-strewn eighty-mile gap between Australia and New Guinea. It was here that one coral reef came close to putting a premature end to the expedition. Both corvettes drove hard on a coral reef at high tide, and it was a desperate four-day struggle to free them. They were pounded hard between swells and reef at half tide, were stranded like beached whales at low tide, and heeled over so far as to be in danger of never floating on the making tide. The outlook was so bleak that d'Urville organized the abandoning of his ships. But the sorely battered corvettes escaped and made for Dutch Timor. Here they wooded and watered before heading for the French island of Bourbon in the Indian Ocean. Then it was on to St. Helena and the obligatory pilgrimage to Longwood and

Napoleon's tomb. It was the last such pilgrimage by a French group. The Prince de Joinville was shortly to arrive at the island and take Napoleon's remains back to France. The corvettes dropped anchor in Toulon Roads on the night of 6 November 1840. It was pouring rain. The last great French exploring expedition under sail, thirty-eight months after sailing from Toulon, had ended.

D'Urville had completed his three great voyages and laid to rest Cook's ghost. And the seaman who had mouthed, *"Oh! ce bonhomme-la ne nous mènera pas loin!"* had been proved wrong. The old boy had taken them very far.

NOTES

1. Discontented Frenchmen, pining for the days of glory under Napoleon, instead of bidding "king of clubs" etc. at cards, would bid "pig of clubs."
2. See Chapter 3 for the 1826–29 *Astrolabe* voyage.
3. Renal problems, next to scurvy and ruptures, appear high on the list of eighteenth- and nineteenth-century sailors' afflictions.
4. *"Oh! ce bonhomme-la ne nous mènera pas loin!"*
5. Louis Philippe, the French king; Prince de Joinville, his brother; and Vice Admiral Claude de Rosamel, the French minister of marine.
6. The marvelously talented twenty-five-year-old Ernest Goupil died at Hobart.
7. For the people of Hobart it was the 2 January. D'Urville had not changed the date on crossing the 180° line of longitude.
8. The French returned to Adélie Land. On 20 January 1950 the Expédition Polaires Françaises (EPF) established a base, Port Martin, which was manned until February 1953, the base being evacuated after a fire. In March 1956 another base, named Dumont d'Urville, was opened on Pointe Géologie, and it has been manned ever since.
9. "The French corvettes *Astrolabe* and *Zélée* left Hobart Town on 25 February 1840, anchored here 11 March, and left on 20 March for New Zealand. From 19 January to 1 February 1840, discovered Adélie Land and determined the south magnetic pole!"

Chapter 13

The Magnetic Crusade

MAGELLAN JACKET. A name given to a watch-coat with a hood, worn in high latitudes—first used by Cook's people.

MAGNETIC NEEDLE. Applied to theodolites, ships' compasses, &c. A balanced needle, highly magnetized, which points to the magnetic pole, when not influenced by the local attraction of neighbouring iron. The magnetism may be discharged by blows, or a fall; hence, after an action at sea, the needles are often found to be useless, until remagnetized.

Admiral W. H. Smyth, *The Sailor's Word-Book*, 1867

ACTS," SAID MR. GRADGRIND in Charles Dickens's *Hard Times*, "facts alone are wanted in life." In the nineteenth century facts made up a large part of science. This was the collectors' century. In museums and genteel drawing rooms the curio and collection cabinets held shells, butterflies, beetles, bones, fossils, and rock samples. Stuffed birds in glass bell cases looked out at viewers with austere and beady eyes. Stuffed Neanderthalish primates, snarling carnivores, lurked on corners and on dim staircases to surprise the unwary.[1]

But natural history made up only a small part of the century's collections. Another was data, facts and figures from which an inference could be drawn, a theory proposed, a pious hope that quantification would lead to understanding.

In 1831 a group of British scientists, frustrated by the elitist torpor of the venerable Royal Society, founded a rival organization, the British Association for the Advancement of Science. An association with such a portentous and weighty name conjures up visions of a gathering composed of frock-coated, top-hatted, muttonchopped sobersides. A reading of the *York Courant*—the first meeting was held in York, far away from the temptations and frivolities of London—suggests otherwise.

The Yorkshire Philosophical Society acted as host, and the week's meetings, according to the *Courant*, were held in the "spacious and elegant theatre of the Museum—brilliantly lighted by gas—thronged till ten o'clock with select company, amongst whom were many ladies, which added much to the brilliance of the scene, and all of whom appeared to enjoy with a high zest the intellectual entertainment provided for them."

The main dinner was held at the York Tavern with Lord Milton in the chair. After dinner came toasts—many toasts, some "3 times 3"[2]—and short speeches, all interspersed with cheers and applause. The *Courant*'s reporter, filled with enthusiasm and toasts, gave his readers a blow-by-blow account. One paragraph gives a flavor for the whole: "Dr. Pearson [an astronomer], in acknowledging the toast, noticed that in the beautiful building of the YPS there was one defect—a cupola (laughter); the situation was admirably calculated for astronomical observations, and he should be happy, if a cupola were raised, to put in a few of his own instruments, (loud cheers). He mentioned that Sir Thomas Brisbane (the former President of the Astronomical Society) was present and he had done more than almost any other person to promote astronomical science (Cheers)."

Reading such a report brings to mind the classic opening pages of *Pickwick Papers* and the formation, in 1827, of the Corresponding Society of the Pickwick Club, but only after Samuel Pickwick, Esq., G.C.M.P.C.[3] had read his paper entitled "Speculations on the Source of the Hampstead Ponds, with Some Observations on the Theory of Tittlebats." The Corresponding Society, as entered in the Transactions of the Pickwick Club, had been formed to extend Mr. Pickwick's travels and for "the advancement of knowledge, and the diffusion of learning," aims little different from those of the younger British Association, which, at the meeting in York, established many committees for the advancement of knowledge and diffusion of learning, one of them being a Committee of Mathematical and Physical Science that listed terrestrial magnetism among its concerns.

More than two centuries before the jovial British Association members reeled out from the York Tavern, Robert Norman, a London instrument and compass maker, had discovered the dip (or inclination) of a balanced magnetized needle from horizontal and then published his *The Newe Attractive* in 1581 with the suggestion that the attraction, and reason, lay in the Earth. Norman then went on to devise a dip circle to measure the amount of dip or inclination. Dr. William Gilbert, physician to Queen Elizabeth I, tested this hypothesis with a scale model. He made a sphere from magnetic lodestone and moved a small compass over its surface. On the sphere he mapped the lines of compass variation and dip. In 1600 he published his scientific treatise *De Magnete* deducing that the Earth was a giant magnet. A century later Edmond Halley's voyages in the *Paramore*, considered the first voyages undertaken for purely scientific purposes, collected data that produced his two famous charts, the Atlantic and World

Charts of 1701 and 1702, showing compass variations from true north. The variations were depicted graphically with what Halley called Curve-Lines—lines joining points of equal magnetic variation. His contemporaries called them Halleyan Lines; today they are known as isogonic lines. Sixteenth- and seventeenth-century concerns with magnetic variation and dip had practical considerations. Navigation across the world's oceans was carried out in a mood of nervous optimism. Charts were poor or nonexistent; instruments were simple and crude: a lead line for depth sounding, useful only in coastal waters; an astrolabe or cross-staff for finding the latitude; an hourglass; a compass.

Martin Frobisher on his first Arctic voyage of 1576 carried twenty compasses, one of them "an Instrument of brasse named Compassum Meridianum," an unusual compass that, by means of a shadow cast across its face at high noon, showed the true north from the magnetic north. (Before sailing from London Frobisher measured the compass variation and found it to be 11 1/2 degrees to the east of true north.)

In 1580 Gerardus Mercator, in a letter to Richard Hakluyt, wrote that "the nearer you come unto it [the North Pole], the more the needle of the compass doth vary from the north, sometimes to the west, and sometimes to the east. . . . This is a very strange alteration and very apt to deceive the sailor unless he know the unconstancy and variation of the compass." Adding to a mariner's woes was the fact that the variation not only changed as his vessel moved across the ocean but changed over the years. (Variation at London in 1580 was 11°15′East. By 1773 it had swept through 32° to 21°09′West.)

As for the dip, measured by a dip circle, this too changed across the surface of the Earth, increasing from the horizontal as vessels sailed closer to the North Pole. In 1608, on his voyage to Spitsbergen, Henry Hudson found the needle on his dip circle very near vertical at 75°N latitude.

Compass variation and dip, to men puzzling over an accurate method of finding a vessel's position at sea, even in cloudy weather, appeared to offer a solution. In 1676 Henry Bond published his *The Longitude Found*. Two years later Bond's theory was taken apart by Peter Blackbarrow in his *The Longitude Not Found*.

All this, plus Halley's theories on terrestrial magnetism, had led British science to take a somewhat proprietorial attitude toward the subject. But the members of the barely weaned British Association were only too aware that France and Germany were now leaders in the field with some very serious players.

Germany had the mathematician, astronomer, and physicist Carl Friedrich Gauss, the physicist Wilhelm Weber, the polymath Alexander von Humboldt. The French had François Arago, director of the Paris Observatory. Even Norway had a magnetic player of note in Christopher Hansteen.

But it was the sixty-two-year-old Humboldt who stood like a colossus across the scientific landscape. This was a man with quiverful of scientific arrows: geology, meteorology, botany, zoology, astronomy, ethnology, linguistics, and magnetism. All facts and data were important, and all had to be collected in the field. Here was a man who combined science with travel and adventure and who, like d'Urville, had been inspired to explore after reading Bougainville and Cook.

In 1790 the twenty-one-year-old budding polymath had traveled with Georg Forster from Germany to England. Forster, after sailing aboard Cook's *Resolution* as a naturalist and assistant to his father, had written a popular account of the voyage that combined travel narrative with scientific comment. Both book and Forster—a man, according to Humboldt, who knew a little about everything—were to affect profoundly Humboldt's holistic view of the world. In London Humboldt met with Sir Joseph Banks and visited his herbarium, then the world's largest. A few years later, in Paris, he met with the hero of his youth, Bougainville. In Paris Humboldt joined the scientific staff of the proposed Baudin expedition with the *Géographe* and the *Naturaliste*. But delays in organizing the expedition led Humboldt—a man, like Banks and Darwin, with a large private income—to travel in Spain, followed by five years roving through Central and South America, years that produced a monumental thirty-volume work and his more accessible and popular *Personal Narrative*, which deeply influenced Charles Darwin, who delighted in reciting whole passages, Alfred Russel Wallace, and a young botanist by the name of Joseph Dalton Hooker. (Years later, in a letter to Darwin, Hooker described Humboldt as one of "our Gods, my friend.")

Before sailing for the Americas, Humboldt had written that his purpose was to "find out about the unity of nature." Terrestrial magnetism, although lacking the immediate visual and romantic appeal of plants and furry creatures, was part and parcel of this unity of nature.

Humboldt, as an exploring scientist, held a great advantage over his earlier fellows. Instrument making had made dramatic advances; year by year instruments were becoming smaller, lighter, and more accurate, John Harrison's chronometer merely being the most famous. (A cynic might suggest that today's technical advances, and our smugness in thinking how clever we are, are little different from the technical advances of the nineteenth century.)

In South America Humboldt and his traveling companion, Aimé Bonpland, were followed by a mule train carrying books, barometers, chronometers, compasses, a dip circle, electrometers, a cynometer (to measure the blueness of the sky),[4] eudiometers (to measure the oxygen in the atmosphere), hygrometers, quadrants, sextants and artificial horizons, telescopes, theodolites, thermometers, rain gauges, a magnetometer, a pendulum, and galvanic batteries.

Magnetic perturbations, occurring across the world at the same time, led Humboldt to think that the cause came from the atmosphere, the cosmos. These violent magnetic fluctuations were due to what he dubbed magnetic storms.[5] But more data were needed, and they had to be collected on an international scale. In 1829 he set off on his last great journey across Russia and Central Asia and organized a chain of magnetic observatories stretching from Moscow through Siberia to Beijing and then across the Pacific to Sitka in Alaska.

This collection of data happened to be meat and drink to a forty-three-year-old captain in the British Army's Royal Artillery, Edward Sabine, fellow of the Royal Society, a member of its council and one of the Admiralty's three scientific advisers. Sabine, like Humboldt, was something of a polymath, and also like Humboldt, he had a wide range of influential friends in military, naval, scientific, and bureaucratic circles. Sabine, in short, was an early networker.

The Royal Artillery and the Royal Engineers tended to attract brighter officers than the guards and cavalry regiments. And Sabine was very bright.[6] Among his disciplines he could number ornithology (*Larus sabini*, Sabine's gull, is named after him), astronomy, meteorology, and geomagnetism. But it was the latter that gripped Sabine with religious fervor. Such was his evangelical approach, akin to the antislavery, temperance, and missionary movements, that his campaigning, along with other magnetic apostles, was termed the Magnetic Crusade and known to the irreverent as the Magnetic Fever.

Sabine, like Humboldt, was no cloistered, deskbound data collector. By 1838 the cheerful, painstaking, organized fifty-year-old could look back on a life of war, exploration, travel, and adventure. As a soldier in Canada he had fought with distinction against the Americans in the War of 1812. In the Arctic he had served as the astronomer, recommended by the Royal Society, with the Royal Navy's post–Napoleonic War attempts to find a Northwest Passage, aboard the *Isabella* in 1818 with Commander John Ross and the *Hecla* in 1819–20 with Lieutenant Commander William Edward Parry. Sabine, during the overwintering of the *Hecla* and the *Griper* in the high Canadian Arctic, had edited the weekly journal entitled the *North Georgia Gazette and Winter Chronicle,* which ran to twenty-one issues and was the forerunner of many such polar publications. One of the midshipmen on both voyages had been a handsome, rosy-cheeked youth by the name of James Clark Ross, a nephew of John Ross's and a man destined to be a comrade-in-arms with Sabine in the Magnetic Crusade but during the 1819–20 overwintering, because of those rosy cheeks, more in demand for the female roles in the expedition's fortnightly theatrical productions.

After his Arctic experiences Sabine was selected to carry out pendulum experiments to calculate the Earth's true shape in warmer climates—West Africa, Brazil, and the Caribbean—followed by a return north with more pendulum measurements in Norway, Greenland, and Spitsbergen. In West Africa, after Sabine had lost his assistant, the captain of the Royal Navy vessel supplied him with Royal Marine helpers. After seeing five of these die from fever, Sabine decided "to do the best I could alone, rather than obtain assistance at such fearful risk to others."

By the time he was thirty-eight years old he had received the prestigious Copley Medal from the Royal Society and the Lalande Gold Medal from the Institute of France. A decade later he was working on a magnetic survey of Ireland with his old sailing companion James Ross and Professor Humphrey Lloyd of Trinity College, Dublin, all part of the British Association's efforts to collect data on terrestrial magnetism. At their 1835 annual meeting, this time held in Dublin, Sabine gave the results of the Irish survey. At the same meeting the association passed the following resolution: "That a representation be made to the Government of the importance of sending an expedition into the Antarctic regions, for the purpose of making observations and discoveries in various branches of Science, as Geography, Hydrography, Natural History and especially Magnetism with a view to determining precisely the place of the Southern Magnetic Pole or Poles, and the direction and intensity of the magnetic force in those regions."

The representation failed to make any headway, the young British Association lacking the Royal Society's influence exercised over the nuts, cigars, and port in discreet and quiet London clubs. Sabine and Lloyd were well aware of this. In 1836, on a trip to Germany with Lloyd, Sabine persuaded Humboldt to write a letter to the Duke of Sussex, president of the Royal Society, asking the society and the British government to establish magnetic observatories in the British colonies to complement the geomagnetic observations of other countries. It would be a grand scientific alliance of Britain, France, Russia, and Germany. Within a month of receiving the letter the Royal Society, swayed by Humboldt's prestige, had printed and circulated hundreds of copies of a resolution supporting his request.

The magnetic snowball, patted into shape and guided by Sabine, gained momentum and adherents, one of them, and a very influential one, being the world-famous astronomer Sir John Herschel.

That same year Charles Wilkes was in London buying charts, instruments, and books for the American expedition and meeting with James Ross and other worthies in the geographic and scientific worlds. An article in the Royal Geographical Society's *Journal* mentioned the visit of Wilkes and the "great gratification" the *Journal* had "in announcing that an expedition on a splendid scale for discovery in the Pacific and Antarctic Oceans, is fitting out in the United States."

Early the next year an anonymous pamphlet, signed A.Z., was sent to the president and council of the Royal Geographical Society. The author—

suspected to be Captain John Washington, the society's secretary and later Admiralty hydrographer—called for a government-sponsored Antarctic expedition. The pamphlet contained a summary of Antarctic exploration with a map showing the tracks of Cook, Biscoe, Weddell, Bellingshausen, and Morrell. Humboldt's letter buttressed the three points of A.Z.'s argument: science, commerce through a revival of sealing, and plain flag-waving patriotism. "All Europe looks to this country to solve the problem of Terrestrial Magnetism; and all Europe, nay all civilized nations, would point to that individual who has already planted the red cross of England on one of the northern Magnetic Poles, as the man best fitted to be leader of an expedition, sent out for such a purpose."

A.Z., in full fervid patriotic flow, concluded with the "earnest hope that through your exertions my wishes may be realized, and that ere long the Southern Cross may shine over an expedition sailing to the Polar Seas . . . and that Cross which I ardently hope will once again shine o'er the 'Meteor Flag of England,' proudly waving o'er Antarctic land, discovered by the zeal and intrepidity of British seamen."

Both the Royal Geographical Society and the government turned deaf ears to A.Z.'s pleas. Sabine, however, was determined to deal with this passivity. A few months later, at the 1837 British Association meeting in Liverpool, he called again for an Antarctic scientific expedition. He resurrected Halley's shade as an example; pointed to Norway's parliament, which had voted funds for a geomagnetic expedition to Siberia while refusing funds to build a new royal palace; and concluded by saying that there was a certain naval officer ideally suited to lead an Antarctic expedition. Moreover, "if fitting instruments make fitting times, none surely can be better than the present."

The naval officer, the "fitting instrument" fingered by Washington and Sabine, was Captain James Clark Ross. The player of female roles in Arctic theatricals had metamorphosed into one of the Royal Navy's most handsome and one of its most scientific officers. He was also, more important, an officer who was something of a hero with the British public. Nineteenth-century Arctic explorers were social lions commanding the respect and adulation handed out to twentieth-century space explorers, and since 1818 the thirty-seven-year-old Ross had spent eight winters and fifteen summers exploring in the Arctic.

Born in London to a Scots family from Galloway, the young Ross, in 1812 and ten days before his twelfth birthday, had entered the Royal Navy under the protective wing of his bluff red-haired uncle Commander John Ross. However, the relationship between the two men, over the many years they were to sail together, both men having strong personalities and prominent egos, was to have its bumpy passages.

In 1827—on James Ross's fifth Arctic exploration voyage—the Royal Navy had made a John Barrow–inspired, futile attempt on the North Pole from a base in Spitsbergen, an attempt, according to William Scoresby, the veteran Arctic whaler and scientist, doomed to failure. Man-hauling two ponderous and heavy sledge-boats over the crumpled and needle-sharp sea ice, Parry and Ross with their seamen managed to reach, after a month of refined torture, 82°43′N before Parry called a halt. He had found they were hauling north over sea ice that was moving south, ice that was moving south sometimes faster than their struggle north.

In 1831, this time on a privately sponsored Arctic expedition (Felix Booth of Booth's gin put up most of the money) with his uncle commanding a side-paddle steamer, the *Victory,* James Ross had sledged to the north magnetic pole, built a cairn, and raised the Union Jack, which he and his uncle later presented to King William IV at Windsor Castle. Like Sabine, Ross was something of an ornithologist (Ross's gull is named after him) and a botanist (Robert Brown, Flinders's old companion and, according to Humboldt, one of the world's leading botanists, had a high opinion of Ross's collecting ability and named an Arctic grass after him).

During the winter of 1835–36 Ross had demonstrated his capabilities as an organizer, seaman, and commander. In early December 1835 a group of Hull shipowners had sent a memorial to the Admiralty pleading for the rescue of eleven whaleships trapped by the ice of an early Arctic winter. Ross offered his services. The Admiralty agreed to supply stores and provisions and pay wages—provided that the shipowners fitted out a ship and manned her with volunteers. Ross selected the Whitby-built *Cove.* Two hundred men worked day and night to strengthen her hull and ready her for the ice; provisions and stores came by steamship from naval dockyards; officers and men were selected. Within two weeks the *Cove* was ready to sail north.

Three weeks out from Hull she ran into a winter storm that one officer, an experienced Arctic whaleship skipper, described as the worst in his memory. One massive wave broke on board, tore away bowsprit and bulwarks, split the stem, swept the deck clean, and slewed the heeled *Cove* broadside to the next huge breaking sea. Ross, in this moment of frightening peril, waiting for a lull, gave his orders coolly and calmly, and the *Cove* payed off before the wind and before the next North Atlantic monster could roll her over. "The captain is," wrote the whaleship skipper, "without exception, the finest officer I have met with, the most persevering indefatigable man you can imagine. He is perfectly idolized by everyone."[7]

A portrait by J. Wildman of this paragon of a naval officer hangs in the National Maritime Museum at Greenwich. The nose is aquiline, the jaw firm, the hair artfully tousled; the eyes are deep-set and dark. A rich fur is draped over Ross's left shoulder, an epaulet gleams on his right, and a ceremonial sword is clasped dramatically across his chest. The polestar glitters in the background, and a bronze and brass dip circle sits on a nearby

Portrait of James Clark Ross

"The Lords Commissioners of the Admiralty being pleased to honour me with the command, I received my commission for Her Majesty's ship *Erebus,* on the 8th of April, 1839, and their Lordships' directions to proceed with the equipment of the expedition upon the most liberal scale."   —James Clark Ross

(Portrait by John Wildman. Courtesy of the National Maritime Museum)

table. This is a romantically Byronic portrait, but one with no hint of the disreputability which surrounds that dangerous poet. Here, in oils, is the very personification of a young maiden's dream of the ideal, gallant, noble Sir Galahad of a naval officer. Certain critics, however, might point to a vanity and pride marching hand in hand with a touch of arrogance in this paragon. But the critics would also have to admit that these were outweighed by his charm, generosity, and obvious abilities.

Sabine's calls for an Antarctic expedition proved as fruitless as Washington's. But as an artilleryman Sabine knew the worth of heavy guns. So he wheeled in a very heavy gun in the shape of Sir John Herschel. The forty-six-year-old astronomer, something of a scientific national hero, had never made a magnetic measurement in his life but carried great gravitas, prestige, and influence in government circles. In August 1838 Humphrey Lloyd wrote to Herschel:

> I rejoice to learn from Major Sabine that you have expressed a strong opinion of the importance of a South Polar Expedition. May we, therefore, hope that you will bring the subject forward at the approaching meeting of the British Association.
>
> It is now three years since the Association resolved to recommend to the Government to undertake an Antarctic Expedition for the purpose of promoting our knowledge of terrestrial magnetism in a region hitherto little explored and to establish one or two observatories in British India. . . . The time, however, has now arrived—and I cannot but think that by a large and well directed expedition on a large and liberal scale Britain might now redeem in the course of two or three years the great distance she has suffered herself to fall behind the nations of the Continent in magnetic discoveries.

The heavy gun agreed to speak, was given a rousing welcome at the 1838 Newcastle meeting, and the association passed a nine-point resolution to be fired at the government. Paragraph Four reads as follows: "That the Association considers it highly important that the deficiency, yet existing in our knowledge of terrestrial magnetism in the southern hemisphere, should be supplied by observations of the magnetic direction and intensity, especially in the high southern latitudes between the meridians of New Holland and Cape Horn; and they desire strongly to recommend to Her Majesty's Government the appointment of a naval expedition expressly directed to that object."

The unborn expedition had been directed close to the theoretical position of the south magnetic pole as calculated by Gauss: 66°S latitude, 146°E longitude, a position thirteen hundred nautical miles south of Tasmania and in an area where no vessels had ever before ventured.

The 154-ton schooner *Eliza Scott* and the 54-ton cutter *Sabrina,* both vessels on a sealing expedition for a group of London merchants, during the week the resolution was passed were heading down the South Atlantic for the Southern Ocean. In a few months they would be sailing very close to Gauss's theoretical position.

At the end of August Herschel wrote to the prime minister, Lord Melbourne, requesting an interview to discuss the association's resolution.

By the middle of October Herschel was dining with the young Queen Victoria and Melbourne at Windsor Castle, where the polar expedition was discussed informally. The conversation led Herschel to believe that Melbourne approved but that it had to be considered by the Cabinet. The Cabinet predictably shied at the cost.[8] For the naval expedition was but a small part of an expensive project that called for observatories in Canada, Ceylon, St. Helena, Tasmania, and Mauritius or the Cape of Good Hope. The naval expedition, subtly baited with the more tangible notions of geographic discoveries, got a tentative grunt of approval.

Among the scientific community only George Airy, the astronomer royal, voiced doubts about the naval expedition. But Herschel, a man ahead of his time and wise to the minds of politicians and those who hold the purse strings, made him toe the line and silenced Airy's objections by persuading him that a "perfect harmony of ideas should subsist between men of science whenever application to Government is in question."

The expedition was given the nod of approval in March 1839, and Ross was appointed its commander a month later. Sabine, Ross, Herschel, and Francis Beaufort, the Admiralty hydrographer, had stormed and taken the scientifically philistine government heights. The Magnetic Crusade had won its first battle—although the Jerusalem of the worldwide range of observatories still had to be won.

Then the crusaders were suddenly thrown into near panic by the resignation of Melbourne's Whig government. For looming over the horizon, ready to replace the Whigs, was that frugal Tory Sir Robert Peel, a man even more of a scientific illiterate than the Whigs and a man who would certainly block the expedition because of its expense.

But by one of those odd quirks of politics and human nature, the expedition was saved by the small, dumpy figure of the nineteen-year-old Queen Victoria. Victoria, a Whig to her fingertips, adored her resigning Melbourne and loathed the graceless Peel, about to usurp his position. Matters came to a head with an episode known to British history with a title more suited to a West End farce than a matter touching on the country's unwritten constitution: The Ladies of the Bedchamber Crisis.

Peel, quite within his powers, requested that some of Victoria's court ladies, Whigs all and married to Whigs, be replaced with Troy ladies. Victoria stuck out her petulant, pendulous lower lip and refused. Peel, flummoxed and taken aback by this unlooked-for change of wind, then declined to form a government. The overjoyed Victoria called back Melbourne to take up his old position as the adored prime minister. The Magnetic Crusaders breathed a collective sigh of relief.

The two ships selected for the expedition were the bomb vessels HMS *Erebus* and HMS *Terror*. Although they were much smaller and slower than Wilkes's *Vincennes* and *Peacock*, their shape and construction made them far more suitable for polar exploration.

Bomb vessels were rather unusual warships designed and constructed to throw high-trajectory mortar bombs at shore installations, as opposed to exchanging broadsides with a floating enemy. To take the massive recoil of the three-ton potbellied mortars, their hulls, decks, frames, and floors were made of gargantuan proportions. Paintings of these vessels in action, spewing forth flame and smoke like volcanoes, set the Admiralty namesmiths, like advertising men, to dream up names that reflected their classical education and the product's attributes, the attributes in this case being fire, destruction, and death. *Erebus* (the dark and gloomy passageway to Hades), *Terror, Beelzebub* (Satan's second-in-command according to Milton in *Paradise Lost*), *Infernal, Fury, Meteor, Hecla, Vesuvius, Aetna, Sulphur, Thunder.*

Bluff-bowed, firm-bilged, the bombs were not the fastest of sailing vessels, a matronly eight knots being considered a most daring speed. But their strong build and carrying capacity made them ideal exploring vessels. Thus, when they were not reducing a fortress to rubble, the Admiralty used them for Arctic exploration and hydrographic survey.

Ross's command, the *Erebus,* launched in 1826, was a 372-ton three-masted barque,[9] 105 feet overall and 29-foot beam. The *Terror,* launched in 1813, was slightly smaller: 326 tons, 102 feet overall, and just over 27-foot beam. Either vessel, if the *Vincennes's* or *Peacock's* deck had been removed, would have fitted into the American hulls with room to spare.

The *Terror,* strongly built as she was, had already been blooded by the Arctic, blooded so badly that after a winter of being crushed by ice, smashed by icebergs, she had pumped her way back across the Atlantic to England. Her cruelly twisted hull, held together by anchor chains passed under her keel, the sea spouting in faster than the pumps could send it back overboard, forced her captain, George Back, to run her aground on a sandy beach in Ireland before she went to the bottom. Since then she had been repaired and strengthened.

Such treatment handed out by the ice had set the Admiralty, awful visions of Antarctic ice dealing similar buffetings, to make both vessels even stronger. Hulls were sheathed with eight-inch-thick English oak planking above the waterline, tapering to three-inch Canadian elm at the keel. Three-inch-thick fir planking was laid diagonally across the decks with a waterproof membrane—fearnought cloth[10] soaked in tallow—laid between. Two watertight bulkheads, constructed like the decks, divided the vessels athwartships, giving three watertight compartments in case the hull was pierced. Beams, struts, pillars, and stanchions braced the hulls internally so much so that the bow and stern sections, the most vulnerable areas, were virtually solid timber. Spare rudders were carried on deck. Each vessel carried nine boats—a pinnace, four cutters, two whaleboats, the captain's galley, all strengthened for work among the ice floes—and a small dinghy. Ice saws, some thirty feet long, were stowed below, according to a *Times* reporter, "looking like the jaws of sharks, competent to cut through any besetting adversary."

Officers and men all berthed and messed on a deck heated by the galley stove and stoves in the captains' cabins and gunroom messes. Both vessels were also fitted with a central heating system devised by a Mr. Sylvester. This system sent warm air circulating around the ships' sides in a square iron duct some one foot in diameter. Mr. Sylvester might have been considered "a strange fellow" by Francis Crozier, the *Terror*'s captain, but his system had been proved in the Arctic aboard the *Hecla* and the *Fury* and was much admired and praised. Large kettles were carried to melt ice into fresh water and to soak the salted meat. But provisioning was not confined to salt meat and pease pudding. The ships were provisioned for three years, and the provisions, measured against the usual seagoing standard, were positively Lucullan.

Salt meat and fish took second place to vast quantities of canned food. (All the tin-plated cans had to be opened with a hammer and chisel.) Fifteen tons of meat (mutton, beef, veal, oxcheek, boiled, roasted, seasoned, some with mixed vegetables); seven tons of vegetables (carrots, turnips, beets, onions, cabbages); three tons of soup and nine tons of concentrated soup. Among the "medical comforts" were tons of cranberries, mixed pickles, pickled walnuts (a valuable antiscorbutic), pickled onions, and pickled cabbage.

Compared with the heavyweight—some American senators would have probably growled "overweight"—United States Exploring Expedition, the British expedition was an anorexic strawweight. The Americans had weighed in with 2,157 tons of ship crewed by 490 men. The British were weighing in with a mere 698 tons of ship crewed by 128 men.

The Admiralty, the expedition landed on its doorstep, turned to the Royal Society for suggestions on the scientific program. In a booklet of one hundred pages the society emphatically stated that "Terrestrial Magnetism" was the great scientific objective, as the "most lamentable deficiencies occur, especially in the Antarctic regions." But meteorology, geology, minerology, botany, vegetable physiology, zoology, and animal physiology were not to be overlooked. In one of the subheadings, "Depth of the Sea," it was suggested (predating the modern echo sounder) that an echo from the seabed might be heard if a shell were exploded just beneath the sea's surface—"as an echo from the earth is heard in the car of a balloon."

Ross, within reason, was given a free hand in choosing officers to carry out the scientific program. Commissioned into the *Terror* went the expedition's second-in-command, Commander Francis Crozier, an old Arctic hand and shipmate of Ross's who had sailed on three of Parry's expeditions. A genial Ulsterman, three years older than Ross, the unmarried Crozier had an Irishman's susceptible heart for flirtatious ladies.

Ross was also unmarried, but his heart was effectively armor-plated against flirts. In 1834 he had met and been instantly smitten by a charming seventeen-year-old girl, Anne Coulman. Unfortunately her father was not so smitten by sailors, however handsome, who vanished into polar regions. James and Anne had thus been forced to carry out a somewhat furtive and circumspect relationship. During Ross's magnetic survey of England the infatuated James had met with Anne at her uncle's house, Wadworth Hall, in the north, a combining of survey with romance. A few months later, in February 1839, he wrote to Anne, referring to both visit and magnetic measurements with a ponderous Victorian pun: "Those *we made together* at Wadworth are inserted although they manifest a considerable degree of *perturbation. . . .*" The perturbations were not restricted to the heart. Ross was also worried that the Admiralty might get wind of his relationship and take away his command.

Other officer Arctic hands were Edward Bird as the *Erebus*'s first lieutenant, Alexander Smith as one of the mates, and Thomas Hallet as purser. Aboard the *Terror* went Archibald McMurdo as first lieutenant and John Davis as second master. Davis had not sailed into the Arctic, but the cheerful and popular surveyor had sailed with FitzRoy on the *Beagle* during the survey of Tierra del Fuego. Among the warrant officers aboard the *Erebus* was the hard-drinking gunner Thomas Abernethy, one of those stalwart noncommissioned officers who are the backbone of all armed forces. An experienced Arctic hand, he had sledged and sailed many miles with Ross, miles that included the sledging trip to the north magnetic pole, and he had every intention of making it to the south magnetic pole.

The expedition's natural history was to be handled by the *Erebus*'s naval surgeon. The thirty-nine-year-old Dr. Robert McCormick, although born in England, came from a family long settled in Ireland. He was a wildly unpredictable man, a man who nursed his grievances with Celtic fervor, and his naval career had been checkered and something of a headache to the naval medical establishment. He had sailed with Parry and Ross in 1827 as assistant surgeon but had taken no part in the failed man-hauling attempt on the North Pole. He had, for a few weeks, sailed aboard the *Beagle* with FitzRoy and Charles Darwin but had left in Rio de Janeiro. Darwin wrote in a letter to John Henslow that "my friend the Doctor is an ass, but we jog along very amicably."

McCormick, in his autobiography, makes no mention of the *Beagle*, FitzRoy, or Darwin, only a passing reference to three years spent in "two miserable craft and for the most part on my old station the West Indies . . . which I can only look back with unavailing regret, as so much time, health and energies utterly wasted." Before joining the *Erebus*, he had been ashore for four years on half pay, walking 3,340 miles throughout England and Wales, following his twin passions of geology and ornithology. But his passion for birds, as later recorded by the *Erebus*'s assistant surgeon, appeared to be confined to blasting them out of the sky with his shotgun.

Chalk portrait of Joseph Hooker
Hooker disliked sitting for portraits and photographs. This one, he thought, made him "a very lackadaisical young man."
(Portrait by George Richmond. Courtesy of the Royal Botanic Gardens, Kew)

The assistant surgeon was the wiry, dreamy-faced, shortsighted twenty-one-year-old Joseph Dalton Hooker. His father, Sir William Jackson Hooker, had been recently knighted for services to botany. Although professor of botany at Glasgow University, the elder Hooker was an Englishman with brewery interests throughout East Anglia, and his appointment to Glasgow had been one of Sir Joseph Banks's last acts of influence—a particularly astute one—before his death. Hooker had turned out to be an inspiring teacher, botanist, and organizer, a man who had quadrupled the number of pupils at his botanical classes and tripled the number of species at the Glasgow Botanic Gardens.

Botany, in those days, was a required subject for medical students so they could recognize and use medicinal plants. The subject, when supervised by Hooker, could be strenuous. On field trips the older Hooker would walk his young students until their legs buckled. The rangy Hooker, according to his son, could cover sixty miles a day with ease. With a summer weekend retreat at Helensburgh, the professor would set off on a Sunday evening to tramp the twenty-two miles to Glasgow for his eight o'clock Monday morning class. His lectures were often attended by his seven-year-old son. By thirteen Joseph was considered an accomplished botanist and well versed in other aspects of natural history.

While studying to take a medical degree, Joseph attended the 1838 British Association meeting at Newcastle, where he found, as he wrote in a letter to his grandfather, that the entertainments of the association's founding in York still continued. For "the scientific department," he noted, "fell far behind the amusement and eating." Also, much to his surprise, he found that the ladies were excluded from some lectures on botany and zoology: "on account of the nature of some of the papers belonging to the latter division." Queen Victoria had only just started her long reign, but the evangelical prudishness was gathering momentum.

Hooker, having heard the resolution for an Antarctic expedition, was suddenly smitten with the idea of joining it. He would be another Charles Darwin. Behind the dreamy exterior lay an iron will. He would travel to Portsmouth and take advice from Dr. John Richardson,[11] a friend of his father's and an old Arctic hand, at the Royal Hospital at Haslar, where young naval surgeons kicked their heels until being appointed to ships. (Coach travel in those days required a tough constitution. Hooker left Newcastle at nine o'clock on a Thursday morning, traveled all night, and arrived in London at eight o'clock Friday evening. He then boarded a coach leaving for Portsmouth, where he arrived at eight o'clock Saturday morning. Total cost: £5 14s or £250 in today's money.)

The old-boy network of Arctic explorers and botanical mutual friends rolled into action. Within a month James Ross had met with Hooker in Glasgow and promised to take him, even though the expedition had no provision for a civilian naturalist. But Hooker, Ross stipulated, had to pass his medical examinations and would then sail as assistant surgeon–naturalist.

Hooker passed his examinations, moved south to Haslar, and then joined the *Erebus*. But botany, it was obvious to Hooker, was low on the Royal Society's list of objectives. At a meeting in London the society gave him advice—all gratuitous and making "much nonsense," according to Hooker—but he felt the lack of cordiality, and when he left the room, "no one even wished me a pleasant or successful voyage." As for the crusty admirals at the Admiralty, one of them made it plain that natural history had no part in a naval expedition. "Which," wrote Hooker, "has annoyed Capt. Ross exceedingly." Moreover, the government's largess for botany consisted of some drying paper for specimens, two collecting vascula, and two Wardian cases[12] for bringing plants home alive. No glass bottles were provided for holding specimens—Hooker used old pickle jars—and the only preserving spirit was rum from the ship's store. It was Hooker's father who provided him with books, microscopes, and instruments, one beautiful instrument being a chronometer-watch that he used for the rest of his life.

Hooker's shipmates proved more congenial than the Admiralty, although Sir William, after a visit to the *Erebus,* "wished to have witnessed their conversation taking a more scientific and soberer turn. Above all I should have liked to have seen them pay more respect to the Sabbath." Even the choleric McCormick had turned a friendly face, though he must have thought another usurping Charles Darwin was hovering on the wing.

By mid-September the two bomb vessels were almost ready to sail. Hooker wrote to his grandfather describing his cabin: six feet by four feet, fitted with a bunk, bookshelf, table, and chair, the light coming from a bull's-eye prism set in the deck (to be removed in the tropics for ventilation). At the same time a small weather-beaten schooner was making her way up the Thames after a circumnavigation that had taken her close to the expedition's Antarctic target zone.

John Balleny and the *Eliza Scott* carried few sealskins but momentous news. Sent off on a sealing expedition with the small cutter-rigged *Sabrina,* they had discovered and landed on islands below the Antarctic Circle, sighted more land below the circle close to the theoretical south magnetic pole, and noted a lessening of the pack ice close to the 180° meridian. The *Sabrina,* alas, had been lost with all hands in a Southern Ocean storm. A hasty copy was made of Balleny's journal and given to Ross. Charles Enderby, one of the partners in the sealing expedition and a member of the Royal Geographical Society, had the satisfaction of seeing it printed later that year in the society's *Journal.* As far as the patriotic Enderby was concerned, a small, privately funded expedition had wiped the eye of the French and American expeditions. It was perhaps but small consolation for a sealing expedition that had sailed at an enormous loss in both lives and money.

But Sir John Herschel, at the 1839 British Association meeting, had unerringly put his finger on the pulse of theories and discoveries: "Great physical theories, with their chains of practical consequences, are preeminently national objects, whether for glory or utility."

NOTES

1. England's most lovable and eccentric naturalist and traveler, Charles Waterton (1782–1865), an ardent Roman Catholic, used to have grotesquely stuffed primates lurking on his stairways in his house in Yorkshire. They were labeled with the names of prominent Protestant churchmen.
2. A rousing ovation, cheer after cheer.

3. General Chairman—Member Pickwick Club.
4. Satirized by Lord Byron in *Don Juan:*

> Humboldt, "the first of travellers," but not
> The last, if late accounts be accurate,
> Invented, by some name I have forgot,
> As well as the sublime discovery's date,
> An airy instrument, with which he sought
> To ascertain the atmospheric state,
> By measuring the intensity of blue.
> Oh Lady Daphne, let me measure you!

5. Humboldt's nomenclature is still used. Magnetic storms occur simultaneously around the Earth. In 1989 one particularly severe storm changed the variation at the Lerwick Observatory by 8° in less than an hour. Magnetic storms adversely affect radio and telegraphic transmissions.

6. It has been suggested that General Sir Edward Sabine (1788–1883), general secretary and then president of the British Association and president of the Royal Society, was the very model for Gilbert and Sullivan's "Modern Major-General."

7. Two whaleships were sunk by the ice with the remainder drifting south, trapped, until reaching open water. The *Cove,* after searching along the edge of the pack ice and reaching 70°N in Baffin Bay, returned to England eight months after sailing on her rescue mission.

8. The naval expedition alone cost close to £110,000.

9. A barque, for those lost in the minefield of nautical terms, is a three-masted vessel, square-rigged on the foremast and mainmast, but only fore-and-aft sails on her mizzen.

10. Fearnought cloth was a thick woolen felt used for hatchway fire screen, port linings, and polar clothing.

11. Dr. John Richardson (1787–1865), later Sir John Richardson, was the pawky Scottish naval surgeon–naturalist on two of Franklin's harrowing Arctic expeditions. He had been appointed physician to the Royal Hospital at Haslar in 1838.

Chapter 14

To the Pillars of the Gateway

NIP. A short turn in a rope. Also, a fishing term for a bite. In Arctic parlance, a nip is when two floes in motion crush by their opposite edges a vessel unhappily entrapped. Also the parts of a rope at the place bound by the seizing, or caught by jambing. Also, *Nip in the hawse:* hence "freshen the nip," by veering a few feet of the service into the hawse.

NORIE'S EPITOME. A treatise on navigation not to be easily cast aside.

Admiral W. H. Smyth, The Sailor's Word-Book, 1867

Y THE END of September the *Erebus* and the *Terror* lay at anchor in Margate Roads waiting for a favorable wind to take them down Channel. They were packed tight as herring barrels with provisions, stores, equipment, and instruments. One new, invaluable instrument was the Fox dip circle, designed to measure the magnetic declination, dip, and intensity at sea, a breakthrough in instrumentation that was to be widely used until the end of the century. The crew had been paid three months' wages in advance, the ships had been swung to determine the effect of the ships' iron on their compasses, and ships and men had been inspected by sightseers, admirals, and reporters.

The 14 September issue of the *Times* had run a column on the expedition and mentioned the discoveries made by John Balleny: "Of these discoveries in the southern hemisphere, Mr. Bates, of the Poultry, has just published an excellent chart, under the superintendence of Captain Beaufort. They appear like the pillars of a gateway, between which the expedition should pass."

On the evening of 30 September 1839, the wind having swung into the east, the two heavily laden vessels weighed anchor, rounded the Foreland, and headed down Channel, bound for Madeira, the Canary Islands, the Cape Verde Islands, Trinidad Island, St. Helena, and the Cape of

Good Hope—Madeira to check the sea rate of their chronometers; St. Helena and the Cape of Good Hope to land and erect permanent magnetic observatories and leave teams of observers.

By the time, nearly six months later, that they came to anchor in Simon's Bay at the Cape of Good Hope, it was obvious that the *Terror* was a much slower sailer than the *Erebus*. If the pace to Simon's Bay had been leisurely, the activity had not. The six months had settled the officers and crews into the routine of discovery ships rather than warships. Towing nets were always over the side, capturing their haul of tiny sea creatures to be drawn and studied by Hooker and Ross, McCormick not showing the least interest. The ocean's temperature, when practical, was taken down to a depth of 600 fathoms. Deep-sea soundings were also taken, and Ross had a hemp line made of 3,600 fathoms—over four miles in length—and fitted with swivels to prevent the line from unlaying on its descent. The soundings were done to music. Forty men, harnessed like donkeys to the line, working to tunes played by the ship's fiddler, took sixteen minutes to haul up 140 fathoms of line. In the South Atlantic, on 3 January 1840, they had made a sounding of 2,425 fathoms. "A depression of the bed of the ocean beneath its surface," an elated Ross pointed out, "very little short of the elevation of Mount Blanc above it." Present-day charts show 2,100 fathoms. In the annals of oceanography it's considered the first deep-sea sounding.

Any possibility of friction between Hooker and McCormick had been eased by Hooker's charm and McCormick's lack of interest in botany and zoology. For, as Hooker noted, McCormick seemed "to care too little about Natural History. . . . He takes no interest but in bird shooting and rock collecting; as of the former he has hitherto made no collection, but I am *nolens volens,* the Naturalist, for which I enjoy no other advantage than the Captain's cabin, and I think myself amply repaid."

Ross, it was obvious, had also accepted Hooker as the expedition's naturalist. Ross had given him a cabinet for his plants, a table under the stern windows, a drawer for microscope, and a locker for papers. Hooker, in his letters home, builds up a cozy domestic scene of the two men working away in the lamplight of the great cabin, often into the early hours of the morning, with Ross writing on one side of the table and Hooker drawing on the other. One day, after hauling aboard masses of seaweed, the two men, with sleeves rolled up, picked through the roots and then deposited the "treasures to be drawn . . . in basins, quietly popping the others into spirits. Some of the seaweeds he [Ross] lays out for himself, often sitting at one end of the table laying them out with infinite pains . . . at which times he is very agreeable and my hours pass quickly and pleasantly."

They had crossed the equator and observed the usual boisterous shavings and dunkings for the initiates. A few days later they had crossed, for Ross, a far more important line: the magnetic equator where the dip circle showed no dip. The Fox dip circles aboard both vessels registered the line simultaneously. For Ross it was a crossing of the Rubicon. He had stood at the north magnetic pole, where the needle pointed vertically downward. He had now crossed the magnetic equator, where the needle lay horizontal. And he was now sailing into the southern magnetic hemisphere where the south-pointing needle was beginning to dip. With luck he would see it stand vertical at the south magnetic pole.

Just over a week had been spent at St. Helena, landing the magnetic instruments and shore party and selecting a site for the permanent observatory. It had been a slow, tedious beat to windward to reach the island, the time made worse by the equally tedious diet. As Hooker wrote to his father, "I cannot tell you how delighted we were to get here, having been upon salt Junk for 74 days, with hard biscuits for vegetables."

Hooker collected plants and, to stop his being called a Goth by his shipmates, visited Napoleon's tomb. He found it to be the center of a flourishing emperor tourist and anecdotal industry. A sentinel showed him the water drunk by the emperor; children tried to sell him the emperor's favorite flowers; on entering a cottage to buy a bottle of ale, he found "the cork was no sooner drawn than out came the Emperor with it; it was the Emperor this, that, and the other thing; our hostess's daughter came in with the Emperor on her lips; his ubiquity astonished me." As Hooker picked some lichens, thinking that the "hero of Marengo could have nothing to do with Lichens on a stone wall," yet another garrulous stranger popped up to inform him that the emperor had been fond of wild plants, including the ones Hooker held in his hand. Hooker, sick and tired of it all, had taken to his heels and fled.

Three weeks were spent at Simon's Bay, the instruments and magnetic party landed, the observatory site selected. McCormick and Dr. John Robertson, the *Terror's* surgeon (regarded by Ross as the expedition's zoologist), climbed Table Mountain and admired the view. Hooker collected three hundred plants to study on the days at sea and sent collections back to London. The day before they sailed three large bullocks took charge of the *Terror's* deck after goring a seaman in the thigh. Also, William Cunningham, the *Terror's* sergeant of marines, had trouble with two deserters—caught by the civil police—and a drunken boat's crew. The usual problems, in short, of a ship in harbor.

The expedition sailed on 6 April bound into the Southern Ocean and the windswept, bleak Kerguelen Island that Cook had named, because of its "stirility," the Island of Desolation. Along their thirty-eight-hundred-mile course lay equally bleak and desolate islands: Prince Edward Island, where Ross hoped to land (he failed); Marion Island; the Crozet Islands. Ross had promised a Cape Town merchant to take provisions (tea and coffee) for an elephant sealing gang working the Crozet Islands' shores.

Running their easting down in the roaring forties, Hooker found his taste buds challenged by the new experience of eating albatross and Cape pigeon. He thought both species, caught by baited hooks slung over the side, then soaked in salt water, made tasty sea pies with no fishiness to the discerning palate. Cape pigeons, however, if cooked without soaking, tasted like fresh herring.

As the ships' noon-to-noon positions angled south, the air and sea temperature, over the course of a week, fell 30°F. Such a drop, to men grown used to warm-water sailing, led Ross to issue the men their cold-weather clothing.

Prince Edward Island, Marion Island, and the Crozet Islands, set close to the Antarctic Convergence, are windswept breeding grounds for a prodigious number of seabirds, penguins, fur seals, and elephant seals. The islands, as the expedition rolled downwind toward them, were in the throes of their second exploitation and on the brink of a third. During the first exploitation American sealers, between 1805 and 1810, had virtually exterminated the fur seals from their breeding rookeries. It was now the turn of the elephant seals to be slaughtered in their thousands, and it would shortly be the turn of migrating right whales.[1]

The boom "elephanting" years, the second exploitation, were to last a decade. By 1843 Ellery Nash, the skipper of the Stonington barque *Bolton*, on arriving at Pig Island in the Crozets, found the Stonington barque *United States* and the New London schooner *Franklin* with all their "men on the beaches . . . taking all the elephant as fast as they can haul." The next day Nash attempted to take seals off the beach occupied by a group of Englishmen and the Americans from the *United States*. Nash was told very forcefully that the beach was divided between them, and the English—"a hard set of men"—told him that they "would be damned if I should have any blubber off that beach . . . and would defend it . . . as long as they could hold a lance." His fellow skipper from the *United States* was no friendlier: "He said if I put men on Long Beach he would work against me in every shape." Nash stayed three months at various islands in the Crozets, meeting with eight New England sealing vessels. At East Island, with no other Americans nearby, he found a beach crammed with three thousand seals. A month later he lost his anchors—and came close to losing his life and vessel—in a violent storm. He managed to get his shore gang off and set sail for home with "only six casks of water and no anchors." But he arrived back at Stonington with fourteen hundred barrels of oil.

Ross spent five very windy days among the Crozets. No landing was made, but the sealers came off to collect their provisions, and Hooker's eyes were opened by the these strange visitors. Ross thought they looked "more like Esquimaux than civilized beings, but filthier far in their dress and persons than any I had ever before seen. Their clothes were literally soaked in oil and smelt most offensively; they wore boots of penguins' skin with their feathers turned inwards." Ross gathered that eleven men were on the island, one of them having been there for three years. They grew no vegetables but lived on a diet of elephant seal tongue and flippers, fish, seabird eggs—an albatross egg weighing in at over a pound—and wild duck. Young albatrosses, taken fresh from the nest, were described as being delicious. "It is possible, however," wrote Ross, no stranger to northern eating, "they may have acquired the Esquimaux taste as well as their habits."

By the second week of May, after a stormy passage from the Crozets, the *Erebus* and the *Terror* were anchored at Kerguelen Island's Christmas Harbor. Cook had spent a few days during the Christmas of 1776 in the harbor, hence the name. He had also taken notice of the vast numbers of seals. Since then the Island of Desolation had become the haunt of American and British sealers.

For Hooker it was the realization of a childhood fantasy. Years later, in a speech at the Royal Society's 1887 anniversary dinner, he told his listeners: "When still a child, I was very fond of Voyages and Travels; and my great delight was to sit on my grand-father's knee and look at the pictures in Cook's 'Voyages.' The one that took my fancy most was the plate of Christmas Harbour, Kerguelen Land, with the arched rock standing out to sea, and the sailors killing penguins; and I thought I should be the happiest boy alive if ever I would see that wonderful arched rock, and knock penguins on the head."

The arch has fallen in since part of Hooker's dream came true. But the wind still howls down the chute formed by the surrounding hills and churns the harbor into a mass of white water, the kelp still surges on the swell, and the penguins still give their mournful croak.

The one reason for calling at this desolate island was to take hourly magnetic observations and on certain designated term days to take them at two-and-a-half-minute intervals throughout the twenty-four hours, at the same time that other British and foreign observatories, in international accord, took the same observations.

Having warped to the head of the bay, the expedition's observatories and huts were landed and erected. Over the two May term days the observing officers noted their instruments recording "strange oscillations and irregular movements." The Earth was being buffeted by one of Humboldt's magnetic storms. Ross was later to find that the Toronto observatory, almost antipodal to Kerguelen, had also recorded the same magnetic storm. The simultaneous disturbances, thought Ross, "afforded one of the most important facts that the still-hidden cause of magnetic phenomena has yet presented."

The island's more obvious windstorms made life a constant struggle. One seaman was blown into the surf and nearly drowned. Ross often hugged the ground to save himself from the same fate. Communications

The arched rock, Kerguelen Island

"My great delight was to sit on my grand-father's knee and look at the pictures in
Cook's 'Voyages.' The one that took my fancy most was the plate of Christmas Harbour, Kerguelen Land, with the arched rock standing out to sea, and the sailors killing
penguins; and I thought I should be the happiest boy alive if ever I would see that wonderful arched rock, and knock penguins on the head."   —Sir Joseph Hooker
(Illustration from *Cook's Voyages,* A. Kippis)

between ships and shore were cut for days at a time, and the ships were
often laid in their beam ends by the violent winds. Although laying on anchors and chain suitable for vessels twice their tonnage, the harried first
lieutenants (left in charge while Ross and Crozier made the magnetic observations) were often forced to drop their sheet anchors, the final and last
hope for dragging ships. Sergeant Cunningham wished he were back in
"Merry England" and recorded in his diary that a geologizing expedition
had returned and "seemed anxious not to go again." But life still held
small delights. The queen's birthday was celebrated with a royal salute,
plum pudding, preserved meat, and a double allowance of grog.

Hooker perhaps was the only happy man. For here was an untouched,
unusual botanical wonderland. William Anderson, Cook's surgeon-
naturalist on the *Resolution,* had identified 18 species of plant. Hooker,
after his first day ashore, returned with 30 species. By the time they sailed
he had brought the total up to 150.

His solitary wanderings to make his collection were usually done in the
endless rain or snow. His lichen collection had to be either hammered out
by the tufts or sat upon until thawed. The Kerguelen cabbage, found by
Cook to be a valuable antiscorbutic, particularly fascinated him. Hooker

gathered seeds that he later sent to his father (now moved from Glasgow to London's Kew Gardens), who had but small success in getting them to grow. Three years later, toward the expedition's end, he had the small pleasure of giving advice to his father on its raising: "Try it again in a cool place very wet and shaded, in black vegetable mould like peat. Do not bury it but lay it on the surface. Depend upon it they will grow if cool and damp enough." He had grown it in a bottle hanging in the rigging and brought it alive to the Falkland Islands. "We used to amuse ourselves planting it here and there where we go."

During their Kerguelen Island stay the cabbage was served out daily to the crew along with their salt beef and salt pork. Not that it was all salted meat. Sheathbills—birds of spotless white plumage, the only claw-footed Antarctic seabird, a great scavenger in penguin colonies, seal rookeries, and eater of unmentionable tidbits—although rather tough eating, went into pies and mulligatawny soup. One lucky favored sheathbill, turned into the crew's pet, used to run about the decks and ate alongside the men at mealtimes, helping itself to rice, raisins, and meat. It was also given a daily grog ration of water, lime juice, and rum. The sailors satisfied their urge to knock penguins on the head (there is no record of Hooker's satisfying all of his childhood dream), and the cooks turned them into stews, pies, curries, and a rich soup that tasted much like hare soup.

They sailed on 20 July, leaving what Ross called "this most dreary and disagreeable harbour," where it had blown a gale for forty-five of their sixty-five-day incarceration, and with only three days free of rain or snow. Sergeant Cunningham dryly noted in his diary that he felt no particular anxiety ever to visit it again. Only Hooker felt sorry at leaving: "By finding food for the mind one may grow attached to the most wretched spots on the globe."

Kerguelen was to perform for Hooker what the Galápagos had done for Darwin. Enough food for the mind had been provided to start the young botanist on his brilliant career as the world's authority on the geographic distribution of plants. Five years later Charles Darwin was writing to Hooker: "I shall live to see you the first authority in Europe on that grand subject, that almost keystone of the laws of creation, geographical distribution."

The thirty-six-hundred-mile passage from Kerguelen to Tasmania was a white-water, booming, downwind run in mountainous seas. At times, with waves breaking over the quarters, the decks lay buried under two feet of water. Steering the bluff-bowed bomb vessels took strength, experience, and confidence. After sighting a small iceberg, and with fifteen hours of darkness, the tense lookouts often had trouble distinguishing between foaming crests and possible ice. During one particularly vicious storm Ross spent all his time on the weather quarter with three turns of the mizzen-staysail halyard lashed around him for support, the tops of the waves driving across the deck in sheets of water.

During one fraught period the *Erebus* lost her boatswain when he fell from the rigging. A life buoy was thrown, and two boats were lowered, but he vanished from sight a few seconds before they reached him. One of the boats was then struck by a cross sea, and four of the crew were washed away. Abernethy went to the rescue in his boat and hauled them aboard, benumbed and stupefied with the cold. But the drama was not finished. The boat, in the violent seas, was swamped again when alongside, but all were saved.

A month after sailing from Christmas Harbor the two vessels were anchored off Hobart, drying out, bending new sails—some sails, torn to shreds, were beyond repair—with the seamen swapping sea stories of the horrors dealt out by the Southern Ocean. But throughout the stormy passage the Fox dip circles had recorded their data. They were indeed, as Ross acknowledged, admirable contrivances.

If Hobart was a welcome change for the expedition after the rigors of Kerguelen Island, their arrival was equally welcome to Lieutenant Governor Sir John Franklin and his wife, Jane. Sir John, much changed since his midshipman days with Flinders and the *Investigator,* was now a stout fifty-four-year-old Arctic hero, a toby jug of a man with an energetic forty-eight-year-old wife. Franklin had been appointed to the penal colony to replace the austere, autocratic Colonel George Arthur, a Calvinistic evangelical convinced of his mission, passed down to him by God, to punish the convicts for their sins. He had been hated and detested by both convicts and free settlers. The self-righteous Arthur, with bureaucratic efficiency, had turned Tasmania into a police state complete with informers and spies, where the government functionaries, many of them his relatives, controlled the supply of convict labor and where Arthur had done his best to muzzle and control the press. Joyous bonfires had flared across the island when his recall had been announced.

But the resident Arthur faction, fiercely opposed to Franklin, whom it despised as a woolly-minded, petticoat-ruled liberal, was turning his tenure of office into a bumpy, uncomfortable ride filled with cunningly placed potholes. For a sensitive man, unused to chicanery and deceit, a penal colony was not the ideal habitat. Jane Franklin thought Tasmania "a country where people should have hearts of stone and frames of iron."

But with the expedition's arrival Franklin's cares dropped away. Jane summed it up in a letter to her father: "The arrival of Captains Ross & Crozier has added much to Sir John's happiness, they all feel towards one another as friends and brothers, & it is the remark of people here that Sir John appears to them in a new light, so bustling & frisky & merry with his new companions."

Franklin had the observatory's framework—no metal in its construction—ready and waiting. It only required Ross to select a site, and within hours two hundred convicts were working on the foundations and raising pillars of freestone for the delicate instruments. Within nine days the building was roofed over—just hours before the August term days. Then the *Hobart Town Courier* urged its readers to "show that Van Diemen's Land, which is the maximum point of intensity in magnetism is not the minimum one in all that appertains to the social relations of life."

Sir John supplied fresh fruits and vegetables for officers and seamen; Government House hosted parties, balls, and dinners; the seamen sampled the delights of Hobart's grogshops and inns. The new Rossbank Observatory in turn played host to the locals, although Jane admitted to being no wiser coming out than when she had entered. An article appeared in the *Hobart Town Advertiser* about one of the "fashionable *belles*" who on "leaning over to obtain 'a sight,' set the instrument vibrating, which afterwards took the officer in charge three days to make good the reckoning. It is said the fair lady had on a steel bust, which did so much unintentional mischief."

Sophia Cracroft, Franklin's niece—and an outrageous flirt, according to Jane—so enamored Crozier that he proposed marriage. But Sophia had no time for Crozier—she thought him a horrid radical and bad speller—and rolled her eyes, much to Jane's annoyance, at the impervious Ross. The young Hooker complained in a letter home about being forced to dance attendance at Government House when aching to be out botanizing. On one picnic party, hosted by Jane, to a 130-acre plot of land still containing remnants of a turnip crop but destined to be a botanical garden, Hooker let out such a scream that Jane, who hated snakes and paid one shilling to the convicts for every dead reptile, thought he had been bitten by one of the hated creatures. He had merely found a new orchid.

Jane's efforts to become the St. Patrick of Tasmania drew a certain amount of sniggers. She herself recognized her scheme as "a little whimsical." The convicts, pragmatists all, thought it manna from heaven. A more serious concern of Jane's—one that appalled the colony's bureaucrats—were her efforts to ease the lot of the female prisoners. If she was to become Tasmania's Elizabeth Fry, a close friend, she had, like Mrs. Fry at Newgate Prison, to visit the inmates. One visit to Cascade Factory with Sir John, his handsome aide-de-camp, and a small party of ladies ended with a touch of ribaldry. The women prisoners listened respectfully to speeches from the Franklins while ogling the handsome aide-de-camp dressed in his scarlet and gold regimentals. The prison chaplain, loathed by the women prisoners, then started to preach. The women started to cough, were warned to silence by the warders, and then, en masse, turned

The Rossbank Observatory, Tasmania

"One of the fashionable *belles* . . . on leaning over to obtain 'a sight,' set the instrument vibrating, which afterwards took the officer in charge three days to make good the reckoning. It is said the fair lady had on a steel bust, which did do much unintentional mischief."   —*Hobart Town Advertiser,* October 16, 1840

(Illustration from Ross's *Voyage,* vol. I)

around, bent down, flipped up their shifts, and smacked their bared bottoms. Sir John was shocked, the chaplain horror-struck; the aide-de-camp roared with laughter; the ladies blushed and giggled.

Less laughter had been evident when the expedition heard of the French and American discoveries. D'Urville's discoveries had been related to Ross by Franklin and read in the saved editions of the Hobart newspapers. Ross, armed with Balleny's journal, thought the western end of d'Urville's Côte Clarie to be the same land seen by Balleny. The information on the American expedition came from Wilkes in a letter and was accompanied by a copy of Wilkes's Antarctic chart. Ross thought the gesture "friendly and highly honourable."

To Beaufort at the Hydrographic Office Ross wrote that he considered both French and Americans had achieved only a little more than Balleny. As for the south magnetic pole, he was convinced that neither d'Urville nor Wilkes had determined its true position. Much later, in his published

Voyage of Discovery, he raised an irritated eyebrow that the Americans and French had chosen to sail into the very area that they well knew "that the expedition under my command was expressly preparing, and thereby forestalling our purposes, did certainly greatly surprise me." It was in fact precisely what they were doing. D'Urville, in a letter to the minister of marine, admitted that his disobeying of his instructions and sailing south from Hobart, instead of to New Zealand, was to forestall Wilkes and Ross.

But if Ross was third on the scene, he held trump cards denied to the Americans and French: two superior vessels, better equipped and strengthened to deal with the ice, and Balleny's journal. The much-studied journal indicated to Ross that a more easterly meridian—170°E—than that chosen by the French and Americans could be the pathway to the south magnetic pole. Balleny had reached 69°S at the 172°E meridian before being stopped by ice. Farther west the Americans and French had failed to get beyond 67°S.

On 11 November Ross was writing to the Admiralty that he intended to sail for the Auckland Islands and then push south to search out the south magnetic pole. The next day, with all the expedition feeling pangs of regret, the two vessels dropped down the Derwent River with Franklin and friends aboard the *Erebus,* followed by the governor's barge. At Storm Bay, the mouth of the river, the Hobart party left to the cheers of the seamen manning the rigging. As Sergeant Cunningham wrote of Franklin, "He is a nice fatherly old man who is much interested in our welfare." The cheers might have been organized cheers, but they came from the heart.

A week later they were at anchor in Sarah's Bosom in the Auckland Islands, where the tyranny of the term days had brought them. An observatory had to be erected ashore with the officers taking their measurements at the exact time other observers, worldwide, were taking theirs. But on coming to anchor, they saw two conspicuous painted boards close to the shore. They proved to be the signboards, now eight months old, left by Ringgold and d'Urville.

Three weeks were spent at the Auckland Islands, the officers taking their measurements and surveying the anchorage and nearby shores—Sarah's Bosom, considered an inappropriate name, being renamed Erebus Cove and Terror Cove—McCormick geologizing and shooting birds, Hooker gathering an astounding number of plants, many of them new to science, and Hallet, the purser, shooting some pigs, now gone wild, that had been left on the island. But their flesh proved to be inferior to that of the ships' well-fed animals.

On 12 December they sailed for Campbell Island, some 120 miles to the south. Only two days were spent at the island, wooding and watering, McCormick blasting away at birds, Hooker in a frenzy of collecting and aided by Ross, who returned, as Hooker wrote to his father, in "his Galley . . . with the bottom like a garden." Campbell Island lay close to Ross's chosen meridian of 170°E. On 17 December the two vessels stood away from the island with a westerly wind and headed south. The voyage, fifteen months out from England, was now set on its prime objective. On board were provisions for three years, and if a safe haven could be found, they would spend the winter as close as possible to the south magnetic pole.

Christmas Day was spent hove to in a northerly gale with rain and snow driving across the decks and the sea temperature down to 32°F. They were now below the Convergence and in the Antarctic. Two days later, sailing south, they came across their first iceberg. Within less than an hour they had counted fifteen. To the Arctic hands these southern icebergs were very different from those of the north. These that they were eyeing were large—several of them were more than two miles in circumference—flat-topped, bounded by perpendicular cliffs, and between 120 feet and 180 feet in height, the classic Antarctic tabular iceberg.

They were also seeing a great many whales—right, sperm, and humpback—and petrels. McCormick, never happier than when shooting birds, had perfected a technique of bringing down birds hovering at the mastheads so that they fell on deck. It was pretty marksmanship in order to avoid both the web of rigging, spars, and sails, plus the first lieutenant's wrath. One calm day, ideal for taking soundings, Ross had 5,000 fathoms of line ready on the reel, the men harnessed, the fiddler sawing away, and they made soundings at 1,560 fathoms (very close to what modern charts indicate).

By New Year's Eve they were at 66°S in clear weather with a strong ice blink to the south. At ten o'clock in the morning of the following day they crossed the Antarctic Circle, the crow's nests were hoisted to the foretopmasts, Ross had the officers to New Year's dinner in the great cabin—fresh roast beef and bullock's heart—and then they sighted a barrier of pack ice stretching across their course. With little wind and a heavy swell making the vessels close to unsteerable, Ross decided to haul north a short distance, away from the pack with the waves swirling across the ice floes, and wait. Because it was New Year's Day, extra rations and grog were issued to the crew along with the cold-weather fearnought jackets, trousers, waterproof boots, scarves, red flannel shirts, and curious worsted wool hats—much beloved by the Royal Navy for cold climates—known as Welsh wigs.

The wait took three days. On 4 January, in good visibility, carrying all sail, the two vessels started their slalom course run through icebergs and streams of floes. That evening the sun's lower limb kissed the horizon three minutes before midnight and rolled along to the eastward for seventeen minutes and thirty seconds before finally vanishing, only to pop up again a few minutes later. For those men unused to the polar regions it was an experience never to be forgotten.

Later that morning they came across the main pack. Here lay Antarctica's main defense system, and the two vessels ranged along the undulating floes searching for weak points—open leads of water between the floes. Ross selected one, made the signal for the *Terror* to follow in his wake, bore away before the wind, and under full sail drove hard at the barrier. After about an hour of hard thumping they found themselves in slightly looser pack ice but still being slammed by violent shocks that only their strengthened bomb vessels could have taken. By noon they were deep in the pack with no open sea visible from the mastheads. Ross was now committed. Any retreat, with the strong northerly, was impossible. Four days later, during the morning of 9 January, they burst out from the pack into an open sea. They had bored their way through a band of pack ice that would have sunk the American and French expeditions. "We had," wrote a jubilant Ross, "accomplished the object of our exertions." The seamen, over those hard pounding days, had entertained themselves by imitating the penguins' cries and then been vastly amused as the small creatures, with their rolling sailor's waddle, toiled across the ice to find out the source before plunging into the open water and porpoising in the ship's wake. The gun room officers, the day before they broke out from the pack, had entertained themselves by getting Billy, the *Erebus*'s pet goat, beastly drunk on port wine so that he staggered around the quarterdeck, according to McCormick, "committing the greatest absurdities." Billy spent the next day suffering from a goatish hangover, bedded in his cask, and that evening McCormick found him dying. Strange seals had been seen hauled out on the ice and collected for science, brained with a handspike by Sergeant Cunningham and then shot by an officer. The unfortunate *Ommatophoca rossi*, the Ross's seal, was about to enter the textbooks.

Seventy years later Ross's remarkable achievement in hammering through the pack was praised by Roald Amundsen: "Few people of the present day are capable of rightly appreciating this heroic deed, this brilliant proof of human courage and energy. With two ponderous craft—regular 'tubs' according to our ideas—these men sailed right into the heart of the pack, which all previous polar explorers had regarded as certain death. It is not merely difficult to grasp this; it is simply impossible—to us, who with a motion of the hand can set the screw going, and wriggle out of the first difficulty we encounter. These men were heroes—heroes in the highest sense of the word."

In poor visibility, cloaked in fog and snow, the only guide the south-pointing needle, the expedition headed for the south magnetic pole. On 11 January, the visibility clearing, Ross suffered a "severe disappointment." Mountainous land lay stretched across their path. By noon Cook's 1774 farthest south—71°15′S—was passed, and more land was appearing across the horizon. That evening they lay six miles off a shore packed with heavy ice and no possibility of making a landing.

The new land of course had to be given names. The highest mountain in the range, and the first peak sighted, became Mount Sabine, named by Ross for "one of the best and earliest friends of my youth and to whom this compliment was more especially due, as having been the first proposer and one of the most active and zealous promoters of the expedition." The high and dark cliff before them became Cape Adare, "after my friend Viscount Adare, M.P. for Glamorganshire, who always evinced a warm interest in our undertaking." The range of mountains, in an astute move by Ross, became the Admiralty Range with its peaks named for the "Lords Commissioners of the Admiralty under whose orders I was serving."

Magnetic observations placed the south magnetic pole some five hundred miles behind these rather daunting but magnificent range of peaks estimated to be between seven and ten thousand feet high. Ross had two choices for an attempt at the magnetic pole: to trace the coast to the west with the hope of turning it and then sailing south or to trace the south-trending coast and then hope to sail west. He adopted the latter, one of the lures being the gain of higher latitudes and the other the possibility of landing on a small group of islands that could be seen lying to the south.

The next day, with the sky taking on an ominous look, the landing was made, and a small group of officers and seamen waded ashore on an island covered with penguins and smothered with guano. The penguins pecked at their legs, the men grimaced at the stench from the thick layer of guano—like walking across a dried-up peat bog, according to Mc-Cormick—the Union Jack was raised, and the land claimed "in the name of our Most Gracious Sovereign, Queen Victoria," followed by a toast to the health, long life, and happiness of both her and her husband, Prince Albert. The officers gave their toast in sherry, and the men in rum. McCormick shot a skua, collected specimens of the black lava rock, banged a penguin on the head with his geological hammer, and stowed the creature away in his haversack. After a half hour stay, the recall signal flying from the *Erebus,* the expedition beat a hasty retreat from this disagreeable, odiferous chunk of land—named Possession Island—with their boats loaded with geological specimens and clubbed penguins. They arrived back on board, after a long, heavy pull, a few minutes before the arrival of a gale of wind and fog.

The next few days were spent riding out a severe storm. The storm over, they closed with the land in sparkling clear weather. On leaving Hobart, McCormick had scribbled an optimistic entry into his diary: "Our future promises to be full of interest, for we may soon make great discoveries in a region of our globe fresh and new as at creation's dawn."

The Victoria Land coast happens to be spectacular and theatrical, a coastline so improbable, especially when the sun tints the mountain peaks, that it could be a stage set showing Creation's first dawn. Ross estimated these improbable snow-covered peaks to be between twelve and fourteen thousand feet high. Everyone stared at them "with feelings of indescribable delight . . . a scene of grandeur and magnificence far beyond anything we had before seen or could have conceived." Hooker thought it one of the most gorgeous sights he had ever seen. Robertson was struck by the range's sense of solitude and "omnipotent grandeur." Cornelius Sullivan, the *Erebus*'s blacksmith, thought it "Quite Enchanting" and would have loved to gaze longer at this "Sublimity of nature—but Lo i had to pull the brails." The sublime peaks were named by Ross after the "eminent philosophers of the Royal Society and British Association, at whose recommendation the government was induced to send forth this expedition," the highest peak being named Mount Herschel.

The next week was spent thumping against southerly winds and adverse currents. But the naming of capes, peaks, and islands continued. On 17 January an island lying some fifteen miles offshore was sighted. Ross, in an effort to oil his gritty relationship with Anne's father, named it Coulman Island. The day being Anne's birthday, the south end was named Cape Anne, and the north end Cape Wadworth—after Wadworth Hall, where he and Anne had taken magnetic observations and which was "a spot of many happy associations."

At noon on 22 January they were at 74°20′S, south of Weddell's magic milestone latitude of 1823. An extra allowance of grog was issued, and its being a Saturday, the seaman's favorite toast of "Sweethearts and wives"—along with the sotto voce "may they never meet"—was heard in what Ross called the "general rejoicing." He spent the evening dining in the gun room with his officers, all drinking the traditional toasts plus one to "Better luck still."

Ten days later luck was with Hooker when he slipped on steep ice-covered rocks while landing through a wicked surf on Franklin Island. Falling into the ice-cold waters, he came close to being crushed to death between rocks and the heavy cutter. His close call was soon forgotten. The following morning, as he wrote to his father, the expedition came across a remarkable sight and, considering the vessels' names, a very appropriate one:

At one time we thought we were really going on to the true South Pole, when we were brought up by the land turning from S. to E., where there was a fine Volcano spouting fire and smoke in 79°S., covered all over with eternal snow, except for just round the crater where the heat had melted it off. I can give you no idea of the glorious views we have here, they are stupendous and imposing, especially when there was any fine weather, with the sun never setting, among huge bergs, the water and sky both as blue, or rather more intensely blue than I have ever seen it in the Tropics, and all the coast one mass of beautiful peaks of snow, and when the sun gets low they reflect the most brilliant tints of gold and scarlet . . . there is a sort of awe that steals over us all considering our own total insignificance and helplessness. Everything beyond what we see is enveloped in a mystery reserved for future voyagers to fathom.

Sullivan, the blacksmith, thought this "Splendid burning mountain"—Mount Erebus—"was truly an imposing Sight." What lay beyond was hidden, but he and all the crew were aware that they were south of the magnetic pole and that it lay miles to the west, blocked from their reaching it by ice and land.

A burning mountain was one imposing sight, but they were soon—the same day—to come upon another. As they sailed closer to Mount Erebus and its smaller, extinct neighbor, Mount Terror, they saw a low white line extending from the land to the east as far as the eye could see. "It presented an extraordinary appearance," wrote Ross, "gradually increasing in height, as we got nearer to it, and proving at length to be a perpendicular cliff of ice, between one hundred and fifty and two hundred feet above the level of the sea, perfectly flat and level at the top, and without any fissures or promontories on its even seaward face. What was beyond it we could not imagine."

Here was yet another disappointment. Such had been their progress that all had been mentally ticking off the degrees to eighty south, and Ross had even appointed a rendezvous there in case of an accidental separation. But faced with this extraordinary barrier (it went down on Ross's chart as "Perpendicular Barrier of Ice" but is now known as the Ross Ice Shelf), the philosophical Ross had to admit that they had as much chance of penetrating it as of sailing through the white cliffs of Dover. His only choice, being blocked by land and ice to the south and west, was to trace the barrier to the east.

Over a week later and some three hundred miles to the east of Mount Erebus, with the temperature down to 12°F, the sea freezing over, the men's jackets crackling in the cold, they sailed through the slush of rapidly forming pancake ice into a bay carved into the barrier. Here the cliff face was lower, and they could see across its flat top from the mastheads. It stretched, flat, limitless, and austere, "an immense plain of frosted silver," according to Ross, south to the distant geographic pole. Sullivan had no doubts of that: "It is quite certain . . . that from the seventy eight Degrees to pole must be one solid continent of Ice and Snow."

Sailing a mere quarter mile off the barrier face, they could see gigantic icicles hanging from every projecting point. It was a scene guaranteed to silence even the most garrulous of sailors. Sullivan, with a poignant cry from his heart, summed up all their emotions:

All hands when they Came on Deck to view this most rare and magnificent Sight that Ever the human Eye witnessed Since the world was created actually Stood Motionless for Several Seconds before he could Speak to the man next to him. Beholding with Silent Surprize the great and wonderful works of nature in this position we had an opportunity to discern the barrier in its Splendid position. Then i wished i was an artist or a draughtsman instead of a blacksmith and armourer . . . we Set a Side all thoughts of mount Erebus and Victorias Land to bear in mind the more Immaginative thoughts of this rare Phenomena that was lost to human view In gone by Ages.

McCormick, amazed at what he was seeing, never left the deck for twenty-four hours and thought it a sight "never to be effaced from memory's tablet to the latest hour of existence . . . scene succeeded scene in nature's unrivalled display of her great Creator's work."

But with pack ice bearing down on the barrier and the small bay freezing over, it now became a struggle to pry themselves out from a dangerous situation. They succeeded and then watched the narrow channel they had wriggled through become shut fast with ice.

Ross was still eager to explore farther east. But after a few days the older pack ice, the younger ice forming along its edge, and the lateness of the season persuaded him to turn west in the hope of finding a safe winter harbor close to the magnetic pole. By 16 February they were in sight of Mount Erebus, still belching out flames and smoke, and discovered an ice-covered bight under the volcano's flank that Ross named McMurdo Bay[2] after the *Terror*'s first lieutenant—"a compliment that his zeal and skill well merited."

But the magnetic pole, the Holy Grail, still beckoned, and with a favorable wind they sailed northwest, shunting aside the loose pack ice, toward it. Within a day Ross was forced to admit defeat. They had managed to sail through old ice and the sludge of new ice to within 10 miles of the low-lying coast behind which lay the Holy Grail. But consolidated pack ice had stopped them. Ross had Crozier come aboard the *Erebus*, and they discussed the situation in the quiet of the great cabin. Calculations put the magnetic pole 160 miles inland. If they had found a safe winter harbor, they could have sent parties in the spring to both Mount Erebus and the magnetic pole.[3] But as the ice held them off from finding any hypothetical harbor, it was patently impossible to overwinter. The Holy Grail lay but a short distance across that frozen landscape, but it was untouchable. Ross's "perhaps too ambitious hope" to plant the Union Jack—the very same flag that he had raised over the north magnetic pole—over both magnetic poles, had to be abandoned.

The retreat proved a struggle. The new ice was thickening fast and held them glued. Ice too thick to sail through. Ice too brittle to stand on and saw. Boats were lowered and broke a passage by stamping and rolling. After a long night of effort they sailed into clear water.

The retracing of their course along what Ross had dubbed Victoria Land was accompanied by the usual naming of prominent features. Mc-Cormick and Hallet got their capes and Robertson his bay. After rounding Cape Adare—no landing because ice extended nine miles offshore—Hooker achieved his cape. Ross was still anxious to find a wintering harbor, but the coast was packed with ice. On 4 March they sighted the Balleny Islands and, after sixty-three days south of it, passed north of the Antarctic Circle.

Two days later, much to their surprise, they were sailing over the land marked down by Wilkes. An extensive search in ideal conditions revealed nothing, and no bottom was found at six hundred fathoms. Ross could only assume that Wilkes, "having but little experience of the delusive appearances in these icy regions," had "mistaken for land some of the dense well-defined clouds which so continually hang over extensive packs of ice." Ross added that they themselves had often been fooled—Cape Flyaway had become a standard joke—until "we actually sailed over the spot." The whole episode, Ross thought, threw doubt on the rest of Wilkes's coastline.

A few days later more pressing—and frightening—problems were facing Ross's men than the one Sullivan called the "Fable the Americans told about their great Discoveries," the dreadful nightmare, one of many, sent to haunt sailors in sailing ships: no wind, a huge swell making towing with boats impossible, and the swell, allied with a strong current, setting your ship onto rocky, sheer cliffs. In this case, it was a massed phalanx of icebergs with the swell breaking at their bases and sending masses of pack ice shooting up their vertical faces. "Sublime and magnificent as such a scene must have appeared under different circumstances," wrote Ross, "to us it was awful, if not appalling." McCormick noted the icebergs to leeward, retired for dinner—roasted fresh beef that McCormick thought very tender, killed in December and aged by being hung under the mizzen top in a bread bag—opened a jar of Tasmanian honey, and broached a bottle of whiskey. As the imperturbable or happily ignorant surgeon downed his drams, a light wind filled the sails, freshened, and the heavy vessels within sound of the surf crept away from certain shipwreck, and the thankful men from certain death.

Ross had established that Gauss's calculated magnetic pole position—66°S latitude and 146°E longitude—was incorrect. The measurements gathered during the voyage indicated a position much farther south, closer to 76°S latitude. Ross conceded that the Americans and French, with much inferior instruments, had made magnetic observations close to the Gauss's position but still thought an inspection "might prove to be of more than ordinary magnetic interest."

By 20 March, after a wet and tedious slog to windward against westerly swells and winds, they were forty-five miles north of the Gauss coordinates, but blocked by heavy pack ice from reaching it. During the uncomfortable thrash to windward Hooker lashed himself, his microscope, and his drawing pad to the table, and set about catching up on plant, trawl, and deep-sea dredge collections. For exercise he heaved—following Sir Francis Drake's dictum that gentlemen should haul and draw with the mariner, and the mariner with the gentlemen—on halyards, tacks, sheets, braces, guys, and bowlines. "Thus my chest expands," he explained to his mother, "my arms get hard, and the former *rings* almost when struck."

It was time to return to Hobart. The zigzag passage back took seventeen days, the course dictated by Ross's desire to cross and recross the magnetic line of no variation, the agonic line where the compass points to the truth north. The days, after the tensions and excitements of their passage to and from the ice barrier, had their minor interests. As they neared the Convergence, wet snow was collected and used for washing to eke out their water ration, now reduced to a half pint a day for every man. One memorable day a huge flock of petrels passed overhead, darkening the sky. The flock was estimated to be six to ten miles in length, two or three miles broad, and took three hours to pass. The crew saw their last iceberg on 1 April, and the next day, being calm, boats were lowered for a deep-sea sounding. It took twenty-four minutes and twenty-nine seconds before the lead line, running off its reel, struck bottom at 1,540 fathoms. That evening the weather changed, and they were hit by a gale and heavy seas that washed away one of their boats.

Just after midnight on 6 April they sighted the glimmer of the lighthouse off the Derwent's entrance. But it was a headwind all the way upriver to Hobart, a tedious beat enlivened by Franklin—he was given three cheers—meeting them in the governor's barge. After a five-month absence the *Erebus* and the *Terror* at last came to anchor off the government gardens and close to the Rossbank Observatory. They had much to tell, Ross to Franklin, the officers to their friends, the men in the grogshops, where, as Cornelius Sullivan put it, "a drop of the Creator soon made our Jolly Tars forget the Cold fingers in the Frozen Regions . . . for very Little they thought of 78 South while Regealing them Selves at Charley Probins the Sign of the Gordon."

NOTES

1. A large elephant seal could produce between six or seven barrels of oil, a barrel holding 32.5 U.S. gallons. During the years 1841–47 American whaleships virtually exterminated the right whale population of the "Crozettes Ground."

2. Now McMurdo Sound and one of Antarctica's historic bodies of water. To its

shores on Ross Island came Captain Robert Scott's expeditions of 1901–04 and 1910–13, and Sir Ernest Shackleton's expeditions of 1907–09 and 1914–16. Today it is home to the American McMurdo Base and the New Zealand Scott-Amundsen Base.

3. Achieved by Shackleton's 1907–09 expedition. Mount Erebus (12,448 feet) was climbed in March 1908, and the south magnetic pole, then at 72°25′S latitude and 155°16′E longitude, was reached in January 1909.

Chapter 15

The Pilgrims of the Ocean

OBSTACLES. Chains, booms, abattis, snags, palisades, or
anything placed to impede an enemy's progress. Unforeseen
hindrances.

ONE, TWO, THREE! The song with which seamen bowse
out the bowlines; the last haul being completed by belay O!

Admiral W. H. Smyth, *The Sailor's Word-Book*, 1867

EN AND SHIPS had returned from the Antarctic in far better physical condition than those of the American and French
expeditions. Ice damage to the ships was minor, requiring no
heaving down, but they were still completely emptied of
stores, provisions, and equipment, which were inspected, cataloged, and
then stored. The seamen set about scrubbing, caulking, and painting the
hulls, stripping, overhauling, and refitting the rigging, all the multitude of
tasks dear to the hearts of first lieutenants and boatswains.

The surgeons and assistant surgeons, with such healthy crews, had
time to botanize, geologize and, for McCormick, never far away from his
double-barreled gun, to wreak havoc among Tasmania's wildlife. Crozier
and the spare officers set up the ships' portable observatories next to those
in the Rossbank Observatory and diligently took measurements. Ross
planned the second Antarctic season and wrote reports to the Admiralty
on the results of the first. In a more personal letter to Beaufort he told of
his disappointment in not reaching the magnetic pole or finding a safe winter haven. He expressed a view that Antarctic navigation was far more difficult than Arctic. "But," he added, "it is our business to endeavour to
overcome not to raise up difficulties." He planned, he wrote, to sail south
again to the most easterly position that they had reached at the ice barrier

and then try to reach Weddell's farthest south by sailing along the barrier, land, or open sea, depending upon whatever might lie in that direction. As for Wilkes's chart and letter, he thought Beaufort would see "the great mistake he has made & the very cursory manner of his proceedings, sufficient I think to throw great doubt over all he has done and I have no doubt that many other of his Mountain Ranges will prove to be delusive appearances by which the unpractised eye in the Icy Regions is so likely to be deceived." Having disposed of Wilkes, he added a postscript: "Crozier hopes to be held in your kind remembrance he is a *regular trump*." In a separate letter to the Admiralty Ross recommended the regular trump for promotion.

Lady Franklin, away on a tour of New Zealand, missed two social highlights of the expedition's three-month stay at Hobart. But accounts, taken from the local newspapers, were printed on pale blue satin and saved for her. The first event was an entertainment presented on 3 May at the Royal Victoria Theatre: "An entirely new nautical Drama entitled the SOUTH POLAR EXPEDITION." The stage set included a "splendid view of the VOLCANIC MOUNTAIN, named by the distinguished Navigators *Mount Erebus.* . . . And in the last scene will be represented a Grand ALLEGORICAL TABLEAU of Science crowning the distinguished Navigators Captains Ross and Crozier at the command of Britannia, and Fame proclaiming their success to the world."

The play ended in tumultuous and patriotic applause with Britannia (a Mrs. Thompson, who had also played Lady Franklin) advancing to the audience, pointing to Ross (played by Mr. Thompson), and declaiming:

> The after ages shall revere his name,
> Crowned as it is on science and by fame.
> His the high guerdon, his the envied prize,
> (Dearer than victory in a conqueror's eyes)
> By genius, science earned—a name that never dies.

The play might have met with Hobart's approval, but the testy McCormick thought it "rather indifferently got up and not much better acted." The evening's entertainment was rounded off with a romantic melodrama—also received with tumultuous applause—entitled *The Robber of the Rhine*, in which a Mr. Booth (Sir John Franklin in the previous production) played Peter the Black, and the ubiquitous Mrs. Thompson the Hag of the Tomb.

To reciprocate Hobart's efforts, the expedition organized a ball, McCormick acting as secretary of the committee, to be held aboard the two ships. It took two weeks of preparation. The ships were moored alongside each other about a hundred feet offshore and connected to the shore by a bridge of boats. This gangway was covered with canvas and flags, decorated with shrubs, and lit by lanterns. A road for carriages was hacked through the trees so that the guests walked into the gangway-grotto and emerged onto the *Erebus*'s awning-covered deck, lit by chandeliers and lamps, acting as the ballroom. The ladies were led away to the captain's cabin or gun room, both of which had been turned into ladies' dressing rooms "with mirrors and most of the etceteras of a lady's toilet," as McCormick delicately put, complete with hairpins, eau de cologne, perfumes, and maidservants from Government House. The music, provided by the Hobart Town Quadrille Band and the band of the 51st Regiment, ended at eleven o'clock when the three hundred guests moved over to the *Terror* and sat down to a supper that had the "French style of variety with the English fashion of plenty." The *Terror*'s deck, packed with tables and chairs, loud with chatter and laughter, colored with the bright splashes of the army's scarlet and gold, the more sober navy's blue and gold, the ladies coquettish in their finery, the flushed faces, the sparkling eyes, the bubbling champagne glasses, all lit by chandeliers made from swords and cutlasses supporting hundreds of candles, and 250 small mirrors (part of the ships' stores to give to friendly natives) each containing two candles, "which reflected double, forming the most brilliant light that could possibly be conceived," made a supper never to be forgotten. After toasts and speeches the company returned to the *Erebus* and danced until daylight with the mellowing McCormick thinking that "the decks of the old ice-and-weatherbeaten ships never before responded to the elastic step of so much female loveliness, as this small island of the Antipodes mustered on the occasion." The *Hobart Town Advertiser* thought it "without exception the most splendid gala ever given in this town, whether as regarded the fitting up of the ships, the quality of the supper, and last, though not least, the attention and politness of the entertainers."

The "Glorious First of June" party, as it was fondly remembered in Hobart, had cost a considerable amount of money—deducted from the officers' pay—and a considerable amount of clearing up. Cunningham's diary entries for 2 June and 3 June are terse. "Clearing away the wrecks—Heads bad." And "Ditto."

Five weeks after the party, on 7 July, the two vessels stood down the Derwent for the last time, bound for Sydney and then New Zealand, before heading for the ice barrier. Sir John Franklin and friends were once more aboard for the sail downriver. The vessels hove to in Storm Bay, and to the cheers of the seamen, the governor's party boarded the government brig for the sail back to Hobart. If they failed to write regularly, the Franklins warned, "we of this household will write in condemning you as very lazy Discovery chaps."

A week later the discovery chaps were in Sydney setting up an observatory on Garden Island for more term day observations. Compared with Hobart, Hooker thought, Sydney, except for its magnificent harbor and few buildings, was a shabby town full of grogshops and the waterfront lined with dirty wharves, a waterfront, where one pitch-black night the short-sighted botanist nearly drowned, and although Sydney's main streets might be wide, gas-lit, and patrolled by police, during the incessant rains they turned into muddy rivers. The expedition, with few regrets after almost three weeks of rain, sailed on 4 August bound for New Zealand's Bay of Islands. The ships were packed with three years' worth of provisions, stores, and fuel.

Twelve days later they were anchored in the Kawa Kawa River at the Bay of Islands. Nearby off Kororarika lay the *Yorktown,* an American sloop of war and virtual sister ship to Hudson's *Peacock.* Over the next few days the American and British officers exchanged visits, Captain John H. Aulick of the *Yorktown* being particularly eager to see Ross's observatory set up on the banks of a tributary stream—named the "muddy-muddy" by the British seamen for its glutinous shores—of the Kawa Kawa.

One meeting in the *Erebus*'s great cabin, instigated by Ross, was to have unfortunate repercussions. The sticky "muddy-muddy" of rival explorers' claims was about to begin. Knowing that Aulick was shortly to sail for Hawaii and see Wilkes, Ross thought the meeting "the most delicate mode of acquainting Lieutenant Wilkes with the circumstances of our having passed over a large space in clear water, where he had placed mountainous land on the chart he sent me." After examining both Ross's and Wilkes's charts laid out on the great cabin table, Aulick and the other American officers could only agree with Ross and Crozier.

The Americans sailed the next day for Hawaii, where Aulick made known what he had learned from Ross, although it was already common knowledge at Hawaii, having been reported in the 2 October 1841 issue of the *Polynesian,* seven days before the *Yorktown*'s arrival. Aulick, in a later issue, confirmed the article. The *Yorktown* sailed from Hawaii a few days before Wilkes's arrival (a passing of ships that some of the exploring expedition thought another stroke of fortune for Wilkes. The senior Aulick would have certainly been more than curious about Wilkes's self-promotion to captain and commodore, flying a blue pennant).

Wilkes heard Aulick's news with fury and rage, ascribing jealousy to Aulic at not commanding the expedition and envy to Ross. Both men, as far as Wilkes was concerned, had now joined the ranks of his enemies.

The British stayed three months at the Bay of Islands, the officers busy with their magnetic and pendulum measurements, the surgeon-naturalists adding to their collections. A small armed party was sent upriver to collect timber for spars, and the officer in charge ran into New Zealand's musket economy. A Maori chief pointed out the best trees that he would allow cut—with the consultation fee to be paid in muskets. The officer agreed. When the chief came aboard the *Erebus* to collect his fee, it appeared that he had wanted *tupara,* the double-barreled musket. Because the muskets were the private property of the officers, loath to give them up, he was persuaded—and happily accepted—two rifles and a complete suit of lieutenant's uniform. The expedition sailed out from the Bay of Islands on 23 November. The crew was healthy, having eaten fresh food, mainly fish, for three months, and packing the decks and quarter boats, so that the ships resembled farmyards or arks more than exploration vessels, were sheep, pigs, cattle, and geese. Also on board the *Erebus* were a chart of the Chatham Islands and a map showing Dumont d'Urville's Antarctic discoveries. Both had been given to Ross by the captain of the *Héroine,* a French corvette, which had arrived at the Bay of Islands with her crew in a sickly condition. The French chart of the islands, lying some five hundred miles east of New Zealand, Ross thought superior to his British chart. It had been made by the *Héroine*'s previous commander, who had sailed to the Chathams on a gunboat mission of revenge after hearing that the crew of a French whaleship had been massacred. The corvette was still in the Pacific, looking after French whaling interests and trying to prevent a cunning fraud. The French government had given a bounty to encourage whaling with the reward graded in proportion to the whaleship's success. But the enterprising whaleship skippers and owners, masters in the French alchemy of turning bureaucratic paper into gold, were buying oil from English and American whaleships and returning with full ships to France, there to collect the maximum bounty.

Ross had hoped to call at the Chatham Islands for land-based magnetic and pendulum observations and to assess the islands as a whaling base. Dense fog and weather prevented him. Hearing, but not seeing, the surf on the many reefs, he bore away south for the Antarctic.

On the way south Ross had towing nets over the side, boats lowered to test for currents, sea temperatures taken down to fifteen hundred fathoms, whales noted and logged. On 13 December the sea surface temperature registered 39°F. By the following day, the weather now becoming foggy, the sea temperature had dropped 5°. They were across the Convergence and back in the Antarctic. On 16 December the sea temperature was close to freezing, and the fog clearing, they saw the first iceberg of their new Antarctic season.

They were close to the 146°W meridian, the one selected by Ross to sail down and reach the barrier, and one far to the east of the previous, so successful season's meridian. A day later pack ice, far to the north of their meeting with the pack of 1840, lay stretched across their course. Ross headed into it. The battle had begun. The ships hammered through it with the ice growling along their hulls like distant gunfire. Davis, the *Terror*'s second master, wrote to his sister that by this time she would never have recognized him: bearded, Jim Crow hat,[1] check shirt, thick boots. But then all the officers and men were wearing an extraordinary variety of costumes. Apart from his chilblains—soaked every night in rum, but to no purpose—Davis's only other problem had been the *Terror's* cat tearing up some of his charts. A few days later she presented the Terrors with three kittens: "We made a bed of furs for her in the berth, for it was very cold for them. Such an event as that you may think nothing of, but to us it is a great deal, for a kitten tends to relieve the monotony of such a cruise as this." The kittens, one day old, were shown to Ross on a warmed plate. Christmas Day was spent locked in the ice, surrounded by sentinel icebergs, fog draped over ships, and ice like a shroud. The gloom was relieved only by Christmas dinner and extra grog. A few days later the gloom was lifted.

The ships, as 1841 came to an end, happened to be moored to a large floe with officers and men exchanging visits, walking across the ice as if it were a quayside, an ideal venue for a New Year's Day party. By one of those happy, serendipitous occasions they also drifted across the Antarctic Circle on the same day that they had crossed it the previous year, although they were now fourteen hundred miles farther to the east.

Hooker and Davis, after a New Year's Eve dinner together, carved out an eight-foot figure of a reclining women in the ice which they called the Venus de Medici. They then built a table of ice to drink the "Old Year out and the New Year in." A few minutes before midnight all hell broke loose: blowing of horns, beating of gongs, squealing of pigs (the seamen, being politically incorrect fellows, picked up pigs and squeezed them like bagpipes, an exercise producing a wail similar to that instrument), followed by the ringing of the traditional nautical forty-two bells for the New Year. Ross and Crozier wished all the men a Happy New Year and then drank to their health. Ross was also given a warm, but very dead, snow petrel. McCormick's itchy trigger finger had shot the ill-fated bird as the ships' bells had started to ring in the New Year. "I presented it to him," wrote the marksman, "as the first victim to science in the new-born year; and, as such, he skinned and preserved it himself." The men's celebrations continued with dancing in the *Erebus's* fo'c'sle. They finished, according to James Savage, "with three or four Pugilastic matches in the Forecastle which peacably Ended."

New Year's Day was spent clearing away snow on the floe to make a dance floor. Surrounding the floor were sofas made from ice and snow and tavern signs on poles. One sign read THE EREBUS AND TERROR, and another displayed the painted figures of Bacchus and Britannia. A third sign, holding all the fo'c'sle's humor and irony, read THE PILGRIMS OF THE OCEAN on one side and THE PIONEERS OF SCIENCE on the other. The seamen, being loyal subjects, also made an ice and snow statue of Queen Victoria and Prince Albert. Flags (including the one hoisted by Ross at the north magnetic pole) and ensigns were hoisted. A table was carved from ice to hold wine bottles and glasses. The *Erebus's* boatswain acted the part of the genial landlord—even padding himself around the waist to give himself that well-fed look—complete with apron and bunches of keys dangling from his belt. Two seamen served as waiters. At eight o'clock in the evening a gun was fired, and the two captains with their officers made their appearance to a rather ragged volley of muskets from a slightly tipsy guard of honor. The New Year's Day party had begun. Ross, reverting to his Arctic female role, with Crozier as his partner, opened the dancing with a quadrille, followed by officers and men, all in their heavy boots, slipping, sliding, skating and falling, to reels, country dances, and waltzes. "Ladies fainting with cigars in their mouths, to cure which the gentlemen would politely thrust a piece of ice down her back. But it would require a 'Boz' to give any idea of the ridiculous scene." So Davis sketched the scene to his sister.

The officers, well knowing when to slip away from an anarchic party, left the seamen to their revels. "So that the Tavern Tap and ball Room, half Empty bottles, in fact the whole ice berg belonged to our Jolly Tars until morning." So dictated James Savage to Sullivan. The same day—although the days were beginning to merge in a haze—the seamen raced in sacks (won by Savage), tried to catch pigs with greased tails (won by Jatter Walsh), and climbed greased poles. The whole marvelous New Year celebrations ended with Ross leaving a record of it enclosed in a cask.

Two weeks later they were still enmeshed in the pack and, what was worse, fifty miles north of their Christmas Day position. At times they had managed to wriggle south through narrow leads by being towed by boats, by hauling the ships with the men in harness, or by sailing with a fair wind and shouldering aside the ice. Then the ice would close in, and the gain south would be lost in the drift north.

Following the unfortunate snow petrel, more birds and seals were sacrificed for science. Emperor penguins—one weighed seventy-eight pounds—proved such tough birds to kill that, once captured, they were given a tablespoon of hydrocyanic acid and died in seconds. One penguin, surfing on his belly across the snow-covered floes, propelled by feet and flipperlike wings, led McCormick a merry chase until the surgeon grabbed him, "and he was finally escorted down to the boat between myself and one of the boat's crew, one having hold of each flipper." Some penguins, instead of being skinned, were headed up in casks of strong pickle for the comparative anatomists back in London.

During the third week of January their worst nightmares came true: hurrican-force winds while still stuck in the pack ice. It proved to be a terrifying experience. Davis thought it the most dangerous gale he had ever suffered through, and young James Savage, the seamen who had joined the *Erebus* at Hobart, likened it to being caught up in a "Steam Engine in a large factory that sets all the machinery in motion," the moving parts in this case being icebergs, growlers, and floes. "An ocean," as Ross suc-

Catching penguins

The end of the chase for an emperor penguin. "And he was finally escorted down to
the boat between myself and one of the boat's crew, one having hold of each flipper."

—Robert McCormick

(Illustration from Ross's *Voyage*, vol. II)

cinctly described it, "of rolling fragments of ice, hard as floating rocks of
granite." Everyone thought the battering so ferocious that the ships would
be holed and sent to the bottom. What the ice did do was to destroy their
most vulnerable mechanisms, the rudders. During the height of the storm
both ships, their rudders smashed, were saved only by the seamanship of
officers and men maneuvering their vessels under scraps of sail alone. The
storm passed, and Ross took stock of his sorely battered expedition. Davis
noted that he had never seen Ross, the usual smile gone, look quite so
careworn and old. Sunday—the hurricane had started on the previous
Wednesday—saw them moored to a floe, the storm damage being repaired, the rudders being replaced. Ross, for the Sunday service, read a
prayer for thanksgiving after a storm at sea from the Book of Common
Prayer, a prayer that Davis, in all his years at sea, had never before heard
read: "O most mighty and gracious good God, thy mercy is over all they
works, but in special manner hath been extended toward us, whom thou
hast so powerfully and wonderfully defended. Thou has shewed us terrible things, and wonders in the deep."

A few days later, the storm having dispersed the ice, they were sailing
in relatively open water, having survived a thousand miles of pack ice.
James Savage was dictating to his friend Sullivan: "Thank God and British
Built Ships we see Our Selves Once more in the boosom of the open Sea
After being closed up in the center of our Enemy for the space of 47
Days."

One enemy could not be defeated: time. It was slipping by, the season shortening, the cold beginning to pinch. By 20 February, skirting the pack, they were still fifty miles north of the barrier. It was bitterly cold with the temperature at 16.5°F and blowing a gale with the sea and spray freezing on contact to decks, hulls, masts, and rigging. Running rigging the thickness of a thumb, unless beaten with a stick, increased to the thickness of a thigh. Trimming, shortening sails, reefing, tacking ship, wearing ship were all time-consuming and painful operations. The men on deck, wrote Davis, "are literally moving lumps of ice." But rigging had to be beaten loose, hulls and decks cleared with axes. Aboard the *Terror,* on this endless exercise, the seamen chipping away at the ice on the bows found a fish frozen in the ice. It was carefully removed and given to Dr. Robertson, who then carried this first fish ever caught below the Antarctic Circle, no matter the strangeness of its capture, into his cabin. There he made a sketch of the six-inch-long find for science and also wrote a brief description. He then put this treasure on a plate to thaw before making a more thorough examination and preserving it in alcohol. The *Terror*'s cat, however, not satisfied with tearing up charts, sneaked in, carried the fish away, and ate it. The thwarted Robertson gave the vanished fish the name *Pagetodes*—"frozen solid" in Greek.[2]

Two days later, the wind having eased off, the thermometer risen two degrees, they sighted the barrier. As the wind was northerly, making the barrier a most dangerous lee shore, they hauled eastward, keeping a few miles off those cliffs of ice. But around them the pancake ice was forming fast and gelling fast. It was like sailing through porridge. The next day, 23 February, the wind veering east, they closed with the barrier, sailed into a large bay filled with ice, and reached their farthest south, six miles beyond their 1841 farthest south, before being stopped by ice. It was a day of brilliant sunshine and intense blue skies. Davis and McCormick made sketches into their pads, and Ross an entry into a small, red morocco-bound, gilt-edged book entitled *The Economy of Human Life.* It was his second entry onto the book's flyleaf. He had taken this tiny book, given to him by his sister Isabella, on the attempt at the North Pole. At the northernmost position, surrounded by the Arctic pack ice, he had penned: "Written on board the *Endeavour* in Latitude 82 3/4°N. 27th July, 1827. Jas. C. Ross." Now, looking at the ice barrier that one day would bear his name, he wrote: "H.M. Ship *Erebus* 23rd of Feb. 1842 in Latitude 78° 10′S. Jas. C. Ross." Two other men could have signed their names alongside Ross's: Thomas Abernethy, the gunner, and Lieutenant Edward Bird. Both had been with Ross and the sledge-boat *Endeavour* on the attempt at the North Pole. Both records, farthest north and farthest south, stood for more than half a century.

With the sea freezing over—from the masthead it was an unbroken expanse of ice—and the pack blocking them off from sailing any farther to the east, it was obviously time to retreat.

Before leaving from New Zealand, Ross had written the Admiralty that he expected to be in the Falkland Islands by the end of April 1842. The islands would be the springboard for the third Antarctic season.

On 24 February, with a favorable southeast wind helping them crump through the ice, Ross made the signal to Crozier to head north, away from the barrier and the danger of being frozen in for the winter. Ross admitted that little had been achieved compared with the previous season. All that could be salvaged, for this season, were more magnetic measurements, new penguins for science, a new record south, and a few more miles of the barrier put on the chart.

They passed north of the Antarctic Circle ten days after leaving the barrier, an event, Ross dryly noted, celebrated with much rejoicing. The next day, with the nights lengthening into eight hours of darkness, they turned due east to follow the 60°S line of latitude, heading for Sabine's calculated position of maximum magnetic intensity, followed by Cape Horn and then the Falkland Islands. With a southerly wind they went booming eastward, the loglines ripping off their reels in a most satisfactory manner, white water about the bluff bows, and, even more satisfactory, not a floe, only the occasional iceberg, to be seen.

On the afternoon of 12 March, an afternoon of fogs and flurries of snow, the vessels running fast before a northwesterly wind, icebergs were spotted. That evening, the wind increasing and the visibility worsening in prolonged snow, sail was reduced. Just before midnight, having seen brash ice indicating icebergs, Ross ordered the topsails to be close-reefed and readied the *Erebus* to be hove to until daylight. Just before the topmen reached the deck, an iceberg was seen dead ahead. The *Erebus* was hauled to the wind on the port tack in an attempt to weather the berg. Then the *Terror,* on the starboard tack, under topsails and foresail, loomed out of the murk, and the two vessels collided head-on. Here again, like the storm in the pack, was a sailor's nightmare come true.

It was a nightmare that Davis, in writing to his sister, called "the awful morning of the 13th . . . for when my thoughts lead me from one circumstance to another connected with it I shudder and feel sick." The *Terror* had also seen the iceberg (there were two bergs with a very narrow opening between them) and also hauled her wind, but onto the starboard tack, and suddenly come upon the *Erebus.* The two ships ground past each other, tearing away catheads and anchors, smashing jibbooms and bowsprits, yardarms striking at every roll, booms and boom irons tumbling from aloft, quarter boats splintering like kindling, ironwork tearing away. At last, after what seemed an eternity to the horrified and terrified crews, the ships drew apart. But the icebergs now loomed frighteningly close under their lee. The Terrors spotted the dark gap between the bergs, and Crozier, wrote Davis, giving his orders as calmly "as if he were steering into any harbour," conned his vessel through an opening little wider than the ship, foam and spray whipping across the deck from the seas

The collision, to windward of the chain of bergs

"And now, my dearest Emily, I approach the awful morning of the 13th; but I must pause and consider how I am to relate it, for when my thoughts lead me from one circumstance to another connected with it I shudder and feel sick."

—John Davis to his sister

(Illustration from Ross's *Voyage,* vol. II)

breaking at the bergs' base. Once under the lee of the berg Crozier ordered a blue light to be lit and, all the Terrors still in a state of shock, waited for the *Erebus.*

Davis's personal experience was typical of many aboard the *Terror:* the cry of "All hands" followed by the throwing on of some clothes, the clamber to the deck to see the bows of the *Erebus,* on top of a sea, come crashing down on his ship. Half-naked seamen rushing around the deck, all sensation of cold gone with the rush of fear-induced adrenaline, shouted orders, the *Erebus* grinding by like a malevolent millstone. The run through the passage was even worse. "I believe myself to be no coward," wrote Davis, "I have often been in danger, and perhaps have had more than my share of it, but never till those moments did I in reality know what fear was."

Crozier admitted to Davis that he had not the slightest idea of what he had done or how the *Terror* got through the gap. Davis, as the blue light flared for the *Erebus,* saw "the ghastly appearance of everyone's face, in which horror and despair were pictured, the half-naked forms of men thrown out by the strong light, oh! it was horrible, truly horrible. That time will never be effaced from my memory."

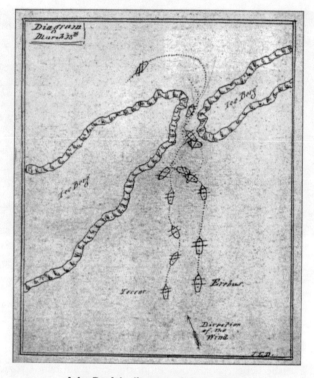

John Davis's diagram of the collision

"Some one regularly screamed out down the fore-hatchway, 'All hands bear a hand on deck, every one'—and immediately after came a crash."   —John Davis.

(Illustration from Davis's *A Letter from the Antarctic*)

McCormick, aboard the *Erebus,* had the same awakening as Davis: the cry "All hands" followed by the throwing on of clothes, the rush to the companionway ladder, where, almost at the top, he was nearly thrown back down by the collision. On deck he found "the massive hull of the *Terror* surging heavily in the swell on our starboard-bow, carrying away our bowsprit, and with it our fore-top-mast; whilst, above all, towered through the mist of a dark, gloomy night, the stupendous form of an enormous iceberg." He noticed an officer clinging to the capstan in his nightshirt, and then the *Terror* vanished "in the surrounding darkness and gloom, like a phantom of ill."

The *Erebus* not only had come off in far worse condition than *Terror* but was in a near checkmate position on the nautical chessboard of sailing

The *Erebus* passing through the chain of bergs

"She dashed through the narrow channel, between two perpendicular walls of ice, and the foaming breakers which stretched across it, and the next moment we were in smooth water under its lee. The *Terror*'s light was immediately seen and answered."

—James Clark Ross

(Illustration from Ross's *Voyage*, vol. II)

moves. A single mistake of judgment in this game, and they all would have been taken off the board. Having lost bowsprit, fore-topmast, and with running and standing rigging snarled into a cat's cradle, chaos on deck, they had drifted into the backwash off the iceberg's base.

Abernethy, out on the *Erebus*'s ice plank,[3] spotted the small gap between the bergs. The only way through was for Ross, now in the impossible position, to pull off a masterstroke of seamanship: a stern board, where a square-rigged vessel goes into reverse. With the yards braced around—it took some time in the chaos on deck and aloft—the *Erebus* gathered sternway, plunging her stern into the seas, washing away her gig and quarter boat, lower yards scraping against the iceberg's face, her hull kept off by the backwash. Just before the narrow opening, going astern, Ross gave his orders, the *Erebus* swung around, and she sailed through as a proper, if battered, sailing vessel.

Once through the opening and in the calm of the iceberg's lee, Ross saw the *Terror*'s blue light and hoisted a blue light of his own. McCormick thought Ross had behaved magnificently throughout the crisis, arms folded across his chest, calmly giving his orders. The *Erebus* was hove to, and the long business of clearing away the wreckage of spars and rigging and their replacement began. One curiosity they did find was their bower anchor some three feet below the waterline, upside down, held by the fluke palms rammed eight inches into the planking. All efforts to remove it failed. But it did drop off, six days and five hundred miles later, after being loosened by a heavy sea and then pried away, according to Mc-Cormick, by "getting a spar wedged against it . . . and sunk in deeper water than it had ever been in before."

James Savage, when dictating to Sullivan, called that night's experience "Our Miraculous Escape from Awful Shipwreck." Like McCormick, he had stumbled onto the dark deck to see the bows of the *Terror* devouring his ship. "My friend the next wave Lifted the Terror above our Main Top mast. The most awful and Tremendous Sight we See yet at this moment, we poor Pilgrims of the Ocean thought it was our last in this Life. Some uttered a feint Shriek through instant Surprize. But the Almighty God helped our Sinking Spirits when we thought we would have a Dreadful Stroke from her. Like a Shot from a gun She made a leep a Stern and the next Sea carried her Quite Clear of us . . . God almighty, My friends, alone that saved us from a miserable death 3000 miles from any land."

One of the pilgrims of the ocean, James Angelly, a popular and much valued quartermaster, had been the man who had spotted the iceberg lying across the *Erebus*'s course. Three weeks later Angelly fell from the main yard during a gale, struck the gunwale—with such force that Mc-Cormick heard it in his cabin below—and bounced overboard. A life buoy (two casks with a red flag on a pole) was thrown overboard and Angelly was seen to reach it. "Abernethy," wrote McCormick, "ever the foremost in all emergencies, was already in the port quarter-boat, with a volunteer crew, all ready for lowering. But Captain Ross deeming it impracticable for a boat to live in the sea that was running, wore the ship round, with the intention of passing close enough to Angelly for a rope to be thrown him." Two hundred yards away—they could see him sitting on the buoy, holding the pole—the wind headed them, and they had to tack. A few minutes later they were over the buoy, but Angelly had vanished. "Several Cape petrels both hovered and swam round the buoy, as it drifted by us," wrote McCormick, "as if singing a last sad *requiem* over the sailor's grave." It was the *Erebus*'s third death by drowning since they had left England, and it cast a deep gloom throughout the whole ship.

A day later they sighted Beauchene Island, the first land they had seen in five months, and the next afternoon were running into Berkeley Sound in fog. "Guided," as Ross acknowledged, "by Captain Fitzroy's excellent chart." At five o'clock in the afternoon of 6 April they came to anchor in five fathoms near the settlement of Port Louis and some miles away from the wreck of Freycinet's *Uranie* and the French campsite of 1820.

James Savage, one of the thankful pilgrims of the ocean, wrote that "if our Ships were Merchantmen this Scribbled Description i give of our Miraculous Escape would never reach Great Britain. But thanks to our noble Strong Barks they done their duty. . . ."

NOTES

1. A floppy hat worn by street clowns.
2. Fifty-seven years later, in 1898, the *Belgica* Antarctic expedition caught a small fish that *was* preserved. Back in Brussels the ichthyologist Louis Dollo pronounced it to be *Pagetodes*, the long-lost food of the *Terror*'s cat. He then gave it the scientific name of *Crydraco antarcticus*.
3. A platform running across the vessel just forward of the mizzenmast. It enabled the ice master to cross over and see ahead and so pilot the vessel clear of ice.

Chapter 16

Perplexing Navigation

PADDY'S HURRICANE. Not enough wind to float the
pennant.

PAYING OFF. The movement by which a ship's head falls
off from the wind, and drops to leeward. Also the paying off
the ship's officers and crew, and the removal of the ship from
active service to ordinary.

Admiral W. H. Smyth, The Sailor's Word-Book, 1867

HE FALKLAND ISLANDS, like Tasmania, boasted a lieutenant governor. There the resemblance ended. The Falkland
ruler was no Arctic hero but an obscure twenty-eight-year-old
lieutenant in the Royal Engineers and an expert on fortifications. Richard Clement Moody (because he had been born in Barbados
and soldiered on St. Vincent, the Colonial Office must have thought him
promising island chief material) had arrived at the Falklands only three
months before Ross and was still grappling with the problems of what the
Dictionary of National Biography delicately calls a "colony . . . almost in
a state of anarchy." To deal with this anarchy, London had assigned him
two thousand pounds, of which six hundred pounds was his salary. Lord
John Russell had written Moody the usual apologetic Colonial Office letter before his departure: "I am perfectly aware that many objects of the
highest importance must be neglected for the present, and must so continue, until you are in possession of funds more adequate to the purposes
of civil government. You will, therefore, clearly understand these inconveniences, whatever they may be, must be borne for a time." Yet another
underfunded proconsul, on his way to administer the Pax Britannica, had
sailed down the Thames to a distant outpost of empire.

London had given Moody three principal tasks: to report on the economic prospects for the islands; to assess the moving of the Port Louis settlement to a more accessible site at another harbor, Port William; and to preserve "the lands, fisheries, and wild cattle from trespass or destruction," the trespass and destruction mainly coming from American whalers and sealers.

Moody's modest little empire, Russell admonished, with more Colonial Office fudge, was to be ruled by "influence, persuasion and example, rather than direct authority; but in the exercise of moral rather than legal power, you must of course be guided by your own discretion, rather than by precise instructions."

The young lieutenant governor's writ extended over forty-seven hundred square miles of treeless land spread over two main islands, East Falkland and West Falkland, plus some two hundred smaller islands. Port Louis, the only settlement, had a handful of stone buildings, thatched or turf-roofed, holding a population of about sixty, twenty of them being government men with their wives and children. Thirty thousand wild cattle, half of them aggressive bulls, roamed the land, but the cows, claimed Moody, "are easily tamed for milking by a fearless person." Three thousand wild horses roamed in herds, and everywhere were thousands of upland geese, birds so tame, wrote Moody, "that the most indifferent sportsman may speedily lade himself with more than he can carry. In unfrequented places they may be knocked down with a stick." Domesticated animals were few: some cattle, horses, sheep—Leicesters and Southdowns, brought from England by a settler—and dogs for hunting. Also at the islands, but rarely at Port Louis, were two Royal Navy surveying ketches, the *Sparrow* and the *Arrow*. (Were the Admiralty's namesmiths relaxing with a little joke?)

The *Erebus* and the *Terror* dropped into this curious backwater like visitors from outer space. As the crew of any one of the vessels outnumbered the settlement's total population, a problem was presented to both Moody and Ross regarding provisioning. The supply ship from South America had failed to arrive, the government store was woefully empty of flour and bread, and the Government House garden could supply only stunted turnips. Port Louis was a meat-eating settlement. In an unusual reversal of roles the expedition now supplied the shore with some essential provisions. Ross also obtained permission to hunt for wild cattle and pay for the meat at government store prices.

But the big disappointment for the ships' crews was the lack of mail. Moody, however, gave them an edition of the Navy List that showed that Crozier, Bird, and Alexander Smith of the *Erebus* had been promoted, as was George Moubray of the *Terror*. Moubray, a well-liked man, could hardly believe his good fortune. Ross immediately gave them all, except for Crozier, acting orders to serve in their new ranks, orders, thought Davis, that were "certainly a great stretch of power and more than an admiral

Hunting wild cattle in the Falkland Islands

"I may give an outline of the general features of a cattle-hunt, as pursued by our sea-men, which differs considerably from that of the Guachoes."   —Joseph Hooker

(Illustration from Ross's *Voyage,* vol. II)

would dare do, but Captain Ross does it on the plea . . . that it would be an act of injustice to let them remain as they were when the Admiralty thought them fit to serve in a higher capacity." McCormick, his nose out of joint, grumbled that the senior medical staff—"as usual"—had been left out in the cold with "their services ignored, notwithstanding they had extra duties to perform, natural history, in addition to their professional routine."

But the Falkland Island cloud had a silver lining for McCormick, who spent the next few months in an orgy of shooting, mainly for the pot. "I had," he later boasted, "with my own gun, alone, contributed no less than four dozen upland geese, forty brace of snipe, two dozen rabbits, be-sides two dozen and a half of the Antarctic geese, and other edible birds, teal, plover, and grey ducks, without limit to our mess."

McCormick's personal game bag did not take into account the tons of beef brought in by the expedition's foraging parties. The officers and men of the *Arrow*, experts in a rather unusual hunting, taught the men from the *Erebus* and the *Terror* the tricks of the chase, for this was how they had provisioned when away surveying the island's bays, harbors, and inlets. They had been doing it for five years.

This was no cowboy or gaucho method using horses and lasso or bolas, but a very English one using dogs. But dogs of no particular breed. These were mongrels with mainly pointer blood, diluted with a heady mixture of Newfoundland, Dalmation, mastiff, bulldog, and bull terrier genes. One, a cross between a pointer and a bull terrier, was so ugly that although its official breeding name for the book happened to be Tom, it was always known as Bully. But no matter what their names—Laporte, Brigand, York—all the dogs were powerfully built, eager, courageous, and fast. The men hunted on foot, dressed in the lightest possible clothing and shoes, even in winter, with a sharp knife strapped at the waist. Two men, usually older, portlier, or better shots, carried double-barreled guns or rifles. The objective was to get as close to the wary herd as possible, then to let slip the dogs, which would all head for one animal, usually a cow, and try to bring it down. The runners, so fit as to be almost as fast as the dogs, on reaching the skirmish, would hamstring the hindlegs and then cut the throat, dodging the horns. Hooker, on one of these expeditions with the Arrows, carrying a rifle and ammunition, puffed along in the rear, taking long shots at three hundred yards, "to the imminent danger of the runners," and then floundered along over balsam bogs, tussock clumps, and diddle-dee bushes, to arrive "thoroughly blown at the top of a hill immediately overlooking the scene of action."

The action at times could be dangerous, particularly when the huge black bulls, "possessed of indomitable courage and untameable ferocity," according to Hooker, decided to charge. One of the survey officers bore a scar on his head, and Abernethy was knocked down and the turf torn up in furrows on each side of his body by the horns of an enraged bull. A shot from the rifleman killed the animal before he could turn and gore the *Erebus*'s gunner. McCormick also had a close encounter with a wounded, charging bull. The account is a perfect example of the "great white hunter" school of writing, complete with faithful follower:

> It was an anxious moment though, as the infuriated beast, tossing his horns, and snorting the blood from his nostrils, tore down upon me, bending his head to the ground for the final charge, for which I had reserved my fire till he had approached very near me. As my own life depended on the accuracy of my aim, this was the moment I seized upon to bring my second barrel to bear upon the region of his heart rather than his head, which had been tossed and lowered too abruptly for a sure aim. He gave a spring upwards as I fired, and came down with such thundering force within a few feet of me as to make the earth tremble beneath my feet. Abernethy, good fellow, who had been a distant observer of the risk I had incurred, and, trusting to his own unerring aim, scarcely allowed time for the report of my gun to reach him before he fired, his ball whizzing rather too close to my ears to be altogether pleasant, striking the bull, however, as he was in the very act of falling with my own ball in his heart. On opening him we found Abernethy's ball (which was a rifle one, and very different to my smoothbore double-barrel one) in the lungs. He was a fine black bull, with a splendid pair of horns, which I preserved as a memento. His companion prudently made off.

Hooker's first botanical impression of the Falklands was one of disappointment. It was impossible, he thought, that these islands could match the botanical paradise of Kerguelen. But over the months his opinion mellowed. The seaweeds, tussock grass, lichens, the fragrant-smelling balsam bog (also known as misery-balls, the hummocked plant usually indicating barren soil), and the heathery diddle-dee, useful as a quick-burning fuel to cook beef after the hunt—for it could be lit even when sodden with rain—perhaps helped the mellowing.

But it was the seaweed—the kelp—and the tussock grass that fascinated him. (These huge beds of kelp still make a natural buoyage system, harbor much marine life, make a fiendish obstacle for small boats, and have given the islanders their present nickname, kelpers.)

For Hooker, gazing down into the clear waters from a small boat, the *Lessonia* was of particular fascination: "The stem or trunk attaches itself by clasping fibres to the rocks, always below high-water mark: it attains a height of eight or ten feet and the thickness of a man's thigh: it branches upwards, and the ends of the branches give out leaves two or three feet long, and barely three inches broad, which, when in the water, hang down like the boughs of a willow." Hooker likened it to a "tree sea-weed," but he had no success in telling the captain of a merchant brig, collecting it from the shore, thinking it would burn like wood, not to waste his time (although knife handles can be made by sticking a naked blade into a moist stem; the stem shrinks and dries, making a handle harder than wood and one needing no fastenings).

Both Hooker and Moody thought the tussock grass a unique feature of the coastal landscape. Much of it has now vanished because of burning and grazing, but it can still be found on many of the smaller islands, and when it is seen from a distance, one can understand why early sailors thought they were looking at trees.

Tussock grows in clumps, the roots forming into an immense ball above ground, a clump that can stand five to six feet high and the same in diameter. On top of this mound grow the tussock leaves, about an inch wide and six to seven feet long. The mounds grow quite close to each other, leaving narrow lanes into which a person can vanish from sight, a magic, mazelike labyrinth, where the unsuspecting wanderer can be startled by penguins or sleeping sea lions.

In a report to London, Moody wrote that the tussock roots were nourishing fodder for cattle, horses, sheep, and pigs, as was evident from the "avidity with which all animals feed, and the rapidity with which they fatten." Other creatures also found it tasty. "For about three or four inches the roots are very agreeable to man, being crisp and of a sweetish nutty flavour, very much resembling the heart of the palm tree in the West Indies, which is called the mountain cabbage."

It was so nutritious that two American sailors, who had deserted from their ship at West Falkland, had lived for fourteen months by eating its roots, diddle-dee berries, and, having no means of lighting a fire, the raw

Tussock grass of the Falkland Islands
"You are considered the fortunate discoverer of the most wonderful grass, that is to
make the fortunes of all Highland or Irish lairds who have bogs."
—Sir William Jackson Hooker to his son Joseph
(Illustration from Ross's *Voyage*, vol. II)

meat of birds and seals. They were described, after their rescue by the
Sparrow, as being "in a good state of health, but from the middle down-
wards were without clothes, and the upper parts were barely covered with
rags." The tussock's mound had provided not only food but, dug out, also
their shelter, with a smaller root ball being rolled into the doorway at
night: a Falkland Island verdant igloo.

Such a wonderful plant led Moody to send his and Hooker's description of the grass to London, where it was read as a paper, by their respective fathers, at a meeting of the Royal Geographical Society. Interest in the
expedition, Hooker's father later wrote to his son, had been "excited by
some little matter which Col. Moody and I laid before the Geo. Soc. from
our sons, relating to the Falkland Islands. *You* are considered (how correctly I won't say) the fortunate *discoverer* of the most wonderful Grass . . .
that is to make the fortune of all Highland or Irish Lairds who have bogs
. . . and said Bogs for hundreds of miles, where nothing has yet grown, will

be clothed with such luxuriant grass as all the cattle in the world cannot keep down. You have no idea of the quantity of letters I have from strangers in all quarters, from the South coast of Kent to John o' Groat's, and from the East of Fife to the west coast of Connaught, humbly begging me, the happy Father of so renowned a son, to give them but the tythe of a fibre of the root, or one seed; or in default of them a piece of a leaf!"

The two young men, Hooker and Moody, got on well together. "Great chums," as Hooker put it, with Hooker having the run of Moody's library (Alexander Pope's *Iliad*, Felicia Henman's poems, John Daniell's *Chemical Philosophy*, Augustus Pugin's *The True Principles of Pointed or Christian Architecture*—a book that Hooker found full of "bigoted Roman Catholicism"—Robert Pollok's *Course of Time*, Joseph Milner's *History of the Church of Christ*—obviously boring reading, for, as he wrote to his mother, "it is too much for me to get through here") and doing his politic best to stay out of the quarrels surging between Moody and Ross.

The cause of the friction is unknown. Interservice rivalry? Simple antipathy? Both men were undoubtedly under considerable stress, the underfunded Moody grappling with the colony's problems; Ross weary after the dangers of the second voyage, holding together a group of men grown tired of one another's company and, more to the point, feeling unappreciated at the lack of recognition of their efforts by both the Admiralty and the British press. Hooker, in a letter to his father, wrote that the press had been full of the French and American expeditions but remarkably coy about theirs. He had given a gentle hint to Ross that notices of the expedition's accomplishments, sent to influential magazines, might be good public relations. But the suggestion had fallen on barren ground. Hooker thought "it would be exceedingly bad taste in me to puff off, through you . . . nothing could induce me to become the mouth-piece of the Voyage."

Rumors were also circulating around the ships that Ross had chosen to winter in the Falklands because the islands could offer no temptations to seamen with notions of deserting. Believing in the adage that "the devil finds work for idle hands to do," Ross set his men to building a magnetic observatory, a meteorological and astronomical observatory, a tidal bench mark[1] and two turf huts to house the observers. He then turned his attention to the ships. A stone pier was built that could be used by the boats at all stages of the tide. Nearby the men also built a large storehouse. The *Erebus* was completely emptied of all stores, provisions, and equipment, which were then inspected and placed in the storehouse. At extreme high water the *Erebus* was beached as high and dry as possible. Carpenters and men from both ships then set about repairing the ice damage to her hull, followed by the hull's being recaulked. She was then hauled off and thoroughly cleansed before being restowed. The same then happened to the *Terror*.

The *Arrow*, at the end of her five years in the Falklands, had sailed for Rio de Janeiro, carrying all the expedition's natural history collections, letters, and a request from Ross to the Royal Navy's South American station commodore for stores, provisions, and a replacement bowsprit for the *Erebus*.

On 23 June HMS *Carysfort*, commanded by Lord George Paulet, a friend of Ross's, arrived at Berkeley Sound, carrying all that Ross had requested. Ross had "no small gratification" in sending across fresh beef for the Carysforts. The few days that they stayed—new faces, talking with old friends—formed what the expedition later called the holiday. The *Carysfort* sailed on 7 July, bound around Cape Horn and into the Pacific.

Ross, at Moody's request, visited Port William and made an assessment of its potential for the site of a new settlement. The navy man came out overwhelmingly in its favor; from a seaman's point of view, the harbor, although the surrounding land was mainly peat bog, had numerous advantages. Moody, initially in favor of the move, was now having second thoughts and was happily drawing up plans to extend Port Louis—to be renamed Anson—and had even given names to his hypothetical streets. Moody later wrote off to London claiming that any site at Port William would require expensive and laborious draining. But Ross's opinion carried greater weight. The terse reply came back from the Colonial Office to make the move. The labor of drainage, according to London, was no different from moving rocks or felling trees. Stanley, the Falklands' new small capital, was born.

On 8 September, intent upon more magnetic observations, the *Erebus* and the *Terror* sailed for Tierra del Fuego. Left behind were an officer and assistants to monitor the Port Louis observatories. The passage to Cape Horn was gale-ridden and uncomfortable, and it was not until 21 September that the two ships were snugly anchored at St. Martin's Cove on the west coast of Hermite Island, some ten miles northwest of Cape Horn. The cove's natives were by now very familiar with these strange white men in their big canoes. This was the Wigwam Cove of James Weddell and Matthew Brisbane in the *Jane* and the *Beaufoy*, the same cove where Henry Foster's *Chanticleer* had been provisioned by Philip Parker King's *Adventure* (provisions that included "Donkin's Preserved Meats which have now found a secure place in vessels sailing from England for extended voyages," and so, continued Webster, the *Chanticleer*'s surgeon, enabling the crew "to have a joint of mutton cooked in London, to eat fresh and good at Cape Horn, which is more than entered the minds of men formerly"), the same cove that had seen FitzRoy's *Beagle* and the young Charles Darwin.

The cove's lineage particularly Darwin's account in his *Journal and Remarks*, appealed to Hooker who had been introduced to Darwin by McCormick in London. The two medical men had been walking through

Charing Cross when they had bumped into Darwin, and the introductions taken place. Hooker, unknown to Darwin, had read the proofs of the *Journal*—he had kept them under his pillow at night so that he might "devour their contents" first thing in the morning—and just before sailing had been given a copy of the final printed edition.

Hooker thought the cove, particularly under the moonlight, one of the most wild and sublime anchorages that the expedition had lain in. The trees alone, none of the men having seen one for a year, were a feast for the eyes, and the roar from the torrents pouring down the mountains reminded him of the Scottish Highlands. Like all visitors, he thought the Fuegians the most "degraded savages" that he had ever seen, an opinion shared by the evangelical Ross, who earnestly hoped that one day they would be given "the blessings of civilization and the joyful tidings of the Gospel."

The observatories took far longer than usual to put in place. The whole ground was a swamp, and the men had to dig down through eight feet of bog before coming on clay. Piles were driven in, and sand-filled casks placed on top of them to make a firm foundation for the instruments. Then a deep trench had to be dug around this construction, isolating it from the bog's upper surface; footsteps on the surface, it was found, disturbed the delicate magnetic instruments.

Five weeks were spent at St. Martin's Cove. McCormick, on his explorations, found the site of the *Chanticleer*'s observatory, was nearly blown off the icy tops of mountains, exchanged his anchor buttons for Fuegian artifacts, and, as usual, shot birds.

For Hooker the island was destined to play an important role in his theories of geographical plant distribution. That Tierra del Fuego shared similar plants to the Falkland Islands, South Georgia, Tristan da Cunha, Kerguelen Island, Campbell Island, and the Auckland Islands was obvious, if not surprising. They had, presumably, "borrowed many plants from this, the great botanical centre of the Antarctic Ocean." The true surprise was the number of common English plants: primroses, dandelions, thrift, wild celery, starworts. Dozens of genera were the same as in England, as were nineteen genera of grasses. The *how* of this borrowing was the question. Wind? Birds, either in crop or on feet? In the stones and earth of icebergs? Drifting on ocean currents and surviving the salt water? Long-sunken land bridges? Years later, after he and Darwin had formed their great personal and professional relationship, the two men spent much time pondering this question. Seeds were sent from Kew to Darwin's home. Here, in an experiment so classic in its simplicity that Asa Gray at Harvard wondered why no one had thought of it before, Darwin popped them into bottles of salt water—the sea salt being bought from a local chemist—and, after days of soaking, took them out to see if they had germinated. An element of rivalry lay in these experiments, for Hooker thought that seawater would kill the seeds and, until proved otherwise, leaned to the sunken land bridge theory of distribution. Darwin told how his children anxiously awaited the results to see if he could "beat Dr. Hooker." Much to Hooker's surprise, nearly all the seeds did germinate. Darwin's experiments became a cottage industry with schoolgirls being paid to collect seeds. Darwin also chaffed Hooker by asking the botanist to send seeds that he expected "to be *most easily killed.*"

The expedition did some of its own plant distribution by digging up eight hundred Hermite Island saplings and taking them to treeless Port Louis for planting. More saplings and plants were earmarked for Kew. Six months later Hooker's mother was writing to her father: "My husband and I were made very happy by the arrival 3 Days ago of 3 Ward's[2] cases of living trees from Cape Horn, which Joseph mentions in his letter as having been filled last October. So valuable a consignment has not been received at the Gardens (his father says) since we came here. The 2 new kinds of Beech & the Winter's Bark Tree (of the latter only one specimen was in the Kingdom before) are growing beautifully. One box weighed upwards of 3 cwt."

The expedition sailed from St. Martin's Cove on 7 November and was back in Port Louis a week later. During their absence HMS *Philomel* had brought dispatches, letters, and a confirmation of the promotions seen in the Navy List. Also, a slight salve to their sensibilities at being ignored, a letter from the Admiralty to Ross expressing their "Lordships' great satisfaction at the successful result of the expedition . . . which, they are satisfied, nothing but unremitting zeal on your part, and that of the officers and crew, could have accomplished on a service of so arduous a nature, wherein difficulties of no ordinary kind were to be encountered and overcome." The letter was dated 12 August 1841. It had taken fifteen months to arrive.

The ships sailed out from Berkeley Sound on 17 December, bound into the Antarctic with a westerly wind, all studding sails set and under a clear sky. They sailed, as Ross put it in his *Voyage,* with not the slightest regret. In a letter to Beaufort he was more forceful: "We are in the best of health and spirits and delighted with the prospects of leaving this vile place. . . ."

The decks, as usual, resembled a mixture of farmyard and butcher's shop. In the *Erebus*'s amidships boat were berthed five sheep and five pigs with a litter of piglets; in the quarter boat roosted turkeys and geese; on deck were three calves and a colt; hanging in the rigging were dead rabbits, geese, snipe, dried fish, seal meat, quarters of veal and beef. Tussock grass lay bundled on deck as fodder.

Ross's plan for their third season was not to follow Weddell's track of 1823—"from which no discovery could be expected"—but to sail down the 55°W meridian and hope to find a continuation of d'Urville's discovery, Louis Philippe's Land, which would lead them south. If that failed, *then* move east and follow Weddell's track.

On 24 December they sighted their first icebergs, and a day later Ross was dining in the *Erebus*'s gun room with McCormick in the president's chair. The Christmas dinner, as McCormick admitted, was a "sumptuous one for these regions, consisting of veal, calf's head, teal and snipe, &c., with a liberal allowance of champagne." Three days later, having skirted the pack, they sighted Joinville Island at the tip of the Antarctic Peninsula. Then started some very tricky sailing along a coastline of icy cliffs, jock-eying the ships across a sea packed with grounded icebergs, the steering made difficult by violent currents swirling into whirlpools. The current almost set them onto a set of low islets—almost hidden by floes—that Ross aptly named the Danger Islets.

The next few weeks held many dangers, perhaps not the concentrated terror of the second voyage, but watch after watch, week after week, of unceasing vigilance. Within a playing field measuring fifty miles by ninety miles, the *Erebus* and the *Terror* dodged, blocked, ran, and tried to outmaneuver a tireless team composed of pack ice, icebergs, strong currents, gales, calms, snow, and fog. Ross's chart of the area, named after his two ships—the Erebus and Terror Gulf—shows a track looking like an exuberant child's first, wild scrawls. Ross, with what can only be described as understatement, called the navigation "perplexing."

His vessels were rammed up against the fast ice (ice attached to the land) by moving pack ice. In this embarrassing position they were heeled over by the pressure and squeezed so tight as to make their timbers crack. Currents swept them against icebergs, and at times they were so beset that Ross feared they might be locked in for the winter. The men acted as donkeys and heaved the ships through narrow leads between the floes. In wider leads the ships were towed by their boats. But Antarctica's team, as usual, proved unbeatable. On 1 February Ross admitted defeat and struggled east into clear water indicated by a water sky. It took them four days of endless labor and difficulty to break clear from the pack "with which we had been so fruitlessly contending for a period of nearly six weeks."

The memorial for those six weeks lies on modern charts. Ross gave over two dozen names to mountains, capes, inlets, islands, and islets. Most of them were named for fellow officers in the Royal Navy, Lord George Paulet getting an island and "our lamented shipmate the late Captain Foster" a cape. Charles Darwin received an islet, and Richard Moody a point.

Before entering the Erebus and Terror Gulf and starting their six-week battle, they had noticed vast numbers of "the largest-sized black whales, so tame they allowed the ships almost to touch them before they would get out of the way." They had found, thought Ross, a "valuable whale-fishery well worth the attention of our enterprising merchants, less than six hundred miles away from one of our own possessions." The suggestion was to lie fallow for fifty years.

One landing had been made, on Cockburn Island, where Hooker had collected twelve different species of terrestrial plant—lichens, mosses, and algae—from the small, ice-free conical island. The landing had set Mc-Cormick, who had not landed, complaining about Ross and his "narrow-minded policy" of always having a medical officer left aboard each ship. As Hooker had been the one to go ashore, the irate surgeon "was left to glean all I could through the medium of the telescope."

A few days later, farther south, they had seen a great number of large icebergs, some four or five miles in diameter, held fast in the pack. Ross thought they must have broken away from "some loftier barrier than we have seen in the vicinity." He was right. Thirty miles away lay the Larsen Ice Shelf, to be discovered fifty years later by a Norwegian whaling captain, Carl Anton Larsen. The lower ice cliffs in the area set Ross to thinking in a letter to the Admiralty that "This was a perfect Barrier in miniature and tended to confirm the opinion I have expressed in my letter of the 6th April 1842 of the existence of an extensive Continent to the Southd. of the great Barrier we discovered in Jany 1841 extending E.S.E. 450 miles from Mount Erebus." He was right again.

Once out from the ice-covered gulf they headed east, pack ice to the south of them, to Weddell's meridian of 40°E, where he had found open water. It was a long, wearisome beat against persistent easterlies, the sailing made worse by thick fog. On 14 February they crossed Weddell's track. But where Weddell had found open water, they found nothing but impenetrable pack. Ross could only conclude that "Weddell was favoured by an unusually fine season, and that we may rejoice that there was a brave and daring seaman on the spot to profit by the opportunity."

But the edge of the pack, happily, now started to trend southward. On 1 March they crossed the Antarctic Circle, heading south, an occurrence noted with mixed feelings by the crew. On the two previous voyages, during March, they had crossed the circle sailing north, away from the Antarctic.

The weather, to lighten their mood, now changed for the better. For more than a month they had sailed in fog and snow. They were now sailing in a new world of sparkling seas and brilliant sun. On 5 March, booming south with all studding sails set, they ran into the pack stretching across their course. From the masthead the outer edge looked navigable with many open leads. Ross ran his ships into the ice for twenty-seven miles before the pack closed in. It was time to haul north now that they had reached a farthest south of 71°30′S at 14°51′W longitude. A cask with a note to that fact was heaved over the side, the signal to Crozier was made to sail for the Cape of Good Hope, an extra issue of grog was issued, and the two vessels started the beat back into clear water, where they were hit by storm-force winds. For a week, with the ships down to scraps of sail, preventer stays rigged, the spray freezing on decks and rigging, they clawed their way off the lee shore of pack ice. On 11 March they passed north of the Antarctic Circle.

Hooker was now writing a long letter to his father, giving a blow-by-blow account of the voyage: "Altogether this is the most detestable climate under the sun:—though whether it be indeed under that luminary, might be doubted by any Astronomer. And I cannot tell you how rejoiced we are to be leaving it for good and all! Capt. Ross says he would not conduct another Expedition to the South Pole for any money & a pension to boot. Nor would any individual of us join it if he did: I am sure I would not for a Baronetcy." Fifty years later, in a talk at the Royal Geographical Society, Hooker's opinion showed no golden glow of old-age reminiscence: "It was the worst season of the three, one of constant gales, fogs, and snow storms. Officers and men slept with their ears open, listening for the lookout man's cry of 'Berg ahead!' followed by 'All hands on deck!' The officers of *Terror* told me their commander never slept in his cot throughout the season in the ice, and that he passed it either on deck or in a chair in his cabin. They were nights of grog and hot coffee, for the orders to splice the main brace were many and imperative, if the crew were to be up to the strain on their nerves and muscles."

They were out of the Antarctic, north of the Convergence during the last week of March. On the evening of 4 April the two weather-beaten ships and their weary crews finally dropped anchor in Simon's Bay. Ross had the satisfaction of reporting to the station's commander in chief that "the expedition had returned for a third time from the arduous service in which it had been engaged, without a single individual of either of the ships on the sick list."

Hooker found the African heat stifling, the ill-paved streets covered with fine red dust, the houses ugly. The enthusiasm for botany, he wrote to his mother, "fairly oozed out of my finger ends." Any enthusiasm for the expedition had long oozed away from the officers and men. Since New Zealand they felt they had been existing in an alien world. But at least the passage back to England would be free of ice.

They sailed from Simon's Bay at the end of April and called at St. Helena, Ascension Island, and Rio de Janeiro. On 2 September, under blue skies, a fair wind, the Channel dotted with the white sails of scores of ships, the men crowded the decks to catch their glimpse of what both Ross and McCormick called the "shores of Old England," the patchwork quilt of Devon's fields and brown cliffs. By 23 September the ships and men had been paid off. The pilgrims of the ocean and the pioneers of science were home after four years and five months of wandering. John Bunyan's line in *Pilgrim's Progress* "As I walk'd through the wilderness of this world" must have struck a responsive chord in them all.

NOTES

1. In 1983 a helicopter flight crew from HMS *Herald* found the position where the tidal tablet had been sited. They also found a horizontal bench mark with the following inscription:

3 feet 8 Inches
above the mean
level of the Ocean
August 1842
HBM Ships
Erebus and Terror

Chapter 17

Antarctic Aftermath

QUARRY. The prey taken by whales; a term borrowed from falconers.

QUARTER-DECKERS. Those officers more remarkable for etiquette than for a knowledge of seamanship.

Admiral W. H. Smyth, *The Sailor's Word-Book*, 1867

HE THREE EXPEDITIONS, French, American, and British, had sailed from their various countries with a certain amount of fanfare. The trumpets, if any, were muted for their return.

The French, first away and first to return, met with a quiet reception. The ailing d'Urville stayed two months at Toulon, with his wife and son, before moving to Paris and reporting on the voyage. At Paris he dined with the king, basked in the praise heaped on him for his Antarctic discoveries, and worked on the voyage's narrative. His requests for his men were granted; he received the Société de Géographie's Gold Medal, was made an officier de la Légion d'Honneur, and was promoted to rear admiral. It was all most gratifying, very different from his cool reception after the 1826–29 *Astrolabe* voyage.

Among his officers the reports of the American and British Antarctic discoveries, and the row between Ross and Wilkes, were met with Gallic shrugs and cynical satisfaction at the Anglo-American squabbling.

On a bright spring day in the May of 1842, with three volumes of his narrative ready for the publishers and a fourth almost completed, d'Urville with his wife and son made an excursion by railway train to Versailles. On the return journey the two speeding locomotive engines jumped the tracks. Fifty-six passengers and the three d'Urvilles died in the inferno made by telescoping wooden carriages piling onto the engines' furnaces. With one of those ironic quirks of history, Dumoutier, the phrenologist who had measured d'Urville's skull so many times, identified it among the burned corpses. By another ironic touch, one of the French expedition's contribution to science—or quantification—was Dumoutier's collection of skulls and head molds to the Paris Musée de l'Homme.

D'Urville's death was a shocking end for one of France's great explorers. Like his hero Cook, he had made three great voyages, and like Cook's, his death was untimely and tragic. But his name lives on at the French Antarctic base of Dumont d'Urville, and his wife's name is immortalized in Antarctica's archetypal bird, the Adélie penguin.

For the United States Exploring Expedition it was inevitable that the press should sniff out its seething rancors. A few days after the *Vincennes*'s return the reporter for the *New York Morning Herald* of 13 June 1842 was licking his chops:

We understand that there is to be a nice mess dished up in a short time in the shape of court martials, court of inquiry, arranging of specimens, rocks, etc., in the eating of which nearly all the officers of the Exploring Expedition are to participate with finger glasses and napkins. It is said that there are at least a bushel and a half of charges already preferred against Lieut. Wilkes, the commander-in-chief, and that several officers of the squadron have come home under arrest. It took four or five years to start this expedition, four years for it to catch Vendovi,[1] knock down a mud village, discover Symmes' Hole, and survey the Sandwich Islands, and five years are to elapse before all is satisfactorily settled with the officers who had command of the fleet.

But the dish served up at the courts-martial made dull eating. What could a reporter do to put spice into the trial of William May, accused of disrespect by Wilkes, which ran for days and hinged on the earthshaking question of whether the marking on a box of seashells was placed faceup or facedown on the deck.

Lieutenant S. F. du Pont, one of the court's officers, was struck by the "bitter & heartburning hostility which pervades the officers of the Exploring Exp. against their commander . . . the indignation which seems to pervade these young men must have sprung from some cause not usual in the Service."

Wilkes, in his final appeal to the court, wrapped himself in patriotism. The country's "honour, its glory, the untarnished lustre of its unconquered flag, have all been assailed through me. With you rests the power of vindicating that honour, exalting that glory, and wiping off any stain which these proceedings have cast upon that banner." He was found not guilty, or the charge not proved, on all but one of the charges brought against him. For illegal punishment of seamen he was sentenced to be publicly reprimanded by the secretary of the navy, Abel Upshur.

Coming on top of what Wilkes considered his cavalier reception by President Tyler—"I found him on entering seated in the center of a semicircle around the fire, and about a dozen of the messiest looking fellows, all squirting their tobacco juice into the fire, and over the white marble hearth. . . . I was literally struck with surprise to find myself in such company at the President's House, it was exactly like a Virginia or North Carolina bar-room . . . the President said be seated Sir! and this was all the recognition I got of my presence"—the reprimand struck home like a well-thrown harpoon. According to du Pont, it pierced Wilkes to the very soul: "Wilkes extreme arrogance, & conviction that he would not only be acquitted, but it would be accompanied with a flourish of trumpets & a swipe at his accusers, has thus rendered his sentence doubly severe to himself—he writhed severely under it, & swears vengeance against Upshur."

As if these blows struck against him were not enough, the question of the land sailed over by Ross still remained, and this, for those Americans who didn't care a hoot for science, was of patriotic importance. When the news of the expedition's Antarctic discoveries had first reached the United States, it had been greeted with much gloating in the press and snide comments made on the ignorance of the British Admiralty about the Antarctic. But that had been in 1840. Two years later the gloss had gone from the expedition. Courts-martial, officers under arrest, conflicting evidence on the sighting of land—no logbook entry of any land sighting was made until 28 January, although Wilkes, in his *Narrative,* claimed 16 January as the start of the American discoveries—were not what the general public wanted. Charts of Pacific islands and the Oregon coast, the magnificent collections embracing botany, zoology, geology, and anthropology counted for nothing among the tobacco-chewing public.

The controversy between Ross and Wilkes was typical of many nineteenth-century geographic wrangles—the Burton and Speke dispute over the source of the Nile springs to mind—and led to the usual intemperate language, fudging of facts, and semantic contortions, in order for the protagonists to prove their point. What was incontrovertible, at least to Ross, was that the British expedition had sailed over land marked down by Wilkes. As far as Ross was concerned, this placed a large question mark over all the American polar discoveries.

Years later Admiral William Smyth, a friend of Ross's, entered the fray with an entry in his *The Sailor's Word-Book:* "COOKING A DAY'S WORK. To save the officer in charge. Reckoning too is cooked, as in a certain Antarctic discovery of land, which James Ross afterwards sailed over."

The din of battle has long since faded. Today's verdict holds that Wilkes, in certain cases, was fooled by one of the polar regions' atmospheric tricks: the looming that brings into view land below the horizon.[2]

Such features as Ringgold's Knoll, Reynolds's Peak, Eld's Peak, Cape Hudson, named and plotted on Wilkes's Antarctic chart, are 75 to 150 miles north of the true Antarctic coastline. Furthermore, Wilkes's Termination Land at the western end does not exist. Later explorers and whalers were to sail across all these features.

If sections of the Wilkes chart of the Antarctic coastline could only deceive the mariner, the same cannot be said of the Pacific island and Oregon coast charts (although one chart of the San Juan Islands, Washington, shows two nonexistent islands drawn in by a resentful officer). American seamen could now sail with American charts. When the U.S. Hydrographic Office was formed in 1871, the core of its copperplate collection came from those produced by the expedition. During World War II the planning for the invasion of Tarawa was done with the only chart available, a Wilkes chart from a century-old survey.

The other legacy, in an age when a weekend sauntering through a museum was considered a way to enlightenment, was the moving, in 1858, of the expedition's vast scientific collection into the newly formed Smithsonian Institution. A more nebulous, less quantifiable legacy was the feeding of O'Sullivan's "Manifest Destiny." America's living space, according to O'Sullivan, should not stop at the Rockies but was destined to spill over into California, Oregon, and Canada. Wilkes, after his Oregon coast survey, urged that the United States boundary be pushed north of 49° to take in Puget Sound. The tobacco-chewing Tyler, in December 1843, claimed a United States right to the coastal region extending to the Russian boundary at 54°40′N. The following year the Democrats fought the election with bellicose slogans, one of which was "Fifty-four forty or fight." But common sense and diplomacy disarmed the saber rattlers, and war with Britain was averted. (The hawks had the satisfaction of reannexing Texas and then waging war on Mexico.)

But the lasting legacy of the United States Exploring Expedition, one that the aging John Quincy Adams had the satisfaction of seeing the first glimmerings of, was his country returning his "light for light." The expedition's scientific publications, produced by scientists distancing themselves from the Sunday Philadelphia dilettantes, ensured that American science had at last come of age.

Charles Wilkes, the United States Navy's stormy petrel, continued his contentious career. In 1861 he took, by force, two Confederate commissioners off the British mail steamer *Trent,* an action that made him an instant hero in the North and gave President Lincoln a severe diplomatic headache in Washington. A year later, operating in the West Indies against Confederate commerce raiders, he managed to offend Great Britain, Spain, France, and Denmark. He was recalled. In 1864 he was again courtmartialed and found guilty on charges of disobedience, disrespect, insubordination, and conduct unbecoming an officer. He was sentenced to be reprimanded and suspended from duty for three years. He died in 1877, a much embittered man, still harboring his grudges, a rear admiral on the retired list.

Perhaps James Dana, of the expedition's scientific staff, should have the last word on this baffling man. In a letter to Asa Gray he wrote: "Wilkes, although overbearing with his officers, and conceited, exhibited through the whole cruise a wonderful degree of energy and was bold even to rashness in his explorations. . . . I much doubt if with any commander that could have been selected we should have fared better or lived together more harmoniously, and I am confident that the Navy does not contain a more daring or driving officer." But his great flaw, according to Dana, was "in never praising his officers but always finding fault with them—and often very unjustly."

The London *Times* gave the British expedition almost three columns in its 11 September 1843 issue; the ships, on passing Gravesend to be paid off, were given a peal of church bells; Hooker, on arriving home in threadbare clothing on a Saturday evening, was given some of his father's clothing for the Sunday church service; and Ross received the Royal Geographical Society's Founder's Medal, the Société de Géographie's Gold Medal, a knighthood, and the hand of Anne Coulman in marriage at Wadworth Hall, with Crozier acting as best man.

Eighteen months later Crozier was captain of the *Terror* once again, this time into the Arctic in search of the Northwest Passage, with Sir John Franklin commanding the expedition aboard the *Erebus*. It was an expedition destined to vanish and lead to the longest and largest search in exploration history. Crozier's last, poignant letter to his great friend and sailing companion was written from the Arctic and brought back to England by the transport *Barretto Junior:*

My dear James,

I cannot allow Transport to leave without writing you a line, altho' I have little to say. . . . How I do miss you—I cannot bear going on board *Erebus*—Sir John is very kind and would have me there dining every day if I would go. . . . All things are going on well and quietly but we are, I fear, sadly late. . . . James, I wish you were here, I would then have no doubt as to our pursuing the proper course. . . . Goodsir in *Erebus* is a most diligent fellow, he seems much in his habits like Hooker, never idle, making perfect sketches of all he collects. . . . All goes on smoothly, but James dear, I am sadly alone, not a soul have I in either ship that I can go and talk to. . . . Well my dear friends I know not what else I can say to you—I feel that I am not in spirits for writing but in truth I am sadly lonely & when I look back to the last voyage I can see the cause and therefore no prospect of having a more joyous feeling. God bless you both not forgetting the Son and believe me ever most sincerely,

F. R. M. Crozier

Ross published the narrative of the Antarctic voyage in 1847. A year later he was sailing into the Arctic in search of his two old friends. The search, by ship and a five-hundred-mile sledge journey by the forty-eight-year-old Ross, produced no sign of the *Erebus* and the *Terror.* By August 1849, after a winter in the Arctic, Ross was back in England.

Twelve years after his return from the Arctic Ross was dealt a blow from which he never recovered. Anne, his adored forty-year-old wife, died from pleural pneumonia. Ross died four years later, a rear admiral, probably hastened into his grave, next to Anne's, by heavy drinking. In an obituary in the Royal Society's *Proceedings* his Antarctic magnetic survey was "justly held to be the greatest work of its kind ever performed." Sabine thought him the "first scientific navigator of his country and his age," an opinion shared by Hooker: "Ross was really the greatest by far of all our scientific navigators, both in point of length of service and span of the globe. Justice has never been done to him."

The last sentence could also apply to Hooker himself. By October 1847 he had completed his two-volume *Flora Antarctica,* cemented his friendship with Darwin, and set off on more travels, this time on a three-year plant collecting trip into the Himalayas. The trip took in Sikkim, Assam, Nepal, and a quick dash into Tibet. In his journeys Hooker climbed higher than any other botanist—or any other climber in Europe—and found, at the top of the 18,466-foot Donkia Pass in Sikkim, identical lichens staining the rocks as orange-red as those he had found at Cockburn Island in the Antarctic. "To find the identical plant," he wrote to his father, "forming the only vegetation at the two extreme limits of vegetable life is always interesting; but to find it absolutely in both instances painting a landscape, so as to render its colour conspicuous in each case five miles off, is wonderful."

Hooker followed his father as director at the Royal Botanic Gardens, Kew. From 1841 to 1885 the Hookers, father and son, directed and molded Kew into what it is today, from what Mea Allan called "eleven acres of royal pleasureground into three hundred acres of a paradise," not to forget its position as one of the world's major scientific botanical institutions.

Sir Joseph Hooker, aged ninety-five, died peacefully in his sleep in 1911. As the world's most eminent botanist he was honored by the Japanese as "one of the twenty-nine Heroes of the World that Modern Time has produced" (although many small children would always remember him by his vastly entertaining ability to pull his shaggy eyebrows down into his mouth and then let them spring back).

As one of the few men who had seen the great ice barrier, the Ross Ice Shelf, he had suggested to Robert Scott that captive military balloons be taken down into the Antarctic to look across the barrier. So, in February

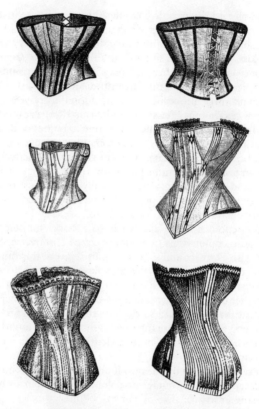

Nineteenth-century corsets

One of the end products of whalebone. Designed to squeeze "the stomach and bowels into as narrow a compass as possible, to procure what is falsely called, a fine shape."

—Dr. William Buchan

1902, with the *Discovery* moored alongside the Ross Ice Shelf, Scott became Antarctica's first aeronaut in an ascent in a balloon named *Eva*. Eight years later, prior to sailing with the *Terra Nova* on his fatal Antarctic expedition, Scott wrote to Hooker: "On Tuesday she will hoist the white ensign under Admiralty warrent. I wonder if there is any possibility that you could hoist our flag on that occasion?" Hooker had to refuse because of old-age frailty, although, as he wrote back to Scott, it was "an honour which would have been the crowning one of my long life could I have accepted it."

After Hooker's leech- and tick-infested Himalayan treks, Humboldt had written to Sir William: "What a notable traveller is Joseph Hooker! What an extent of acquired knowledge does he bring to bear on the observations he makes, and how marked with sagacity are the views he puts forward." Darwin also admired Hooker for those sagacious views. A man, thought Darwin, of somewhat "peppery" temper, which blew over very quickly, but the most pleasant and kindhearted of companions: "One of my best friends throughout life."

Linked with Thomas Huxley—another man who had served his time as a surgeon-naturalist in the Royal Navy—Hooker and Darwin became the theory of evolution's Three Musketeers, cutting and thrusting against the reactionary forces roused by Darwin's revolutionary work of scientific imagination. Both Hooker and Huxley were pallbearers at Darwin's funeral service in Westminster Abbey.

James Cook's eighteenth-century narratives had brought the sealers south into the Antarctic. James Ross's nineteenth-century narrative helped bring the whalers south. But it took some time before his comments on the vast number of whales found their mark, one of the reasons being the fluctuations in women's fashions and the price of whalebone.

The French Revolution, with its radical ideas, had led to an unloosening of stays, girdles, and also, as some would have it, morals. But the evangelical Victorian male was determined to put women back on a high moral pedestal. On the pedestal she went, wasp-waisted, corseted and armored with whalebone. It happened to be good news for whaleship owners, but bad news for their daughters and wives.

Whalebone, the baleen plates from the right and bowhead whale, softened by heat, retains any curve when held in that shape until cold. This quality makes it ideal for shaping corsets, bodices, bustles, crinolines, and boned petticoats.

George du Maurier poked gentle fun at the outrageous fashions with his cartoons in *Punch*. One such drawing shows a wasp-waisted, bustled lovely, being guided to a sofa by her male companion. The text reads: "I should like to sit down but my dressmaker says I mustn't."

The return of the whalebone-molded figure would have had the eighteenth-century Rousseau and Dr. William Buchan throwing up their hands in collective horror. Rousseau, in his novel *Émile,* had loosed a blast at "those frames of whalebone in which our women distort rather than display their figures. It seems to me that this abuse, which is carried to an incredible degree of folly in England, must sooner or later lead to the production of a degenerate race." Buchan, in his popular *Domestic Medicine,* was blunter. The doctor fulminated against fashion's follies and called them "highly pernicious" to health. In the language of a more robust age, language that would have brought blushes to the cheeks of Victorian ladies teetering on their pedestals, the doctor warmed to his subject:

"The most destructive [fashion] in this country is that of squeezing the stomach and bowels into as narrow a compass as possible, to procure, what is falsely called, a fine shape. By this practice the action of the stomach and bowels, the motion of the heart and lungs, and almost all the vital functions are obstructed. Hence proceed indigestions, syncopes, or fainting fits, consumption of the lungs &c."

In 1874, after trawling through Ross's and other Antarctic narratives, David and John Gray, whaleship owners from Peterhead in Scotland, published a short pamphlet entitled *Report on New Whaling Grounds in the Southern Seas.* In the waters of Antarctica, according to the Grays, lay a fortune waiting to be caught in the shape of the right whale with its oil and increasingly valuable whalebone. As the price of whalebone increased fivefold under the pressure of ladies' fashions, and the Arctic catch declined, the Grays' pamphlet began to take on a golden glow. In 1892 a four-vessel whaling expedition sailed from Dundee for the Weddell Sea. All the vessels had auxiliary steam engines. From Norway sailed the auxiliary steam-engined *Jason* with the thirty-two-year-old Carl Anton Larsen as skipper. The two expeditions found few right whales with those baleen plates that could ooze money, but they did take note of the many fast-swimming rorquals: blue, sei, fin. Whales, alas, beyond their catching capabilities. Both expeditions returned with seal oil.

But the Norwegians had the technology and the expertise to deal with the rorquals and had been doing it for thirty years off Norway and Scotland: steam-powered whale catchers firing explosive-headed harpoon guns, whale lines attached to winches running off the main engine, the whale line itself running through a block suspended from the mast by stout rubber strops, this to absorb the shock from the sudden titanic jerks from the world's largest animal.

Whaling is an industry that, over the centuries, has kept on reinventing itself. Early whaling was shore-based, small boats harpooning their quarry close to shore and the whale being towed back. The Basques—who have given us the word *harpoon*—at the end of the sixteenth century invented pelagic whaling: whale catching on the high seas with the blubber being rendered down aboard ship. Over the centuries, depending on the quarry—sperm, right whale, bowhead, humpback—the whaling business fluctuated between shore and ocean. By the close of the nineteenth century and the beginning of the twentieth the Norwegians, the world's leading whaling nation, with a technology forged by Svend Foyn and led into the Antarctic by Carl Larsen, had floating factory ships anchored in bays, shore-based factories, and whale catchers scouring the waters around South Georgia and the South Shetlands.

In 1923 Larsen brought pelagic whaling to the Ross Sea. On 30 November the factory ship *Sir James Clark Ross* steamed out of Hobart, followed by five whale catchers and headed south to meet the pack on 15 December. Towing the catchers, the factory ship pushed through the pack, taking five days, and then headed for the Ross Ice Shelf. The flensing of the whales was done alongside the *Sir James Clark Ross*. It was done in cold so bitter that the blubber froze hard as iron and had to be hacked away with axes, the flensing knives being useless. By 7 March Larsen called an end to it and headed for New Zealand. Aboard the factory ship was a disappointing 17,300 barrels of oil from 10 fin whales and 211 blue whales. One of the blue whales had been 106 feet long, a foot longer than the *Erebus*.

Larsen was back in the Ross Sea for the 1924–25 season. It was his last voyage. He died in his cabin a few days after the expedition had broken through the pack. The whaling conditions were ideal: calm water between the floes, light winds, mild temperatures, plus hundreds of whales, most of them blue whales. The tally at season's end was 31,850 barrels of oil from 417 whales. The following seasons were even better with new factory ships having slipways to haul the whales on deck. From 1923 to 1930 the Norwegians turned the Ross Sea into a blue whale killing ground with 6,111 whales killed and an uncounted number lost. Modern whaling had arrived.

The Norwegian Road Amundsen, the first man to the South Pole, had combed Ross's narrative as well as other Antarctic literature, combed it so well that when he arrived at the Ross Ice Shelf in the *Fram*, he felt as if he had known it for years. Shackleton's 1908 Bay of Whales—so named because of the vast number of whales—was obviously the same bay in the Ross Ice Shelf recorded by Ross. Here Amundsen thought the Ross Ice Shelf to be aground. He was wrong, but it was here that he chose to make his base for the South Pole journey. "A whole degree," as he noted, "farther south than Scott could hope to get in McMurdo Sound." Amundsen was also convinced that if Shackleton, who had played with the idea, *had* made his base at the Bay of Whales in 1908 instead of McMurdo Sound, "the problem of the South Pole would probably have been solved long before December, 1911." The Bay of Whales also saw the return of Americans to Antarctica with Commander Richard E. Byrd's 1928–30 expedition and flight to the South Pole.

James Clark Ross, with the *Erebus* and the *Terror*, had led explorers and whalers into the heart of the Antarctic and to the South Pole.

NOTES

1. Vendovi, a Fijian chief, was thought to have have been responsible for the 1834 murder of American seamen from the brig *Charles Daggett*. Captured and held aboard the *Vincennes*, the chief died three days after his arrival in New York. The

New York Herald thought his death a "consequence . . . of having no human flesh to eat." His skull, months later, found its way into the expedition's ethnological collection.

2. Ross, like Wilkes, had also been fooled by Antarctica's visual tricks. Beyond Mount Erebus, and across the ice barrier, Ross had seen a mountain range running southward and named them the Parry Mountains. Sixty years later Scott found no mountains existed and thought that Ross had been fooled by a mirage of the Minna Bluff promontory.

Epilogue

N 9 JANUARY 1845 the 362-ton barque *Pagoda* sailed from Simon's Bay in South Africa bound for the high latitudes of the Indian Ocean. Hired by the Royal Navy and manned by Royal Navy volunteers, she was commanded by Lieutenant Thomas Moore, who had sailed on the *Terror*'s Antarctic voyages as one of the mates.

Ross's expedition had left a gap in magnetic measurements in the southern reaches of the Indian Ocean, a gap that Sabine, the great quantifier, was determined to fill. Pressure was brought to bear, and the Admiralty, bowing to the inevitable, had chartered the *Pagoda* for the last, if small, voyage of scientific exploration under sail. The Admiralty—even though Cook, Biscoe, and Ross had found the prevailing winds blowing from the east in the high southern latitudes—perversely ordered Moore to sail east and battle against these prevailing winds. Moore carried out his orders, sailed south of the Antarctic Circle (to within forty-five miles of the Antarctic coast, but failed to see it in poor visibility), gathered his magnetic data, saw more icebergs than on his three voyages in the *Terror*, and, in one of those ironic twists in which Antarctic exploration is steeped, sailed through more degrees of longitude south of 60°S than Cook, Bellingshausen, Biscoe, Balleny, Ross, Wilkes, or d'Urville.

The *Pagoda* returned to Simon's Bay after a six-month voyage with all the crew in good health and all the magnetic measurements to satisfy the demanding Sabine. As an Antarctic voyage it has always been consigned to oblivion, but it does have a significance.

Halley and the *Paramore*, in 1698, had sailed on the first ever voyage for science. Moore and the *Pagoda*, in 1845, ended the sailing tradition. With pleasing symmetry, both voyages had been sent out on a tide of magnetic curiosity. All future scientific voyages would have the benefits of auxiliary power.

For fifty years the waters surrounding Antarctica, except for sealing and whaling expeditions and the *Challenger* hydrographic expedition, lay untouched and unfrequented. Any British polar concerns lay in the north

with the search for Sir John Franklin and the *Erebus* and the *Terror.* Other
countries had concerns other than polar. The United States, after being
torn apart by a civil war, looked toward its own vast continent; the French,
still hankering for the glorious years of the emperor Napoleon, achieved
an imitation under his nephew, and a second empire with colonial expan-
sion into the Pacific, Africa, and Indochina. Except for whales and seals the
Antarctic appeared to be destitute of anything to entice imperialist, merchant, explorer, or adventurer, a pariah continent with nothing to offer.
Roald Amundsen, however, thought the continent a sleeping beauty
awaiting her kiss.

The kiss came in September 1895, when the assembled delegates to
the London Sixth International Geographical Congress adopted a resolution: "That the Congress record its opinion that the exploration of the
Antarctic Regions is the greatest piece of geographical exploration still to
be undertaken."

One of the speakers at the Congress had been Sir Joseph Hooker, now
the oldest Antarctic expert, and Carsten Borchgrevink, a thirty-one-year-
old Norwegian who had sailed aboard the whaling reconnaissance vessel
the *Antarctic* and had landed at Cape Adare (named by Ross in 1841) on
24 January 1895, making what was thought to be the first ever landing on
the continent. (New England sealers in fact had landed on the Antarctic
Peninsula in 1821.) Women's fashions and the demand for whalebone
had led the *Antarctic* south in search of right whales and their valuable
baleen.

Over the next twenty years fourteen expeditions sailed to the Antarctic: four British, two French, two German, one Australian, one Belgian,
one Japanese, one Norwegian, one Scottish, and one Swedish. Five of the
expeditions were to be trapped in the ice, beset, with only three escaping.
The unlucky expeditions abandoned their vessels before they were crushed
and sunk by the ice of the Weddell Sea. All these vessels had auxiliary
power and were lured into the ice to a position where no sailing vessel
could ever have found herself. But their steam engines—engines with far
less horsepower than is tucked away in the hull of a modern cruising
yacht—were not powerful enough to ram through and escape when the
pack ice closed in. A classic case of a too touching faith's being placed in
a new technology.

But the 1897–99 Belgian expedition of the *Belgica* (beset but survived), the 1901–03 German expedition in the *Gauss* (beset but survived),
the 1901–04 Swedish expedition in the *Antarctic* (beset and sunk), the
1911–12 German expedition in the *Deutschland* (beset but survived), and
the 1914–17 British Shackleton expedition with the *Endurance* (beset
and sunk) and the *Aurora* (beset but survived) encapsulated what has become known as the Heroic Age of Antarctic exploration. The types of
story all the survivors could tell, stories of fortitude, courage, leadership,

madness, and despair, were the same as those outlined by Richard Hakluyt in the 1598 preface to the second edition of his *Principal Navigations,* which contained narratives of expeditions into the Arctic: "Into what dangers and difficulties they plunged themselves, I tremble to recount . . . unto what drifts of snow and mountains of ice . . . unto what hideous overfalls, uncertain currents, dark mists and fogs, and divers other fearful inconveniences they were subject and in danger of, I wish you rather to learn. . . ."

Maps

Australia and New Zealand to the Antarctic.

Matthew Flinders's track with the *Investigator*, 1801–03

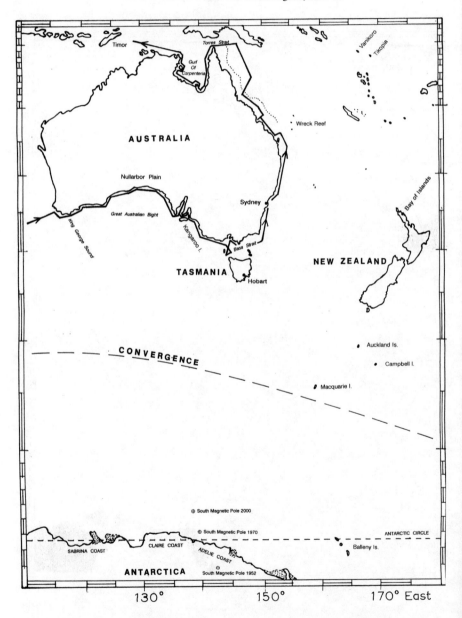

John Balleny's track with the *Eliza Scott* and the *Sabrina*, January 1839–March 1839

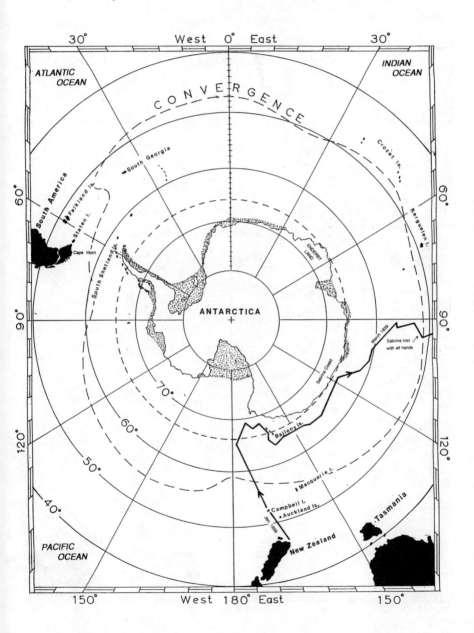

Dumont d'Urville's track with the *Astrolabe* and the *Zélée*, and the attempt to beat
James Weddell's farthest south of 1823, January 1838–March 1838

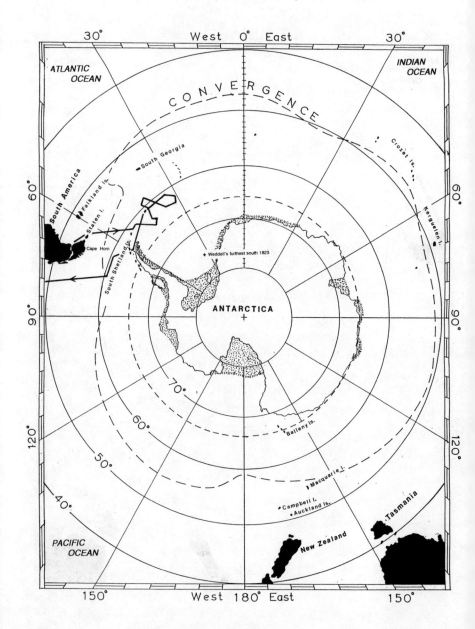

Dumont d'Urville's track with the *Astrolabe* and the *Zélée*,
January 1840–February 1840

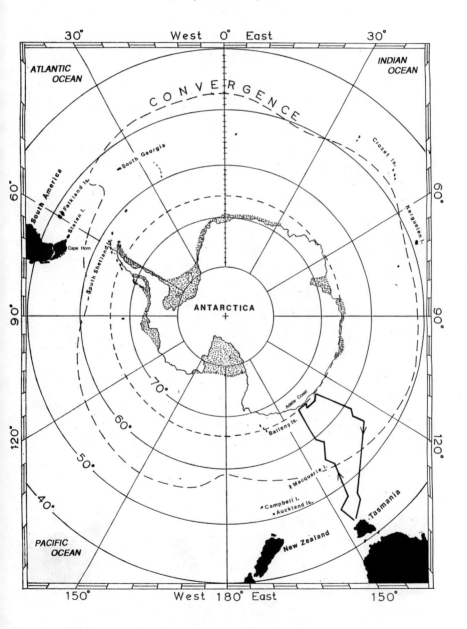

United States Exploring Expedition and the attempt to beat James Cook's farthest
south of 1774. William Walker's track with the *Flying Fish*, February 1839–April 1839

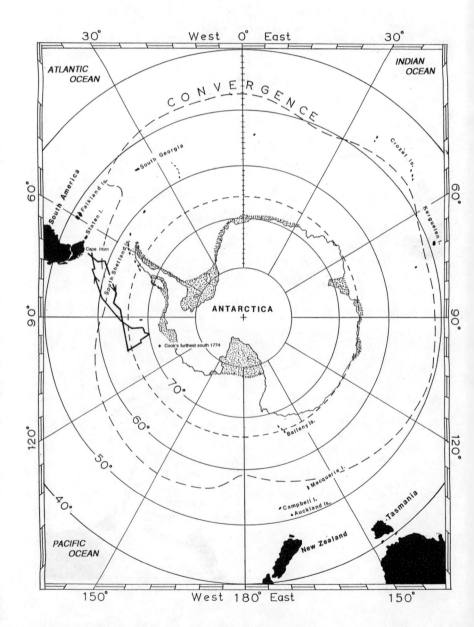

United States Exploring Expedition. Charles Wilkes's track with the *Vincennes,*
December 1839–March 1840

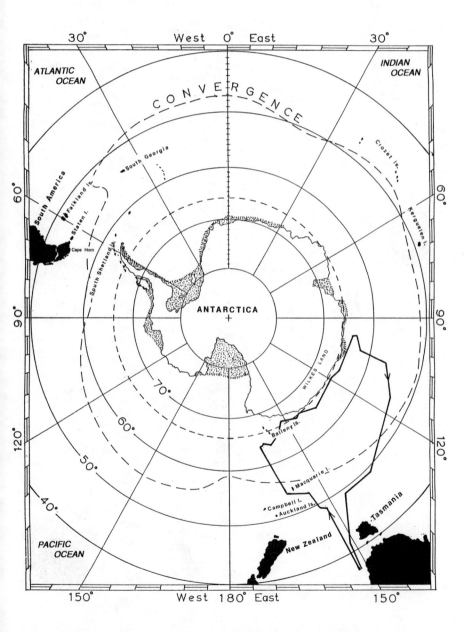

James Clark Ross's track with the *Erebus* and the *Terror*, Novermber 1840–April 1841

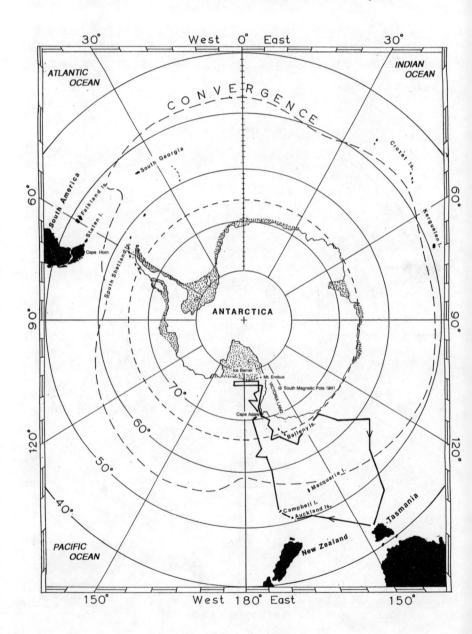

James Clark Ross's track with the *Erebus* and the *Terror*, Novermber 1841–April 1842

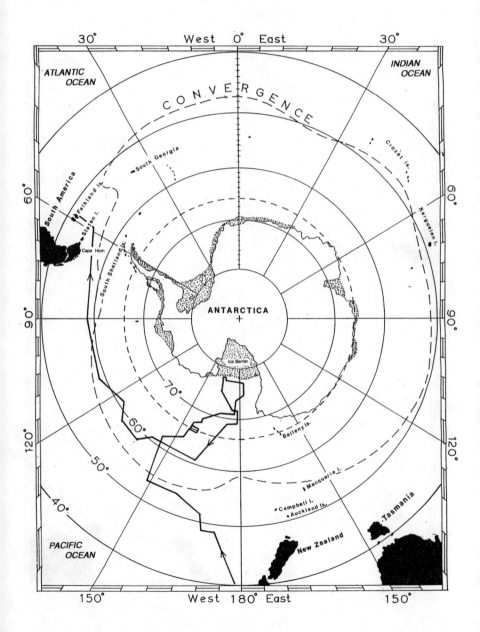

James Clark Ross's track with the *Erebus* and the *Terror,* December 1842–April 1843

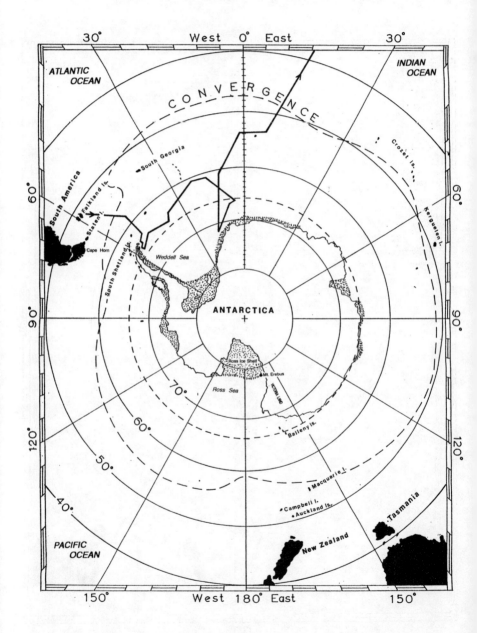

Tierra del Fuego to the Antarctic Peninsula

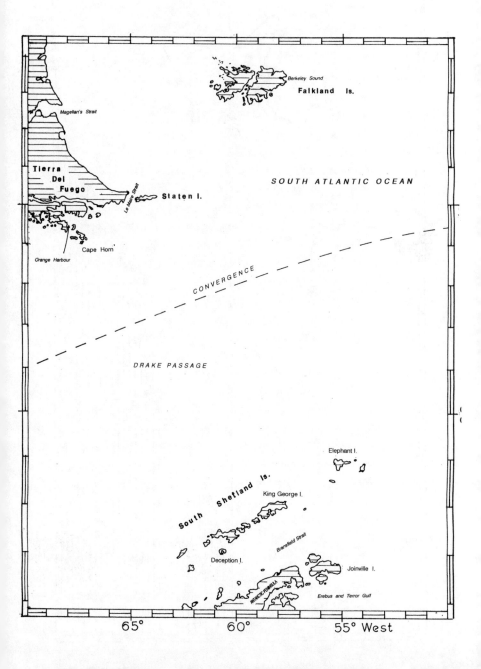

The cause of the argument between Wilkes and Ross. Eastern section of the supposed
Antarctic coastline laid down by Wilkes and then sailed over by Ross.

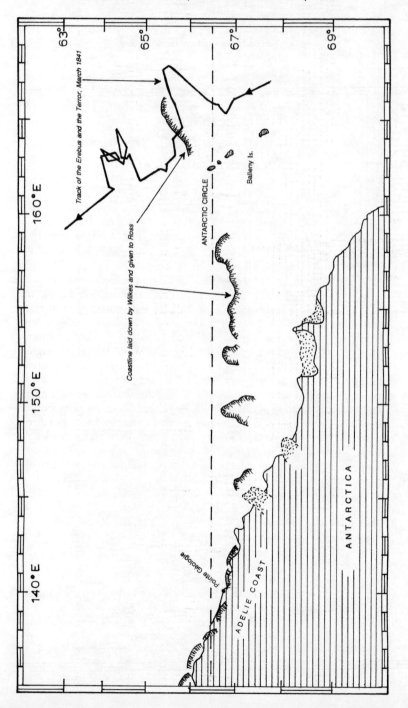

Bibliography

HIS BIBLIOGRAPHY would not be complete without a few words on Admiral W. H. Smyth, who has appeared with regularity—perhaps depressing regularity for some readers—at the head of each chapter. William Henry Smyth (1788–1865) was born in London and claimed descent from Captain John Smith of Virginia fame. He went to sea at an early age and saw service during the Napoleonic Wars in Indian, Chinese, and Australian waters. He is best remembered, however, for his surveys of the Italian, Sicilian, Greek, and African coasts. Such was his expertise in these waters that his contemporaries called him Mediterranean Smyth. During World War II his original surveys were studied when landings on the Sicilian coastline were under discussion. As well as being a brilliant hydrographer Smyth was an astronomer (he had his own observatory), an antiquarian, a founder member and later president of the Royal Geographical Society, a Fellow of the Royal Society as well as its vice-president, and a vice-president and director of the Society of Antiquities. A most serious, dull fellow, one might think. Not so. All of Smyth's friends commented on his impish sense of humor and beguiling anecdotes. His *Sailor's Word-Book* was published posthumously.

Alexander, Michael. Omai "Noble Savage." London, 1977.

Allan, Mea. *The Hookers of Kew: 1785–1911*. London, 1967.

Amundsen, Roald. *The South Pole*. London, 1912.

Anderson, Bern. *Surveyor of the Sea*. Toronto, 1960.

Anderson, J. R. L. *The Ulysses Factor*. New York, 1970.

Ansel, Willits D. *The Whaleboat*. Mystic, Conn., 1978.

Arago, Jacques. *Narrative of a Voyage round the World . . . during the Years 1817, 1818, 1819, and 1820*. London, 1823.

Balleny, J. "Discoveries in the Antarctic Ocean, in February, 1839." *Journal of the Royal Geographical Society*. London, 1839.

Banks, Joseph. *The "Endeavor" Journal of Joseph Banks*. Edited by J. C. Beaglehole. 2 vols. Sydney, Australia, 1962.

Barrow, J. *An Autobiographical Memoir of Sir John Barrow.* London, 1847.
Bauer, K. Jack. *A Maritime History of the United States.* Columbia, S.C., 1988.
Beaglehole, J. C. *The Exploration of the Pacific.* London, 1975.
————. *The Life of Captain James Cook.* London, 1974.
Bernacchi, Louis. *To the South Polar Regions.* London, 1901.
Bertrand, Kenneth J. *Americans in Antarctica 1775–1948.* New York, 1971.
Besant, W. *Captain Cook.* London, 1890.
Blewitt, Mary. *Surveys of the Seas.* London, 1957.
Borchgrevink, C. E. *First on the Antarctic Continent.* London, 1901.
Bowden, Keith Macrae. *George Bass 1771–1803.* Melbourne, Australia, 1952.
Bridges, E. Lucas. *Uttermost Part of the Earth.* New York, 1950.
Brooks, Van Wyck. *The World of Washington Irving.* New York, 1946.
Browne, J. Ross. *Etchings of a Whaling Cruise.* New York, 1846.
Buchan, William. *Domestic Medicine.* London, 1769.
Bull, H. J. *The Cruise of the "Antarctic."* London, 1896.
Bullen, F. T. *The Cruise of the Cachalot.* New York, 1925.
Burney, Fanny. *Early Diaries.* Edited by A. R. Ellis. London, 1889.
Cawkell, M. B. R., D. H. Maling; and E. M. Cawkell. *The Falkland Islands.* London, 1960.
Cawood, J. "The Magnetic Crusade: Science and Politics in Early Victorian Britain." *Isis.* Vol. 70, 1979.
————. "Terrestrial Magnetism and the Development of International Collaboration in the Early Nineteenth Century." *Annals of Science.* Vol. 34, 1977.
Chapelle, Howard. *American Small Sailing Craft.* New York, 1951.
————. *The History of the American Sailing Navy.* New York, 1949.
Chatterton, E. Keble. *Whalers and Whaling.* London, 1925.
Colby, B. L. *For Oil and Buggy Whips.* Mystic, Conn., 1990.
Collins, David. *An Account of the English Colony in New South Wales.* 2 vols. London, 1798, 1802. Reprinted Sydney, Australia, 1975.
Colman, George. *Random Records.* London, 1830.
Cook, Frederick A. *Through the First Antarctic Night 1898–1899.* London, 1900.
Cook, James. *The Journals of Captain James Cook on His Voyages of Discovery.* Edited by J. C. Beaglehole. 4 vols. Cambridge, England, 1955, 1961, 1967 (Hakluyt Society).
Crawford, Janet. *That First Antarctic Winter.* Christchurch, New Zealand, 1998.
Dakin, W. J. *Whalemen Adventurers.* Sydney, Australia, 1934.
Dampier, William. *A New Voyage round the World.* London, 1697. Reprint 1998.

Darwin, Charles. *The Autobiography of Charles Darwin 1809–1882.* Edited by N. Barlow. New York, 1969.

———. *The Origin of Species.* London, 1859. Reprint 1976.

———. *The Voyage of the Beagle.* New York, 1962.

Davis, John Edward. *A Letter from the Antarctic.* London, 1901. Privately printed.

Defense Mapping Agency. *Sailing Directions for Antarctica.* Washington, D.C., 1976.

Dening, Greg. *Mr. Bligh's Bad Language.* Cambridge, England, 1992.

Desmond, Adrian, and James Moore. *Darwin.* London, 1992.

Desmond, Ray. *Sir Joseph Dalton Hooker: Traveller and Plant Collector.* Antique Collectors' Club, Woodbridge, England, 1999.

Dixon, Norman F. *On the Psychology of Military Incompetence.* New York, 1976.

Dunmore, John. *French Explorers in the Pacific.* 2 vols. London 1969.

D'Urville, J. S.-C. D. *Two Voyages to the South Seas.* Edited and translated by H. Rosenman. Melbourne, Australia, 1987.

Earle, Augustus. *A Narrative of a Nine Month's Residence in New Zealand in 1827.* Christchurch, New Zealand, 1909.

Edgell, Vice-Admiral Sir John. *Sea Surveys.* London, 1965.

Erskine, Charles. *Twenty Years before the Mast.* Washington, D.C., 1985.

Eyre, John Edward. *Journals of Expeditions of Discovery into Central Australia and Overland from Adelaide to King George's Sound 1840–1841.* 2 vols. London, 1845.

Fanning, Edmund. *Voyages round the World.* New York, 1833. Reprint by Gregg Press, Upper Saddle River, N.J., 1970.

Fitzpatrick, K. *Sir John Franklin in Tasmania 1837–1843.* Melbourne, Australia, 1949.

FitzRoy, Captain Robert, R.N. *Narrative of the Surveying Voyages of His Majesty's Ships* Adventure *and* Beagle *between the Years 1826 and 1836.* 3 vols. London, 1839.

Flinders, Matthew. *A Voyage to Terra Australis.* 2 vols. London, 1814.

Fogg, G. E. *A History of Antarctic Science.* Cambridge, England, 1992.

Freycinet, Rose de. *Journal de Madame Rose de Saulces de Freycinet, d'après le manuscrit original accompagné de notes.* Edited by Charles Duplomb. Paris, 1927.

———. *A Woman of Courage.* Translated by Marc Serge Rivière. Canberra, Australia, 1996.

Friendly, Alfred. *Beaufort of the Admiralty.* New York, 1977.

Gilman, D. C. *The Life of James Dwight Dana.* New York, 1899.

Gould, R. T. "Bligh's Notes on Cook's Last Voyage." *Mariner's Mirror.* Vol. 14, London, 1928.

Grant, James. *The Narrative of a Voyage of Discovery, Performed in His Majesty's Vessel the Lady Nelson . . .* London, 1803.

Haldane, Charlotte. *Tempest over Tahiti*. London, 1963.

Hakluyt, Richard. *The Principal Navigations, Voyages, Traffiques and Discoveries of the English Nation*. London, 1907.

Hakluyt Society. *The World Encompassed by Sir Francis Drake* . . . Edited by W. S. W. Vaux. London, 1854.

Harrison, Tom. *Savage Civilisation*. London, 1937.

Headland, R. K. *Chronological List of Antarctic Expeditions*. Cambridge, England 1989.

Henderson, Daniel. *The Hidden Coasts*. New York, 1953.

Hobbs, William H. *American Antarctic Discoveries 1819–1940*. Proceedings Eighth American Scientific Congress, 1940.

——. "Wilkes Land Rediscovered." *Geographical Review*. Vol. 22, 1932.

Hogben, Lancelot. *Science for the Citizen*. London, 1944.

Hohman, E. P. *The American Whaleman*. New York, 1928.

Hooker, J. D. *The Botany of the Antarctic Voyage of H.M. Discovery Ships Erebus and Terror in the Years 1839–1843*

Part 1. *Flora Antarctica*. 2 vols. London, 1844–47.

Part 2. *Flora Novae-Zelandiae*. 2 vols. London, 1852–55.

Part 3. *Flora Tasmaniae*. 2 vols. London, 1855–59.

——. *Himalayan Journals*. London, 1891.

Howe, K. R. *Where the Waves Fall*. Sydney, Australia, 1984.

Hughes, Robert. *The Fatal Shore*. London, 1987.

Huxley, Leonard. *Life and Letters of Sir Joseph Dalton Hooker*. 2 vols. London, 1918.

Ingleton, Geoffrey C. *Matthew Flinders, Navigator and Chartmaker*. Guildford, England, 1986.

Hydrographic Department. *The Antarctic Pilot*. London, 1948.

——. *The Antarctic Pilot*. Taunton, England, 1974.

Jackson, Gordon. *The British Whaling Trade*. London, 1978.

Jones, A. G. E. *Polar Portraits*. Caedmon of Whitby, England, 1992.

——. *Ships Employed in the South Seas Trade*. Canberra, Australia, 1986.

La Pérouse, Jean-François. *The Journal of Jean-François de Galaup de la Pérouse 1785–1788*. Translated by John Dunmore. 2 vols. London, 1994. (Hakluyt Society.)

Lee, Jack. *"I Have Named It the Bay of Islands. . . ."* Auckland, New Zealand, 1983.

Lever, Darcy. *The Young Sea Officer's Sheet Anchor*. London, 1808.

McCabe, James D. *Lights and Shadows of New York Life*. New York, 1872.

McCormick, Robert. *Voyages of Discovery in the Arctic and Antarctic Seas and round the World*. 2 vols. London, 1884.

McFee, William. *The Life of Sir Martin Frobisher*. New York, 1928.

Mack, James D. *Matthew Flinders 1774–1814*. Melbourne, Australia, 1966.

Macy, Obed. *History of Nantucket and of the Whale Fishery*. Boston, Massachusetts, 1835.

Maning, Frederick Edward. *Old New Zealand: A Tale of the Good Old Times.* Auckland, New Zealand, 1948.

Marryat, Frederick. *A Diary in America.* London, 1839.

Mellersh, H. E. L. *FitzRoy of the Beagle.* London, 1968.

Melville, Herman. *Moby-Dick; or, The Whale.* New York, 1851. Reprint 1986.

Mill, Hugh R. "A Relic of Ross." *Polar Record.* Vol. 3, No. 21, January 1941. Cambridge, England.

———. *The Siege of the South Pole.* London, 1905.

Miller, S. "Sir James Clark Ross's Tidal Tablets, Port Louis 1842." *Falkland Islands Journal,* 1984.

Mitterling, Philip I. *America in the Antarctic to 1840.* Urbana, Ill., 1959.

Moody, R. C. "A Despatch by Governor Moody to Lord Stanley, 1842." *Falkland Islands Journal,* 1969.

Moorehead, Alan. *The Fatal Impact.* New York, 1966.

Morrell, Abby Jane. *Narrative of a Voyage . . . in the Years 1829, 1830, 1831.* New York, 1833.

Morrell, Benjamin. *A Narrative of Four Voyages . . . from the Year 1822 to 1831.* New York, 1832. Reprint 1970.

Murray, G. (editor). *The Antarctic Manual.* Royal Geographical Society. London, 1901.

North American Review. *Narrative of the United States Exploring Expedition.* July 1845.

———. *Synopsis of the Cruise of the United States Exploring Expedition.* April 1843.

Nozikov, N. *Russian Voyages round the World.* Translated by Ernst and Mira Lesser. London, 1945.

Oliver, Douglas L. *The Pacific Islands.* New York, 1961.

Orange, Claudia. *The Treaty of Waitangi.* Wellington, New Zealand, 1987.

Palmer, James C. *Thulia: A Tale of the Antarctic.* New York, 1843.

Poesch, Jessie. *Titian Ramsay Peale and His Journals of the Wilkes Expedition.* Philadelphia, 1961.

Price, A. G. *The Winning of Australian Antarctica.* Sydney, Australia, 1962.

Quigley, Hugh. *Passchendaele and the Somme.* London, 1928.

Reynolds, Jeremiah N. *Address on the Subject of a Surveying and Exploring Expedition to the Pacific Ocean and South Seas.* New York, 1836.

———. *Pacific and Indian Oceans.* New York, 1841.

Reynolds, William. *Voyage to the Southern Ocean: The Letters of Lieutenant William Reynolds from the U.S. Exploring Expedition, 1838–1842.* Edited by A. H. Cleaver and E. J. Stann. Annapolis, Md., 1988.

Richards, R. *The Commercial Exploitation of Sea Mammals at Îles Crozet and Prince Edward Islands before 1850.* Polar Monograph No. 1, Cambridge, England.

Ritchie, G. S. *The Admiralty Chart.* Durham, England, 1995.

Ross, J. C. *A Voyage of Discovery and Research in the Southern and Antarctic Regions during the Years 1839–43*. 2 vols. London 1847. Reprint 1969.

Ross, M. J. *Polar Pioneers: John Ross and James Clark Ross*. London, 1994.
———. *Ross in the Antarctic*. Caedmon of Whitby, England, 1982.

Royal Society. *Report . . . of the Royal Society on the Instructions to be Prepared for the Scientific Expedition to the Antarctic Regions*. London, 1839.

Russell, Lord John. "Correspondence Relative to the Falkland Islands." *Falkland Islands Journal*, 1968.

Savours, Ann. "Two Unpublished Accounts of the British Antarctic Expedition, 1839–43." *Polar Record*. Vol. 10, No. 69, September 1961. Cambridge, England.

———, and Anita McConnell. "The History of the Rossbank Observatory, Tasmania." *Annals of Science*. Vol. 39, 1982.

Scott, E. *The Life of Captain Matthew Flinders*. Sydney, Australia, 1914.

Scott, Robert F. *The Voyage of the "Discovery."* 2 vols. London, 1905.

Shackleton, Ernest H. *The Heart of the Antarctic*. 2 vols. London, 1909.

Sinclair, K. *A History of New Zealand*. London, 1980.

Smyth, William Henry. *The Sailor's Word-Book*. London, 1867. Reprint Conway Maritime Press, 1996.

Spears, John R. *Captain Nathaniel Brown Palmer*. New York, 1922.

Stackpole, E. A. *The Sea Hunters*. New York, 1953.

Stamp, T. and C. *William Scoresby, Arctic Scientist*. Caedmon of Whitby, England, 1975.

Stanton, William. *The Great United States Exploring Expedition of 1838–1842*. Berkeley, Calif., 1975.

Starbuck, Alexander. *History of the American Whale Fishery*. Waltham, Mass., 1878. Reprint Secaucus, N.J., 1989.

Thomson, Keith S. *HMS Beagle*. New York, 1995.

Tocqueville, Alexis de. *Democracy in America*. Edited by J. P. Mayer, translated by George Lawrence. London, 1994.

Tønnessen, J. N., and A. O. Johnsen. *The History of Modern Whaling*. Translated by R. I. Christophersen. London, 1982.

Trollope, Fanny. *Domestic Manners of the Americans*. London, 1832.

Turrill, W. B. *Joseph Dalton Hooker*. London, 1963.

Tyler, David B. *The Wilkes Expedition*. Philadelphia, 1968.

Vancouver, George. *A Voyage of Discovery to the North Pacific Ocean and round the World . . .* 3 vols. London, 1798.

Vergniol, C. *Dumont d'Urville*. Paris, 1931.

Viola, H. J., and C. Margolis (editors). *Magnificent Voyagers: The U.S. Exploring Expedition, 1838–1842*. Washington, D.C., 1985.

Wallace, Alfred Russel. *The Malay Archipelago*. London, 1913.

Ware, Chris. *The Bomb Vessel*. London, 1994.

Waters, D. W. *The Art of Navigation in England in Elizabethan and Early Stuart Times.* London, 1958.

Waugh, Norah. *Corsets and Crinolines.* London, 1954.

Webster, W. H. *Narrative of a Voyage to the Southern Atlantic Ocean, in the Years 1828, 1829, and 1839, Performed in H.M. Sloop Chanticleer, Under the Command of Captain Henry Foster, F.R.S., etc.* London, 1834. Reprint 1970.

Weddell, James. *A Voyage towards the South Pole Performed in the Years 1822–24.* London, 1825. Reprint 1970.

Whipple, A. B. C. *Yankee Whalers in the South Seas.* London, 1957.

Wilkes, Charles. *Autobiography of Rear Admiral Charles Wilkes, U.S. Navy 1798–1877.* Edited by W.J. Morgan, D. B. Tyler, J. L. Leonhart, and M. F. Loughlin. Washington, D.C., 1978.

————. *The Narrative of the United States Exploring Expedition during the Years 1838, 1839, 1840, 1841, 1842.* 5 vols. Philadelphia, 1845.

Woodward, F. J. *Portrait of Jane: A Life of Lady Franklin.* London, 1951.

Index